NYSTCE 005

Social Studies CST

Teacher Certification Exam

By: Sharon Wynne, M.S
Southern Connecticut State University

"And, while there's no reason yet to panic, I think it's only prudent that we make preparations to panic."

XAMonline, INC.

Boston

To obtain permission(s) to use the material from this work for any purpose including workshops or seminars, please submit a written request to:

XAMonline, Inc.
21 Orient Ave.
Melrose, MA 02176
Toll Free 1-800-509-4128
Email: info@xamonline.com
Web www.xamonline.com
Fax: 1-781-662-9268

Library of Congress Cataloging-in-Publication Data
Wynne, Sharon A.
CST Social Studies (005): Teacher Certification / Sharon A. Wynne. -2nd ed.
ISBN 978-1-58197-265-8
1.CST Social Studies (005). 2. Study guides. 3. NYSTCE 4. Teachers' Certification & Licensure.
5. Careers

Managing Editor	Dr. Harte Weiner, Ph. D.
Senior Editor	Zakia Hyder
Copy Editor	Ira Glasser, B.A.
Assistant Editor	Kerrie Forbes, B.A.

Disclaimer:
The opinions expressed in this publication are the sole works of XAMonline and were created independently from the National Education Association, Educational Testing Service, or any State Department of Education, National Evaluation Systems or other testing affiliates. Between the time of publication and printing, state specific standards as well as testing formats and website information may change that is not included in part or in whole within this product. Sample test questions are developed by XAMonline and reflect similar content as on real tests; however, they are not former tests. XAMonline assembles content that aligns with state standards but makes no claims nor guarantees teacher candidates a passing score. Numerical scores are determined by testing companies such as NES or ETS and then are compared with individual state standards. A passing score varies from state to state.

Printed in the United States of America   œ-1

NYSTCE: CST Social Studies 005
ISBN: 978-1-58197-265-8

About the Subject Assessments

Subject Assessment in the Social Studies (005) examination

Purpose: The assessments are designed to test the knowledge and competencies of prospective secondary level teachers. The question bank from which the assessment is drawn is undergoing constant revision. As a result, your test may include questions that will not count toward your score.

Time Allowance, Format, and Length: You will have four hours to complete the test. The questions are presented in a 90-question multiple-choice format and one constructed-response (written) assignment.

Content Areas: Each test is designed to measure areas of knowledge called domains. These are:

Domain I.   History
Domain II.   Geography
Domain III.   Economics
Domain IV.   Civics, Citizenship, and Government
Domain V.   Social Studies Skills
Domain VI.   History: Constructed-Response Assignment

Within each domain, statements of important knowledge and skills, called objectives, define the content of the test. Each test objective is followed by focus statements that provide examples of the range, type, and level of content that may appear on the test for questions measuring that objective. The approximate percentage of the test corresponding to each domain is:

Domain I.   35%
Domain II.   15%
Domain III.   12%
Domain IV.   16%
Domain V.   12%
Domain VI.   10%

Test Taxonomy: Both versions of the subject assessments are constructed on the comprehension, synthesis and analysis levels of Bloom's Taxonomy. In many questions, the candidate must apply knowledge of more than one discipline in order to correctly answer the questions.

Additional Information about the New York Assessments: The New York series subject assessments are developed by the *New York Department of Education* of Albany, NY. They provide additional information on the Social Studies CST (05) series assessments, including registration, preparation and testing procedures, and study materials such as topical guides that are about 52 pages of information with approximately 22 additional sample questions.

Topical guides versus study guides. The latest topical guide developed by the State of New York is presented below. The topics are in bold type. The numbers following the competencies represent the interpretation of the major topics by the State of New York test preparation staff.

Table of Contents

Great Study and Testing Tips!

What to study in order to prepare for the subject assessments is the focus of this study guide, but equally important is *how* you study.

You can increase your chances of truly mastering the information by taking some simple, but effective steps.

Study Tips:

1. Some foods aid the learning process. Foods such as milk, nuts, seeds, rice, and oats help your study efforts by releasing natural memory enhancers called CCKs (*cholecystokinin*) composed of *tryptophan*, *choline*, and *phenylalanine*. All of these chemicals enhance the neurotransmitters associated with memory. Before studying, try a light, protein-rich meal of eggs, turkey, and fish. All of these foods release memory-enhancing chemicals. The better the connections, the more you comprehend.

Likewise, before you take a test, stick to a light snack of energy-boosting and relaxing foods. A glass of milk, a piece of fruit, or some peanuts all release various memory-boosting chemicals and help you to relax and focus on the subject at hand.

2. Learn to take great notes. A byproduct of our modern culture is that we have grown accustomed to getting our information in short doses (i.e., TV news sound bites or newspaper articles of *USA Today* style).

Consequently, we've subconsciously trained ourselves to assimilate information better in neat little packages. If your notes are scrawled all over the paper, it fragments the flow of the information. Strive for clarity. Newspapers use a standard format to achieve clarity. Your notes can be much clearer through use of proper formatting. A very effective format is called the "Cornell Method."

Take a sheet of loose-leaf, lined notebook paper and draw a line all the way down the paper about 1-2" from the left-hand edge.

Draw another line across the width of the paper, about 1-2" up from the bottom. Repeat this process on the reverse side of the page.

Look at the highly effective result. You have ample room for notes, a left-hand margin for special-emphasis items or inserting supplementary data from the textbook, a large area at the bottom for a brief summary, and a little rectangular space for just about anything you want.

3. <u>Get the concept, then the details.</u> Too often, we focus on the details and don't gather an understanding of the concept. However, if you memorize only dates, places, or names, you may well miss the whole point of the subject.

A key way to understand things is to put them in your own words. If you are working from a textbook, automatically summarize each paragraph in your mind. If you are outlining text, don't simply copy the author's words.

Rephrase the text in your own words. You remember your own thoughts and words much better than someone else's, and subconsciously tend to associate the important details to the core concepts.

4. <u>Ask Why?</u> Pull apart written material paragraph by paragraph and don't forget the captions under the illustrations.

Example: If the heading is "Stream Erosion," flip it around to read "Why do streams erode?" Then answer the questions.

If you train your mind to think in a series of questions and answers, not only will you learn more, you will get used to answering questions and thereby lessen your test anxiety.

5. <u>Read for reinforcement and future needs.</u> Even if you only have 10 minutes, put your notes or a book in your hand. Your mind is similar to a computer; you have to input data in order to have it processed. *By reading, you are creating the neural connections for future retrieval.* The more times you read something, the more you reinforce the learning of ideas.

Even if you don't fully understand something on the first pass, *your mind stores much of the material for later recall.*

6. <u>Relax to learn, so go into exile.</u> Our bodies respond to an inner clock called biorhythms. Burning the midnight oil works well for some people, but not everyone.

If possible, set aside a particular place to study that is free of distractions. Shut off the television, cell phone, and pager and exile your friends and family during your study period.

If you really are bothered by silence, try background music. Light classical music at a low volume has been shown to aid in concentration over other types.

Music that evokes pleasant emotions without lyrics is highly suggested. Try just about anything by Mozart. It relaxes you.

7. <u>Use arrows, not highlighters.</u> At best, it's difficult to read a page full of yellow, pink, blue, and green streaks.

Try staring at a neon sign for a while and you'll soon see my point; the horde of colors obscures the message.

A quick note, a brief dash of color, an underline, and an arrow pointing to a particular passage is much clearer than a horde of highlighted words.

8. <u>Budget your study time.</u> Although you shouldn't ignore any of the material, *allocate your available study time in the same ratio that topics may appear on the test.*

Testing Tips:

1. Get smart, play dumb. Don't read anything into the question. Don't assume the test writer is looking for something other than what is asked. Stick to the question as written and don't read extra things into it.

2. Read the question and all the choices _twice_ before answering the question. You may miss something by not carefully reading, and then re-reading, both the question and the answers. If you really don't have a clue as to the right answer, leave it blank on the first time through. Go on to the other questions, as they may provide a clue as to how to answer the skipped questions. If, later on, you still can't answer the skipped questions, just _guess_. The only penalty for guessing is that you _might_ get it wrong. Only one thing is certain; if you don't put anything down, you will get it wrong!

3. Turn the question into a statement. Look at the way the questions are worded. The syntax of the question usually provides a clue. Does it seem more familiar as a statement rather than as a question? Does it sound strange? By turning a question into a statement, you may be able to spot if an answer sounds right, and it may also trigger memories of material you have read.

4. Look for hidden clues. It's actually very difficult to compose multiple-foil (choice) questions without giving away part of the answer in the options presented.

In most multiple-choice questions you can often readily eliminate one or two of the potential answers. This leaves you with only two real possibilities, and automatically your odds go to fifty-fifty for very little work.

5. Trust your instincts. For every fact you have read, you subconsciously retain something of that knowledge. On questions you aren't really certain about, go with your basic instincts. Your first impression on how to answer a question is usually correct.

6. Mark your answers directly on the test booklet. Don't bother trying to fill in the optical scan sheet on the first pass through the test.

Just be very careful not to miss-mark your answers when you eventually transcribe them to the scan sheet.

7. Watch the clock! You have a set amount of time to answer the questions. Don't get bogged down trying to answer a single question at the expense of 10 questions you can more readily answer.

<u>DOMAIN I.</u>   HISTORY

**COMPETENCY 1   UNDERSTAND KEY HISTORICAL TERMS AND
CONCEPTS, THE SPECIALIZED FIELDS OF HISTORICAL
STUDY, AND HISTORIOGRAPHY**

**Skill 1.1   Apply key concepts to the analysis of general historical
phenomena and specific historical events**

HISTORY is the study of the past, political and economic events as well as
cultural and social conditions. Students study history through textbooks,
research, field trips to museums and historical sites, and other methods. Most
nations set the requirements in history to study the country's heritage, usually to
develop an awareness and feeling of loyalty and patriotism. History is generally
divided into the three main divisions: (a) time periods, (b) nations, and (c)
specialized topics. Study is accomplished through research, reading, and writing.

History is, without doubt, an integral part of every other discipline in the social
sciences. Knowing the historical background on anything and anyone anywhere
goes a long way toward explaining that what happened in the past leads up to
and explains the present.

Causality: The reason something happens is a basic category of human
thinking. We want to know the causes of some major event in our lives. Within
the study of history, causality is the analysis of the reasons for change. The
questions we ask are why and how a particular society or event developed in the
particular way it did given the context in which it occurred.

Conflict: Conflict within history is the opposition of ideas, principles, values, or
claims. Conflict may take the form of internal clashes of principles, ideas, or
claims within a society or group, or it may take the form of opposition between
groups or societies.

Bias: A prejudice or a predisposition either toward or against something. In the
study of history, bias can refer to the persons or groups studied, in terms of a
society's bias toward a particular political system, or it can refer to the historian's
predisposition to evaluate events in a particular way.

Interdependence: A condition in which two things or groups rely upon one
another—as opposed to independence, in which each thing or group relies only
upon itself.

Identity: The state or perception of being a particular thing or person. Identity can also refer to the understanding or self-understanding of groups, nations, etc.

Nation-state: A particular type of political entity that provides a sovereign territory for a specific nation in which other factors also unite the citizens (e.g., language, race, ancestry, etc.).

Culture: The civilization, achievements, and customs of the people of a particular time and place.

Herodotus was the first major Greek historian who wrote the account of the wars between the Greeks and Persians; often called the "Father of History."

Thucydides wrote an authentic account of the war between Athens and Sparta, titled "History of the Peloponnesian War."

Livy was a Roman historian who wrote "History from the Founding of the City."

Eusebius wrote "Ecclesiastical History," a history of Christianity, showing God's control of human events.

Bede was the Middle Ages' greatest historian who wrote "Ecclesiastical History of the English Nation" (731 A.D.); he is still considered the principal source for English history up to that time.

Ibn Khaldun was a great Arab historian who wrote a seven-volume study of world civilization entitled "Universal History."

Edward Gibbon was a British scholar who wrote the masterpiece "History of the Decline and Fall of the Roman Empire," which showed bias against Christianity and blamed Christianity in part for the fall of the Roman Empire.

Leopold von Ranke is considered the "Father of Modern History." He conceived the basic methods modern historians used to analyze and evaluate historical documents and introduced seminars to train future historians in how to do research.

Skill 1.2   Examine reasons for dividing history into various periods and epochs

The practice of dividing history into a number of discrete periods or blocks of time is called "periodization." Because history is continuous, all systems of periodization are arbitrary to some extent. However, dividing time into segments facilitates understanding of changes that occur over time and helps identify similarities of events, knowledge, and experience within the defined period. Further, some divisions of time into these periods apply only under specific circumstances.

Divisions of time may be determined by date, cultural advances or changes, historical events, the influence of particular individuals or groups, or geography. Speaking of the World War II era defines a particular period of time in which key historical, political, social, and economic events occurred. Speaking of the Jacksonian Era, however, has meaning only in terms of American history. Defining the "Romantic Period" makes sense only in England, Europe, and countries under their direct influence.

Many of the divisions of time that are commonly used are open to some controversy and discussion. The use of BC and AD dating, for example, has clear reference only in societies that account time according to the Christian calendar. Similarly, speaking of "the year of the pig" has greatest meaning in China.

An example of the kind of questions that can be raised about designations of time periods can be seen in the use of "Victorian." Is it possible to speak of a Victorian era beyond England? Is literature written in the style of the English poets and writers "Victorian" if it is written beyond the borders of England?

Some designations also carry both positive and negative connotations. "Victorian" is an example of potential negative connotations, as well. The term is often used to refer to class conflict, sexual repression, and heavy industry. These might be negative connotations. In contrast, the term "Renaissance" is generally read with positive connotations.

Sometimes, several designations can be applied to the same period. The period known as the "Elizabethan Period" in English history is also called "the English Renaissance." In some cases, the differences in designation refer primarily to the specific aspect of history that is being considered. For example, one designation may be applied to a specific period of time when one is analyzing cultural history, while a different designation is applied to the same period of time when considering military history.

Skill 1.3 Compare the characteristics, uses, advantages, and limitations of typical source materials employed by historians in various fields of historical research

The resources used in the study of history can be divided into two major groups: primary sources and secondary sources. Primary sources are works, records, etc. that were created during the period being studied or immediately after it. Secondary sources are works written significantly after the period being studied and based upon primary sources. "Primary sources are the basic materials that provide the raw data and information for the historian. Secondary sources are the works that contain the explications of, and judgments on, this primary material." [Source: Norman F Cantor & Richard I. Schneider. HOW TO STUDY HISTORY, Harlan Davidson, Inc., 1967, pp. 23-24.]

Primary sources include the following kinds of materials:

- Documents that reflect the immediate, everyday concerns of people: memoranda, bills, deeds, charters, newspaper reports, pamphlets, graffiti, popular writings, journals or diaries, records of decision-making bodies, letters, receipts, snapshots, etc.
- Theoretical writings that reflect care and consideration in composition and an attempt to convince or persuade. The topic is generally deeper and has more pervasive values than is the case with "immediate" documents. These may include newspaper or magazine editorials, sermons, political speeches, philosophical writings, etc.
- Narrative accounts of events, ideas, trends, etc. written with intentionality by someone who has contemporary knowledge of the events described.
- Statistical data, although statistics may be inaccurate
- Literature and non-verbal materials, including novels, stories, poetry, and essays from the period, as well as coins, archaeological artifacts, and art produced during the period.

Guidelines for the use of primary resources:

1. Be certain that you understand how language was used at the time of writing and that you understand the context in which it was produced.
2. Do not read history blindly; be certain that you understand both explicit and implicit references in the material.
3. Read the entire text you are reviewing; do not simply extract a few sentences to read.
4. Although anthologies of materials may help you identify primary source materials, the full original text should be consulted.

Secondary sources include the following kinds of materials:

- Books written on the basis of primary materials about the period of time
- Books written on the basis of primary materials about persons who played a major role in the events under consideration
- Books and articles written on the basis of primary materials about the culture, the social norms, the language, and the values of the period
- Quotations from primary sources
- Statistical data on the period
- The conclusions and inferences of other historians
- Multiple interpretations of the ethos of the time

Guidelines for the use of secondary sources:

1. Do not rely upon only a single secondary source.
2. Check facts and interpretations against primary sources whenever possible.
3. Do not accept the conclusions of other historians uncritically.
4. Place greatest reliance on secondary sources created by the best and most respected scholars.
5. Do not use the inferences of other scholars as if they were facts.
6. Ensure that you recognize any bias the writer brings to his/her interpretation of history.
7. Understand the primary point of the book as a basis for evaluating the value of the material presented in it to your questions.

Skill 1.4 Recognize approaches and resources of specialized fields of historical study

Specialized fields of historical study include the following:

- Social History: the approach to the study of history that views a period of time through the eyes of everyday people and is focused on emerging trends; the study of societies in the past.
- Archaeology: study of prehistoric and historic human cultures through the recovery, documentation, and analysis of material remains and environmental data.
- Art History: the study of changes in and social context of art.
- Big History: study of history on a large scale across long time frames (since the Big Bang and up to the future) through a multidisciplinary approach.
- Chronology: science of localizing historical events in time.
- Cultural History: the study of culture in the past.
- Diplomatic History: the study of international relations in the past.
- Economic History: the study of economies in the past.
- Military History: the study of warfare and wars in history.
- Naval History: sometimes considered to be a sub-branch of military history.
- Paleography: study of ancient texts.
- Political History: the study of politics in the past.
- Psychohistory: study of the psychological motivations of historical events.
- Historiography of Science: study of the structure and development of science.
- World History: the study of history from a global perspective.

Skill 1.5   Recognize the existence of conflicting perspectives on historical experience and analyze various interpretations of historical movements and events

Varying perspectives on the study of history may be summarized by one of three definitions:

1. History is the study of what persons have done, said, and thought in the past.
2. History is a creative attempt to reconstruct the lives and thoughts of particular persons who lived at specific times (biography).
3. History is the study of the social aspects of humans, both past and present.

The first definition essentially applies to the *narrative school of history*. This approach attempts to provide a general account of the most important things people have said, done, written, etc. in the past. Several schools fall within this category:

- The political-institutional school believes that what has occurred in government and law is the most important.
- The school of intellectual history (the history of ideas) finds greatest importance in the emergence of higher thought and feeling (including philosophy, art, science, literature).
- Economic historians are most concerned with the way humans have controlled the environment and made a living.
- Cultural historians focus on the development of ideas within the total context of a social, economic, and political situation.

The second definition understands history as a biography of important persons. These historians fall into one of two schools:

- Psychologizing approaches – historians who believe the motivations and actions of people in the past can be understood and explained in terms of modern psychological theories.
- Non-psychologizing approaches – historians who believe it is impossible to psychoanalyze people who are dead and that people of the past must be understood in terms of the theories of personality and motivation that were accepted at the time.

The third definition essentially equates history with sociology. This approach believes it is possible to study history to observe forms of social change that are relevant to current social problems. This group is also divided:

- One group uses the Marxist doctrine of dialectical materialism to explain social change.
- Another group believes that each society is unique and distinctive.
- Comparative sociological historians study history to identify consistent patterns that run through all or several societies.

COMPETENCY 2   UNDERSTAND THE MAJOR POLITICAL, SOCIAL,
ECONOMIC, SCIENTIFIC, AND CULTURAL
DEVELOPMENTS AND TURNING POINTS
THAT SHAPED THE COURSE OF WORLD HISTORY
THROUGH 1500

Skill 2.1   Recognize the principal characteristics and important cultural
contributions of ancient world civilizations and compare
important developments and major civilizations from different
historical periods

Prehistory is defined as the period of human achievement before the
development of writing. In Stone Age cultures, there were three different periods.
In the first, the **Lower Paleolithic Period**, crude tools were used. The second,
the **Upper Paleolithic Period**, exhibited a greater variety of better-made tools
and implements, the wearing of clothing, highly organized group life, and skills in
art. In the third period, the **Neolithic Period**, humans domesticated animals;
mastered food production; engaged in the arts of knitting, spinning and weaving
cloth, starting fires through friction, and building houses rather than living in
caves; and developed institutions such as the family, religion, and a form of
government (the origin of the state).

Ancient civilizations were cultures that developed to a greater degree and were
considered advanced. These included the following, with their respective
accomplishments:

Egypt made numerous significant contributions—including construction of the
great pyramids, development of hieroglyphic writing, preservation of bodies after
death, making paper from papyrus, contributing to developments in arithmetic
and geometry, the invention of the method of counting in groups of 1-10 (the
decimal system), completion of a solar calendar, and laying the foundation for
science and astronomy.

The ancient civilization of the **Sumerians** invented the wheel; developed
irrigation through use of canals, dikes, and devices for raising water; devised the
system of cuneiform writing; learned to divide time; and built large boats for
trade. The **Babylonians** devised the famous "Code of Hammurabi," a code of
laws.

The ancient **Assyrians** were warlike and aggressive, with a highly organized
military, and used horse-drawn chariots.

The **Hebrews**, also known as the ancient Israelites, instituted "monotheism,"
which is the worship of one God, Yahweh. They compiled a collection of sacred
writings containing worship texts, historical accounts, prophecy, instructive
writings and law, including the Ten Commandments.

The **Minoans** had a system of writing using symbols to represent syllables in
words. They built palaces with multiple levels, featuring many rooms, water and
sewage systems with flush toilets, bathtubs, hot and cold running water, and
bright paintings on the walls.

The **Mycenaeans** changed the Minoan writing system to aid their own language and used symbols to represent syllables.

The **Phoenicians** were sea traders well known for their manufacturing skills in glass and metals and the development of their famous purple dye. They became so proficient in the skill of navigation that they were able to sail by the stars at night. Further, they devised an alphabet using symbols to represent single sounds, which was an improved extension of the Egyptian writing system.

In **India**, the caste system was developed to structure society and the principle of zero in mathematics was discovered. Hinduism was the predominant religion, though challenged by the rise of Buddhism. Industry and commerce developed along with extensive trade with the Near East. Outstanding advances in the fields of science and medicine were made, along with leadership and dominance in navigation and maritime enterprises during this time.

China began building the Great Wall, practiced crop rotation and terrace farming, increased the importance of the silk industry, and developed caravan routes across Central Asia for extensive trade. Also, they increased proficiency in rice cultivation and developed a written language based on drawings or pictographs (no alphabet symbolizing sounds as each word or character had a form different from all others).

The ancient **Persians** developed an alphabet; contributed the religions/philosophies of **Zoroastrianism**, **Mithraism**, and **Gnosticism**; and allowed conquered peoples to retain their own customs, laws, and religions.

The classical civilization of **Greece** reached the highest levels in human achievement based on the foundations already laid by such ancient groups as the Egyptians, Phoenicians, Minoans, and Mycenaeans.

Among the more important contributions of Greece was the Greek alphabet, derived from the Phoenician letters, which formed the basis for the Roman alphabet and our present-day alphabet. Extensive trading and colonization resulted in the spread of the Greek civilization. The love of sports, with emphasis on a sound body, led to the tradition of the Olympic Games. Greece was responsible for the rise of independent, strong city-states. Note the complete contrast between independent, freedom-loving Athens with its practice of pure democracy (i.e. direct, personal, active participation in government by qualified citizens) and the rigid, totalitarian, militaristic Sparta. Other important areas that the Greeks are credited with influencing include drama, epic and lyric poetry, fables, myths centered on the many gods and goddesses, science, astronomy, medicine, mathematics, philosophy, art, architecture, and recording historical events. The conquests of Alexander the Great spread Greek ideas to the areas he conquered and brought to the Greek world many ideas from Asia—including the value of ideas, wisdom, curiosity, and the desire to learn as much about the world as possible.

Characteristic of Greek, Hellenistic, and Roman civilizations was an almost religious devotion to the state, which was practiced alongside a large number of personal religions and cults (often called "mystery" religions). No single religion dominated the culture or the political life of these civilizations.

China is considered by some historians to be the oldest, uninterrupted civilization in the world and was in existence around the same time as the ancient civilizations founded in **Egypt**, **Mesopotamia**, and the **Indus Valley**. The Chinese studied nature and weather; stressed the importance of education, family, and a strong central government; followed the religions of Buddhism, Confucianism, and Taoism; and invented such things as gunpowder, paper, printing, and the magnetic compass.

The civilization of **Japan** at this time borrowed much of its culture from China. It was the last of these classical civilizations to develop. Although they used, accepted, and copied Chinese art, law, architecture, dress, and writing, the Japanese refined these into their own unique way of life, including incorporating the religion of Buddhism into their culture.

The civilizations in **Africa**, south of the Sahara, were developing the refining and use of iron, especially for farm implements and later for weapons. Trading was conducted overland using camels and at important seaports. The Arab influence was extremely important, as was their later contact with Indians, Christian Nubians, and Persians. In fact, their trading activities were probably the most important factor in the spread of and assimilation of different ideas and stimulation of cultural growth.

The **Vikings** had a lot of influence at this time, spreading their ideas and knowledge of trade routes and sailing, first through their conquests and later through trade.

Major civilizations in other parts of the world were the **Byzantine** and **Saracenic** (or Islamic) civilizations, both dominated by religion. The major contributions of the Saracens were in the areas of science and philosophy, including accomplishments in astronomy, mathematics, physics, chemistry, medicine, literature, art, trade and manufacturing, agriculture, and a marked influence on the Renaissance period of history.

The **Byzantines** (Christians) made important contributions in art and the preservation of Greek and Roman achievements, including architecture (especially in Eastern Europe and Russia) and the Code of Justinian and Roman law.

The ancient empire of **Ghana** occupied an area that is now known as Northern Senegal and Southern Mauritania. There is no absolute certainty regarding the origin of this empire. Oral history dates the rise of the empire to the seventh century BCE. Most believe, however, that the date should be placed much later. Many believe the nomads who were herding animals on the fringes of the desert posed a threat to the early Soninke people, who were an agricultural community. In times of drought, it is believed the nomads raided the agricultural villages for water and other places to pasture their herds. To protect themselves, it is believed that these farming communities formed a loose confederation that eventually became the empire of ancient Ghana.

The word "Ghana" means king or war chief. It is believed that the Arabs and Europeans took this reference to the king to be the name of the society. These rulers conquered neighboring communities and thus extended the boundaries of the growing empire. The purpose of expansion was to gain control of trade routes. By the fifth century (some say the seventh century), a kingdom had been established. This kingship was significantly different from most other kingships of the time. First, kingship was matrilineal. The sister of the king provided the heir to the throne. Second, the king ruled in conjunction with a People's Council chosen from all social strata.

The empire's economic vitality was determined by geographical location. It was situated midway between the desert, which was the major source of salt and the gold fields. This location along the trade routes of the camel caravans provided exceptional opportunity for economic development. The caravans brought copper, salt, dried fruit, clothing, manufactured goods, etc. For these goods, the people of Ghana traded kola nuts, leather goods, gold, hides, ivory, and slaves. In addition, the empire collected taxes on every trade item that entered the boundaries of the empire.

With the revenue from the trade goods tax, the empire supported a government, an army that protected the trade routes and the borders, the maintenance of the capital, and primary market centers. But it was control of the gold fields that gave the empire political power and economic prosperity. The location of the gold fields was a carefully guarded secret. By the 10th century, Ghana was very rich and controlled an area about the size of the state of Texas. Demand for this gold sharply increased in the ninth and 10th centuries as the Islamic states of Northern Africa began to mint coins. As the gold trade expanded, so did the empire.

The availability of local iron ore enabled the early people of the Ghana kingdom to make more efficient farm implements and effective weapons. But in the 11th century, the Berbers attacked the empire in an attempt to gain control of the gold fields and to purify Islam as it was practiced in Ghana. They eventually withdrew, but left behind a greatly weakened empire. Later, invasions and internal rebellions further weakened the empire and made the trade routes quite dangerous. The merchants moved east and the empire began to crumble. A serious drought compounded the disintegration of the empire through deterioration of the environment and overgrazing. By the middle of the 13th century, the empire was just a memory.

The **Tang Dynasty** extended from 618 to 907. Its capital was the most heavily populated of any city in the world at the time. Buddhism was adopted by the imperial family (Li) and became an integral part of Chinese culture. The emperor, however, feared the monasteries and began to take action against them in the 10th century. Confucianism experienced a rebirth during the time of this dynasty as an instrument of state administration. Following a civil war, the central government lost control of local areas. Warlords arose in 907, and China was divided into north and south. These areas came to be ruled by short-lived minor dynasties. A major political accomplishment of this period was the creation of a class of career government officials, who functioned between the populace and the government. This class of "scholar-officials" continued to fulfill this function in government and society until 1911.

The period of the Tang Dynasty is generally considered a pinnacle of Chinese civilization. Through contact with the Middle East and India, the period of the Tang Dynasty was marked by great creativity in many areas. Block printing was invented, and made much information and literature available to wide audiences.

In science, astronomers calculated the paths of the sun and the moon, as well as the movements of the constellations. This facilitated the development of the calendar. In agriculture, such technologies as cultivating the land by setting it on fire, the curved-shaft plow, separate cultivation of seedlings, and sophisticated irrigation system increased productivity. Hybrid breeds of horses and mules were created to strengthen the labor supply. In medicine, there were achievements like the understanding of the circulatory system and the digestive system and great advances in pharmacology. Ceramics was another area in which great advances were made. A new type of glazing was invented that gave Tang Dynasty porcelain and earthenware its unique appearance through three-colored glazing.

In literature, the poetry of the period is generally considered the best in the entire history of Chinese literature. The rebirth of Confucianism led to the publication of many commentaries on the classical writings. Encyclopedias on several subjects were produced, as well as histories and philosophical works.

Skill 2.2   Identify key factors in the rise and decline of the Roman Empire and the Han dynasty and evaluate major legal, artistic, architectural, technological, and literary achievements of these societies

Rome was one of the early Italian cities conquered by the Etruscans, who ruled over Rome until 509 BCE when they were overthrown by the Roman Republic. The Etruscans had absorbed and modified Greek civilization. Such elements of Greek culture as writing, certain religious practices, and engineering skills were passed on to the Italian peoples during their rule.

The period prior to the establishment of the Republic remains a mystery to modern historians. The following has been reconstructed: Rome was composed of three tribes each divided into clans. Clans were composed of groups of families. There was a division into a class of nobles and the class of commoners very early. The nobles, called **patricians** (fathers), appear to have been the privileged class that functioned as an advisory council to the king and had certain political rights. There was no protective function in the government. Thus, there was no army. Protection of the citizenry was the responsibility of the father of the family, who was also the priest of the religious cult of the home. The father was also a patron to commoner clients. In exchange for services to the family, these clients were given political and legal protection. The family unit, then, was composed of the family itself, free clients, and slaves (once wars of conquest began). The early kings were elected by the nobles and ruled with supreme power in legal matters and in time of war. They were advised by the council, or the senate, which was composed of 30 senators (10 to each tribe). The religion of the early Romans was animistic; they believed that everything was inhabited by a spirit. These were not personified or anthropomorphic until just prior to the birth of the Republic. The religion absorbed a number of Greek and Etruscan elements. The household religion was devoted to household gods, called *lares* and *Penates*. They were believed to protect the household. Ancestors were worshiped and their death masks were maintained in an in-house chapel.

The primary factors that led to the overthrow of the last king and the establishment of the Roman Republic appear to be: (1) a desire to be free of the Etruscans; (2) a desire to put an end to the tyranny of the last king; and (3) the kind of political evolution that occurred elsewhere as the noble classes wanted to cast aside the control of the monarch and establish an aristocratic form of government.

The factors that enabled Rome to conquer Italy were:

- Geographical location in the center of the peninsula, with no mountain barriers.
- A sturdy citizen army and superior military tactics.
- The disunity of their enemies.
- The use of a superior form of imperialism, by which military veterans settled in conquered areas, providing structure and guidance that allowed self-government to local peoples.
- A highly disciplined family structure and a very powerful Patrician.
- A superior form of government, the republic

The structure of the early Republic was clearly aristocratic. The nobles subjugated the commoners and dominated both the consuls and the Senate. In 450 BC, a written law gave new rights to the common people: the right to popular assembly, the creation of *tribunes* to protect the rights of all citizens, and the creation of special new officials (judges and treasury officials) who were to make government fairer and more efficient. By 287 BC, the *Hortensian law* allowed nobles and commoners to intermarry and permitted commoners to hold public offices.

The next 275 years were occupied with expansion. This involved numerous wars of conquest. By 100 BC, Rome controlled most of the Hellenistic world. This rapid conquest was one of the factors in the decline of the Republic. The Republic did not have the infrastructure to absorb the conquered people. In addition, there was political decay, vast economic and social change, and military failure. In politics, the Senate refused to grant rights to the mass of the populace. A civil war erupted between rival factions. Lacking adequate infrastructure, Rome was not able to provide good government to conquered territories. Heavy taxation of these territories, oppression by the government, and corrupt resident government officials led to decay. Critical social and economic changes included the ruin of small farmers by importing slaves from conquered areas, a vast migration of the poor to the city of Rome, a failure to encourage and invest in industry and trade, the dissatisfaction of the new business class, and a general decline in morale among all classes of citizens. At the same time, the Republic experienced a vast slave uprising in Southern Italy and faced the first attacks from Germanic invaders.

The end of the Republic was marked by two significant power struggles. The first was the grasp of power by the *First Triumvirate* in 59 BCE. The Triumvirate consisted of Caesar, Pompey and Crassus. Caesar eliminated Pompey and attempted to establish a dictatorship. Caesar made many reforms, including reducing the power of the Senate, but he was killed in the Senate in 44 BCE.

The following year experienced the rise of the *Second Triumvirate*, composed of Octavian, Mark Antony, and Lepidus. Octavian (later called Augustus) emerged victorious from the ensuing power struggle and became ruler of Rome in 31 BCE. Octavian (Augustus) established a "disguised monarchy" in which he appeared to share power with the Senate, though he withheld most power. He established the boundaries of Rome on the Rhine and Danube rivers, improved government, and extended citizenship rights to all Roman soldiers. The power of the emperor was gradually enlarged by his successors. Finally, the empire reached its greatest heights under "the five good emperors" – Nerva, Trajan, Hadrian, Antoninus Pius, and Marcus Aurelius.

The major contributions of the Roman Empire are:

- Peace and prosperity (the *Pax Romana*)
- The codification of Roman law
- A unified empire that allowed much self-government to component city-states
- The introduction of the idea of separation of powers and popular sovereignty
- The development of the "science" of public administration
- Formalized methods of tax collection
- Construction of an extensive civil-service program
- Tolerance and the granting of citizenship rights to all inhabitants
- Engineering and construction of excellent roads, bridges, aqueducts, and sanitation systems
- Construction of massive buildings: coliseums, public baths, basilicas
- Architectural innovations in the use of vaults and arches
- Preservation of Greek artistic techniques
- Development of education
- Refinement of rhetoric
- Literature: Cicero, Caesar, Lucretius, Virgil, Juvenal, Livy, Plutarch
- Extension of philosophy in the Greek tradition

The reasons for the decline of the Roman Empire are still a matter of debate. However, they may be classified under the following major headings:

Political: a period of anarchy and military emperors led to war and destruction. Diocletian reconstructed the empire, establishing a "divine-right" absolute monarchy, a new imperial bureaucracy, and new administrative divisions to lessen the burden of ruling. Diocletian also reorganized the army and established a new and efficient, but very oppressive, taxation system. Constantine reunited the empire, but moved the capital to the East. All of this reform demoralized the city-states.

Economic: the rise of large villas owned and controlled by landlords who settled poor people on the land as hereditary tenants who lived under conditions of partial servitude; use of wasteful agricultural methods; a decline of commerce; skilled workers bound to jobs and forced to accept government wages and prices; corruption; lack of productivity and inadequate investment of capital; and the draining of gold from the western part of the empire through unfavorable trade balances with the East.

Biological, ecological and social: deforestation, bad agricultural methods, diseases (particularly malaria), earthquakes, immorality, brutal treatment of the masses in the cities, and demoralization of the upper classes. This was accompanied by the decay of pagan beliefs and Roman ideals with the rise of Christianity.

The beginning of the barbarian infiltrations and invasions further weakened the sense of Roman identity. All of these factors contributed to an empire that was ill equipped to contend with invaders.

The **Han Dynasty** in China lasted from 206 BCE to 220 CE. The Dynasty was founded by the family known as the Liu clan. Within China, the period of the Han Dynasty (some 400 years) is generally considered one of the greatest periods in Chinese history. During this period, China officially became a Confucian state. The empire was prosperous and commerce flourished. The empire also extended its influence, both culturally and politically, over Mongolia, Korea, Vietnam, and Central Asia.

Following the death of Emperor Qin Shi Huang of the Qin Dynasty, there was widespread unrest. The resulting revolts were led by peasants, prisoners, soldiers, and descendants of the nobles of the "Six Warring States." These ongoing uprisings toppled the Qin dynasty in 206 BCE. The leader of the insurgents divided the country into 19 feudal states. What followed was five years of war among the states. The struggle was essentially between Chu Han and Liu Bang. Liu Bang eventually won the struggle and became the first emperor of the Han dynasty.

The new empire maintained the administrative structure of the previous dynasty, but established vassal states for the sake of political expediency. Emperor Gao (Liu Bang) divided the country into "feudal states" to appease his wartime allies. His intention, however, was to consolidate his power and then to consolidate the empire. After his death, his successors tried to rule China by combining legalist methods with the Taoist philosophical ideals. This produced a stable centralized government, revival of the agricultural sector, and the break-up of the "feudal states."

Prior to Emperor Wu, the government reduced taxation, reduced the government's control over the lives of the people, created stability, and assumed a subservient relationship to neighboring tribes. Under Emperor Wu, who led the most prosperous period of the Dynasty, the empire fought back and gained control of present day Qinghai, Gansu, and northern Vietnam. He also made China a Confucian state. This enabled Confucian scholars to gain prominence as the core of the civil service. Emperor Wu also sent an envoy to the West and pioneered the route known as the **Silk Road**. To finance his program of expansion, Emperor Wu gave control of land to merchants. This resulted in legalizing the privatization of land. Land taxes were based on the size of fields rather than income. This led to the rise of a landholding class.

Major accomplishments of the Han Dynasty include:
- Development of a strong military
- Westward expansion
- Enabling of secure caravan traffic across Central Asia
- Development of a "tributary system" with non-Chinese local powers that allowed these non-Chinese states autonomy in exchange for symbolic recognition of Han overlordship
- Creation of the Silk Road
- Conversion to a Confucian state
- The invention of paper
- Intellectual, literary and artistic revival
- Introduction of a policy of the government buying surplus commodities and selling them in periods of want to prevent hunger and speculation
- Restricting the coining of metal to the government
- Ssu-ma Chien's narrative of the history of China up to his own time
- Production of one of the world's first dictionaries
- The scientists of the period came close to working out the true length of the solar year
- First observation of sunspots
- The assertion that eclipses were not the warnings of Providence, but natural phenomena
- Artistic carving in stone depicted realistic action
- Making of mirrors, glass and lacquered objects
- The introduction of Buddhism into China

After the death of Wu Ti in 87 BCE, the Han dynasty experienced a rapid decline. In 9 CE, Wang Mang seized the throne and ruled as emperor for almost 15 years. He tried to introduce dramatic innovations and by doing so became very unpopular with the rich. His reforms included ending slavery, dividing large estates, and price-fixing. When he was killed, the Han line was restored.

The later Han rulers were relatively weak and incompetent. An insurrection by the Taoist Red Turbans contributed to the decline of the dynasty. Further weakening resulted from internal corruption and political infighting. The dynasty ended when its capital was captured by the Huns.

Skill 2.3 **Demonstrate an understanding of the principal teachings and historical development of major belief systems**

Judaism: Judaism is the oldest of the Western world's three monotheistic religions. It developed from the ancient religion of the Hebrews or Israelites. This early religion shared a number of common elements and primordial stories with neighboring peoples, especially the Mesopotamian and Babylonian cultures. Judaism's sacred writing, the Hebrew Scripture, is generally referred to as *Torah* or *Tannakh*. It consists of 24 books, which are divided into three sections: Law (*Torah*), Prophets (*Nevi'im*), and Writings (*Ketuvim*).

The word and law of God were transmitted orally for many generations prior to the writing of the Hebrew Scripture. The *Mishna* is the collection of the oral tradition. The *Gemara* is a collection of commentary by the rabbis (teachers). The tradition of living interpretation and commentary continued through the centuries. *Halakah* is the tradition of interpretation of law, history and practice. *Kabbalah* is a body of Jewish mystical literature. *Kabbalah* arose from a movement in France in the 11th Century that discovered an esoteric system of symbolic interpretation of scripture.

Judaism is centered in belief in a single, all-powerful, all-seeing, and all-knowing God. God chose the Hebrew people from all the people of the earth and entered into a covenant with them. "I will be your God, and you will be my people." This covenant implies special privileges, but it also implies certain obligations of the people. The life of the people is to be structured around the promises and commandments of God. The Law provides the structure of religious practice and daily life. The Law is the guide for making ethical choices that reflect and demonstrate their unique character as the chosen people of God. Failure to act in accordance with God's law is a willful act, called sin. Sin destroys the proper relationship between the person and God. It is, however, possible to return from willful rebellion and restore the broken relationship. Judaism is also marked by a strong sense of communal identity, and sin can be either individual or communal.

The Hebrew people, as the chosen people of God, are to remain separate or apart from other peoples in several ways. First, the Hebrews are to avoid marriage to persons outside the faith. Second, they are to observe certain dietary restrictions The rules for **kosher** (ritually correct) food preparation and consumption are quite detailed and include prohibitions against eating certain animals, including pork and shellfish, specifications for the slaughter and butchering of meat, and a prohibition against mixing meat and dairy products. Third, they shall not marry foreigners (this protects the faith of the community against other influences and conflicting ideas). Fourth is the circumcision of all males (this is both an act of obedience to the covenant and an indication of the separateness of the people).

Among devout Jews, special times for prayer are at dawn, noon, dusk and, for some, bedtime. The Jewish Sabbath is observed from sunset on Friday until sunset on Saturday. The Sabbath is a day of rest. Many observant Jews gather on the Sabbath for worship in synagogues, where a Rabbi leads them in readings from the Scriptures, prayer, and singing. The Jewish religious calendar is based on a lunar calendar, so the dates of religious holidays vary from year to year. With the exception of the New Year observance and the Day of Atonement, most holidays are based on either seasonal or historical events. The frequent prohibitions against idolatry in Hebrew Scripture reflect a deep and abiding concern that no limited entity or belief be mistaken for the one true God by God's chosen people.

The basic beliefs of Judaism are:

(1) There is one and only one God with whom each believer has direct personal experience and to whom prayers may be addressed.
(2) God is the ultimate authority and possesses final dominion over the universe, which God created.
(3) Life is holy.
(4) The **Torah** is a guide to correct living and a source of continued revelation of the word of God.
(5) Group worship and prayer are indispensable elements of a righteous life.
(6) Jews share a broad common diversity and a sense of collective purpose and responsibility to one another.

Today, there are three basic branches or schools of Jewish belief and practice.

Orthodox Judaism is the most rigorous and the smallest branch. This group conducts worship in Hebrew and interprets the Law very strictly and literally. **Reform** Judaism, which originated in the 18th century, attempted to integrate Judaism into the mainstream European culture. Law, doctrine, and ritual are more liberally interpreted, and dietary laws generally are not observed. **Conservative** Judaism combines doctrinal reform with traditional observance. This attempt to retain much of the old orthodoxy while also staying in touch with contemporary culture has made Conservatives slower in embracing most of the changes of Reform Judaism.

Christianity: Christianity grew out of Judaism and its belief that God would send a Messiah ("anointed one") who would establish the Kingdom of God on earth. Jesus of Nazareth appeared in the early years of the first century CE, preaching repentance in preparation for the arrival of the Kingdom of God. His brief (about three years) ministry of teaching, preaching, healing, and miracles gathered followers from among the common and the despised of his day, as well as non-Jews and the wealthy. This ministry was confined to the areas of Galilee and northwest Palestine. According to Christian writings, Jesus eschewed the separatism of Judaism and reached out to the poor, the sick, and the social outcasts. He preached a Kingdom of God not of this world, which ran contrary to Jewish expectation of a political Messiah who would establish an earthly kingdom. As the movement grew, the teachings of Jesus were perceived as a danger to the political order by both the Jews and the Roman government. Jesus was handed over to the authorities by one of his closest followers, arrested, tried, and crucified. According to Christian belief, Jesus rose from the dead on the third day, appeared to his disciples, and then ascended to heaven.

Christians believe that Jesus is the Son of God; he died on the cross as an offering and sacrifice that saved humankind from sin. Those who believe in him will be saved. Christian scripture (**the Bible**) consists of two major parts: the Old Testament, which is an adaptation of the Hebrew Scripture, and the New Testament, which consists of 27 books. As an outgrowth of Judaism, Christianity accepts many of the beliefs—though not the practices—of Judaism. Fundamental beliefs of Christianity are: (1) There is one God who is the creator and redeemer of humankind; God is all-knowing, all-powerful, and all-present. (2) Jesus Christ is the unique Son of God who is the savior of humankind. The doctrine of the Trinity teaches that the one God has three natures through/by which God is active in the world: God the Father, the creator and governor of creation, is the judge of humankind; God the Son (Jesus) is God in the flesh, who came among humankind to save them from sin; and God the Holy Spirit is the invisible presence of God that provides believers strength, faith, and guidance.

Christians observe Sunday as the Sabbath because Jesus was believed to have risen from the dead on a Sunday morning. Christian worship consists of the reading of scripture, the proclamation of the word of God, prayer, and the observance of the Sacraments. The Roman Catholic and Eastern Orthodox churches recognize seven sacraments: baptism, confirmation, marriage, ordination, anointing and absolution of the sick and dying, the confession of sins, and the Eucharist or Holy Communion. Protestant churches recognize only two sacraments: baptism and Holy Communion. Christians believe that each human being has an eternal soul that will be judged by God after death. The soul will then be "rewarded" or "punished" according to one's faith and actions in life. Roman Catholics and Eastern Orthodox also believe in the existence of a purgatory, which is a state in which some souls are purified for entry to heaven.

Christian ethics are based on the **Ten Commandments** of the Old Testament and the teachings of Jesus, which include the "Golden Rule" (Do unto others as you would have them do unto you") and a broader application of the commandments.

Until 1054, there was one Christian Church. In 1054, the Eastern Orthodox Church split from the Roman Catholic Church over several issues of belief and practice. In the 16th century, several reformers split from the Roman Catholic Church, again over issues of belief and practice, in what is known as the Protestant Reformation.

Islam: In about 610 CE, an orphan in Mecca, named **Mohammed,** began to preach Islam, a religion believed to have been revealed to him over a period of 23 years through the angel Gabriel. The word "Islam" is derived from an Arabic word meaning "peace." Literally meaning "submission to the will of God," Islam is considered by its followers as the final culmination and fulfillment of the same truths revealed through Moses, Jesus, and other chosen prophets of God. When Mohammed received his first revelation, it is believed that it was his cousin-in-law—a devout Christian of that time—who pronounced him prophet.

Like Judaism and Christianity, Islam traces its roots to Abraham. While Moses and Jesus descended from Abraham's son Isaac, Mohammed descended from his son Ishmael. When Mohammed began to preach, his followers suffered bitter persecution. So, in 622, the Muslim community left their city of Mecca for Medina, about 260 miles to the north. This migration event, called "hijrah," marks the beginning of the Muslim calendar. After several years of living in Medina, where Jews are believed to have been among the tribes that welcomed the Muslims, Mohammed returned to Mecca. Having learned that God loved patience and forgiveness, he forgave his enemies and succeeded in establishing Islam in Mecca as well.

Islam is founded on these primary beliefs:

(1) There is one God for all. He is unique, incomparable and merciful.

(2) God has created angels.

(3) God has sent many prophets to humankind with his message. Prophet Mohammed, the last messenger, reconfirmed what was revealed prior to him.

(4) All people will be judged on the Day of Judgment. All individuals are accountable for their particular intentions and actions.

(5) God has complete authority over destiny, be it good or bad.

(6) This world is a temporary place; there's life after death.

Mohammed left behind a collection of divine revelations (*surahs*) he believed were delivered by the angel Gabriel. These revelations make up Islam's holy scripture, the *Koran* (reading). In addition, Muslims have access to the *Sunnah,* a record of the practices and traditions of Mohammed, and the *Hadith*, a record of Mohammed's sayings. While the *Koran* is the ultimate authority, the *Sunnah* and *Hadith* serve as guides in understanding the Koran in context.

The *Koran* mainly emphasizes the relationship between God and His creatures, but also addresses basic human concerns such as wisdom, worship, and law. It is considered a guide to a just society, proper human conduct, and equitable economic principles. As a guide to Muslim life, it sets forth five basic principles:

(1) There is one God (*Allah*). Mohammed, the last messenger of Allah, summed up the eternal truths revealed by previous prophets. .

(2) One is obliged to pray five times a day at prescribed intervals, facing Mecca. Prayer is a direct link between the worshipper and God. All worshippers facing Mecca is symbolic of the idea that all are children of God and that there is one God for all. There are no distinctions of any kind.

(3) One should practice charity for the welfare of the community. It is believed that setting aside a proportion of personal wealth for those in need purifies possessions and encourages new and fair growth.

(4) Fasting is prescribed from sunrise to sunset every day during the holy month of Ramadan to cleanse the spirit. It is said that fasting helps a person focus on his or her real purpose in life by staying away from worldly pleasures. It makes one more considerate toward the poor and hungry.

(5) Pilgrimage to Mecca should be made if it is physically and financially possible. Mecca is where the "father" of monotheistic religion—Abraham—built the "Kaabah," a house of worship to the one God. Pilgrims wear simple garments that are said to remove all distinctions of class and culture so that all stand equal before God..

The moral principles of Islam are to practice charity, humility, and patience; forgive enemies; avoid avarice, lying, and malice; and stay away from drinking alcohol, eating pork, and gambling. According to the *Koran*, all souls will be judged on the Day of Judgment on the basis of their true and honest "intentions" in this world. Ultimately, God alone will determine who is faithful, just and honest. These people will see their rewards in heaven, while those who are swayed by worldly gain alone and engage in unjust and selfish practices will be given due punishment. Mohammed repeatedly instructed people to use their powers of intelligence and observation. He said God has bestowed humans with the ability to learn, so it is their obligation to seek knowledge. Islam, therefore, puts special emphasis on education.

The *Koran* also mentions the concept of "jihad," which literally means "struggle." This could be a personal and inner struggle against evil within oneself; a struggle for goodness and righteousness on the social level; or struggle on the battlefield, only if and when necessary for self defense. Even in combat, Muslims must follow strict rules. They are prohibited from harming civilians or destroying crops, trees and livestock.

The *Koran* elevates the level of women—although the treatment of women in many Muslim societies today is reflective of cultural practices rather than authentic Islamic teaching. In Islam, women are given the rights to earn their own living, choose their marriage partners, and own and dispose of their personal property and earnings as they wish. Roles of men and women are seen as complementary and collaborative. Their rights and responsibilities are to be equitable and balanced in society.

According to Islam, the family is the foundation of society. Marriage is encouraged as both a sacred act and a legal agreement between the partners. The groom is asked to give a marital gift to the bride for her own use, and she may keep her own family name instead of adopting her husband's.

Although allowed as a last resort in troubled relationships, divorce is considered as "despised" by God and as a betrayal of a sacred relationship. Emphasis is placed on love, fairness, and harmony in the relationship.

Both men and women are expected to dress and act in a modest and dignified manner. However, specific traditions of dress that have evolved over time may once again reflect cultural practices.

Hinduism: Hinduism is unique among the major religions of the world in that it has no identifiable founder, no single theological system, no single code of ethics, and no central religious organization. Modern Hinduism evolved from an ancient religion called Vedism, which dates from around 1500 BCE. Hinduism is expressed in many forms, most of which are "henotheistic" – recognizing a single God that is manifested or expresses itself in other gods and goddesses.

Hinduism recognizes several sacred writings: the Vedas (the chants of the priestly class of the Aryan or "noble" people who introduced Vedism into the Indian subcontinent), with their four central texts – the **Rig Veda** ("hymn knowledge"), the **Yajur Veda** ("ceremonial knowledge"), the **Sama Veda** ("chant knowledge") and the **Atharva Veda** ("knowledge from Atharve," a Vedic teacher); the **Brahmana** and **Aranyakas**, which are ceremonial rules that were later added to the other Vedas; and the **Upanishads**, which is a collection of poetry and prose that explores the basic philosophical and spiritual concepts of Hinduism. The Upanishads teach that spiritual mastery is achievable by all who practice correct meditation and discipline. Two other important Hindu texts are the **Ramayana** and the **Mahabharata**, which includes the **Bahagavad Gita**. The Bhagavad Gita teaches that duty (dharma) and action are equal to prayer and sacrifice as paths to spiritual perfection.

Hinduism is a very complex and very diverse religion. Beliefs and practices vary from one school to another. Central beliefs are:

(1) Worship is an individual or family matter.
(2) Atman and **Brahman** are generally understood as "soul" and "divine spirit."
(3) Brahman is the course and substance of all existence; when it is understood as the "self" of humans, it is called Atman.
(4) The spiritual goal of Hinduism is to understand and experience that there is no difference between one's self and the rest of the universe.
(5) **Maya**, which is used to describe the world, comes from the concepts of magic and matter and is often translated as "illusion." This belief is that the world has a single spiritual nature and is not divided into "things."
(6) **Karma** is the moral consequence of every act in the course of human life.
(7) **Samsara** is the cycle of birth and rebirth in life. The path of the soul through rebirth is determined by the individual's karma.
(8) **Moksha**, which means "liberation" or "freedom," refers to the soul breaking free of the endless cycle of rebirth in life. Moksha is attained by freeing oneself of egotism and anger and losing one's sense of individuality in Maya. The ultimate goal of Hinduism is the achievement of recognition that one's self is indistinguishable from Brahman.

In addition, Hindus also believe in pursuing worldly goals, including religious and social duty, economic security and power, and pleasure, all of this according to one's place in society. The **caste** system provides the framework of society and this process. The society is divided into four major "castes" that are defined by social standing and occupation. These are the priestly class; the aristocratic protectors of society; the class of merchants, landowners and moneylenders; and the laborers. Those outside the caste system were the "Untouchables."

Yoga is an active path to spiritual perfection. Evolving around the cults of anthropomorphic gods, there are three major theistic traditions. Vishnu is the force of preservation, Shiva is a god of destruction, and Brahma is the creative force. Hindus honor a number of incarnations of these gods, including Rama and Krishna. Hindus believe that all living things share a common element of Brahman, and thus are to be respected. Some animals are understood to be manifestations of certain deities. The most honored animal is the cow.

Buddhism: Buddhism was developed and taught by Siddhartha Gautama in what is now Nepal around 563 BCE. Upon consideration of the suffering of people in the world, he traveled widely, studying and meditating. He experienced "enlightenment" and thus earned the name *Buddha*, which means "the awakened one" or "the enlightened one." He then created an order of monks and taught the Buddhist philosophy of escape from life's cycle of suffering through compassion, nonviolence, and moderate living.

The central written text of Buddhism is called the **Tipitaka**, the "three baskets" or collections of Buddhist thought. Although these were not written down until many years after the death of the Buddha, these texts are accepted as his exact words. The three baskets are: the **sutras**, which are the teachings in the form of dialogues and sermons; the **vinaya**, which are the rules for monastic life; and the **abhidharma**, a systematic ordering of the lessons of the sutras.

Buddism shared a number of beliefs and ideas with Hinduism. These include the cycle of birth and rebirth. The idea of **nirvana** is quite similar to moksha in the Hindu tradition, which is an escape from the cycle of rebirth. However, Buddhism teaches that nothing is permanent, including the universal spirit or the self. The Buddha taught that there is constant change in the universe and that all things will, in time, decay and disappear. Because nothing can endure unchanged forever, desire is infinite and insatiable. Peace and enlightenment are thus possible only by renouncing desire and accepting that existence is not permanent.

The **Three Jewels of Buddhism** are the three things that are the heart of Buddhist belief:

(1) the Buddha is the model of what all humans should aspire to be or become
(2) the overarching Buddhist worldview and way of life

(3) the community of Buddhist nuns and monks

The **Four Noble Truths** summarize the Buddhist worldview: All life involves suffering; suffering is caused by desire; desire can be overcome; the way to overcome desire is to follow the eightfold path.

The **Noble Eightfold Path** summarizes the steps one should practice simultaneously to understand the universe, to live compassionately, and to achieve peace and enlightenment: right views, right intentions, right speech, right conduct, right work, right effort, right meditation, and right contemplation.

There are three major schools or branches of Buddhism:

Theravada Buddhism (Doctrine of the Elders) adheres most closely to the earliest practices. The monastic life has special importance in this branch. The ideal is a person who has attained perfect enlightenment and the end of all desire.
Mahayana Buddhism (Greater Vehicle) focuses on compassion for others over personal progress toward enlightenment. The ideal of this branch is the "bodhisattva," an enlightened person who postpones entry into Nirvana to help others.
Vajrayana Buddhism (Tantric Buddhism) emphasizes ritual, including the use of mantras (chants), hand gestures, mandalas (icons of the universe), and prayer wheels.

Confucianism: This is a Chinese religion based on the teachings of the Chinese philosopher Kung Fu-Tzu (translated, Confucius). There is no clergy, no organization, and no belief in a deity or in life after death. Confucius took a code of ethics and the teaching of a scholarly tradition, and systematized it. The teachings of Confucius were written down in the *Analects*. These writings deal with individual morality, ethics, and the correct exercise of power by rulers.

Confucianism was primarily a philosophical and ethical system until about the first century CE, when Buddhism was introduced into China. It gradually began to take on aspects of a religion.

Confucianism is essentially a "humanitarian ethical system" built on five key values:

(1) **Ren**: reciprocal human feeling
(2) **Yi**: righteousness
(3) **Li**: propriety, which includes ritually correct behavior
(4) **Zhi**: knowledge
(5) **Xin**: trustworthiness

These five values enable one to exercise the virtues of *Xiao*, filial piety, and *Wen*, civilization.

Taoism: This is a native Chinese religion with worship of more deities than almost any other religion. It is believed to have been founded by Lao Tzu, who is believed to have been a contemporary of Confucius. The word Tao means path or way. The central writing of Taoism is the *Tao Te Ching* (*The Way and its Power*). The 81 brief chapters, in poetry, discuss the nature of the Tao, which is the source and essence of all being. Primary Taoist concepts, practices and beliefs are: (1) Tao is the first cause of the universe and the force that flows through all life; (2) the goal of each believer is to develop harmony with the Tao; (3) there are many gods, which are manifestations of the one Tao; (4) answers to life's problems are to be sought through inner meditation and outward observation; (5) time is cyclical, not linear; (6) health and vitality are to be strengthened; (7) the five main organs and orifices of the body correspond to the five parts of the universe – fire, water, metal, earth, and wood; (8) the development of virtue is the chief goal of believers; (9) the three "Jewels" to be cultivated in life are moderation, humility, and compassion; (10) humans should allow nature to take its course; (11) one should carefully consider each action in advance; (12) one should be kind to others; and (13) people are compassionate by nature. A basic Taoist symbol is the Yin and Yang. It represents the balance and the essential unity of opposites in the universe.

Shinto: Shinto is a native religion of Japan that developed from native folk beliefs and involved the worship of spirits and demons in animals, trees, and mountains. According to its mythology, deities created Japan and its people, which resulted in worshipping the emperor as a god. Shinto was strongly influenced by Buddhism and Confucianism, but never had strong doctrines on salvation or life after death.

There are "Four Affirmations" in Shinto: (1) tradition and the family (the family is the primary mechanism for preserving traditions); (2) love of nature (nature is sacred. To be in contact with nature is to be close to the gods, who reside in natural objects); (3) physical cleanliness; and (4) "Matsuri" (the honor and worship of the Kami and the ancestral spirits). Morality in Shinto is defined by what is in the best interest of the group.

Skill 2.4 Evaluate the impact of Islam and the role of trade on the growth and development of sub-Saharan African civilizations

During the 14th and 15th centuries, the Muslim Empire experienced great expansion. The conquest of Ghana by Muslim Berbers in 1076 permitted rule to devolve to a series of lesser successor states. By the 13th century, the successor state of Kangaba established the **Kingdom of Mali.** This vast trading state extended from the Atlantic coast of Africa to beyond Gao on the Niger River in the east.

Much of the history of Mali was preserved by Islamic scholars because the Mali rulers converted to Islam and were responsible for the spread of Islam throughout Africa. The expansion of the Mali kingdom began from the city of Timbuktu and gradually moved downstream along the Niger River. This provided increasing control of the river and the cities along its banks, which were critical for both travel and trade. The Niger River was a central link in trade for both west and north African trade routes. The government of the Mali kingdom was held together by military power and trade. The kingdom was organized into a series of feudal states that were ruled by a king. Most of the kings used the surname "Mansa" (meaning "sultan"). The most powerful and effective of the kings was Mansa Musa.

The religion and culture of the kingdom of Mali was a blend of Islamic faith and traditional African belief. The influence of the Islamic empire provided the basis of a large and very structured government, which allowed the king to expand both territory and influence. The people, however, did not follow strict Islamic law. The king was thought of in traditional African fashion as a divine ruler removed from the people. A strong military and control of the Niger River and the trade that flourished along the river enabled Mali to build a strong feudal empire.

Farther to the east, the king of **the Songhai people** had earlier converted to Islam in the 11th century. Songhai was at one time a province of Mali. By the 15th century, Songhai was stronger than Mali and emerged as the next great power in western Africa. Songhai was situated on the great bend of the Niger River. From the early 15th to the late 16th centuries, the Songhai Empire stood, one of the largest empires in the history of Africa. The first king, Sonni Ali, conquered many neighboring states, including the Mali Empire. This gave him control of the trade routes and cities like Timbuktu. He was succeeded by Askia Mohammad, who initiated political reform and revitalization. He also created religious schools, built mosques, and opened his court to scholars and poets from all parts of the Muslim world.

During the same period, **the Zimbabwe kingdom** was built. "Great Zimbabwe" was the largest of about 300 stone structures in the area. This capital city and trading center of the Kingdom of Makaranga was built between the 12th and 15th centuries. It was believed to have housed as many as 20,000 people. The structures are built entirely of stone, without mortar. The scanty evidence that is available suggests that the kingdom was a trading center that was believed to be part of a trading network that reached as far as China.

The area known today as the Republic of Benin was the site of an early African kingdom known as **Dahomey**. By the 17th century, the kingdom included a large part of West Africa. The kingdom was economically prosperous because of slave trading relations with Europeans, primarily the Dutch and Portuguese, who arrived in the 15th century. The coastal part of the kingdom was known as "the Slave Coast." This kingdom was known for a very distinct culture and some very unusual traditions. In 1729, the kingdom started a female army system. A law was passed stating that females would be inspected at the age of 15. Those thought beautiful were sent to the Palace to become wives of the king. Those who were sick or were considered unattractive were executed. The rest were trained as soldiers for two years. Human sacrifice was practiced on holidays and special occasions. Slaves and prisoners of war were sacrificed to gods and ancestors.

The slave trade provided economic stability for the kingdom for almost 300 years. The continuing need for human sacrifices caused a decrease in the number of slaves available for export. As many colonial countries declared the trade of slaves illegal, demand for slaves subsided steadily until 1885 when the last Portuguese slave ship left the coast. With the decline of the slave trade, the kingdom began a slow disintegration. The French took over in 1892.

Skill 2.5   Compare the social and cultural characteristics of Asian empires during the 14th and 15th centuries

The Ottoman Empire is to be noted for its ability to unite a highly varied population as it grew through conquest and treaty arrangement. This ability is attributed to military strength, a policy of strict control in recently invaded territories, and an Islamic belief that stated that all Muslims, Christians, and Jews were related because they were all "People of the Book." The major religious groups were permitted to construct their own semi-autonomous communities. Conquering armies immediately repaired buildings, roads, bridges, and aqueducts, or built them where needed. They also built modern sanitary facilities and linked the city to a supply structure that was able to provide for the needs of the people. This religious and ethnic tolerance was the basis upon which a heterogeneous culture was built. It quickly transformed the Turkish empire into the Ottoman Empire.

In time, the attitude of tolerance and respect for diverse ethnic and cultural groups produced a rich mix of people that was reflected in multicultural and multi-religious policies based on recognition and respect for different perspectives. Ottoman architecture, although influenced by Seljuk, Byzantine and Arab styles, developed a unique style of its own. Music was important to the elites of the empire. Two primary styles of music that developed were Ottoman classical music and folk music. Again, both styles reflect a basis in the diversity of influences that came together in the unified empire.

The Mongol Empire, founded by Genghis Khan, included the majority of the territory from Southeast Asia to central Europe during the height of the empire. One of the primary military tactics of conquest was to annihilate any cities that refused to surrender.

Government was by decree on the basis of a code of laws developed by Genghis Khan. It is interesting that one of the tenets of this code was that the nobility and the commoners shared the same hardship. The society, and the opportunity to advance within the society, was based on a system of meritocracy. The carefully structured and controlled society was efficient and safe for the people. Religious tolerance was guaranteed. Theft and vandalism were strictly forbidden. Trade routes and an extensive postal system were created, linking the various parts of the empire. Taxes were quite onerous, but teachers, artists, and lawyers were exempted from paying taxes. Mongol rule, however, was absolute. The response to all resistance was collective punishment in the form of destruction of cities and slaughter of the inhabitants.

The lasting achievements of the Mongol Empire include:

- Reunification of China and expansions of its borders
- Unification of the Central Asian Republics that later formed part of the USSR
- Expansion of Europe's knowledge of the world

The Ming Dynasty in China followed the Mongol-led Yuan Dynasty. In addition to its expansion of trade and exploration of surrounding regions, the period is well known for its highly talented artists and craftsmen. The Hongwu emperor rose from peasant origins. He distributed land to small farmers in an effort to help them support their families. To further protect these family farms, he proclaimed title of the land non-transferable. He also issued an edict by which anyone who cultivated wasteland could keep the land as their property and would never be taxed. One of the major developments of the time was the development of systems of irrigation for farms throughout the empire. Hongwu maintained a strong army by creating military settlements. During peacetime, each soldier was given land to farm and, if he could not afford to purchase equipment, it was provided by the government.

The legal code created during the period is generally considered one of the greatest achievements of the dynasty. The laws were written in understandable language and in enough detail to prevent misinterpretation. The law reversed previous policy toward slaves and promised them the same protection as free citizens. Emphasis was placed on family relations clearly based on Confucian ideas. The other major accomplishment of this dynasty was the decision to begin building the Great Wall of China to provide protection from northern horsemen.

The Moghul Empire reached its height during the reign of Akbar. In the administration of the empire, Akbar initiated two approaches that are notable. First, he studied local revenue statistics for the various provinces within the empire. He then developed a revenue plan that matched the revenue needs of the empire with the ability of the people to pay the taxes. Although the taxes were heavy (one third to one half of the crop), it was possible to collect the taxes and meet the financial needs of the empire. Second, he created a rank and pay structure for the warrior aristocracy that was based on number of troops and obligations.

He introduced a policy of acceptance and assimilation of Hindus, allowed temples to be built, and abolished the poll tax on non-Muslims. He devised a theory of "rulership as a divine illumination" and accepted all religions and sects. He encouraged widows to remarry, discouraged marriage of children, outlawed the practice of "sati," and persuaded the merchants in Delhi to recognize special market days for women who were otherwise required to remain secluded at home. The empire supported a strong cultural and intellectual life. He sponsored regular debates among religious and scholarly individuals with different points of view.

The unique style of architecture of the Moghul Empire was its primary contribution to South Asia. The Taj Mahal was one of many monuments built during this period. The culture was a blend of Indian, Iranian, and Central Asian traditions. Other major accomplishments were:
- Centralized government
- Blending of traditions in art and culture
- Development of new trade routes to Arab and Turkish lands
- A unique style of architecture
- Landscape gardening
- A unique cuisine
- The creation of two languages (Urdu and Hindi) for the common people

Skill 2.6   Analyze the structure and development of feudal societies in different areas of the world

Between 1000 and 1500 CE, the system of **feudalism** became the dominant feature. It was a system of loyalty and protection. The strong protected the weak that returned the service with farm labor, military service, and loyalty. Life was lived out on a vast estate, owned by a nobleman and his family, called a "manor." It was a complete village supporting a few hundred people, mostly peasants. Improved tools and farming methods made life more bearable, although most never left the manor or traveled from their village during their lifetime. In feudal societies, a very small number of people (or no one) owned land. Instead, they held it as a hereditary trust from some social or political superior in return for services. The superiors were a small percentage of the people, a fighting and ruling aristocracy. The vast majority of the people were simply workers. One of the largest landowners of the time was the Roman Catholic Church. It was estimated that during the 12th and 13th centuries the Church controlled one third of the useable land in Western Europe.

Other important elements from this time period were knighthood and its code of chivalry, as well as the tremendous influence of the Roman Catholic Church. Until the period of the Renaissance, the Church was the only place where people could be educated. The Bible and other books were hand-copied by monks in the monasteries. Cathedrals were built and were decorated with art depicting religious subjects.

With the increase in trade and travel, cities sprang up and began to grow. Craft workers in the cities developed their skills to a high degree, eventually organizing guilds to protect the quality of the work and to regulate the buying and selling of their products. City government developed centered on strong town councils, which consisted of the wealthy businessmen who made up the rising middle class.

The end of the feudal manorial system was sealed by the outbreak and spread of the infamous **Black Death**, which killed over one-third of the total population of Europe. Those who survived and were skilled in any job or occupation were in demand and many serfs or peasants found freedom and, for that time, a decidedly improved standard of living. Strong nation-states became powerful and people developed a renewed interest in life and learning

From its beginnings, Japan morphed into an imperial form of government, with the divine emperor being able to do no wrong and, therefore, serving for life. **Kyoto**, the capital, became one of the largest and most powerful cities in the world. The rich and powerful landowners, the nobles, grew powerful. Eventually, the nobles had more power than the emperor, which required an attitude change in the minds of the Japanese people.

The nobles were lords of great lands and were called **Daimyos**. They were of the highest social class and people of lower social classes worked for them The Daimyos had warriors serving them, known as **Samurai**, who were answerable only to the Daimyo. The Samurai code of honor was an exemplification of the overall Japanese belief that every man was a soldier and a gentleman.

The main economic difference between imperial and feudal Japan was that the money that continued to flow into the country from trade with China, Korea, and other Asian countries and from plunder on the high seas, made its way into the pockets of the Daimyos rather than the emperor's coffers.

Feudalism developed in Japan later than it did in Europe and lasted longer. Japan deflected Mongol invasion because of the famed **kamikaze**, or "divine wind," in the 12th century. Japan was thus free to continue to develop on its own terms and to refrain from interacting with the West. This isolation continued until the 19th century.

COMPETENCY 3 **UNDERSTAND THE MAJOR POLITICAL, SOCIAL, ECONOMIC, SCIENTIFIC, AND CULTURAL DEVELOPMENTS AND TURNING POINTS THAT SHAPED THE COURSE OF WORLD HISTORY FROM 1500 THROUGH 1850**

Skill 3.1 **Analyze the influence of the Renaissance on European political, artistic, and scientific beliefs and practices, including the emergence of modern nation-states**

The Reformation period consisted of two phases: the **Protestant Reformation** and the **Catholic Counter-Reformation**. The Protestant Reformation came about because of religious, political, and economic factors. The religious reasons stemmed from abuses in the Catholic Church, including fraudulent clergy with their scandalous immoral lifestyles; the sale of religious offices, indulgences, and dispensations; different theologies within the Church; and frauds involving sacred relics.

The political reasons for the Protestant Reformation involved the increase in the power of rulers, considered "absolute monarchs," who desired all power and control, especially over the Church. The growth of "nationalism" or patriotic pride in one's own country was another contributing factor.

Economic reasons included the greed of ruling monarchs to possess and control all lands and wealth of the Church, the deep animosity against the burdensome papal taxation, the rise of the affluent middle class and its clash with medieval Church ideals, and the increase of an active system of "intense" capitalism.

The Protestant Reformation began in Germany with the revolt of Martin Luther against Church abuses. It spread to Switzerland, where it was led by Calvin. It began in England with the efforts of King Henry VIII to have his marriage to Catherine of Aragon annulled so he could wed another and have a male heir. The results were the increasing support given not only by the people but also by nobles and some rulers, and of course, the attempts of the Church to stop it.

The Catholic Counter-Reformation was undertaken by the Church to "clean up its act" and to slow or stop the Protestant Reformation. The major efforts to this end were supplied by the Council of Trent and the Jesuits. Seven major results of the Reformation included:

A) End of many abuses
B) Religious freedom
C) Religious tolerance
D) More opportunities for education
E) Power and control of rulers limited
F) Increase in religious wars
G) An increase in fanaticism and persecution

A number of individuals and events led to the time of exploration and discoveries. The Vivaldo brothers and Marco Polo wrote of their travels and experiences. From the Crusades, the survivors made their way home to different places in Europe bringing with them fascinating, new information about exotic lands, people, customs, and desired foods and goods such as spices and silks.

The **Renaissance** was a time of curiosity, learning, and incredible energy sparking the desire for trade to procure these new, exotic products and to find better, faster, cheaper trade routes to get to them. The work of geographers, astronomers and mapmakers made important contributions and many studied and applied the work of such men as Hipparchus of Greece, Ptolemy of Egypt, Tycho Brahe of Denmark, and Fra Mauro of Italy.

The word, Renaissance, literally means "rebirth." It was a time of renewed interest in the glory of ancient classical Greek and Roman civilizations. It was the period in human history that gave birth to many new ideas and innovations.

The Renaissance began in Italy, particularly in Florence, which was controlled by the Medici family. Education included reading, writing, math, the study of law, and the writings of classical Greek and Roman writers.

Renaissance artists, most notably Leonardo da Vinci, Michelangelo, Raphael, Titian, Donatello, and Rembrandt, pioneered a new method of painting and sculpture—people and events were realistically portrayed rather than idealized. Michelangelo's *David* is a perfect example of this trend.

In Literature, humanists including Petrarch, Boccaccio, Erasmus, and Sir Thomas More shifted the focus to life on earth, realistically portrayed, rather than heaven and its rewards. The monumental works of Shakespeare, Dante, and Cervantes found their origins in these ideas as well. The invention of the printing press made these literary works more generally available to the people.

The Renaissance changed music as well. No longer written primarily in the service of the Church, music complemented every aspect of life. Musicians worked for themselves, rather than for the churches, and began to experiment with new styles for the sake of the art itself.

Science advanced considerably during the Renaissance, especially in the area of physics and astronomy. Copernicus, Kepler, and Galileo led a Scientific Revolution in proving that the earth was round and that it was not the center of the universe.

All of these things encouraged people to see the world and their place within it in a new way.

Contributions of the Italian Renaissance period were in:

Art - the more important artists were **Giotto**, known for his development of perspective in paintings; **Leonardo da Vinci**, who was not only an artist but also a scientist and inventor; and **Michelangelo**, a sculptor, painter, and architect. Others important artists included **Raphael**, **Donatello**, **Titian**, and **Tintoretto**.

Political philosophy - the writings of **Machiavelli**

Literature - the writings of **Petrarch** and **Boccaccio**

Science - **Galileo**

Medicine - the work of Brussels-born **Andrea Vesalius** earned him the title of "father of anatomy" and had a profound influence on the Spaniard **Michael Servetus** and the Englishman **William Harvey**.

In Germany, Gutenberg's invention of the **printing press** with movable type facilitated the rapid spread of Renaissance ideas, writings and innovations, thus ensuring the enlightenment of most of Western Europe. Contributions were also made by Durer and Holbein in art and by Paracelsus in science and medicine.

The effects of the Renaissance in the Low Countries can be seen in the literature and philosophy of **Erasmus** and the art of **van Eyck** and **Breughel the Elder**. **Rabelais** and **de Montaigne** in France also contributed to literature and philosophy. In Spain, the art of **El Greco** and **de Morales** flourished, as did the writings of **Cervantes** and **De Vega**. In England, **Sir Thomas More** and **Sir Francis Bacon** wrote and taught philosophy inspired by **Vesalius**. **William Harvey** made important contributions in medicine. The greatest talent in literature and drama was seen in the works of **Chaucer, Spenser, Marlowe, Jonson**, and **Shakespeare**.

Skill 3.2   Compare and contrast the exercise of power by world political leaders and analyze challenges to absolutism

Louis XIV acceded to the throne shortly before his fifth birthday. His mother and the First Minister, Mazarin, controlled the government until Mazarin's death in 1661, at which time Louis XIV declared that he would rule the country. He has been referred to alternately as Louis the Great, the Great Monarch, and The Sun King. During his reign, France attained cultural dominance, as well as military and political superiority. Louis XIV created a centralized government that he ruled with absolute power. He is often considered "the archetype of an absolute monarch." He is quoted as claiming "I am the State." However, many scholars believe this statement was falsely attributed to him by political opponents. It did, however, summarize the absolute power he held.

Mazarin was hated and distrusted in most political circles because he was not French born. The absolute rule exercised by Anne (his mother) and Mazarin was very unpopular among the people. At about the time the Thirty Years' War ended (1648), a civil war, known as the *Fronde*, broke out in France. Mazarin continued the policies of his predecessors in trying to expand the power of the Crown at the expense of the nobles. He tried to impose a tax on the members of the Parliament. Parliament refused to pay the tax and ordered all of his previous financial edicts burned. Mazarin responded by arresting several members of the Parliament. The result was insurrection and rioting in Paris. The royal family fled. When the war ended the French army was available to aid and protect the royal family. By January 1649, the conflict was temporarily ended with the Peace of Rueil.

The second Fronde broke out in 1650. This was a revolt of the nobility and the clergy against the crown. During these times of rebellion, the Queen sold jewels to feed her family. Louis XIV emerged from these years of internal rebellion with a strong distrust of both the nobility and the common people.

Louis XIV reigned as an absolute monarch. To be sure, he and his advisors moved France to economic strength, political power, and influence in Europe. His claim of absolute power by divine right combined with his distrust of others led to unique actions to maintain power and control over any who might instigate rebellion against him. One of his tactics to control the nobility was to require them to remain at the Palace of Versailles, where he could watch them and prevent them from plotting unrest in their communities. He spent lavishly on parties and distractions to keep the nobility occupied and to strengthen his control over them. He was determined to undercut the power and influence of the nobility. He tried to fill high offices with commoners or members of the new aristocracy because he believed that if commoners got out of hand, they could be dismissed. He knew he could not mitigate the influence of great nobles. By forcing the powerful nobles to remain at court, he effectively reduced their power and influence. By appointing commoners and new aristocracy to government functions, he increased his control over both the functions and those who held them. He controlled the nobles to such an extent that he was able to ensure that there would never be another Fronde.

Louis also tried to control the Church. He called an assembly of the clergy in 1681. By the time the assembly ended, he had won acceptance of the "Declaration of the Clergy of France," by which the power of the Pope was greatly reduced and his power was greatly enhanced. This Declaration was never accepted by the Pope.

Perhaps the great mistake of Louis' reign was his attitude toward Protestantism and his handling of the Huguenots. In 1685 he revoked the Edict of Nantes. This resulted in the departure from the country of these French Protestants, who were among the wealthiest and most industrious people in the nation. He also alienated the Protestant countries of Europe, particularly England.

Catherine the Great (Catherine II) has often been called the "enlightened despot." She came to power through a coup that removed her husband (Peter III) from the throne and had herself proclaimed Empress with the help of the military and other politically powerful persons with whom Catherine had cultivated relationships. Shortly after the coup, Peter was murdered.

Catherine revised Russian law in an effort to make it more logical and more humane. She built many hospitals and orphanages, encouraged the people to be inoculated against smallpox, and wanted to establish schools throughout the nation to teach the people the responsibilities of citizenship. Despite her sympathy for the peasants, she did nothing to free them from serfdom. In fact, to maintain control of the nobility, she made large land grants, which increased serfdom. She divided Russia into 50 provinces. She claimed to want each district to control its own local affairs, yet she empowered the governors she appointed. The end result was broader despotism rather than enlightenment.

Because Catherine's power relied upon the loyalty of the nobles, they had to be pleased with land grants. She did not enforce her more humanitarian ideas when her subordinates did not enforce them. Although she was "enlightened," she never forgot that she ruled an empire of "barbarous peoples." She corresponded with leading thinkers of the day throughout Europe and read widely. This resulted in some influence of European culture and technology, philosophy, and social theory. However, the influence of these ideas was limited to a very small number of professional and intellectual circles.

Tokugawa Ieyasu came to power in Japan in 1600 by defeating a coalition that sought political power in Japan. His rise to power marks the beginning of the Tokugawa shogunate, which held power as military rulers in Japan until 1868. In the 16th century, Japan had absorbed a great deal of European influence. The Portuguese had arrived in 1543 and Francis Xavier, a Jesuit priest, brought a mission to Japan in 1549. By 1600 there were about 300,000 Christians, including a number of the military aristocracy. Hideyoshi began to suppress Christianity as a foreign threat in 1587, and banished the Portuguese missionaries. The Tokugawa shoguns persecuted Christianity more extensively by executing thousands of Christians and driving the Church underground. An uprising in 1637-38 culminated in a massive slaughter. After this event, foreigners were banned from the country, except for a small number of Dutch merchant traders who were strictly confined to an island.

This military dictatorship adopted the existing social class hierarchy that was in place. The warrior-caste of samurai was at the top of the hierarchy. Next were farmers, artisans, and traders. This very tightly controlled hierarchy eventually led to conflict. The peasants were taxed in fixed amounts. There was no variation in the amount of the tax. As monetary values changed, this resulted in less support for the samurai who collected the taxes. There were a number of confrontations between the samurai, who were growing steadily poorer, and the peasants, who were growing steadily wealthier. None of these conflicts had significant results until the arrival of foreign power and influence.

A rebellion by the "titular Emperor" and several of the powerful nobles resulted in the Boshin War. The war ended in the Meiji Restoration and the overthrow of the Tokugawa shogunate. Foreign travel was banned, as well as foreign books. This permitted a flourishing of local culture. Although the government was stable, the financial situation of the government was slowly declining, resulting in higher taxes. The tax increases caused riots among the farmers and peasants. A number of natural disasters caused years of famine and deepening financial difficulties. The merchant class claimed greater power and many samurai became financially dependent upon them. The second part of the Edo era was marked by corruption, decline of morality, and government incompetence.

The financial difficulties and the inability of the government to respond to numerous natural disasters and famine produced growing anti-government sentiment. Movements arose that tried to limit Western influence and to restore control of the government to the imperial line. Others wanted greater openness to Western ideas and technology.

Skill 3.3   Analyze major causes and consequences of European expansion and colonialism and examine economic, political, and cultural relations among peoples of Europe, Africa, Asia, the Pacific, and the Americas

In the century and a half after 1520, European nations began to reap the benefits of the age of exploration and discovery. They began a period of economic and colonial expansion that spread European civilization throughout the world. Europeans invaded the Far East and the unknown areas to the West, pillaging, trading, colonizing, and introducing Christianity to native peoples. Capitalism spread to an extent that essentially dominated the economic activities of the nations. Considering the rate of expansion of overseas trade, the great increase in the volume and variety of goods transported, and the resulting increase in the wealth of European nations, it seems appropriate to speak of a commercial revolution. Several factors fueled this desire for expansion: the desire for knowledge, the desire to convert the heathen natives to Christianity, the lust for gold and silver, and the capitalist desire to reap the benefits of trade.

In the early years of expansion, the most active peoples were the Spanish, the Portuguese, and the Dutch. In fact, in 1494, the Pope divided the planet between Spain and Portugal. The French and English did not become active players in the competition for foreign colonies and domination until the 17th century. By 1600, foreign trade was becoming more important to both nations. The English East India Company was typical of the way this expansion was occurring. This was a chartered company, rather than a government effort, that became the agency of expansion.

The first Europeans in the New World were **Norsemen** led by Eric the Red and later, his son Leif the Lucky.

Portugal made the start under the encouragement, support, and financing of Prince Henry the Navigator. The better known explorers who sailed under the flag of Portugal included Cabral, Diaz, and Vasco da Gama, who successfully sailed all the way from Portugal, around the southern tip of Africa, to Calcutta, India.

Christopher Columbus, who sailed for **Spain**, is credited with the discovery of America, although he never set foot on its soil. Magellan is credited with the first circumnavigation of the earth. Other Spanish explorers made their marks in parts of what are now the United States, Mexico, and South America.

For **France**, claims to various parts of North America were the result of the efforts of such men as Verrazano, Champlain, Cartier, LaSalle, Father Marquette, and Joliet.

Dutch claims were based on the work of one Henry Hudson.

John Cabot gave **England** its stake in North America along with John Hawkins, Sir Francis Drake, and the half-brothers Sir Walter Raleigh and Sir Humphrey Gilbert.

The ancestors of today's Native Americans and Latin American Indians crossed the Bering Strait from Asia to Alaska, eventually settling in all parts of the Americas.

Competition for trade monopolies in the East led to a struggle between the English and the Dutch. England's first Navigation Act (1651) was directed against the Dutch. There was rivalry with Spain for control of various areas on the part of the Dutch and the English. This was superseded by the *Anglo-Dutch Wars*. There were a number of issues in this conflict: slave trade of Africa, Atlantic fisheries, North American settlements, and trade. The Dutch East India Company had shut off the Spice Islands from the English. The final result was an English trading post in the Spice Islands.

England and France had stood together to evict the Dutch from the North American mainland. Numerous changes were occurring, however, within England, eventually bringing William of Orange to the throne. William and Louis XIV were bitter enemies, and opinion turned toward the view that the true enemy of England was France. This resulted in the Anglo-French Conflict. Both nations had adopted mercantilist policies. Both countries had competing colonies and trading interests in the New World, Asia, and the West Indian islands. On the North American mainland, English settlements essentially controlled the Atlantic coast from Maine to Georgia. These areas were well populated and provided fish, tobacco, and trade. Although less densely populated, the French had claims of a large area of land. The Louisiana Territory was under French control. Competition between England and France for land, sugar, and furs was intense. The English colonies were barred from westward expansion by French territory, which was being protected by a strong line of military defenses. India, which was densely populated and in possession of a strong culture, was also highly prized by both nations. By 1689 the English had established outposts at Bombay, Madras, and Calcutta. The French had come to India somewhat later and established their outposts in two areas near Calcutta and Madras. Both nations saw these outposts as entry points for greater penetration of India. These areas were the loci of the conflicts that ensued.

The first struggle was *The War of the League of Augsburg,* which occurred in Acadia. The Treaty of Ryswick restored the previous division of territory. The second was *The War of the Spanish Succession.* English and Dutch sea power prevailed over French and Spanish. The Treaty of Utrecht gave England clear possession of Acadia (New Scotland), Newfoundland, Hudson Bay, and St. Kitts in the West Indies. The third conflict was *The War of the Austrian Succession.* This was a resumption of the hostilities between England and Spain. It merged into the European War. France and England were at odds again in North America and in India. The treaty of Aix-la-Chapelle restored pre-war territorial holdings. The French had, however, strengthened their positions in the Louisiana territory. The issue of control of the Ohio Valley led to the French and Indian Wars. Spain tried to intervene on behalf of France, but it was too late. The war in India, at about the same time, ended with the British dominating the east coast of India. Both of these struggles came to be incorporated into the Seven Years' War in Europe. The Treaty of Paris (1763) restored peace at a very high cost to France. The treaty essentially ended France's claim to be an imperial power. When the American colonies declared independence thirteen years later, the assistance of the French was critical to the success of the colonies. With the decline of French power, England was able to expand her empire and consolidate her interests.

Skill 3.4   Identify major causes and consequences of the scientific, agricultural, and industrial revolutions and evaluate their impact on human society and the physical world

The **Scientific Revolution** was characterized by a shift in scientific approach and ideas. Near the end of the 16th century, Galileo Galilei introduced a radical approach to the study of motion. He moved from attempts to explain why objects move the way they do and began to use experiments to describe precisely how they move. He also used experimentation to describe how forces affect non-moving objects. Other scientists continued in the same approach. Outstanding scientists of the period included Johannes Kepler, Evangelista Torricelli, Blaise Pascal, Isaac Newton, and Gottfried Leibniz. This was the period when experiments dominated scientific study. This method was particularly applied to the study of physics.

The **Agricultural Revolution** occurred first in England. It was marked by experimentation that resulted in increased production of crops from the land and a new and more technical approach to the management of agriculture. The revolution in agricultural management and production was hugely enhanced by the Industrial Revolution and the invention of the steam engine. The introduction of steam-powered tractors greatly increased crop production and significantly decreased labor costs. Developments in agriculture were also enhanced by the Scientific Revolution and the learning from experimentation that led to philosophies of crop rotation and soil enrichment. Improved systems of irrigation and harvesting also contributed to the growth of agricultural production.

The **Industrial Revolution**, which began in Great Britain and spread elsewhere, was the development of power-driven machinery (fueled by coal and steam) leading to the accelerated growth of industry with large factories replacing homes and small workshops as work centers. The lives of people changed drastically and a largely agricultural society changed to an industrial one. In Western Europe, the period of empire and colonialism began. The industrialized nations seized and claimed parts of Africa and Asia in an effort to control and provide the raw materials needed to feed the industries and machines in the "mother country". Later developments included power based on electricity and internal combustion, replacing coal and steam.

Skill 3.5   Examine the origins of the Enlightenment and French Revolution and analyze their influence on world history

The period from the 1700s to the 1800s was characterized in Western countries by opposing political ideas of democracy and nationalism. This resulted in strong nationalistic feelings and people of common cultures asserting their belief in the right to have a part in their government.

The **Enlightenment** was a period of intense self-study that focused on ethics and logic. Scientists and philosophers questioned cherished truths, widely held beliefs, and their own sanity in an attempt to discover why the world worked—from within. "I think, therefore I am" was one of the famous sayings from this era. It was uttered by Rene Descartes, a French scientist-philosopher whose dedication to logic and the rigid rules of observation were a blueprint for the thinkers who came after him.

One of the giants of the era was England's **David Hume**. Hume, a pioneer of the doctrine of empiricism (believing things only when you've seen the proof for yourself), was also a prime believer in the value of skepticism. In other words, he was naturally suspicious of things other people told him and constantly set out to discover the truth for himself. These two related ideas influenced many great thinkers after Hume and his writings.

Immanuel Kant of Germany was both a philosopher and a scientist. He took a scientific view of the world. He wrote the movement's most famous essay, "Answering the Question: What Is Enlightenment?" and he answered his famous question with the motto "Dare to Know." For Kant, the human being was a rational being capable of hugely creative thought and intense self-evaluation. He encouraged all to examine themselves and the world around them. He believed that the source of morality lay not in nature or in the grace of God, but in the human soul itself. He believed that man believed in God for practical, not religious or mystical, reasons.

Also prevalent during the Enlightenment was the idea of the **social contract**, the belief that government existed because people wanted it to, that the people had an agreement with the government that they would submit to it as long as it protected them and didn't encroach on their basic human rights. This idea was first made famous by the Frenchman Jean-Jacques Rousseau, but was also adopted by England's **John Locke** and America's Thomas Jefferson. John Locke was one of the most influential political writers of the 17th century who emphasized human rights and put forth the belief that when governments violate those rights people should rebel. In 1960, he wrote the book *Two Treatises of Government*, which influenced political thought in the American colonies and helped shape the U.S. Constitution and Declaration of Independence.

The **American Revolution** resulted in the successful efforts of the English colonists in America to win their freedom from Great Britain. After more than 100 years of mostly self-government, the colonists resented the increased British meddling and control, they declared their freedom, won the Revolutionary War with aid from France, and formed a new independent nation.

The **French Revolution** was the revolt of the middle and lower classes against the gross political and economic excesses of the rulers and the supporting nobility. It ended with the establishment of the first in a series of French Republics. Conditions leading to revolt included extreme taxation, inflation, lack of food, and the total disregard for the impossible, degrading, and unacceptable condition of the people on the part of the rulers, nobility, and the Church.

The **Russian Revolution** occurred first in March (or February on the old calendar) 1917 with the abdication of Tsar Nicholas II and the establishment of a democratic government. Those who were the extreme Marxists and had a majority in Russia's Socialist Party, the Bolsheviks, overcame opposition, and in November (October on the old calendar), did away with the provisional democratic government and set up the world's first Marxist state.

Skill 3.6   Analyze the roles, contributions, and diverse perspectives of individuals and groups involved in independence struggles in Latin America

The major turning point for Latin America, already unhappy with Spanish restrictions on trade, agriculture, and the manufacture of goods, was Napoleon's move into Spain and Portugal. Napoleon's imprisonment of King Ferdinand VII made the local agents of the Spanish authorities feel that they were in fact agents of the French. Conservative and liberal locals joined forces, declared their loyalty to King Ferdinand, and formed committees, known as *Juntas*. Between May of 1810 and July of 1811, the juntas in Argentina, Chile, Paraguay, Venezuela, Bolivia, and Colombia all declared independence. Fighting erupted between Spanish authorities in Latin America and the members and followers of the juntas. In Mexico City, another junta declared loyalty to Ferdinand and independence.

Society in Latin America was sharply distinguished according to race and the purity of Spanish blood. **Miguel Hidalgo**, a 60-year-old priest and enlightened intellectual, disregarded the racial distinctions of the society. He had been fighting for the interests of the Indians and part Indian/part white citizens of Mexico, including a call for the return of land stolen from the Indians. He called for an uprising in 1810.

Simon Bolivar was born into Venezuela's wealthy society and educated in Europe. With Francisco de Miranda, he declared Venezuela and Columbia to be republics and removed all Spanish trading restrictions. They removed taxes on the sale of food, ended payment of tribute to the government by the local Indians, and prohibited slavery. In March 1812 Caracas was devastated by an earthquake. When the Spanish clergy in Caracas proclaimed the earthquake God's act of vengeance against the rebel government, they provided support for the Spanish government officials, who quickly regained control.

When Ferdinand returned to power in 1814, it was no longer possible for the rebel groups to claim to act in his name. Bolivar was driven to Colombia, where he gathered a small army that returned to Venezuela in 1817. As his army grew, Spain became concerned and the military moved into the interior of Venezuela. This action aroused the local people to active rebellion. As he freed slaves, he gained support and strength. Realizing that he did not have the strength to take Caracas, Bolivar moved his people to Colombia. Bolivar's forces defeated the Spanish and organized "Gran Colombia" (which included present-day Ecuador, Colombia, and Panama), and became president in 1819. When Ferdinand encountered difficulties in Spain, the soldiers assembled to be transported to the Americas revolted. Several groups in Spain joined the revolt and drove Ferdinand from power. Bolivar took advantage of the opportunity and took his army back to Venezuela. In 1821, Bolivar defeated the Spanish, took Caracas, and established Venezuelan freedom from Spanish rule.

In Peru, **San Martin** took his force into Lima amid celebration. Bolivar provided assistance in winning Peru's independence in 1822. Bolivar now controlled Peru. By 1824, Bolivar had combined forces with local groups and rid South America of Spanish control.

In 1807, Queen Maria of Portugal fled to escape Napoleon. The royal family sailed to Brazil, where they were welcomed by the local people. Rio de Janeiro became the temporary capital of Portugal's empire. Maria's son, Joao, ruled as regent. He opened Brazil's trade with other nations, gave the British favorable tax rates in gratitude for their assistance against Napoleon, and opened Brazil to foreign scholars, visitors, and immigrants. In 1815, he made Brazil a kingdom that was united with Portugal. By 1817, there was economic trouble in Brazil and some unrest over repression (censorship). This discontent became a rebellion that was repressed by Joao's military. When Napoleon's forces withdrew from Portugal, the British asked Joao to return. Liberals took power in both Portugal and Spain and both drafted liberal constitutions.

By 1821, Joao decided to return to Portugal as a constitutional monarch. He left his oldest son Pedro on the throne in Brazil. When Portugal tried to reinstate economic advantages for Portugal and restrict Brazil, resistance began to grow. Pedro did not want to be controlled by Portugal and was labeled a rebel. When he learned that Portuguese troops had been sent to arrest him, he prohibited the landing of the ship, sent them back to Portugal, and declared independence in 1922. Within two months, he was declared Emperor of Brazil.

COMPETENCY 4   UNDERSTAND THE MAJOR POLITICAL, SOCIAL, ECONOMIC, SCIENTIFIC AND CULTURAL DEVELOPMENTS AND TURNING POINTS THAT SHAPED THE COURSE OF WORLD HISTORY FROM 1850 TO THE PRESENT

Skill 4.1   Recognize major geopolitical developments, social movements, and political/economic initiatives since 1850 and evaluate the effect of these developments, movements and initiatives on peoples and nations

Until the early years of the 20th century, Russia was ruled by a succession of Tsars. The Tsars ruled as autocrats or, sometimes, despots. Society was essentially feudalistic and was structured into three levels. The top level was held by the Tsar, the second level was composed of the rich nobles who held government positions and owned vast tracts of land, and the third level was composed of the remaining people who lived in poverty as peasants or serfs.

There was discontent among the peasants. There were several unsuccessful attempts to revolt during the 19th century, but they were quickly suppressed. The revolutions of 1905 and 1917, however, were quite different.

The causes of the 1905 Revolution were:
- Discontent with the social structure
- Discontent with the living conditions of the peasants
- Discontent with working conditions despite industrialization
- The general discontent was aggravated by the Russo-Japanese War (1904-1905) with inflation, rising prices, etc. Peasants who had been able to eke out a living began to starve
- Many of the fighting troops were killed in battles Russia lost to Japan because of poor leadership, lack of training, and inferior weaponry
- Czar Nicholas II refused to end the war despite setbacks
- Port Arthur fell in January 1905

A trade union leader (Father Gapon) organized a protest to demand an end to the war, industrial reform, more civil liberties, and a constituent assembly. Over 150,000 peasants joined a demonstration outside the Czar's Winter Palace. Before the demonstrators even spoke, the palace guard opened fire on the crowd. This destroyed the people's trust in the Czar. Illegal trade unions and political parties formed and organized strikes to gain power. The strikes eventually brought the Russian economy to a halt. This led Czar Nicholas II to sign the October Manifesto, which created a constitutional monarchy, extended some civil rights, and gave the parliament limited legislative power. In a very short period of time, the Czar disbanded the parliament and violated the promised civil liberties. This violation contributed to foment the 1917 Revolution.

The **Russian Revolution** occurred in March (or February on the old calendar) 1917 with the abdication of Tsar Nicholas II and the establishment of a democratic government. Those who were the extreme Marxists and had a majority in Russia's Socialist Party, the Bolsheviks, overcame opposition, and in November (October on the old calendar), did away with the provisional democratic government and set up the world's first Marxist state.

Russia's harsh climate, tremendous size, and physical isolation from the rest of Europe, along with the brutal despotic rule and control of the tsars over enslaved peasants, contributed to the final conditions leading to revolution. Despite the tremendous efforts of Peter the Great to bring his country up to the social, cultural, and economic standards of the rest of Europe, Russia always remained a hundred years or more behind. Autocratic rule, the existence of the system of serfdom or slavery of the peasants, lack of money, defeats in wars, lack of enough food and food production, little industrialization--all of these contributed to conditions ripe for revolt.

By 1914, Russia's industrial growth was even faster than Germany's and agricultural production was improving, along with better transportation. However, the conditions of poverty were horrendous. The Orthodox Church was steeped in political activities and the absolute rule of the tsar was the order of the day. By the time the nation entered World War I, conditions were just right for revolution. Marxist socialism seemed to be the solution or answer to all the problems. Russia had to stop participation in the war. Industry could not meet the military's needs.

Transportation by rail was severely disrupted and it was most difficult to procure supplies from the Allies. The people had had enough of war, injustice, starvation, poverty, slavery, and cruelty. The support for and strength of the Bolsheviks were mainly in the cities. After two or three years of civil war, fighting foreign invasions, and opposing other revolutionary groups, the Bolsheviks were finally successful in making possible a type of "pre-Utopia" for the workers and the people.

The causes of the 1917 Revolution were:

- The violation of the October Manifesto.
- Defeats on the battlefields during WWI caused discontent, loss of life, and a popular desire to withdraw from the war.
- The Czar continued to appoint unqualified people to government posts and handle the situation with general incompetence.
- The Czar also listened to his wife's (Alexandra) advice. She was strongly influenced by Rasputin. This caused increased discontent among all level of the social structure
- WWI had caused another surge in prices and scarcity of many items. Most of the peasants could not afford to buy bread.

Workers in Petrograd went on strike in 1917 over the need for food. The Czar again ordered troops to suppress the strike. This time, the troops sided with the workers. The revolution then took a unique direction. The parliament created a provisional government to rule the country. The military and the workers also created their own governments called soviets (popularly elected local councils). The parliament was composed of nobles who soon lost control of the country when they failed to comply with the wishes of the populace. The result was chaos.

The political leaders who had previously been driven into exile returned. Lenin, Stalin and Trotsky won the support of the peasants with the promise of "Peace, Land, and Bread". The parliament, on the other hand, continued the country's involvement in the war. Lenin and the Bolshevik party gained the support of the Red Guard and together overthrew the provisional government. In short order they had complete control of Russia and established a new communist state.

The most significant differences between the 1905 and 1917 revolutions were the formation of political parties and their use of propaganda and the support of the military and some of the nobles in 1917.

As succeeding Marxist or Communist leaders came to power, the effects of this violent revolution were felt all around the earth. From 1989 until 1991, Communism eventually gave way to various forms of democracies and free enterprise societies in Eastern Europe and the former Soviet Union. The foreign policies of all free Western nations were directly and immensely affected by the Marxist-Communist ideology. Its effect on Eastern Europe and the former Soviet Union was felt politically, economically, socially, culturally, and geographically. The people of ancient Russia simply exchanged one autocratic dictatorial system for another and its impact on all of the people on the earth is still being felt to this day.

The time from 1830 to 1914 is characterized by the extraordinary growth and spread of patriotic pride in a nation along with intense, widespread imperialism. Loyalty to one's nation included national pride, extending and maintaining sovereign political boundaries, and unification of smaller states with common language, history, and culture into a more powerful nation. As part of a larger multicultural empire, there were smaller groups who wished to separate into smaller, political, cultural nations. Examples of major events of this time resulting from the insurgence of nationalism include:

Territorial expansion in the western United States under the banner of "Manifest Destiny." In addition, the U.S. was involved in the War with Mexico, the Spanish-American War, and support of the Latin American colonies of Spain in their revolt for independence. In Latin America, the Spanish colonies were successful in their fight for independence and self-government.

In Europe, Italy and Germany were each totally united into one nation from many smaller states. There were revolutions in Austria and Hungary, the Franco-Prussian War, the dividing of Africa among the strong European nations, interference and intervention of Western nations in Asia, and the breakup of Turkish dominance in the Balkans.

In Africa, France, Great Britain, Italy, Portugal, Spain, Germany, and Belgium controlled the entire continent except Liberia and Ethiopia.

In Asia and the Pacific Islands, only China, Japan, and present-day Thailand (Siam) kept their independence. The others were controlled by the strong European nations.

An additional reason for European imperialism was the harsh, urgent demand for the raw materials needed to fuel and feed the great Industrial Revolution. These resources were not available in the huge quantity so desperately needed which necessitated (and rationalized) the partitioning of the continent of Africa and parts of Asia. In turn, these colonial areas would purchase the finished manufactured goods.

World War I 1914 to 1918

Causes of World War I were the surge of nationalism, the increasing strength of military capabilities, massive colonization for raw materials needed for industrialization and manufacturing, and military and diplomatic alliances.

The initial spark, which started the conflagration, was the assassination of Austrian Archduke Francis Ferdinand and his wife in Sarajevo.

There were 28 nations involved in the war, not including colonies and territories. It began July 28, 1914 and ended November 11, 1918 with the signing of the Treaty of Versailles. Economically, the war cost a total of $337 billion; increased inflation and huge war debts; and caused a loss of markets, goods, jobs, and factories. Politically, old empires collapsed and many monarchies disappeared; smaller countries gained temporary independence; Communists seized power in Russia; and, in some cases, nationalism increased. Socially, total populations decreased because of war casualties and low birth rates. There were millions of displaced persons, and villages and farms were destroyed. Cities grew while women made significant gains in the work force and the ballot box. There was less social distinction and classes. Attitudes completely changed and old beliefs and values were questioned. The peace settlement established the League of Nations to ensure peace, but it failed to do so.

World War II 1939 to 1945

Ironically, the Treaty of Paris, the peace treaty ending World War I, ultimately led to the Second World War. Countries that fought in the first war were either dissatisfied over the "spoils" of war, or were punished so harshly that resentment continued building to an eruption twenty years later.

The economic problems of both winners and losers of the first war were never resolved and the worldwide Great Depression of the 1930s dealt the final blow to any immediate rapid recovery. Democratic governments in Europe were severely strained and weakened, which in turn gave strength and encouragement to those political movements that were extreme and made promises to end the economic chaos in their countries.

Nationalism, which was a major cause of World War I, grew even stronger and seemed to feed the feelings of discontent, which became increasingly rampant.

Because of unstable economic conditions and political unrest, harsh dictatorships arose in several of the countries, especially where there was no history of experience in democratic government.

Countries such as Germany, Japan, and Italy began to aggressively expand their borders and acquire additional territory.

In all, 59 nations became embroiled in World War II, which began September 1, 1939 and ended September 2, 1945. These dates include both the European and Pacific settings of war. The horrible, tragic results of this second global conflagration were more deaths and more destruction than in any other armed conflict. It completely uprooted and displaced millions of people. The end of the war brought renewed power struggles, especially in Europe and China, with many Eastern European nations as well as China coming under complete control and domination of the Communists, supported and backed by the Soviet Union. With the development of and deployment of two atomic bombs against two Japanese cities, the world found itself in the **Nuclear Age**. The peace settlement established the United Nations Organization, which still exists and operates today.

Korean War 1950 to 1953

Korea was under control of Japan from 1895 to the end of the Second World War in 1945. At war's end, the Soviet and U.S. military troops moved into Korea with the U.S. troops in the southern half and the Soviet troops in the northern half with the 38 degree North Latitude line as the boundary.

The General Assembly of the UN in 1947 ordered elections throughout all of Korea to select one government for the entire country. The Soviet Union would not allow the North Koreans to vote, so they set up a Communist government there. The South Koreans set up a democratic government, but both claimed the entire country. At times, there were clashes between the troops from 1948 to 1950. After the U.S. removed its remaining troops in 1949 and announced in early 1950 that Korea was not part of its defense line in Asia, the Communists decided to act and invaded the south.

Participants were: North and South Korea, United States of America, Australia, New Zealand, China, Canada, France, Great Britain, Turkey, Belgium, Ethiopia, Colombia, Greece, South Africa, Luxembourg, Thailand, the Netherlands, and the Philippines. It was the first war in which a world organization played a major military role and it presented quite a challenge to the UN, which had only been in existence five years.

The war began June 25, 1950 and ended July 27, 1953. A truce was created and an armistice agreement was signed to end the fighting. A permanent treaty of peace has never been signed and the country remains divided between the Communist North and the Democratic South. It was a very costly and bloody war destroying villages and homes, displacing and killing millions of people.

The Vietnam War 1957 to 1973 (U.S. Involvement)
U.S. involvement was the second phase of three in Vietnam's history. The first phase began in 1946 when the Vietnamese fought French troops for control of the country. Prior to 1946, Vietnam had been part of the French colony of Indochina (since 1861, along with Laos and Kampuchea or Cambodia). In 1954, the defeated French left and the country became divided into Communist North and Democratic South. United States' aid and influence continued as part of the U.S. "Cold War" foreign policy to help any nation threatened by Communism.

The second phase involved the U.S. commitment. The Communist Vietnamese considered the war one of national liberation, a struggle to avoid continual dominance and influence of a foreign power. A cease-fire was arranged in January 1973 and a few months later, U.S. troops left for good. The third and final phase consisted of fighting between the Vietnamese, but ended April 30, 1975, with the surrender of South Vietnam, which left the entire country united under Communist rule.

Participants were the United States of America, Australia, New Zealand, South and North Vietnam, South Korea, Thailand, and the Philippines. With active U.S. involvement from 1957 to 1973, it was the longest war participated in by the U.S. It was tremendously destructive and completely divided the American public in their opinions and feelings about the war. Many were frustrated and angered by the fact that it was the first war fought on foreign soil in which U.S. combat forces were totally unable to achieve their goals and objectives.

Returning veterans faced not only readjustment to normal civilian life, but also faced bitterness, anger, rejection and no heroes' welcomes. Many suffered severe physical and deep psychological problems. The war set a precedent with Congress and the American people actively challenged U.S. military and foreign policy. The conflict, though tempered markedly by time, still exists and still has a definite effect on people.

The struggle between the Communist world under Soviet Union leadership and the non-Communist world under Anglo-American leadership resulted in what became known as the Cold War. Communism crept into the Western Hemisphere with Cuban leader Fidel Castro and his regime. Most colonies in Africa, Asia, and the Middle East gained independence from European and Western influence and control. In South Africa in the early 1990s, the system of racial segregation, known as apartheid, was abolished.

The Soviet Union was the first industrialized nation to successfully begin a program of space flight and exploration, launching Sputnik and sending the first man to space. The United States also experienced success in its space program, successfully landing space crews on the moon. In the late 1980s and early 1990s, the Berlin Wall was torn down and Communism fell in the Soviet Union and Eastern Europe. The 15 republics of the former USSR became independent nations with varying degrees of freedom and democracy in government and together formed the Commonwealth of Independent States (CIS). The former Communist nations of Eastern Europe also emphasized their independence with democratic forms of government.

Tremendous progress in communication and transportation has tied all parts of the earth and drawn them closer. There are still vast areas of the former Soviet Union that have unproductive land, extreme poverty, food shortages, rampant diseases, violent friction between cultures, the ever-present nuclear threat, environmental pollution, rapid reduction of natural resources, urban over-crowding, acceleration in global terrorism and violent crimes, and a diminishing middle class.

Skill 4.2 **Relate important developments in the arts, literature, popular culture, religion, and philosophy to the social, economic, and political history of this period**

The last century and a half has been a time of rapid and extensive change on almost every front. Notably, there has been a growing concern for human rights and civil rights. The end of imperialism and the liberation of former colonies and territorial holdings have created new nations and increased communication and respect among the nations of the world. Democracy has grown; Communism has risen and almost fallen. Nations are no longer ruled by distant mother countries or their resident governors. Both political and individual freedoms have been won through struggle and at the cost of human lives. Nationalism has risen and created new states and nations have cultivated a national identity. Yet these individual nations have been brought into contact and cooperation in ways never before experienced in human history. Scientific and technological developments, new thinking in religion and philosophy, and new political and economic realities have combined to begin to create a global society that must now learn to define itself and understand how to cooperate and respect diversity in new ways.

After the defeat of Napoleon in 1815, Europe began a 100-year period of relative peace. There were vast changes in agricultural technology, new policies of land tenure, and the rise of both capitalism and mercantilism. Liberal and democratic institutions began to exercise greater influence throughout the world.

The developing technologies of war have moved society from battle with swords and spears to battle with single-shot muskets and cannon. From cannon and muskets came repeating rifles and the Gatling gun, which in turn allowed the development of automatic weapons. Cannons were replaced by missiles and rockets that were able to be propelled farther. Bombs became more and more powerful, culminating into the atomic bomb. In every development, the act of war became more remote for those engaging in it. The cost of war could be counted, but the fighters were becoming more removed from it.

Developments for war, however, also brought benefits. Plastics, alloys, and electronic devices used in war were now being perfected for industrial or medical purposes. The use of the radio is a good case in point. Developed to a new extent during WWI, the radio offered new applications for peacetime communication and entertainment. Sadly, throughout the **Cold War** and the **Arms Race,** more attention and money were devoted to the development of weapons than to the conditions of human existence.

Deeper human problems—the growing divide between the rich and the poor, the conditions of life in the cities and in third-world countries, etc.—have been more seriously addressed only since the end of the Cold War and the Arms Race. Recent, massive relocations from the farm to the city have changed the way people think about the environment, values, and other people.

The literature of this period reflects this change in people's thinking by inviting readers to ponder the nature and the cost of war, the meaning of the human struggle for freedom, and the possibility of everyone enjoying basic human and civil rights. Literature has both cried out against and embraced change. By the beginning of the 20th century, literature was reflecting the struggle of the modern individual to find a place and a meaning in a new world that seemed foreign. Literature has reflected the observation that not only does the modern human not know how to find meaning, he/she does not actually know what he/she is seeking. It is this crisis of identity that has been the subject of most modern literature. This theme can be seen in the writings of Joseph Conrad, Sigmund Freud, James Joyce, Eugene O'Neill, Luigi Pirandello, Samuel Beckett, George Bernard Shaw, T.S. Eliot, Franz Kafka, Albert Camus, Boris Pasternak, Graham Greene, Tennessee Williams, and many others.

In art and architecture, there has been a search for new forms and for basic symbols that would speak a universal language. This fragmentation and anxiety has found expression in cubism and surrealism. In painting, one need only consider the works of Cezanne and Picasso and Dali. In Sculpture, artists took one of two directions: either looking back and preserving the conventional ideals of beauty, or experimenting with distortion and the abstract concepts of time and force. Architecture tended to move toward more functional lines and expressions.

In religion and philosophy there have been great changes as well. For much of the period, religious interpretation tended to swing like a pendulum between the liberal and the conservative. By the end of the 20th century, however, the struggle for meaning and identity had resulted in a generalized conservative trend. This tendency can be seen in most religions today. Religion and philosophy are, to be sure, the means of self-definition and the understanding of one's place in the universe. Recent conservative trends, however, have had a polarizing effect. Issues of the relationship of Church and State have arisen and been resolved in most countries during this period. At the same time, there has been an increasing effort to understand the religious beliefs of others, either to create new ways to define one's religion over and against other religions, or as the basis of new attacks on the values and teachings of other religions. This same struggle resulted in the rise of the philosophical movement known as existentialism, as seen in the writings of Soren Kierkegaard, Karl Jaspers, and Jean-Paul Sartre.

Skill 4.3   Compare major international conflicts and political revolutions of the 20th century and analyze factors that influenced their outcomes

The **Mexican Revolution** was a response to Mexico's long history under Spanish control which placed power, control, wealth and land in the hands of a small minority, leaving the majority in poverty. Under General Diaz, the distinction grew between rich and poor, and with this growing divide the lower classes were losing any voice in politics. Opposition to Diaz began when Francisco I. Madero led a series of strikes throughout Mexico. Madero gained a following and brought pressure to bear on Diaz until an election was held in 1910. Madero won a large number of votes. Diaz had Madero imprisoned and claimed that the Mexican people were not prepared for democracy.

As soon as Madero was released from prison, he began an attempt to have Diaz overthrown. At about this time two other local heroes emerged – Pancho Villa and Emiliano Zapata. Villa and Zapata harassed the Mexican army and eventually won control of regions in the north and in the south. Unable to control the spread of the insurgence, Diaz resigned in 1911. Madero and Zapata ran for president of Mexico; Madero won. Madero had a plan of land reform that was too slow in Zapata's opinion. Within a matter of months, Zapata denounced Madero and claimed the presidency. With control of the state of Morelos, he deported the wealthy land owners and divided their lands among the peasants. He was assassinated in 1919.

Many factions began to arise, and guerilla units roamed the country pillaging and destroying large haciendas and ranchos. Madero was executed, leaving the country in disarray for several years, allowing Pancho Villa free reign in the north. Various factions vied for control of the government until Venustiano Carranza emerged and became president. He called a constitutional convention resulting in the 1917 Constitution (still in effect). One of the provisions of the Constitution was land reform. The Constitution created the *ejido*, a farm cooperative program that redistributed much of the land among the peasants.

The **Iranian Revolution** in 1979 transformed a constitutional monarchy, led by the Shah, into an Islamic populist theocratic republic. The new ruler was Ayatollah Ruhollah Khomeini. This revolution occurred in two essential stages. In the first, religious, liberal and leftist groups cooperated to oust the Shah (king). In the second stage, the Ayatollah rose to power and created an Islamic state.

The Shah had faced intermittent opposition from the middle classes in the cities and from Islamic figures. These groups sought a limitation of the Shah's power and a constitutional democracy. The Shah enforced censorship laws and imprisoned political enemies. At the same time, living conditions of the people improved greatly and several important democratic rights were given to the people. Iranian Mullahs fiercely opposed giving women the right to vote.

The Shah was said to be a puppet of the U.S. government. A series of protests in 1978 was sparked by a libelous story about the Ayatollah Khomeini that was published in the official press. The protests escalated until December of that year when more than two million people gathered in Tehran in protest against the Shah. On the advice of Prime Minister Shapour Bakhtiar, who was an opposition leader, the Shah and the empress left Iran. Bakhtiar freed the political prisoners, permitted Khomeini to return from exile, and asked Khomeini to create a state modeled on the Vatican. Bakhtiar promised free elections and called for the preservation of the Constitution. Khomeini rejected Bakhtiar's demands and appointed an interim government. In a very short period of time, Khomeini gathered his revolutionaries and completed the overthrow of the monarchy.

The revolution accomplished certain goals: reduction of foreign influence and a more even distribution of the nation's wealth. It did not change repressive policies or levels of government brutality. It reversed policies toward women, restoring ancient policies of repression. Religious repression became rife, particularly against members of the Bahai Faith. The revolution has also isolated Iran from the rest of the world, being rejected by both capitalist and communist nations. This isolation, however, allowed the country to develop its own internal political system, rather than having a system imposed by foreign powers.

The **Chinese Revolution** was a response to imperial rule under the Qing Dynasty. Numerous internal rebellions caused widespread oppression and death. Conflicts with foreign nations had tended to end with treaties that humiliated China and required the payment of reparations that amounted to massive cost. In addition, there were popular feelings that political power should be restored from the Manchus to the Han Chinese. There was some attempt at reform, but it was undercut by the conservative supporters of the dynasty. The failures in modernization and liberalization, and the violent repression of dissidents moved the reformers toward revolution.

The most popular of the numerous revolutionary groups was led by Sun Yat-sen, whose movement was supported by Chinese who were living outside China and by students in Japan. He won the support of regional military officers. Sun's political philosophy consisted of the three principles of the people: (1) nationalism, which called for ousting of the Manchus and putting an end to foreign hegemony; (2) democracy, to establish a popularly elected government; (3) people's livelihood, or socialism, which was designed to help the common people by equalizing the ownership of land and the tools of production.

Revolution began with the discontented army units. This was called the Wuchang Uprising. The uprising spread to other parts of China. It was suppressed by the Qing Court within 50 days. During this time, however, a number of other provinces declared independence of the Qing Dynasty. A month later Sun Yat-sen was elected the first Provisional President of the new Republic of China. Yuan Shikai, who had control of the Army, tried to prevent civil war and possible intervention by foreign governments. He claimed power in Beijing. Sun agreed to unite China under a government headed by Yuan, who became the second provisional president of the Chinese republic.

Yuan quickly gathered more power than was controlled by the Parliament. He revised the constitution and became a dictator. In the national elections of 1912, Sung Jiaoren led the new Nationalist Party in winning the majority of seats in the parliament. A month later, Yuan had Sung assassinated. This increased Yuan's unpopularity. Several leadership missteps of a dictatorial nature aroused greater discontent. A second revolution began in 1913. This resulted in the flight to Japan of Sun Yat-sen and his followers. While Yuan pursued an imperialistic policy, Sun gathered more followers. Yuan alienated the parliament and the military. When WWI broke out, Japan issued the "Twenty-one Demands." Yuan agreed to many of the demands, further alienating the people of China.

Several southern provinces declared independence. In 1916, Yuan repudiated monarchy and stepped down as emperor.

A period of struggle between rival warlords followed. By the end of WWI, Duan Qirui had emerged as the most powerful Chinese leader. He declared war on Germany and Austria-Hungary in 1917 in the hope of getting loans from Japan. His disregard for the constitution led Sun Yat-sen and others to establish a new government and the Constitutional Protection Army. Sun established a military government. The Constitutional Protection War continued through 1918. The result was a divided China, along the north-south border.

By 1921, Sun had become president of a unified group of southern provinces. He was unable to obtain assistance from Western nations, and turned to the Soviet Union in 1920. The Soviets supported both Sun and the newly established Communist Party in China. This set off a power struggle between the Communists and the Nationalists. In 1923, Sun and a Soviet representative promised Soviet support for the re-unification of China. The soviet advisers sent Chiang Kai-shek to Moscow to be trained in propaganda and mass mobilization. Sun died in 1925.

Chiang was commander of the National Revolutionary Army, and began to take back the Northern provinces from the warlords. By 1928, all of China was under Chiang's control and his government was recognized internationally.

Skill 4.4   Analyze the effects of independence movements on African and Asian societies

The achievement of independence by the colonies and protectorates of European countries in Africa and Asia is called **decolonization**. Most of the decolonization occurred in the period following the conclusion of WWII. Decolonization was achieved in one of three ways: (1) by attaining independence, (2) by establishing a "free association" status, or (3) by integrating with the governing or administrative power of another state. Decolonization affects self-determination. Decolonization may be peacefully negotiated or may result from revolt and armed struggle of varying degrees of intensity.

There was a beginning of movement toward decolonization following WWI and the creation of the League of Nations. In theory, there was an intention to prepare the colonies for self-government. In fact, however, the League merely redistributed the former colonies of Germany and the Ottoman Empire.

The reasons for decolonization are primarily a matter of investing the former colonies with independence and self-determination. The colonizing countries benefit, however, from the ability to free themselves of the costs of maintaining the colonies. In many cases, a relationship continues to exist between the two countries.

Decolonization is a process rather than a solitary event. Colonial areas tend to move through a series of steps that provide increasing autonomy.

In Africa, opposition to colonial rule took several forms during the years between WWI and WWII:

- Demands for opportunity and inclusion
- Economic opposition
- Religious opposition
- Mass protests

The effect of WWII on Africa was profound. Not only were several important battles fought in Africa, but the English and French actively recruited soldiers from their African colonies. When the soldiers returned home, they questioned why they were fighting for the freedom of other countries if they could not have it themselves. Further, the proliferation of news and information during and after WWII made many Africans, especially those who served in the military, aware of the content of the *Atlantic Charter*. The third paragraph of the charter states that the Allies "respect the right of all peoples to choose the form of government under which they will live; and they wish to see sovereign rights of self-government restored to those who have been forcibly deprived of them." Many Africans saw this as a commitment by the British to end colonial rule in Africa.

European colonies in Asia were demanding and earning independence from Europe, particularly India, which was freed from British rule in 1947. The partitioning of India and Pakistan was viewed by many Africans as a model of what could be achieved in their own countries. In the late 1940s and early 1950s, new political organizations emerged throughout Africa with the support of the broader populace. These organizations demanded political freedom and the end of colonial rule. Libya and Egypt were the first African nations to win independence. Ghana gained independence in 1957. Fourteen African countries won independence in 1960, and by 1966, all but six countries were independent.

Skill 4.5   Assess how science and technology have influenced social attitudes and beliefs in the 20th century

New technologies have made production faster, easier, and more efficient. People found their skills and their abilities replaced by machines that were faster and more accurate. To some degree, machines and humans have entered an age of competition; yet these advances have facilitated greater control over nature, lightened the burden of labor, and extended human life span. These advances in science, knowledge, and technology have also called into question many of the assumptions and beliefs that have provided meaning for human existence. The myths that provided meaning in the past have been exposed and there are no new structures of belief to replace them. Without the foundational belief structures that have given meaning to life, an emptiness and aimlessness has arisen. Technology and science have extended life and made life easier. They have provided power and knowledge, but not the wisdom to know how to use it effectively. It was not accompanied by self-mastery, or the willingness to prevent class conflicts and prejudice, or to stop war, cruelty and violence.

The extraordinary advances in science and technology opened new frontiers and pushed back an ever-growing number of boundaries. These influences have had a profound effect in shaping modern civilization. Each discovery, machine, or insight was built upon other new discoveries, insights, or machines. By the 20th century, the rate of discovery and invention became literally uncontrollable. The results have, in many cases, been beneficial. But others have been horrifying.

Advances in biology and medicine have decreased infant mortality and increased life expectancy dramatically. Antibiotics and new surgical techniques have saved countless lives. Inoculations have essentially erased many dreadful diseases, yet others have resulted from the careless disposal of byproducts and the effects of industrialization upon the environment and the individual.

Progress in communication and transportation has tied all parts of the earth and drawn them closer. There are still vast areas of the former Soviet Union that have unproductive land, extreme poverty, food shortages, rampant diseases, violent friction between cultures, the ever-present nuclear threat, environmental pollution, rapid reduction of natural resources, urban over-crowding, acceleration in global terrorism and violent crimes, and a diminishing middle class.

New technologies have changed the way of life for many. This is the computer age, and even some grade schools have computers. Technology makes the world seem like a much smaller place. Even children have cell phones today. The existence of television and modern technology has us watching a war while it is in progress. Outsourcing is now popular because of technological advances. Telemarketing or "call centers" for European, American and other large countries are now located in India, Pakistan, and many other places. Multinational corporations located plants in foreign countries to lower costs.

In many places technology has resulted in a mobile population. Popular culture has been shaped by mass production and the mass media. Mass production and technology has made electronic goods affordable to most. This is the day of the **cell phone** and the **PDA**. The **Internet** allows people anywhere in the world to be in touch and allows people to learn about world events. In both industrial and many other countries, the popular culture is oriented towards the electronic era.

Skill 4.6   Recognize the interdependence of human societies in the 21st century and analyze the impact of globalization on the contemporary world

Globalization refers to the complex social, political, technological, and economic changes that result from increasing contact, communication, interaction, integration and interdependence of peoples of disparate parts of the world. The term is generally used to refer to the process of change or to the result of turbulent change. Globalization may be understood in terms of positive social and economic change, as in the case of a broadening of trade resulting in an increase in the standard of living for developing countries. Globalization may also be understood negatively in terms of the abusive treatment of developing countries in the interest of cultural or economic imperialism. These negative understandings generally point to cultural assimilation, plunder and profiteering, the destruction of the local culture and economy, and ecological indifference.

The period of European peace after the defeat of Napoleon and the reliance upon the gold standard in that time is often referred to as "The First Era of Globalization." This period began to disintegrate with the crisis of the gold standard in the late 1920s and early 1930s. This period of globalization included Europe, several European-influenced areas in the Americas and Oceania. The exchange of goods based upon the common gold standard resulted in prosperity for all countries involved. Communication and the exchange of ideas between these countries also prospered. Since WWII, globalization of trade has been accomplished primarily through trade negotiations and treaties.

Globalization also involves exchange of money, commodities, information, ideas, and people. Much of this has been facilitated by the great advances in technology in the last 150 years. The effects of globalization can be seen across all areas of social and cultural interaction. Economically, it brings about broader and faster trade and flow of capital, increased outsourcing of labor, the development of global financial systems (such as the introduction of the Euro), the creation of trade agreements and the birth of international organizations to moderate the agreements. From a social and cultural point of view, globalization results in greater exchange of all segments of the various cultures, including ideas, technology, food, clothing, fads, etc. Travel and migration create multicultural societies. The media facilitates the exchange of cultural and social values. As values interact, a new universal set of values begins to emerge.

In theory, globalization is creating a new international society. Occurring at a rapid pace, it is changing the composition of individual societies as it is creating a new international society. Trade and economic interests will undoubtedly continue to impel society forward on this course. The issues the world society must confront in the 21st century are: What is a human being? What gives meaning to human existence? How are human beings of different cultures, value systems, religious beliefs, and political interests to live together in peace?

COMPETENCY 5 UNDERSTAND THE MAJOR POLITICAL, SOCIAL, ECONOMIC, SCIENTIFIC AND CULTURAL DEVELOPMENTS AND TURNING POINTS IN U.S. HISTORY UP TO 1815

Skill 5.1   Demonstrate an understanding of Native American societies, cultures, and interrelationships before European contact

Though not greatly differing from each other in degree of civilization, the native peoples north of Mexico varied widely in customs, housing, dress, and religion. Among the native peoples of North America, there were at least 200 languages and 1500 dialects. Each of the hundreds of tribes was somewhat influenced by its neighbors. Communication between tribes that spoke different languages was conducted primarily through a very elaborate system of sign language. Several groups of tribes can be distinguished.

The Woods Peoples occupied the area from the Atlantic to the Western plains and prairies. They cultivated corn and tobacco, fished and hunted.

The Plains Peoples, who populated the area from the Mississippi River to the Rocky Mountains, were largely wandering and warlike, hunting buffalo and other game for food. After the arrival of Europeans and the re-introduction of the horse, they became great horsemen.

The Southwestern Tribes of New Mexico and Arizona included Pueblos, who lived in villages constructed of *adobe* (sun-dried brick), cliff dwellers, and nomadic tribes. These tribes had the most advanced civilizations.

The California Tribes were separated from the influence of other tribes by the mountains. They lived primarily on acorns, seeds and fish, and were probably the least advanced civilizations.

The Northwest Coast Peoples of Washington, British Columbia and Southern Alaska were not acquainted with farming, but built large wooden houses and traveled in huge cedar canoes.

The Plateau Peoples lived between the plains and the Pacific coast. They lived in underground houses, or brush huts, and subsisted primarily on fish.

The native peoples of America, like other peoples of the same stage of development, believed that all objects, both animate and inanimate, were endowed with certain spiritual powers. They were intensely religious, and lived every aspect of their lives as their religion prescribed. They believed a soul inhabited every living thing. Certain birds and animals were considered more powerful and intelligent than humans and capable of influence for good or evil. Most of the tribes were divided into clans of close blood relations, whose *totem* was a particular animal from which they were often believed to have descended. The sun and the four principal directions were often objects of worship. The *shaman*, a sort of priest, was often the *medicine-man* of a tribe. Sickness was often supposed to be the result of displeasing some spirit and was treated with incantations and prayer. Many of the traditional stories resemble those of other peoples in providing answers to primordial questions and guidance for life. The highest virtue was self-control. Hiding emotions and enduring pain or torture unflinchingly was required of each. Honesty was also a primary virtue, and promises were always honored no matter what the personal cost.

The communities did not have any strict form of government. Each individual was responsible for governing oneself, particularly with regard to the rights of other members of the community. The chiefs generally carried out the will of the tribe. Each tribe was a discrete unit, with its own lands. Boundaries of tribal territories were determined by treaties with neighbors. There was an organized confederation among certain tribes, often called a nation. The Iroquois confederation was often referred to as The Five Nations (later The Six Nations).

Customs varied from tribe to tribe. One consistent cultural element was the smoking of the calumet, a stone pipe, at the beginning and end of a war. In Native American communities, no individual owned land. The plots of land that were cultivated were, however, respected. Wealth was sometimes an honor, but generosity was more highly valued. Agriculture was quite advanced and irrigation was practiced in some locations. Most tribes practiced unique styles—either in terms of shape or decoration—of basket work, pottery and weaving.

Skill 5.2 Analyze the interactions among Native Americans, Europeans, and Africans in early North American colonial societies

Spain's influence was in Florida, the Gulf Coast from Texas all the way west to California, south to the tip of South America, and some of the islands of the West Indies. French control centered from New Orleans north to what is now northern Canada including the entire Mississippi Valley, the St. Lawrence Valley, the Great Lakes, and the land that was part of the Louisiana Territory. A few West Indies islands were also part of France's empire. England settled the eastern seaboard of North America, including parts of Canada and from Maine to Georgia. Some West Indies islands also came under British control. The Dutch had New Amsterdam for a period but later ceded it into British hands. One interesting aspect of this was each of these three nations, especially England, claimed land that extended partly or all the way across the continent, regardless of the fact that the others claimed the same land. The wars for dominance and control of power and influence in Europe would undoubtedly and eventually extend to the Americas, especially North America.

The part of North America claimed by **France** was called New France and consisted of the land west of the Appalachian Mountains. This settlement included the St. Lawrence Valley, the Great Lakes, the Mississippi Valley, and the entire region of land westward to the Rocky Mountains. The French established the permanent settlements of Montreal and New Orleans, thus gaining control of the two major gateways into the heart of North America, as well as the vast, rich interior. The St. Lawrence River, the Great Lakes, and the Mississippi River, along with its tributaries, made it possible for the French explorers and traders to roam at will, virtually unhindered in exploring, trapping, trading, and furthering the interests of France.

Most of the French settlements were in Canada along the St. Lawrence River. Only scattered forts and trading posts were found in the upper Mississippi Valley and Great Lakes region. The rulers of France originally intended New France to have vast estates owned by nobles and worked by peasants who would live on the estates in compact farming villages--the New World version of the Old World's medieval system of feudalism. However, it didn't work out that way. Each of the nobles wanted his estate to be on the river for ease of transportation. The peasants working the estates also wanted the prime waterfront location. The result of all this real estate squabbling was that New France's settled areas wound up mostly as a string of farmhouses stretching from Quebec to Montreal along the St. Lawrence and Richelieu Rivers.

In the non-settled areas in the interior were the French fur traders. They befriended the friendly tribes of Indians, spending the winters with them and obtaining the furs needed for trade. In the spring, they would return to Montreal in time to take advantage of trading their furs for the products brought by the cargo ships from France, which usually arrived at about the same time. Most of the wealth for New France and its "Mother Country" was from the fur trade, which provided a livelihood for many people. Manufacturers, ship owners, merchants, fur traders and their Indian allies, and workmen back in France all benefited. However, the freedom of roaming and trapping in the interior was a strong enticement for the younger, stronger men and resulted in the French not strengthening the areas settled along the St. Lawrence.

Into the 18th century, the rivalry with the British was getting stronger. New France was united under a single government and enjoyed the support of many Indian allies. The French traders were very diligent in not destroying the forests and driving away game upon which the Indians depended for life. It was difficult for the French to defend all of their settlements as they were scattered over half of the continent. However, by the early 1750s, France was the most powerful nation in Western Europe. Its armies were superior to all others and its navy was giving the British stiff competition for control of the seas. The stage was set for confrontation in both Europe and America.

Spanish settlement had its beginnings in the Caribbean with the establishment of colonies on Hispaniola (at Santo Domingo, which became the capital of the West Indies), Puerto Rico, and Cuba. There were a number of reasons for Spanish involvement in the Americas, to name just a few:

• The spirit of adventure
• The desire for land
• Expansion of Spanish power, influence, and empire
• The desire for great wealth
• Expansion of Roman Catholic influence and conversion of native peoples

The first permanent settlement in what is now the United States was in 1565 in St. Augustine, Florida. A later permanent settlement in the southwestern United States was in 1609 in Santa Fe, New Mexico. At the peak of Spanish power, the area in the United States claimed, settled, and controlled by Spain included Florida and all land west of the Mississippi River. Of course, France and England also lay claim to the same areas. Nonetheless, ranches and missions were built and the Indians who came in contact with the Spaniards were introduced to animals, plants, and seeds from the Old World that they had never seen before. Animals brought in included: horses, cattle, donkeys, pigs, sheep, goats, and poultry.

Spain's control over her New World colonies lasted more than 300 years, longer than England or France. To this day, Spanish influence remains in names of places, art, architecture, music, literature, law, and cuisine. The Spanish settlements in North America were not commercial enterprises, but were for protection and defense of the trading and wealth from their colonies in Mexico and South America. The Russians hunting seals came down the Pacific coast, the English moved into Florida and west into and beyond the Appalachians, and the French traders and trappers were making their way from Louisiana and other parts of New France into Spanish territory. The Spanish never realized or understood that self-sustaining economic development and colonial trade was so important. Consequently, the Spanish settlements in the U.S. never really prospered.

Before 1763, when England was rapidly on the way to becoming the most powerful of the three major Western European powers, its 13 colonies, located between the Atlantic and the Appalachians, physically occupied the least amount of land. Moreover, it is interesting that even before the Spanish Armada was defeated, two Englishmen, Sir Humphrey Gilbert and his half-brother Sir Walter Raleigh were unsuccessful in their attempts to build successful permanent colonies in the New World. Nonetheless, the 13 English colonies were successful and, by the time they had gained their independence from Britain, were more than able to govern themselves. They had a rich historical heritage of law, tradition, and documents leading the way to constitutional government conducted according to laws and customs. The settlers in the British colonies highly valued individual freedom, democratic government, and getting ahead through hard work.

The English colonies, with only a few exceptions, were considered commercial ventures to make a profit for the crown, the company, or whoever financed its beginnings. One was strictly a philanthropic enterprise and three others were primarily for religious reasons, but the other nine were started for economic reasons. Settlers in these unique colonies came for different reasons:

    a) Religious freedom
    b) Political freedom
    c) Economic prosperity
    d) Land ownership

The colonies were divided generally into the three regions of **New England, Middle Atlantic, and Southern**. The culture of each was distinct and had affected attitudes and ideas toward politics, religion, and economic activities. The geography of each region also contributed to its unique characteristics.

The **New England colonies** consisted of Massachusetts, Rhode Island, Connecticut, and New Hampshire. Life in these colonies was centered on the towns. What farming was done was by each family on its own plot of land, but a short summer growing season and limited amount of good soil gave rise to other economic activities such as manufacturing, fishing, shipbuilding, and trade. The vast majority of the settlers shared similar origins, coming from England and Scotland. Towns were carefully planned and laid out the same way. The form of government was the town meeting, where all adult males met to make the laws. The legislative body, the General Court, consisted of an Upper and Lower House.

The **Middle or Middle Atlantic colonies** included New York, New Jersey, Pennsylvania, Delaware, and Maryland. New York and New Jersey were at one time the Dutch colony of New Netherlands, and Delaware at one time was New Sweden. These five colonies, from their beginnings, were considered "melting pots" with settlers from many different nations and backgrounds. The main economic activity was farming, with the settlers scattered over the countryside cultivating large farms. The Indians were not as much of a threat as in New England, so they did not have to settle in small farming villages. The soil was very fertile, the land was gently rolling, and a milder climate provided a longer growing season.

These farms produced a large surplus of food, not only for the colonists themselves, but also for sale. This colonial region became known as the "breadbasket" of the New World, and the New York and Philadelphia seaports were constantly filled with ships being loaded with meat, flour, and other foodstuffs for the West Indies and England. There were other economic activities such as shipbuilding, iron mines, and factories producing paper, glass, and textiles. The legislative body in Pennsylvania was unicameral or consisted of one house. In the other four colonies, the legislative body had two houses. Also, units of local government were in counties and towns.

The **Southern colonies** were Virginia, North and South Carolina, and Georgia. Virginia was the first permanent successful English colony and Georgia was the last. The year 1619 was a very important year in the history of Virginia and the United States, with three very significant events. First, 60 women were sent to Virginia to marry and establish families, Second, 20 Africans, the first of thousands, arrived, Third, most importantly, the Virginia colonists were granted the right to self-government. They began by electing their own representatives to the House of Burgesses, their own legislative body.

The major economic activity in this region was farming. Here, the soil was very fertile and the climate was very mild with an even longer growing season. The large plantations that would eventually require large numbers of slaves were found in the coastal or tidewater areas. Although the wealthy slave-owning planters set the pattern of life in this region, most of the people lived inland and away from coastal areas. They were small farmers and very few owned slaves.

The settlers in these four colonies came from diverse backgrounds and cultures. Virginia was colonized mostly by people from England, while Georgia was started as a haven for debtors from English prisons. Pioneers from Virginia settled in North Carolina, while South Carolina welcomed people from England, Scotland, , Germany, France, and islands in the West Indies. Products from farms and plantations included rice, tobacco, indigo, cotton, and some corn and wheat. Other economic activities included lumber and naval stores (tar, pitch, rosin, and turpentine) from the pine forests and fur trade on the frontier. Cities, such as Savannah and Charleston, were important seaports and trading centers.

In the colonies, the daily life differed greatly between the coastal settlements and the inland, or interior. The Southern planters and the people living in the coastal cities and towns had a way of life similar to that in towns in England. The influence was seen and heard in how people dressed and talked. The architectural styles of houses and public buildings, and the social divisions or levels of society, mimicked that of England. Both the planters and city dwellers enjoyed an active social life and had strong emotional ties to England.

On the other hand, life inland on the frontier had marked differences. All facets of daily living--clothing, food, housing, economic and social activities--were all connected to what was needed to sustain life and survive in the wilderness. These people practically produced everything themselves. They were self-sufficient and extremely individualistic and independent. There were little, if any, levels of society or class distinctions. People were considered equal to each other, regardless of station in life. The roots of equality, independence, individual rights and freedoms were strong and well developed. People were not judged by their fancy dress, expensive homes, eloquent language, or titles following their names.

The colonies from 1607 to 1763 had to develop, refine, practice, experiment, and experience life in a rugged, uncivilized land. The Mother Country had virtually left them on their own. In 1763, when Britain decided she needed to regulate, she was surprised to discover that she had a losing fight on her hands.

By the 1750s, Spain was no longer the most powerful nation and not even considered a contender. The remaining rivalry was between Britain and France. For nearly 25 years, between 1689 and 1748, a series of "armed conflicts" involving these two powers had been taking place. These conflicts had spilled over into North America. The War of the League of Augsburg in Europe, 1689 to 1697, had been King William's War. The War of the Spanish Succession, 1702 to 1713, had been Queen Anne's War. The War of the Austrian Succession, 1740 to 1748, was called King George's War in the colonies. The two nations fought for possession of colonies, especially in Asia and North America, and for control of the seas, but none of these conflicts proved to be decisive.

The final conflict, which decided once and for all who was the most powerful, began in North America in 1754, in the Ohio River Valley. It was known in America as the **French and Indian War** and in Europe as the Seven Years' War, since it began there in 1756. In America, both sides had advantages and disadvantages. The British colonies were well established and consolidated in a smaller area. British colonists outnumbered French colonists 23 to 1. Except for a small area in Canada, French settlements were scattered over a much larger area (roughly half of the continent) and were smaller. However, the French settlements were united under one government and were quick to act and cooperate when necessary. In addition, the French had many more Indian allies than the British. The British colonies had separate, individual governments and very seldom cooperated, even when needed. In Europe, at that time, France was the more powerful of the two nations.

The French depended on the St. Lawrence River for transporting supplies, soldiers, and messages—the link between New France and the Mother Country. Tied into this waterway system were the connecting links of the Great Lakes and the Mississippi River and its tributaries, along which were scattered French forts, trading posts, and small settlements.

In 1758, the British captured Louisburg on Cape Breton Island and New France was doomed. Louisburg gave the British navy a base of operations preventing French reinforcements and supplies getting to their troops. Other forts fell to the British: Frontenac, Duquesne, Crown Point, Ticonderoga, Niagara, those in the upper Ohio Valley, and, most importantly, Quebec and finally Montreal. Spain entered the war in 1762 to aid France, but it was too late. British victories occurred all around the world: in India, the Mediterranean, and Europe.

In 1763, Spain, France, and Britain met in Paris to sign the Treaty of Paris. The terms of this treaty specified that Great Britain would retain control of India and all of North America east of the Mississippi River, except for New Orleans. Britain received control of Florida and returned Cuba and the islands of the Philippines to Spain. France lost nearly all of its territories in America and India, but was allowed to keep four islands: Guadeloupe, Martinique, Haiti on Hispaniola, and Miquelon and St. Pierre. France gave Spain New Orleans and the vast territory of Louisiana, west of the Mississippi River. Britain was now the most powerful nation.

Where did all of this leave the British colonies? Their colonial militias had fought with the British and they too benefited. The militias and their officers gained much experience in fighting, which would be very valuable to them later. The 13 colonies began to realize that cooperating with each other was the only effective form of defense.. At the start of the war in 1754, Benjamin Franklin proposed to the 13 colonies that they unite permanently to be able to defend themselves. This was after the French and their Indian allies had defeated Major George Washington and his militia at **Fort Necessity**. This left the entire northern frontier of the British colonies vulnerable and open to attack.

Delegates from seven of the 13 colonies met in Albany, New York, along with the representatives from the **Iroquois Confederation** and British officials. Franklin's proposal, known as the Albany Plan of Union, was rejected by the colonists, along with a similar proposal from the British. They simply did not want each of the colonies to lose its right to act independently. However, the seed was planted.

Skill 5.3   Analyze the movement for American independence and the factors contributing to its success

Great Britain founded, populated and supported the American colonies primarily for economic reasons. The valuable raw materials taken from the new world or produced by the colonists would be used by the manufacturing and industrial concern in England. Finished goods would then be sold throughout the world. Economic success depended upon a favorable balance of trade. Control of shipping, trade, raw materials, and manufactured goods was critical to a favorable balance of trade.

In the early years of colonization, Great Britain enacted several laws to protect the favorable balance of trade. These were called the **Navigation Acts**:

1651 – All shipping and trade within the British Empire must use British ships.

1660 -- Colonial products could only be sold to England.

1663 – Colonies could buy manufactured goods only from England, and any European goods bound for the Colonies must go to England first.

As the colonies grew and began to develop their own industries, these laws restricted access to some raw materials and restricted trade of manufactured goods.

The colonies grew to enjoy relatively greater autonomy than colonies in other parts of the world. The Enlightenment had introduced new ways of thinking about the world and about the inherent rights and dignity of the individual. The Protestant Reformation had introduced new ideas as well. These new ways of thinking had been carried into the American colonies. Several factors and influences created a somewhat different mindset in the American colonies:

1. The founding and settlement of colonies as a quest for religious freedom and toleration
2. The belief that government originates from the governed, that rulers are obligated to protect the individual rights of the people, and that the people have the right to choose their rulers
3. Trading companies practiced the right to make decisions and shape policies affecting their lives
4. Colonists were familiar with English law that protected the right of ownership of private property
5. The population became more diverse and a larger percentage of the people felt no strong loyalty to England
6. The colonies were practicing a local, representative government.

The end of the war in Europe between England and France and of the French and Indian War left both England and the colonies with significant war debt. King George III decided to pay off the war debt through taxes. These taxes were imposed upon the colonists.

In 1763, King George III issued a proclamation that the land between the Allegheny Mountains and the Mississippi River should be reserved for the Native American peoples. He wanted to limit colonization to the coastal areas because it would be easier to control them. The English government declared its intent to maintain a standing army of 10,000 troops to protect the colonists from the Indians and to protect the Canadian border. The colonists would pay for this army by paying a stamp tax. The colonists refused to pay the tax, stating that they had no interest in Canada and that they could protect themselves from the Indians.

The colonists agreed to pay import and export taxes, but refused to pay taxes to England on local industries. They then demanded representation in Parliament if a taxation policy was to be enforced. The rallying cry that resulted was: "No taxation without representation."

The Sugar Act of 1764 required the colonists to pay a tax on any molasses brought into the colonies. It also gave English officials the right to search the premises of anyone suspected of breaking the law.

The Stamp Act was passed in 1765, requiring the colonists to attach stamps, ranging in value from a halfpenny to 50 dollars, on all legal papers, insurance policies, newspapers and advertising sheets. Merchants threatened not to buy English goods; the "Sons of Liberty" burned the stamps and forced officials to agree to abide by the will of the people. The reaction to the act alarmed the king, and the stamp act was repealed in 1766.

The Townshend Act was passed the next year. It stipulated that the colonists must pay the salaries of the governors, vice-governors, and judges sent by the king of England. The colonists had no voice in selecting the people or in determining the number of people sent. The colonies again threatened to boycott England's merchants; the act was repealed, except a provision relating to a tax on tea. The response to the continuing tax on tea was **The Boston Tea Party.**

In 1766 England imposed the **Quartering Act**, which required the colonists to provide for the king's soldiers. Two years later, a mob in Boston attacked the soldiers with clubs and dared them to fire. The troops fired, killing several, in what came to be known as the **Boston Massacre**.

Boston created a Committee of Correspondence to state the rights of the colonists. This committee rapidly grew to include other towns and colonies.

The First Continental Congress met in Philadelphia in 1774, adopting a "Declaration of Colonial Rights." It declared that the colonies alone had the right to enact local laws and levy taxes, the people of the colonies were entitled to protection under the common law of England and to trial by jury in the colonies, and the laws passed by Parliament were straining the loyalty of the colonists.

The reply from King George III was an insistence that the colonies submit to British rule or be crushed. With the start of the Revolutionary War on April 19, 1775, the Second Continental Congress began meeting in Philadelphia on May 10 of that year to conduct the business of war and government for the next six years.

By 1776, the colonists and their representatives in the Second Continental Congress realized that things were past the point of no return. **The Declaration of Independence** was drafted and declared July 4, 1776. George Washington labored against tremendous odds to wage a victorious war. The turning point in the Americans' favor occurred in 1777 with the American victory at Saratoga. This victory decided for the French to align themselves with the Americans against the British. With the aid of Admiral DeGrasse and French warships blocking the entrance to Chesapeake Bay, British General Cornwallis trapped at Yorktown, Virginia, surrendered in 1781 and the war was over. **The Treaty of Paris**, which officially ended the war, was signed in 1783.

Most important battles of the Revolutionary War: Bennington, Brandywine, Bunker Hill, Germantown, Guilford Courthouse, Lexington, Monmouth, Princeton, Saratoga, Ticonderoga, Trenton, White Plains, and Yorktown.

The success of the colonists in the conduct of the war can be attributed to a number of factors:

1. **Ideology** -- The enlightenment and the Protestant Reformation had produced new ideas about the freedoms and rights of the individual and the need for a limited role of government in the daily life of the citizen. There was great support for the ideological basis of the Revolutionary War.
2. **Tactics** – The colonists had learned new battle tactics from the Native Peoples of North America. The English army still fought in open set formations. The colonists had learned to fight from protected positions.
3. **Passion** – The colonists were passionately committed to the cause for which they were fighting. This passion was shared throughout all of the colonies and enabled the government to raise an army of strong and committed fighters.
4. **Homeland advantage** – The colonists were fighting for their homes and their families, certainly part of the passion of their commitment. They knew the land and how to move about undetected. They also had avid support and assistance immediately at hand.

Skill 5.4   Recognize basic principles of the Articles of Confederation and the U.S. Constitution, evaluate the strengths and weaknesses of the Articles of Confederation, and analyze issues related to the creation and ratification of the U.S. Constitution

Articles of Confederation - This was the first political system under which the newly independent colonies tried to organize themselves. It was drafted after the Declaration of Independence in 1776, passed by the Continental Congress on November 15, 1777, ratified by the 13 states, and brought into effect on March 1, 1781.

The newly independent states were unwilling to give too much power to a national government. After many debates, the form of the Articles was accepted. Each state agreed to send delegates to the Congress. Each state had one vote in the Congress. The Articles gave Congress the power to declare war, appoint military officers, and coin money. The Congress was also responsible for foreign affairs. The Articles of Confederation limited the powers of Congress by giving the states final authority. Although Congress could pass laws, at least nine of the 13 states had to approve a law before it went into effect. Congress could not pass any laws regarding taxes. To get money, Congress had to ask each state for it and no state could be forced to pay.

Thus, the Articles created a loose alliance among the 13 states. The national government was weak, partly because it didn't have a strong chief executive to carry out laws passed by the legislature. This weak national government might have worked if the states were able to get along with each other. However, many different disputes arose and there was no way of settling them.

The central government of the new United States of America consisted of a Congress of two to seven delegates from each state with each state having just one vote. The government under the Articles solved some of the postwar problems, but had serious weaknesses. Some of its powers included: borrowing and coining money, directing foreign affairs, declaring war and making peace, building and equipping a navy, regulating weights and measures, and asking the states to supply men and money for an army. The delegates to Congress had no real authority, as each state carefully and jealously guarded its own interests and limited powers under the Articles. Also, the delegates to Congress were paid by their states and had to vote as directed by their state legislatures. The serious weaknesses were the lack of power: to regulate finances, over interstate trade, over foreign trade, to enforce treaties, and over the military. Something better and more efficient was needed.

In May of 1787, delegates from all states (except Rhode Island) began meeting in Philadelphia. At first, they met to revise the Articles of Confederation as instructed by Congress, but they soon realized that much more was needed. Abandoning the instructions, they set out to write a new Constitution for the foundation of all government in the United States and a model for representative government throughout the world.

The first order of business was the agreement among all the delegates that the convention would be kept secret. No discussion of the convention outside of the meeting room would be allowed. They wanted to be able to discuss, argue, and agree among themselves before presenting the completed document to the American people.

The delegates were afraid that if the people were aware of what was taking place before it was completed, the entire country would be plunged into argument and dissension. It would be extremely difficult, if not impossible, to settle differences and come to an agreement. The official notes kept at that time, along with the complete notes of later President James Madison, make up a good historical record of the events of the Philadelphia Convention..

All Convention attendees agreed on a strong central government, but not one with unlimited powers. They also agreed that no one part of government could control the rest. It would be a republican form of government (sometimes referred to as representative democracy) in which the supreme power was in the hands of the voters who would elect the men who would govern for them.

One of the first serious controversies involved the small states versus the large states over representation in Congress. Virginia's Governor Edmund Randolph proposed that state population determine the number of representatives sent to Congress, also known as the Virginia Plan. New Jersey delegate William Paterson countered with what is known as the New Jersey Plan, each state having equal representation.

After much argument and debate, the Great Compromise was devised, known also as the Connecticut Compromise, as proposed by Roger Sherman. It was agreed that Congress would have two houses. With two senators each in the Senate, the states would have equal powers in this house of Congress. The House of Representatives, on the other hand, would have its members elected based on each state's population. Both houses could draft bills to debate and vote on—with the exception of bills pertaining to money, which must originate in the House of Representatives.

Another controversy involved economic differences between the North and South. One concerned the counting of the African slaves for determining representation in the House of Representatives. The southern delegates wanted this representation, but didn't want it to determine the taxes to be paid. The northern delegates argued the opposite: Count the slaves for taxes, but not for representation. The resulting agreement was known as the "three-fifths" compromise. Three-fifths of the slaves would be counted for both taxes and determining representation in the House.

The last major compromise, also between the North and South, was the Commerce Compromise. The economic interests of the northern part of the country were ones of industry and business, whereas the south's economic interests were primarily in farming. The northern merchants wanted the government to regulate and control commerce with foreign nations and with the states. Southern planters opposed this idea, as they felt that any tariff laws passed would be unfavorable to them. The acceptable compromise to this dispute was that Congress was given the power to regulate commerce with other nations and the states, including levying tariffs on imports. However, Congress did not have the power to levy tariffs on any exports. This increased southern concern about the effect it would have on the slave trade. The delegates finally agreed that the importation of slaves would continue for 20 more years with no interference from Congress. Any import tax could not exceed 10 dollars per person. After 1808, Congress would be able to decide whether to prohibit or regulate any further importation of slaves.

Of course, when work was completed and the document was presented, nine states needed to approve it for it to go into effect. The opposition had three major objections:

1) The states seemed as if they were being asked to surrender too much power to the national government.
2) The voters did not have enough control and influence over the men who would be elected by them to run the government.
3) There was a lack of a bill of rights guaranteeing hard-won individual freedoms and liberties.

Eleven states finally ratified the document, and the new national government went into effect. It was no small feat that the delegates were able to produce a workable document that satisfied all opinions, feelings, and viewpoints. The separation of powers of the three branches of government and the built-in system of checks and balances to keep power balanced were a stroke of genius. It provided for both the individuals and the states, while also establishing an organized central authority to keep a young, inexperienced nation on track. It created a system of government so flexible that it has continued in its basic form to this day. In 1789, the Electoral College unanimously elected George Washington as the first president and thereby created the new nation.

Of this new document, Benjamin Franklin said: *"Though it may not be the best there is, ... wasn't sure that it could be possible to create one better."* It is truly a living document because of its ability to remain strong while allowing itself to be changed with changing times.

Ratification of the U.S. Constitution was by no means a foregone conclusion. The representative government had powerful enemies, especially those who had seen firsthand the failure of the Articles of Confederation. The strong central government had powerful enemies, including some of the guiding lights of the American Revolution.

Those who wanted to see a strong central government were called Federalists because they wanted to see a federal government reign supreme. Among the leaders of the Federalists were Alexander Hamilton and John Jay. These two, along with James Madison, wrote a series of letters to New York newspapers, urging that that state ratify the Constitution. These became known as the **Federalist Papers**.

In the Anti-Federalist camp were Thomas Jefferson and Patrick Henry. These men and many others like them were worried that a strong, national government would descend into the kind of tyranny that they had just worked so hard to abolish. In the same way that they took their name from their foes, they wrote a series of arguments against the Constitution called the **Anti-Federalist Papers.**

In the end, both sides got most of what they wanted. The Federalists got their strong, national government, which was held in place by the famous "checks and balances." The Anti-Federalists got the Bill of Rights, the first 10 Amendments to the Constitution and a series of laws that protect some of the most basic of human rights. The states that were in doubt for ratification of the Constitution signed on when the Bill of Rights was promised.

Legislative – Article I of the Constitution established the legislative or law-making branch of the government called the Congress. It is made up of two houses, the House of Representatives and the Senate. Voters in all states elect the members who serve in each respective House of Congress. The Legislative branch is responsible for making laws, raising and printing money, regulating trade, establishing the postal service and federal courts, approving the president's appointments, declaring war and supporting the armed forces. The Congress also has the power to change the Constitution itself, and to *impeach* (bring charges against) the president. Charges for impeachment are brought by the House of Representatives, and are then tried in the Senate.

Executive – Article II of the Constitution created the Executive branch of the government, headed by the president, who leads the country, recommends new laws, and can veto bills passed by the legislative branch. As the chief of state, the president is responsible for carrying out the laws of the country and the treaties and declarations of war passed by the legislative branch. The president also appoints federal judges and is commander-in-chief of the military when it is called into service. Other members of the Executive branch include the vice-president, also elected, and various cabinet members as the president might appoint—ambassadors, presidential advisors, members of the armed forces, and other appointed and civil servants of government agencies, departments and bureaus. Though the president appoints them, they must be approved by the Legislative branch.

Judicial – Article III of the Constitution established the Judicial Branch of government headed by the Supreme Court. The Supreme Court has the power to rule that a law passed by the legislature, or an act of the Executive branch is illegal and unconstitutional. Citizens, businesses, and government officials can in an appeal capacity, ask the Supreme Court to review a decision made in a lower court if someone believes that the ruling by a judge is unconstitutional. The judicial branch also includes lower federal courts known as federal district courts that have been established by the Congress. These courts try lawbreakers and review cases referred from other courts.

Powers delegated to the federal government:	Powers reserved to the states:
1. To tax	1. To regulate intrastate trade
2. To borrow and coin money	2. To establish local governments
3. To establish postal service	3. To protect general welfare
4. To grant patents and copyrights	4. To protect life and property
5. To regulate interstate & foreign commerce	5. To ratify amendments
6. To establish courts	6. To conduct elections
7. To declare war	7. To make state and local laws
8. To raise and support the armed forces	
9. To govern territories	
10. To define and punish felonies and piracy on the high seas	
11. To fix standards of weights and measures	
12. To conduct foreign affairs	

Concurrent powers of the federal government and states:

1. Both Congress and the states may tax.
2. Both may borrow money.
3. Both may charter banks and corporations.
4. Both may establish courts.
5. Both may make and enforce laws.
6. Both may take property for public purposes.
7. Both may spend money to provide for the public welfare.

Implied powers of the federal government:

1. To establish banks or other corporations—implied from delegated powers to tax, borrow, and regulate commerce
2. To spend money for roads, schools, health, insurance, etc.—implied from powers to establish roads, to tax to provide for general welfare and defense, and to regulate commerce
3. To create military academies—implied from powers to raise and support an armed force
4. To locate and generate sources of power and sell surplus—implied from war powers, powers to dispose of government property, and power to conduct commerce
5. To assist and regulate agriculture—implied from power to regulate commerce and tax and spend for general welfare

The first amendment guarantees the basic rights of freedom of religion, freedom of speech, freedom of the press, and freedom of assembly.

The next three amendments came out of the colonists' struggle with Great Britain. For example, the third amendment prevents Congress from forcing citizens to keep troops in their homes. Before the Revolution, Great Britain tried to coerce the colonists to house soldiers.

Amendments five through eight protect citizens who are accused of crimes and are brought to trial. Every citizen has the right to due process of law (due process as defined earlier, being that the government must follow the same fair rules for everyone brought to trial). These rules include the right to a trial by an impartial jury, the right to be defended by a lawyer, and the right to a speedy trial.

The last two amendments limit the powers of the federal government to those that are expressly granted in the Constitution. Any rights not expressly mentioned in the Constitution, thus, belong to the states or to the people. In regards to specific guarantees:

Freedom of Religion: Religious freedom has not been seriously threatened in the United States historically. The policy of the government has been guided by the premise that church and state should be separate. When religious practices have been at cross purposes with attitudes prevailing in the nation at particular times, there have been restrictions placed on these practices. Some of these have been restrictions against the practice of polygamy that is supported by certain religious groups. The idea of animal sacrifice that is promoted by some religious beliefs is generally prohibited. The use of mind-altering and illegal substances that some have used in religious rituals has been restricted. In the United States, all recognized religious institutions are tax-exempt in following the idea of separation of church and state, and therefore, there have been many quasi-religious groups that have in the past tried to take advantage of this fact. All of these issues continue, and most likely will continue to occupy both political and legal considerations for some time to come.

Freedom of Speech, Press, and Assembly: These rights historically have been given wide latitude in their practice, though there have been instances when one or the other has been limited for various reasons. The classic limitation, for instance, in regards to freedom of speech, has been the famous precept that an individual is prohibited from yelling "Fire!" in a crowded theatre. This prohibition is an example of the state saying that freedom of speech does not extend to speech that might endanger other people. There is also a prohibition against slander, where one party may knowingly state a falsehood against another. Also, there are many regulations regarding freedom of the press, the most common being the various laws against libel (the printing of a known falsehood). In times of national emergency, various restrictions have been placed on the rights of press, speech, and sometimes assembly.

All these ideas found their final expression in the United States Constitution's first 10 amendments, known as the Bill of Rights. In 1789, the first Congress passed these first amendments and by December 1791, three-fourths of the states at that time had ratified them. The Bill of Rights protects certain liberties and basic rights. James Madison, author of the amendments, said that the Bill of Rights does not give Americans these rights. People, Madison said, already have these rights. They are natural rights that belong to all human beings. The Bill of Rights simply prevents the government from taking away these rights.

Skill 5.5   Recognize major accomplishments and failures of early presidential administrations and examine factors that influenced the emergence of political parties

George Washington faced a number of challenges during his two terms as President. There were boundary disputes with Spain over the Southeast and wars with the Indians on the western frontier. The French Revolution and the ensuing war between France and England created great turmoil within the new nation. Thomas Jefferson, Secretary of State, was pro-French and believed the U.S. should enter the fray. Alexander Hamilton, Secretary of the Treasury, was pro-British and wanted to support England. Washington took a neutral course, believing the U.S. was not strong enough to be engaged in a war. Washington did not interfere with the powers of the Congress in establishing foreign policy. Two political parties were beginning to form by the end of his first term. In his farewell address he encouraged Americans to put an end to regional differences and exuberant party spirit. He also warned the nation against long-term alliances with foreign nations.

John Adams, of the Federalist Party, was elected President in 1796. When he assumed office, the war between England and France was in full swing. The British were seizing American ships that were engaging in trade with France. France, however, was refusing to receive the American envoy and had suspended economic relationships. The people were divided in their loyalties to either France or England. Adams focused on France and the diplomatic crisis known as the XYZ Affair. During his administration, Congress appropriated money to build three new frigates and additional ships, authorized the creation of a provisional army, and passed the Alien and Sedition Acts which were intended to drive foreign agents from the country and to maintain dominance over the Republican Party. When the war ended, Adams sent a peace mission to France. This angered the Republicans. The Election of 1800 pitted a unified and effective Republican Party against a divided and ineffective Federalist Party.

Thomas Jefferson won the election of 1800. Jefferson opposed a strong centralized government as a champion of States' Rights. He supported a strict interpretation of the Constitution. He reduced military expenditures, made budget cuts, and eliminated a tax on whiskey. At the same time, he reduced the national debt by one third. The Louisiana Purchase doubled the size of the nation. During his second term, the administration focused on keeping the U.S. out of the Napoleonic Wars. Both the French and the British were seizing American ships and trying to deny the other access to trade with the U.S. Jefferson's solution was to impose an embargo on all foreign commerce. The cost to the northeast was great and the embargo was both ineffective and unpopular.

James Madison won the election of 1808 and inherited the foreign policy issues with England. During the first year of his administration, trade was prohibited with both Britain and France. In 1810, Congress authorized trade with both England and France. They directed the President that if either nation would accept America's view of neutrality, he was to forbid trade with the other nation. Napoleon pretended to comply. Madison thus banned trade with Great Britain. The British continued to harass American ships and captured sailors and forced them to become members of the British Navy (impressment). In June of 1812, Madison asked Congress to declare war on Great Britain. The nation was not prepared to fight a war, especially with the strong British army. The British were successful in blockading U.S. ports and troops entered Washington and burned the White House and the Capitol. There were some notable American victories in the war, particularly Andrew Jackson's victory at New Orleans. This victory encouraged Americans to believe the war had been successful. The result was a tremendous rise in nationalism. The war ended with the **Treaty of Ghent**, in which Britain finally accepted U.S. independence. The war had been strenuously opposed by the Federalist Party, which even began to speak of secession. By the time the war was over, the party had been so deeply embarrassed and discredited that it was no longer a national political party.

The political party system in the U.S. has five main objects or lines of action:

(1) To influence government policy.
(2) To form or shape public opinion.
(3) To win elections.
(4) To choose between candidates for office.
(5) To procure salaried posts for party leaders and workers

The first domestic challenges of the new nation dealt with finances--paying for the war debts of the Revolutionary War and managing other financial needs. Alexander Hamilton, the Secretary of Treaury, wanted the government to increase tariffs and put taxes on certain products made in the U.S., such as liquor. This money would be used to pay war debts of the federal government as well as those of the states. There would be money available for expenses and needed internal improvements.

To provide for this, Hamilton favored a national bank. Secretary of State Thomas Jefferson, along with southern supporters, opposed many of Hamilton's suggested plans. Later, Jefferson relented and gave support to some proposals in return for Hamilton and his northern supporters agreeing to locate the nation's capital in the South. Jefferson continued to oppose a national bank, but Congress set up the first one in 1791, chartered for the next 20 years. In 1794, Pennsylvania farmers, who made whiskey, their most important source of cash, refused to pay the liquor tax and started what came to be known as the **Whiskey Rebellion**. Troops sent by President Washington successfully put it down with no lives lost, thus demonstrating the growing strength of the new government.

The **Judiciary Act** set up the U.S. Supreme Court by providing for a Chief Justice and five associate justices. It also established federal district and circuit courts. One of the most important acts of Congress was the first 10 amendments to the Constitution called the **Bill of Rights**, which emphasized and protected the rights of individuals.

Under President John Adams, a minor diplomatic upset occurred with the government of France. By this time, the two major political parties called Federalists and Democratic-Republicans had fully developed. Hamilton and his mostly northern followers had formed the Federalist Party, which favored a strong central government and was sympathetic to Great Britain and its interests. The Democratic-Republican Party had been formed by Jefferson and his mostly Southern followers, and they wanted a weak central government and stronger relations with France. In 1798, the Federalists, in control of Congress, passed the **Alien and Sedition Acts** written to silence vocal opposition. These acts made it a crime to voice any criticism of the president or Congress and unfairly treated all foreigners.

The legislatures of Kentucky and Virginia protested these laws, claiming they attacked freedoms, and challenged their constitutionality. These Resolutions stated mainly that the states had created the federal government, which was considered merely as an agent for the states and was limited to certain powers and could be criticized by the states, if warranted. They went further, stating that states' rights included the power to declare any act of Congress null and void if the states felt it unconstitutional. The controversy died down as the Alien and Sedition Acts expired, one by one, but the doctrine of states' rights was not finally settled until the Civil War.

Supreme Court Chief Justice John Marshall made extremely significant contributions to the American judiciary. He established three basic principles of law, which became the foundation of the judicial system and the federal government. He started the power of judicial review, the right of the Supreme Court to determine the constitutionality of laws passed by Congress. He stated that the Supreme Court had the power to set aside laws passed by state legislatures only if and when they contradicted the U.S. Constitution. He established the right of the Supreme Court to reverse decisions of state courts.

After the U.S. purchased the Louisiana Territory, Jefferson appointed Captains **Meriwether Lewis and William Clark** to explore it, to find out exactly what had been bought. The expedition went all the way to the Pacific Ocean, returning two years later with maps, journals, and artifacts. This led the way for future explorers to make available more knowledge about the territory and resulted in the Westward Movement and the later belief in the doctrine of Manifest Destiny.

Skill 5.6   Analyze the causes and consequences of the War of 1812

United States' unintentional and accidental involvement in what was known as the **War of 1812** came about due to the political and economic struggles between France and Great Britain. Napoleon's goal was complete conquest and control of Europe, including and especially Great Britain. Although British troops were temporarily driven off the mainland of Europe, the navy still controlled the seas, the seas across which France had to bring the products needed. America traded with both nations, especially with France and its colonies. The British decided to destroy the American trade with France, mainly for two reasons:

(a) Products and goods from the U.S. gave Napoleon what he needed to keep up his struggle with Britain.
(b) Britain felt threatened by the increasing strength and success of the U.S. merchant fleet.

The British issued the **Orders in Council,** which was a series of measures prohibiting American ships from entering any French ports, including those in India and the West Indies. At the same time, Napoleon began efforts for a coastal blockade of the British Isles. He issued a series of Orders prohibiting all nations, including the United States, from trading with the British. He threatened seizure of every ship entering French ports after they stopped at any British port or colony, even threatening to seize every ship inspected by British cruisers or that paid any duties to their government. The British stopped American ships and impressed American seamen to service on British ships. Americans were outraged.

In 1807, Congress passed the Embargo Act forbidding American ships from sailing to foreign ports. It couldn't be completely enforced and it really hurt business and trade in America. So, in 1809, it was repealed. Two additional acts passed by Congress after James Madison became president attempted to regulate trade with other nations and to get Britain and France to remove the restrictions they had put on American shipping. The catch was that whichever nation removed restrictions, the U.S. agreed not to trade with the other one. Napoleon was the first to do this, prompting Madison to issue orders prohibiting trade with Britain, ignoring warnings from the British not to do so. Of course, this didn't work either and although Britain eventually rescinded the Orders in Council, war came in June of 1812 and ended on Christmas Eve, 1814, with the signing of the Treaty of Ghent.

During the war, Americans were divided over not only whether or not it was necessary to even fight, but also over what territories should be fought for and taken. The nation was still young and not prepared for war. The primary American objective was to conquer Canada, but it failed. Two naval victories and one military victory stand out for the United States. Oliver Perry gained control of Lake Erie and Thomas MacDonough fought on Lake Champlain. Both of these naval battles successfully prevented the British invasion of the United States from Canada. Nevertheless, the troops did land below Washington on the Potomac, marched into the city, and burned the public buildings, including the White House. Andrew Jackson's victory at New Orleans was a great morale booster to Americans, giving them the impression the U.S. had won the war. The battle actually took place after Britain and the United States had reached an agreement and it had no impact on the war's outcome. The peace treaty did little for the United States other than bringing peace, releasing prisoners of war, restoring all occupied territory, and setting up a commission to settle boundary disputes with Canada. Interestingly, the war proved to be a turning point in American history. European events had profoundly shaped U.S. policies, especially foreign policies.

COMPETENCY 6   UNDERSTAND THE MAJOR POLITICAL, SOCIAL, ECONOMIC, SCIENTIFIC, AND CULTURAL DEVELOPMENTS AND TURNING POINTS IN U.S. HISTORY FROM 1815 TO 1900

Skill 6.1   Analyze issues and events related to the emergence of the political party system in the United States

During the colonial period, political parties did not exist. The issues, which divided the people, were centered on the relations of the colonies to the mother country. There was initially little difference of opinion on these issues. About the middle of the 18th century, after England began to develop a harsher colonial policy, two factions arose in America. One favored the attitude of home government and the other declined to obey and demanded a constantly increasing level of self-government. The former came to be known as **Tories**, the latter as **Whigs**. During the course of the American Revolution, a large number of Tories left the country either to return to England or move to Canada.

From the beginning of the Confederation, there were differences of opinion about the new government. One faction favored a loose confederacy in which the individual state would retain all powers of sovereignty except the absolute minimum required for the limited cooperation of all the states. (This approach was tried under the Articles of Confederation.) The other faction, which steadily gained influence, demanded that the central government be granted all the essential powers of sovereignty and what should be left to the states was only the powers of local self-government.

The first real party organization developed soon after the inauguration of Washington as president. His cabinet included people of both factions. Hamilton was the leader of the **Nationalists** – the **Federalist Party** – and Jefferson was the spokesman for the Anti-Federalists, later known as **Republicans**, **Democratic-Republicans**, and finally **Democrats**.   **(Also refer to Skill 5.5)**

The Anti-Masonic Party came into being to oppose the Freemasons, who they accused of being a secret society trying to take over the country. The Free Soil Party existed for the 1848 and 1852 elections only. They opposed slavery in the lands acquired from Mexico. The Liberty Party of this period was also abolitionist.

In the mid-1850s, the slavery issue was beginning to heat up. In 1854, those opposed to slavery, the Whigs, and some Northern Democrats opposed to slavery united to form the **Republican Party**. Before the Civil War, the Democratic Party was more heavily represented in the South and was thus pro-slavery for the most part. The American Party was called the "Know Nothings." They lasted from 1854 to 1858 and were opposed to Irish-Catholic immigration.

The **Constitution Union Party** was formed in 1860. It was made up of entities from other extinguished political powers. They claim to support the Constitution above all and thought this would do away with the slavery issue. The **National Union Party** of 1864 was formed only for the purpose of the Lincoln election. Other political parties came and went in the post-Civil War era. The **Liberal Republican** Party formed in 1872 to oppose Ulysses S. Grant. They thought that Grant and his administration were corrupt and sought to displace them. The Anti-Monopoly Party of 1789 was more short-lived than the previous one. It billed itself as progressive and supported things like a graduated income tax system, the direct election of senators, etc. The **Greenback Party** was formed in 1878 and advocated the use of paper money. The Populist Party was a party consisting mostly of farmers who opposed the gold standard.

The process of political parties with short life spans continued in the 20th century. Most of this is due to the fact that these parties come into existence in opposition to some policy or politician. Once the "problem" is gone, so is the party that opposed it. The Farmer-Labor Party was a Minnesota-based political party. It supported farmers and labor and social security. It had moderate success in electing officials in Minnesota and merged with the Democratic Party in 1944. The **Progressive Party** was formed in 1912 due to a rift in the Republican Party that occurred when Theodore Roosevelt lost the nomination. This is not the same as the Progressive Party formed in 1924 to back LaFollette of Wisconsin. The Social Democratic Party was an outgrowth of a social movement and didn't have much political success.

There have also been other parties that have had a short life in the years following the Great Depression. The **American Labor Party** was a socialist party that existed in New York for a while. The American Workers Party was another socialist party based on Marxism. They also were short-lived. The **Progressive Party** came into being in 1948 to run candidates for president and vice president. The Dixicrats or States Rights Democratic Party also formed in 1948. They were a splinter group from the Democrats who supported Strom Thurmond. They also supported Wallace in 1968. There have been various Workers' Parties that have come and gone. Most of these have had left-wing tendencies.

There are other political parties, but they are not as strong as the Republicans and the Democrats. The Libertarian Party represents belief in the free rights of individuals to do as they wish without the interference of government. They favor a small government and propose a much lower level of government spending and services. The Libertarians are the third largest political party in America. The Socialist Party is also a political party. They run candidates in the elections. They favor the establishment of a radical democracy in which people control production, as well as the setting up of communities for all and not for the benefit of a few.

The **Communist Party** is also a political party advocating very radical changes in American society. They are concerned with the revolutionary struggle and moving through Marx's stages of history. There are many other parties. The American First Party is conservative as is the American Party. The American Nazi Party is also active in politics. Preaching fascism, they run candidates for elections and occasionally win. The Constitution Party is also representative of conservative views. The **Reform Party** was founded by Ross Perot, after his bid for President as an Independent. The list goes on. Many of these parties are regional, small, and not on the national scene. Many of them form for a purpose, such as an election, and then dwindle.

Skill 6.2 Examine the impact of major social, technological, and political developments on U.S. society

After 1815, the U.S. became more independent from European influence and was treated with growing respect by European nations who were impressed by the fact that the young United States showed no hesitancy in going to war with the world's greatest naval power.

The Red River cession was the next acquisition of land and came about as part of a treaty with Great Britain in 1818. It included parts of North and South Dakota and Minnesota. In 1819, Florida, both east and West, was ceded to the U.S. by Spain along with parts of Alabama, Mississippi, and Louisiana. Texas was annexed in 1845 and after the war with Mexico in 1848, the government paid $15 million for what would become the states of California, Utah, Nevada, and parts of four other states. In 1846, the Oregon Country was ceded to the U.S., which extended the western border to the Pacific Ocean. The northern U.S. boundary was established at the 49th parallel. The states of Idaho, Oregon, and Washington were formed from this territory. In 1853, the **Gadsden Purchase** rounded out the present boundary of the 48 conterminous states with payment to Mexico of $10 million for land that makes up present New Mexico and Arizona.

The election of Andrew Jackson as President signaled a swing of the political pendulum from government influence of the wealthy, aristocratic Easterners to the interests of the Western farmers and pioneers and the era of the "common man." Jacksonian democracy was a policy of equal political power for all. After the War of 1812, Henry Clay and supporters favored economic measures that came to be known as the American System. This involved tariffs that protected American farmers and manufacturers from having to compete with foreign products, while stimulating industrial growth and employment. With more people working, more farm products would be consumed, prosperous farmers would be able to buy more manufactured goods, and the additional monies from tariffs would make it possible for the government to make the needed internal improvements. To get this going, in 1816, Congress not only passed a high tariff, but also chartered a second Bank of the United States. Upon becoming president, Jackson fought to get rid of the bank.

One of the many duties of the bank was to regulate the supply of money for the nation. The President believed that the bank was a monopoly that favored the wealthy. Congress voted in 1832 to renew the bank's charter, but Jackson vetoed the bill, withdrew the government's money, and the bank finally collapsed. Jackson also faced the "null and void," or nullification issue from South Carolina. In 1828 Congress passed a law placing high tariffs on goods imported into the United States. Southerners, led by South Carolina's then vice president of the United States, John C. Calhoun, felt that the tariff favored the manufacturing interests of New England. Calhoun denounced it as an abomination, and claimed that any state could nullify any of the federal laws it considered unconstitutional.

The tariff was lowered in 1832, but not enough to satisfy South Carolina, which promptly threatened to secede from the Union. Although Jackson agreed with the rights of states, he also believed in preservation of the Union. A year later, the tariffs were lowered and the crisis was averted.

Many social reform movements began during this period, including those related to education, women's rights, labor and working conditions, temperance, prisons and insane asylums. But the most intense and controversial was the abolitionists' efforts to end slavery, an effort alienating and splitting the country, hardening Southern defense of slavery, and leading to four years of bloody war. The abolitionist movement had political fallout, affecting admittance of states into the Union and the government's continued efforts to keep a balance between total numbers of free and slave states. Congressional legislation after 1820 reflected this.

The **Industrial Revolution** had spread from Great Britain to the United States. Before 1800, most manufacturing activities were done in small shops or in homes. However, starting in the early 1800s, factories with modern machines were built making it easier to produce goods faster. The eastern part of the country became a major industrial area although some developed in the West. At about the same time, improvements began to be made in building roads, railroads, canals, and steamboats. The increased ease of travel facilitated the westward movement and boosted the economy with faster and cheaper shipment of goods and products, covering larger areas.

Westward expansion occurred for a number of reasons, most important being economic. Cotton had become very important to most of the people who lived in the southern states. The effects of the Industrial Revolution, which began in England, were now being felt in the United States. With the invention of power-driven machines, the demand for cotton fiber greatly increased for the yarn needed in spinning and weaving. Eli Whitney's cotton gin made the separation of the seeds from the cotton much more efficient and faster. This, in turn, increased the demand and more farmers became involved in the raising and selling of cotton.

The innovations and developments of better methods of long-distance transportation moved the cotton in greater quantities to textile mills in England as well as the areas of New England and Middle Atlantic States in the U.S. As prices increased along with increased demand, southern farmers began expanding by clearing increasingly more land to grow more cotton. Movement, settlement, and farming headed west to utilize the fertile soils. This increased need for a large supply of cheap labor. The system of slavery expanded, both in numbers and in the movement to lands "west" of the South.

Cotton farmers and slave owners were not the only ones heading west. Many, in other fields of economic endeavor, began the migration: trappers, miners, merchants, ranchers, and others were all seeking their fortunes. The Lewis and Clark expedition stimulated the westward push. Fur companies hired men, known as "Mountain Men," to go westward, searching for the animal pelts to supply the market and meet the demands of the East and Europe. These men explored and discovered the many passes and trails that would eventually be used by settlers in their trek to the west. The California gold rush also had a very large influence on the movement west.

There were also religious reasons for westward expansion. Increased settlement was encouraged by missionaries who traveled west with the fur traders. They sent word back east for more settlers and the results were tremendous. By the 1840s, the population increases in the Oregon country alone were at a rate of about a 1000 people a year. People of many different religions and cultures as well as Southerners with black slaves made their way west, which led to a third reason, political.

It was the belief of many that the United States was destined to control all of the land between the two oceans—or, as one newspaper editor termed it, "Manifest Destiny." This mass migration westward put the U.S. government on a collision course with the Indians, Great Britain, Spain, and Mexico. The fur traders and missionaries ran up against the Indians in the northwest and the claims of Great Britain for the Oregon country.

The U.S. and Britain had shared the Oregon country. By the 1840s, with the increase in the free and slave populations and the demand of the settlers for control and government by the U.S., the conflict had to be resolved. In a treaty, signed in 1846 by both nations, a peaceful resolution occurred with Britain giving up its claims south of the 49th parallel.

In the American southwest, the results were exactly the opposite. Spain had claimed this area since the 1540s, had spread northward from Mexico City, and, in the 1700s, had established missions, forts, villages, towns, and very large ranches. After the purchase of the Louisiana Territory in 1803, Americans began moving into Spanish territory. A few hundred American families in what is now Texas were allowed to live there, but had to agree to become loyal subjects to Spain. In 1821, Mexico successfully revolted against Spanish rule, won independence, and chose to be more tolerant towards the American settlers and traders. The Mexican government encouraged and allowed extensive trade and settlement, especially in Texas. Many of the new settlers were southerners and brought with them their slaves. Slavery was outlawed in Mexico and technically illegal in Texas, although the Mexican government looked the other way.

With the influx of so many Americans and the liberal policies of the Mexican government, there came to be concern over the possible growth and development of an American state within Mexico. Settlement restrictions, cancellation of land grants, the forbidding of slavery, and increased military activity brought everything to a head. The order of events included the fight for Texas independence, the brief Republic of Texas, eventual annexation of Texas, statehood, and finally, war with Mexico. The Texas controversy was not the sole reason for war. Since American settlers had begun, pouring into the Southwest, the cultural differences played a prominent part. Language, religion, law, customs, and government were totally different and opposite between the two groups. A clash was bound to occur.

Robert Fulton's "**Clermont**," the first commercially successful steamboat, demonstrated the newest, fastest, and therefore most important way to ship goods. Later, steam-powered railroads soon became the biggest rival of the steamboat as a means of shipping, eventually being the most important transportation method opening the West. Expansion into the interior of the country, made the United States the world's leading agricultural nation. The hardy pioneer farmers produced a vast surplus and emphasis went to producing products with a high-sale value. These implements, such as the cotton gin and reaper, improved production. Travel and shipping were greatly assisted in areas not yet touched by railroad or, by improved or new roads, such as the National Road in the East and in the West the Oregon and Santa Fe Trails.

People were exposed to works of literature, art, newspapers, drama, live entertainment, and political rallies. With better communication and travel, more information was desired about previously unknown areas of the country, especially the West. The discovery of gold and other mineral wealth resulted in a literal surge of settlers and even more interest.

Public schools were established in many of the states with more children being educated. With more literacy and more participation in literature and the arts, the young nation was developing its own unique culture becoming less and less influenced by and dependent on that of Europe.

More industries and factories required more labor. Women, children, and, at times, entire families worked the long hours and days. By the 1830's, the factories were getting even larger and employers began hiring immigrants, who were coming to America in huge numbers. Before then, efforts were made to organize a labor movement to improve working conditions and increase wages. It never really caught on until after the Civil War, but the seed had been sown.

In between the growing economy, expansion westward of the population, and improvements in travel and mass communication, the federal government did face periodic financial depressions. Contributing to these downward spirals were land speculations, availability and soundness of money and currency, failed banks, failing businesses, and unemployment. Sometimes conditions outside the nation would help trigger it; at other times, domestic politics and presidential elections affected it. The growing strength and influence of two major political parties with opposing philosophies and methods of conducting government did not ease matters at times.

As 1860 began, the nation had extended its borders north, south, and west. Industry and agriculture were flourishing. Although the U.S. did not involve itself actively in European affairs, the relationship with Great Britain was much improved and it and other nations that dealt with the young nation accorded it more respect and admiration. Nevertheless, war was on the horizon. The country was deeply divided along political lines concerning slavery and the election of Abraham Lincoln.

Skill 6.3   Evaluate the influence of religious ideas on social and political reform movements in the United States prior to 1860

Social and political movements are group actions in which large informal groups or persons and organizations focus on specific social or political issues and work for either implementing or undoing some form of change. The social movement originated in England and North America during the first decades of the 19th century.

Several types of social and political movements are often identified and distinguished by key factors:

1. Distinguished by *Scope*
   (a) Reform movements aim to change some norms
   (b) Radical movements seek to change some value systems
2. Distinguished by *Type of Change*
   (a) Innovation movements attempt to introduce new norms or values
   (b) Conservative movements want to preserve existing norms or values
3. Distinguished by *Target group*
   (a) Group-focused movements attempt to affect either society in general or specific groups
   (b) Individual-focused movements seek to transform individuals

4. Distinguished by *Method of action*
   (a) Peaceful movements
   (b) Violent movements
5. Distinguished by *time*
   (a) Old movements – prior to the 20th century
   (b) New movements – since the second half of the 20th century
6. Distinguished by *Range*
   (a) Global movements
   (b) Local movements

The role of religion in political movements or as a basis for political action can be quite varied, depending upon the religion and the exigencies of the time. In general, one's interpretation of how people should act within the political sphere will take one of three approaches:

(1) Withdrawal from politics (and sometimes from the world)
(2) Quietism
(3) Activism

Religion has always been a factor in American life. Many early settlers came to America in search of religious freedom. Religion, particularly Christianity, was an essential element of the value and belief structure shared by the Founding Fathers. Yet, the Constitution prescribes a separation of Church and State. Religion is a basis for the actions of believers, no matter which religion is practiced. Because religion determines values and ethics, it drives individuals and groups to work to change conditions that are perceived to be wrong.

The **First Great Awakening** was a religious movement within American Protestantism in the 1730s and 1740s. This was primarily a movement among Puritans seeking a return to strict interpretation of morality and values, as well as emphasizing the importance and power of personal religious or spiritual experience. Many historians believe the First Great Awakening unified the people of the original colonies and supported the independence of the colonists.

The **Second Great Awakening** (the Great Revival) was a broad movement within American Protestantism that led to several kinds of activities that were distinguished by region and denominational tradition. In general, the Second Great Awakening, which began in the 1820s, was a time of recognition that "awakened religion" must weed out sin on both a personal and a social level. It inspired a wave of social activism. In New England, the Congregationalists established missionary societies to evangelize the West. Publication and education societies arose, most notably the American Bible Society. This social activism gave rise to the temperance movement, prison reform efforts, and help for the handicapped and mentally ill. This period was notable for the abolition movement. In the Appalachian region, the camp meeting was used to revive religion. It became a primary method of evangelizing new territory.

The **Third Great Awakening** (the Missionary Awakening) gave rise to the Social Gospel Movement. This period (1858 to 1908) resulted in a massive growth in membership of all major Protestant denominations through their missionary activities. This movement was partly a response to claims that the Bible was fallible. Many churches attempted to reconcile or change biblical teaching to fit scientific theories and discoveries. Colleges associated with Protestant churches began to appear rapidly throughout the nation. In terms of social and political movements, the Third Great Awakening was the most expansive and profound. Coinciding with many changes in production and labor, it won battles against child labor and stopped the exploitation of women in factories. Compulsory elementary education for children came from this movement, as did the establishment of a set work day. Much was also done to protect and rescue children from abandonment and abuse, improve the care of the sick, prohibit the use of alcohol and tobacco, and prohibit numerous other "social ills."

Skill 6.4   Analyze the environmental consequences of U.S. expansion into the Great Plains and the effects of that expansion on indigenous populations

Numerous conflicts, often called the "Indian Wars," broke out between the U.S. army and many different native tribes. Many treaties were signed with the various tribes, but most were broken by the government for a variety of reasons. Two of the most notable battles were the Battle of Little Bighorn in 1876, in which native people defeated General Custer and his forces, and the massacre of Native Americans in 1890 at Wounded Knee. In 1876, the U.S. government ordered all surviving Native Americans to move to reservations. This forced migration of the Native Americans to lands that were deemed marginal, combined with the near-extermination of the buffalo, caused a downturn in Prairie Culture that relied on the horse for hunting, trading, and traveling.

In the late 19th century, the avid reformers of the day instituted a practice of trying to "civilize" Indian children by educating them in Indian Boarding Schools. The children were forbidden to speak their native languages, they were forced to convert to Christianity, and generally forced to give up all aspects of their native culture and identity. There are numerous reports of abuse of the Indian children at these schools.

During World War I, a large number of Native Americans were drafted into military service. Most served heroically. This fact, combined with a growing desire to see the native peoples effectively merged into mainstream society, led to the enactment of The Indian Citizenship Act of 1924, by which Native Americans were granted U.S. citizenship.

Until recent years, the policy of the federal government was to segregate and marginalize Native Americans. Their religion, arts, and culture have been largely ignored until recent years. Safely restricted to reservations in the "Indian territory," various attempts were made to strip them of their inherited culture, just as they were stripped of their ancestral lands. Life on the reservations has been difficult for most Native Americans. The policies of extermination and relocation, as well as the introduction of disease among them, significantly decimated their numbers by the end of the 19th century.

Skill 6.5   Recognize the experiences and contributions of diverse individuals and groups to the development of the United States during the 19th century

Following is just a partial list of well-known Americans who contributed their leadership and talents in various fields and reforms:

Lucretia Mott and **Elizabeth Cady Stanton** for women's rights

Emma Hart Willard, Catharine Esther Beecher, and **Mary Lyon** for education of women

Dr. Elizabeth Blackwell, the first woman doctor

Antoinette Louisa Blackwell, the first female minister

Dorothea Lynde Dix for reforms in prisons and insane asylums

Elihu Burritt and **William Ladd** for peace movements

Robert Owen for a Utopian society

Horace Mann, Henry Barmard, Calvin E. Stowe, Caleb Mills, and **John Swett** for public education

Benjamin Lundy, David Walker, William Lloyd Garrison, Isaac Hooper, Arthur and Lewis Tappan, Theodore Weld, Frederick Douglass, Harriet Tubman, James G. Birney, Henry Highland Garnet, James Forten, Robert Purvis, Harriet Beecher Stowe, Wendell Phillips, and **John Brown** for abolition of slavery and the **Underground Railroad**

Louisa Mae Alcott, James Fenimore Cooper, Washington Irving, Walt Whitman, Henry David Thoreau, Ralph Waldo Emerson, Herman Melville, Richard Henry Dana, Nathaniel Hawthorne, Henry Wadsworth Longfellow, John Greenleaf Whittier, Edgar Allan Poe, Oliver Wendell Holmes, famous writers

John C. Fremont, Zebulon Pike, Kit Carson, explorers

Henry Clay, Daniel Webster, Stephen Douglas, John C. Calhoun, American statesmen

Robert Fulton, Cyrus McCormick, Eli Whitney, inventors

Noah Webster, American dictionary and spellers

Hispanic Americans have contributed to American life and culture since before the Civil War. Hispanics have distinguished themselves in every area of society and culture. Mexicans taught Californians to pan for gold and introduced the technique of using mercury to separate silver from worthless ores. Six state names are of Hispanic origin.

Native Americans have made major contributions to the development of the nation and have been contributors, either directly or indirectly in every area of political and cultural life. In the early years of European settlement, Native Americans were both teachers and neighbors. Even during periods of extermination and relocation, their influence was profound.

Asian Americans, particularly in the West and in large cities, have made significant contributions despite immigration bans, mistreatment, and confinement. Asians were particularly important in the construction of the trans-continental railroad, mining metals, and providing other kinds of labor and service.

> **Skill 6.6** **Analyze the causes, key events, and major consequences of the Civil War and the impact of Reconstruction on U.S. social, political, and economic life**

One historian has stated that before 1865, the nation referred to itself as "the United States are ... ," but after 1865, "the United States is. ..." It took the Civil War to finally and completely unify all states into one Union.

The drafting of the Constitution, its ratification and implementation, united 13 different, independent states into a Union under one central government. The two crucial compromises of the convention delegates concerning slaves pacified Southerners, especially the slave owners, but the issue of slavery was not settled. From then on, **sectionalism** became stronger and more apparent each year and put the entire country on a collision course.

Slavery in the English colonies began in 1619, when 20 Africans arrived in the colony of Virginia at Jamestown. From then on, slavery had a foothold, especially in the agricultural South, where a large amount of slave labor was needed for the extensive plantations. Free men refused to work for wages on the plantations when land was available for settling on the frontier. Therefore, slave labor was the only recourse. If it had been profitable to use slaves in New England and the Middle Colonies, then without doubt slavery would have been more widespread.

By 1860, the country was made up of three major regions. The people in all three regions had a number of beliefs and institutions in common. Of course, there were major differences with each region having its own unique characteristics. The basic problem was their development along very different lines.

The North was industrial with towns and factories growing and increasing rapidly. The South had become agricultural, eventually becoming increasingly dependent on cotton. In the West, restless pioneers moved into new frontiers seeking land, wealth, and opportunity. Many were from the South and were slave owners, and brought their slaves with them. Views on tariffs, public lands, internal improvements at federal expense, banking and currency, and the issue of slavery were decidedly different. This period of U.S. history was a period of compromises, breakdowns of the compromises, desperate attempts to restore and retain harmony among the three sections, short-lived intervals of the uneasy balance of interests, and ever-increasing conflict.

At the Constitutional Convention, one of the slavery compromises concerned counting slaves for deciding the number of representatives for the House and the amount of taxes to be paid. Southerners pushed for counting the slaves for representation, but not for taxes. The Northerners pushed for the opposite. The resulting compromise, sometimes referred to as the "three-fifths compromise," was that both groups agreed that three-fifths of the slaves would be counted for both taxes and representation.

The other compromise over slavery was part of the disputes over how much central government would control commercial activities such as trade with other nations and the slave trade. It was agreed that Congress would regulate commerce with other nations including taxing imports. Southerners were worried about taxing slaves and the possibility of Congress prohibiting the slave trade altogether. The agreement reached allowed the states to continue importation of slaves for the next 20 years until 1808, at which time Congress would make the decision as to the future of the slave trade. During the 20-year period, no more than $10 per person could be levied on slaves coming into the country.

These two "slavery" compromises were a necessary concession to have Southern support and approval for the new document and new government. Many Americans felt that the system of slavery would eventually die out in the U.S., but by 1808, cotton was becoming increasingly important in the primarily agricultural South and the institution of slavery had become firmly entrenched in Southern culture. It is also evident that as early as the Constitutional Convention, active anti-slavery feelings and opinions were very strong, leading to extremely active groups and societies.

The first serious clash between the North and South occurred in 1819-1820 during the Monroe administration concerning admitting Missouri as a state. In 1819, the U.S. consisted of 21 states: 11 free states and 10 slave states. The Missouri Territory allowed slavery and if admitted would cause an imbalance in the number of U.S. Senators. The first Missouri Compromise resolved the conflict by approving the admission of Maine as a free state along with Missouri as a slave state. The balance of power in the Senate continued with the same number of free and slave states.

An additional provision of this compromise was that with the admission of Missouri, slavery would not be allowed in the rest of the Louisiana Purchase territory north of latitude 36 degrees 30'. In its state constitution, Missouri discriminated against the free blacks. Anti-slavery supporters in Congress went into an uproar, determined to exclude Missouri from the Union. Henry Clay, known as the Great Compromiser, then proposed a second Missouri Compromise.

His proposal stated that the Constitution of the United States guaranteed protections and privileges to citizens of states and Missouri's proposed constitution could not deny these to any of its citizens. The acceptance in 1820 of this second compromise opened the way for Missouri's statehood.

The issue of tariffs also was a divisive factor during this period, especially between 1829 and 1833. The Embargo Act of 1807 and the War of 1812 had completely cut off the source of manufactured goods for Americans, so it was necessary to build factories to produce what was needed. To protect and encourage its own industries and their products, Congress passed the Tariff of 1816, which required high duties to be levied on manufactured goods coming into the United States. Southern leaders, such as John C. Calhoun of South Carolina, supported the tariff with the assumption that the South would develop its own industries.

For a brief period after 1815, the nation enjoyed the "Era of Good Feelings." People were moving into the West; industry and agriculture were growing; a feeling of national pride united Americans in their efforts and determination to strengthen the country. However, over-speculation in stocks and lands for quick profits backfired. Cotton prices were rising, so many Southerners bought land for cultivation at inflated prices. Manufacturers in the industrial North purchased land to build more plants and factories as an attempt to have a part of this prosperity. Settlers in the West rushed to buy land to reap the benefits of the increasing prices of meat and grain. To have the money for all of these economic activities, all of these groups were borrowing heavily from the banks and the banks themselves encouraged this by giving loans on insubstantial security.

In late 1818, the Bank of the United States and its branches stopped renewal of personal mortgages and required state banks to immediately pay their bank notes in gold, silver, or in national bank notes. Unable to do this, state banks closed. Since mortgages could not be renewed, people lost all their properties and foreclosures were rampant throughout the country. At the same time, cotton prices collapsed in the English market. Its high price had caused the British manufacturers to seek cheaper cotton from India for their textile mills. With the fall of cotton prices, the demand for American manufactured goods declined, revealing how fragile the economic prosperity had been.

Congress passed a higher tariff in 1824 favoring the financial interests of the manufacturers in New England and the Middle Atlantic States. The 1824 tariff was closely tied to the presidential election of that year. Before becoming law, Calhoun had proposed the high tariffs in an effort to get Eastern business interests to vote with the agricultural interests in the South (who were against it).

By the time the higher 1828 tariff was passed, feelings were extremely bitter in the South, due to a belief that the New England manufacturers greatly benefited from it. Vice-President Calhoun, also speaking for his home state of South Carolina, promptly declared that if any state felt that a federal law was unconstitutional, that state could nullify it. In 1832, Congress took the action of lowering the tariffs to a degree but not enough to please South Carolina, which promptly declared the tariff null and void, and threatened to secede from the Union.

In 1833, Congress lowered the tariffs again to a level acceptable to South Carolina. Although President Jackson believed in states' rights, he also firmly believed in the preservation of the Union. A constitutional crisis had been averted but sectional divisions were getting deeper and more pronounced. The abolition movement was growing rapidly and becoming an important issue in the North.

By 1836, Texas was an independent republic with its own constitution. During its fight for independence, Americans were sympathetic to and supportive of the Texans, and some recruited volunteers who crossed into Texas to help the struggle. Problems arose when the state petitioned Congress for statehood. Texas wanted to allow slavery, but Northerners in Congress opposed admission to the Union because it would disrupt the balance between free and slave states and give Southerners in Congress increased influence. Others believed that granting statehood to Texas would lead to a war with Mexico. Mexico had refused to recognize Texas independence. Statehood was denied.

Friction increased between land-hungry Americans swarming into western lands and the Mexican government, which controlled these lands. The clash was political, cultural and economic. Spanish influence permeated all parts of southwestern life: law, language, architecture, and customs. By this time, the doctrine of Manifest Destiny was in the hearts and on the lips of those seeking new areas of settlement and a new life. Americans were demanding U.S. control of not only the Mexican Territory but also Oregon. Peaceful negotiations with Great Britain secured Oregon, but it took two years of war to gain control of the southwestern U.S.

The Mexican government owed debts to U.S. citizens whose property was damaged or destroyed during its struggle for independence from Spain. By the time war broke out in 1845, Mexico had not paid its war debts. The government was weak, corrupt, irresponsible, torn by revolutions, and in poor financial condition. Mexico was also bitter over American expansion into Texas and the 1836 revolution, which resulted in Texas independence. In the 1844 presidential election, the Democrats pushed for annexation of Texas and Oregon and after winning, they started the procedure to admit Texas to the Union.

When statehood occurred, diplomatic relations between the U.S. and Mexico ended. President Polk wanted U.S. control of the entire southwest, from Texas to the Pacific Ocean. He sent a diplomatic mission with an offer to purchase New Mexico and Upper California but the Mexican government refused to even receive the diplomat. Consequently, in 1846, each nation claimed aggression on the part of the other and war was declared. The treaty signed in 1848 and a subsequent one in 1853 established the southwestern boundary of the United States as the Pacific Ocean.

It was obvious that the newly acquired land would be divided up into territories and later become states. Factions of Northerners advocated prohibition of slavery and Southerners favored slavery. A third faction arose supporting the doctrine of "popular sovereignty" which stated that people living in territories and states should be allowed to decide for themselves whether or not slavery should be permitted. In 1849, California applied for admission to the Union and the furor began.

The result was the Compromise of 1850, a series of laws designed as a final solution to the issue. Concessions made to the North included the admission of California as a free state and the abolition of slave trading in Washington, D.C. The laws also provided for the creation of the New Mexico and Utah territories. As a concession to Southerners, the residents there would decide whether to permit slavery when these two territories became states. In addition, Congress authorized implementation of stricter measures to capture runaway slaves.

A few years later, Congress took up admission of new territories between Missouri and present-day Idaho. Again, heated debate arose over slavery, Those opposed to slavery used the Missouri Compromise to argue that the land being considered was part of the area the Compromise had been designated barring to slavery. On May 25, 1854, Congress passed the infamous Kansas-Nebraska Act which nullified the provision creating the territories of Kansas and Nebraska. This provided for the people of these two territories to decide for themselves whether or not to permit slavery. Kansas was called "Bleeding Kansas" because of the extreme violence and bloodshed throughout the territory because two governments existed there, one pro-slavery and the other anti-slavery.

The Supreme Court, in 1857, handed down a deeply controversial decision in the case of Dred Scott. Scott was a slave whose owner had taken him from (slave state) Missouri, then to (free state Illinois), into Minnesota Territory, (free under the provisions of the Missouri Compromise), then finally back to (slave state) Missouri. Abolitionists presented a court case, stating that since Scott had lived in a free state and free territory, he was in actuality a free man. The Supreme Court decided that residing in a free state and free territory did not make Scott a free man because Scott (and all other slaves) was not a U.S. citizen or a citizen of Missouri. Therefore, he did not have the right to sue in state or federal courts. The Court went a step further and ruled that the old Missouri Compromise was now unconstitutional because Congress did not have the power to prohibit slavery in the Territories.

Anti-slavery supporters were stunned. They had just recently formed the new Republican Party and one of its platforms was keeping slavery out of the Territories. Now, according to the decision in the Dred Scott case, this basic party principle was unconstitutional. The only way to ban slavery in new areas was by a Constitutional amendment, requiring ratification by three-fourths of all states. At this time, this was out of the question because the supporters would be unable to get a majority due to Southern opposition.

In 1858, Abraham Lincoln and Stephen A. Douglas were running for the office of U.S. Senator from Illinois and participated in a series of debates, which directly affected the outcome of the 1860 Presidential election. Douglas, a Democrat, was up for re-election and knew that if he won this race, he had a good chance of becoming President in 1860. Lincoln, a Republican, was not an abolitionist but he believed that slavery was wrong morally and he firmly believed in and supported the Republican Party principle that slavery must not be allowed to extend any further.

Douglas, on the other hand, originated the doctrine of "popular sovereignty" and was responsible for supporting and getting through Congress the inflammatory Kansas-Nebraska Act. In the course of the debates, Lincoln challenged Douglas to show that popular sovereignty reconciled with the Dred Scott decision. Either way he answered Lincoln, Douglas would lose crucial support from one group or the other. If he supported the Dred Scott decision, Southerners would support him but he would lose Northern support. If he stayed with popular sovereignty, Northern support would be his but Southern support would be lost. His reply to Lincoln, stating that Territorial legislatures could exclude slavery by refusing to pass laws supporting it, gave him enough support and approval to be re-elected to the Senate. But it cost him the Democratic nomination for president in 1860.

In 1859, abolitionist John Brown and his followers seized the federal arsenal at Harper's Ferry in what is now West Virginia. His purpose was to take the guns stored in the arsenal, give them to slaves nearby, and lead them in a widespread rebellion. He and his men were captured by Colonel Robert E. Lee of the United States Army and after a trial with a guilty verdict, he was hanged. Most Southerners felt that the majority of Northerners approved of Brown's actions but in actuality, most of them were stunned and shocked. Southern newspapers took great pains to quote a small but well-known minority of abolitionists who applauded and supported Brown's actions. This merely served to widen the gap between the two sections.

The final straw came with the election of Lincoln to the presidency the next year. Due to a split in the Democratic Party, there were four candidates from four political parties. With Lincoln receiving a minority of the popular vote and a majority of electoral votes, the Southern states, one by one, voted to secede from the Union, as they had promised they would do if Lincoln and the Republicans were victorious. The die was cast.

South Carolina was the first state to secede from the Union and the first shots of the war were fired on Fort Sumter in Charleston Harbor. Both sides quickly prepared for war. The North had more in its favor: a larger population; superiority in finances and transportation facilities; and manufacturing, agricultural, and natural resources. The North possessed most of the nation's gold, about 92% of all industries, and almost all known supplies of copper, coal, iron, and various other minerals. Most of the nation's railroads were in the North and mid-West; men and supplies could be moved wherever needed; food could be transported from the farms of the mid-West to workers in the East and to soldiers on the battlefields. Trade with nations overseas could go on as usual due to control of the navy and the merchant fleet. The Northern states numbered 24 and included western (California and Oregon) and border (Maryland, Delaware, Kentucky, Missouri, and West Virginia) states.

The Southern states numbered 11 and included South Carolina, Georgia, Florida, Alabama, Mississippi, Louisiana, Texas, Virginia, North Carolina, Tennessee, and Arkansas, making up the Confederacy. Although outnumbered in population, the South was completely confident of victory. They knew that all they had to do was fight a defensive war and protect their own territory. The North had to invade and defeat an area almost the size of Western Europe. They figured the North would tire of the struggle and give up. Another advantage of the South was that a number of its best officers had graduated from the U.S. Military Academy at West Point and had had long years of army experience. Many had exercised varying degrees of command in the Indian Wars and the war with Mexico. Men from the South were conditioned to living outdoors and were more familiar with horses and firearms than men from northeastern cities. Since cotton was such an important crop, Southerners felt that British and French textile mills were so dependent on raw cotton that they would be forced to help the Confederacy in the war.

The South had specific reasons and goals for fighting the war, more so than the North. The major aims of the Confederacy never wavered: to win independence, gain the right to self government, preserve states' rights, and preserve slavery. The Northerners were not as clear in their reasons for conducting war. At the beginning, most believed, along with Lincoln, that preservation of the Union was paramount. Only a few extremely fanatical abolitionists looked on the war as a way to end slavery. However, by war's end, more and more northerners had come to believe that freeing the slaves was just as important as restoring the Union.

The war strategies for both sides were relatively clear and simple. The South planned a defensive war, wearing down the North until it agreed to peace on Southern terms. The only exception was to gain control of Washington, D.C., go north through the Shenandoah Valley into Maryland and Pennsylvania in order to drive a wedge between the Northeast and mid-West, interrupt the lines of communication, and end the war quickly. The North had three basic strategies:

1. Blockade the Confederate coastline in order to cripple the South
2. Seize control of the Mississippi River and interior railroad lines to split the Confederacy in two
3. Seize the Confederate capital of Richmond, Virginia, and drive southward to join the Union forces coming east from the Mississippi Valley

Though it had not been an initial aim of the war, the issue of emancipation quickly became a major issue for the North. No longer needing to placate the Southern members of Congress or their states, Congress passed legislation providing for the emancipation of captured "contraband" slaves. President Lincoln took this a step further, and on January 1, 1863 he issued the **Emancipation Proclamation**, freeing all slaves in the Union. While it had no immediate effect on the South, it provided moral support to the war effort, and also effectively kept Britain – itself an anti-slave nation – from supporting the Confederacy. It also meant that all slaves in Union states were immediately free. When the South finally surrendered, the acceptance of emancipation (by then codified in the 13th Amendment) was one of the major requirements for re-admittance to the Union of the former Confederate States.

Working against the North were Lincoln's choice of commanders, McDowell and McClellan, who were less than desirable, whereas neither Burnside and Hooker were what was needed at the time. On the other hand, Jefferson Davis, President of the Confederation, had chosen Robert E. Lee to lead the Confederate Army. Unlike the problems with command in the Union forces, Lee had many able officers to depend on, including Stonewall Jackson and J.E.B. Stuart. When Jackson died at Chancellorsville he was replaced by James Longstreet. Under Lee's leadership, the South won decisively until the Battle of Gettysburg, July 1 - 3, 1863.. Four things worked against Lee at Gettysburg:

1) The Union troops gained the best positions and the best ground first, making it easier to make a stand there.

2) Lee's move into Northern territory put him and his army a long way from food and supply lines. They were more or less on their own.

3) Lee thought that his Army of Northern Virginia was invincible and could fight and win under any conditions or circumstances.

4) Lee's decision to invade the North depended on Stuart and his cavalry to keep him informed of the location of Union troops and their strengths. Stuart and his men did not arrive at Gettysburg until the end of the second day of fighting and by then, it was too little too late. He and the men had had to detour around Union soldiers and he was delayed getting the information Lee needed.

Though Longstreet advised following the strategy of regrouping back into Southern territory to the supply lines, Lee felt that regrouping was retreating and almost an admission of defeat. He was convinced the army would be victorious. Longstreet was concerned about the Union troops occupying the best positions and felt that regrouping to a better position would be an advantage. He was also very concerned about the distance from supply lines.

It was not the intention of either side to fight there, but the fighting began when a Confederate brigade, who were looking for shoes, stumbled into a Union cavalry unit. The third and last day, Lee launched the final attempt to break Union lines. General George Pickett sent his division of three brigades under Generals Garnet, Kemper, and Armistead against Union troops on Cemetery Ridge under command of General Winfield Scott Hancock. Union lines held and Lee and the defeated Army of Northern Virginia made their way back to Virginia. Although Lincoln's commander George Meade successfully turned back a Confederate charge, he and the Union troops failed to pursue Lee and the Confederates. This battle was the turning point for the North. After this, Lee never again had the troop strength to launch a major offensive.

Four months after the battle, President Lincoln delivered a speech at the dedication of a national cemetery at Gettysburg. Lincoln's speech was short, only about two minutes, but it laid out what would become the defining vision of the United States and its founding principles. The speech also conferred a sense of moral righteousness upon the Civil War. This speech, **Gettysburg Address**, remains one of the most famous American speeches ever.

The day after Gettysburg, on July 4, Vicksburg, Mississippi surrendered to Union General Ulysses Grant, thus severing the western Confederacy from the eastern part. In September 1863, the Confederacy won its last important victory at Chickamauga. In November, the Union victory at Chattanooga made it possible for Union troops to go into Alabama and Georgia, splitting the eastern Confederacy in two. Lincoln gave Grant command of all Northern armies in March of 1864. Grant led his armies into battles in Virginia while Phil Sheridan and his cavalry did as much damage as possible. In a skirmish at a place called Yellow Tavern, Virginia, Sheridan's and Stuart's forces met, with Stuart being fatally wounded.

The Union won the Battle of Mobile Bay and in May 1864, William Tecumseh Sherman began his march to successfully demolish Atlanta, then on to Savannah. He and his troops turned northward through the Carolinas to Grant in Virginia. On April 9, 1865, Lee formally surrendered to Grant at Appamattox Courthouse, Virginia.

The Civil War took more American lives than any other war in history, the South losing one-third of its' soldiers in battle compared to about one-sixth for the North. More than half of the total deaths were caused by disease and the horrendous conditions of field hospitals. Both sides paid a tremendous economic price but the South suffered more severely from direct damages. Destruction was pervasive with towns, farms, trade, industry, lives and homes of men, women, children all destroyed and an entire Southern way of life was lost. The South had no voice in the political, social, and cultural affairs of the nation, lessening to a great degree the influence of the more traditional Southern ideals. The Northern Yankee Protestant ideals of hard work, education, and economic freedom became the standard of the United States and helped influence the development of the nation into a modem, industrial power.

The effects of the Civil War were tremendous. It changed the methods of waging war and has been called the first modern war. It introduced weapons and tactics that, when improved later, were used extensively in wars of the late 1800s and 1900s. Civil War soldiers were the first to fight in trenches, first to fight under a unified command, first to wage a defense called "major cordon defense", a strategy of advance on all fronts. They were also the first to use repeating and breech loading weapons. Observation balloons were first used during the war along with submarines, ironclad ships, and mines. Telegraphy and railroads were put to use first in the Civil War. It was considered a modern war because of the vast destruction and was "total war", involving the use of all resources of the opposing sides. There was no *way* it could have ended other than total defeat and unconditional surrender of one side or the other.

By executive proclamation and constitutional amendment, slavery was officially ended, although there remained deep prejudice and racism. The Union was preserved and the states were finally truly united. Sectionalism, especially in the area of politics, remained strong for another 100 years but not to the degree and with the violence that existed before 1861. It has been noted that the Civil War may have been American democracy's greatest failure for, from 1861 to 1865, calm reason, basic to democracy, fell to human passion. Yet, democracy did survive. The victory of the North established that no state has the right to end or leave the Union. Because of unity, the U.S. became a major global power. Lincoln never proposed to punish the South. He was most concerned with restoring the South to the Union in a program that was flexible and practical rather than rigid and unbending. In fact he never really felt that the states had succeeded in leaving the Union but that they had left the "family circle" for a short time. His plans consisted of two major steps:

- All Southerners taking an oath of allegiance to the Union and promising to accept all federal laws and proclamations dealing with slavery would receive a full pardon. The only ones excluded from this were men who had resigned from civil and military positions in the federal government to serve in the Confederacy, those who were part of the Confederate government, those in the Confederate army above the rank of lieutenant, and Confederates who were guilty of mistreating prisoners of war and blacks.

- A state would be able to write a new constitution, elect new officials, and return to the Union fully equal to all other states on certain conditions: A minimum number of persons (at least 10% of those who were qualified voters in their states before secession from the Union who had voted in the 1860 election) would have to take an oath of allegiance.

While the war dragged on to its bloody and destructive conclusion, Lincoln was very concerned and anxious to get the states restored to the Union. He showed flexibility in his thinking as he made changes to his Reconstruction program to make it as easy and painless as possible. Congress had final approval of many actions. It would be interesting to know how differently things might have turned out if Lincoln had lived to see some or all of his kind policies, supported by fellow moderates, put into action. After Andrew Johnson became President and the radical Republicans gained control of Congress, the harsh measures of radical Reconstruction were implemented.

The economic and social chaos in the South after the war was unbelievable with starvation and disease rampant, especially in the cities. The U.S. Army provided some relief of food and clothing for both white and blacks but the major responsibility fell to the Freedmen's Bureau. Though the bureau agents helped some southern whites, their main responsibility was to the freed slaves. They were to assist the freedmen to become self-supporting and protect them from being taken advantage of by others. Northerners looked on it as a real, honest effort to help the South out of its chaos. Most white Southerners charged the bureau with causing racial friction, deliberately encouraging the freedmen to consider former owners as enemies.

As a result, as southern leaders began to be able to restore life as it had once been, they adopted a set of laws known as "black codes," containing many of the provisions of the prewar "slave codes." There were certain improvements in the lives of freedmen, but the codes denied the freedmen their basic civil rights. In short, except for the condition of freedom and a few civil rights, white Southerners made every effort to keep the freedmen in a way of life subordinate to theirs.

Radicals in Congress pointed out these illegal actions by white Southerners as evidence that they were unwilling to recognize, accept, and support the complete freedom of black Americans and could not be trusted. Therefore, Congress drafted its own program of Reconstruction, including laws that would protect and further the rights of blacks. Three amendments were added to the Constitution: the 13th Amendment of 1865 outlawed slavery throughout the entire United States. The 14th Amendment of 1868 made blacks American citizens. The 15th Amendment of 1870 gave black Americans the right to vote and made it illegal to deny anyone the right to vote based on race.

Federal troops were stationed throughout the South and protected Republicans who took control of Southern governments. Bitterly resentful, white Southerners fought the new political system by joining a secret society called the Ku Klux Klan, using violence to keep black Americans from voting and getting equality. However, before being allowed to rejoin the Union, the Confederate states were required to agree to all federal laws. Between 1866 and 1870, all of them had returned to the Union, but Northern interest in Reconstruction was fading. Reconstruction officially ended when the last Federal troops left the South in 1877. It can be said that Reconstruction had a limited success as it set up public school systems and expanded legal rights of black Americans. Nevertheless, white supremacy came to be in control again.

Lincoln and Johnson had considered the Civil War a "rebellion of individuals." Congressional Radicals, such as Charles Sumner in the Senate, considered the Southern states as complete political organizations that were now in the same position as any unorganized Territory and should be treated as such. Radical House leader Thaddeus Stevens considered the Confederate States not as Territories, but as conquered provinces. He felt they should be treated that way. President Johnson refused to work with Congressional moderates, insisting on having his own way. As a result, the Radicals gained control of both houses of Congress; when Johnson opposed their harsh measures, they came within one vote of impeaching him. General Grant was elected President in 1868, serving two scandal-ridden terms. He was himself an honest and upright person, but he greatly lacked political experience and his greatest weakness was a blind loyalty to his friends. He absolutely refused to believe that his friends were not honest and stubbornly would not admit to their using him to further their own interests. One of the sad results of the war was the rapid growth of business and industry, with large corporations controlled by unscrupulous men. However, after 1877, some degree of normalcy returned and there was time for rebuilding, expansion, and growth.

There was a marked degree of industrialization before and during the Civil War, but at war's end, industry in America was small. After the war, dramatic changes took place. Machines replaced hand labor; extensive nationwide railroad service allowed wider distribution of goods; new inventions resulted in larger quantities of new products; and large amounts of money from bankers and investors made possible the expansion of many business operations. American life was definitely affected by this phenomenal industrial growth. Cities became the centers of this new business activity. People moved to cities in masses, and the cities experienced tremendous growth. This new boom in business resulted in huge fortunes for some Americans and extreme poverty for many others. The discontent this caused resulted in a number of new reform movements from which came measures controlling the power and size of big business and helping the poor.

Of course, industry before, during, and after the Civil War was centered mainly in the North, especially the tremendous industrial growth after. The late 1800s and early 1900s saw the U.S. increasing its military strength and emerging as a world power.

The use of machines in industry enabled workers to produce a large quantity of goods, much faster than by hand. With the increase in business, hundreds of workers were hired, assigned to perform a certain job in the production process. This method of organization, called "division of labor," helped businesses increase their rate of production, lower prices, and make their products more affordable for more people. As a result, sales and businesses were increasingly successful and profitable.

A great variety of new products or inventions became available, such as: the typewriter, the telephone, barbed wire, the electric light, the phonograph, and the gasoline automobile. Of these, the one that had the greatest effect on America's economy was the automobile.

The increase in business and industry was greatly affected by the many rich natural resources that were found throughout the nation. The industrial machines were powered by the abundant water supply. The construction industry as well as products made from wood depended heavily on lumber from the forests. Coal and iron ore in abundance were needed for the steel industry, which profited and increased from the use of steel in such things as skyscrapers, automobiles, bridges, railroad tracks, and machines. Other minerals such as silver, copper, and petroleum played a large role in industrial growth, especially petroleum, from which gasoline was refined as fuel for the increasingly popular automobile.

Skill 6.7   Demonstrate an understanding of U.S. imperialism and examine the experience of the United States as a colonial power

During the period of 1823 to the 1890s, the major interests and efforts of the American people were concentrated on expansion, settlement, and development of the continental United States. The Civil War, 1861-1865, preserved the Union and eliminated the system of slavery. From 1865 onward, the focus was on taming the West and developing industry. During this period, travel and trade between the United States and Europe were continuous. By the 1890s, American interests turned to areas outside the boundaries of the United States. The West was developing into a major industrial area and people in the United States became very interested in selling their factory and farm surplus to overseas markets. In fact, some Americans desired getting and controlling land outside the U.S. boundaries. Before the 1890s, the U.S. had little, if anything to do with foreign affairs, was not a strong nation militarily, and had inconsequential influence on international political affairs. In fact, the Europeans looked on the American diplomats as inept and bungling in their diplomatic efforts and activities. However, all of this changed and the **Spanish-American War of 1898** saw the entry of the United States as a world power.

It was the belief of many that the United States was destined to control all of the land between the two oceans—or, as one newspaper editor termed it, "Manifest Destiny." This mass migration westward put the U.S. government on a collision course with the Indians, Great Britain, Spain, and Mexico. The fur traders and missionaries ran up against the Indians in the northwest and the claims of Great Britain for the Oregon country.

In the American southwest, Spain had claimed this area since the 1540s, had spread northward from Mexico City, and, in the 1700s, had established missions, forts, villages, towns, and very large ranches. After the purchase of the Louisiana Territory in 1803, Americans began moving into Spanish territory. A few hundred American families in what is now Texas were allowed to live there but had to agree to become loyal subjects to Spain. In 1821, Mexico successfully revolted against Spanish rule, won independence, and chose to be more tolerant towards the American settlers and traders. The Mexican government encouraged and allowed extensive trade and settlement, especially in Texas. Many of the new settlers were southerners and brought with them their slaves. Slavery was outlawed in Mexico and technically illegal in Texas, although the Mexican government rather looked the other way.

With the influx of so many Americans and the liberal policies of the Mexican government, there came to be concern over the possible growth and development of an American state within Mexico. Settlement restrictions, cancellation of land grants, the forbidding of slavery and increased military activity brought everything to a head. The order of events included the fight for Texas independence, the brief Republic of Texas, eventual annexation of Texas, statehood, and finally war with Mexico.

The Texas controversy was not the sole reason for war. Since American settlers had begun, pouring into the Southwest the cultural differences played a prominent part. Language, religion, law, customs, and government were totally different between the two groups. A clash was bound to occur.

Friction increased between land-hungry Americans swarming into western lands and the Mexican government, which controlled these lands. The clash was not only political but also cultural and economic. The Spanish influence permeated all parts of southwestern life: law, language, architecture, and customs. By this time, the doctrine of Manifest Destiny was in the hearts and on the lips of those seeking new areas of settlement and a new life.

During the 1890s, Spain controlled such overseas possessions as Puerto Rico, the Philippines, and Cuba. Cubans rebelled against Spanish rule and the U.S. government found itself besieged by demands from Americans to assist the Cubans in their revolt. When the U.S. battleship Maine blew up off the coast of Havana, Cuba, Americans blamed the Spaniards for it and demanded American action against Spain. Two months later, Congress declared war on Spain and the U.S. quickly defeated them. The peace treaty gave the U.S. possession of Puerto Rico, the Philippines, Guam and Hawaii, which was annexed during the war.

Most students of American history are aware of the tremendous influx of immigrants to America during the 19th century. It is also a known fact that the majority settled in the ethnic neighborhoods and communities of the large cities, close to friends, relatives, and the work they were able to find. After the U.S. Congress passed the 1862 Homestead Act after the Civil War ended, the West began to open up for settlement. More than half of the hardy pioneers who went to homestead and farm western lands were European immigrants: Swedes, Norwegians, Czechs, Germans, Danes, Finns, and Russians.

By far, the nation's immigrants were an important reason for America's phenomenal industrial growth from 1865 to 1900. They came seeking work and better opportunities for themselves and their families. What they found in America was suspicion and distrust because they were competitors with Americans for jobs, housing, and decent wages. Their languages, customs, and ways of living were different. Until the early 1880s, most immigrants were from northwestern Europe.

After 1890, the new arrivals increasingly came from eastern and southern Europe. Chinese immigrants on the Pacific coast, so crucial to the construction of the western part of the first transcontinental railroad, were the first to experience this increasing distrust which eventually erupted into violence and bloodshed. From about 1879 to the present time, the U.S. Congress made, repealed, and amended numerous pieces of legislation concerning quotas, restrictions, and other requirements pertaining to immigrants. The immigrant laborers, both skilled and unskilled, were the foundation of the modern labor union movement as a means of gaining recognition, support, respect, rights, fair wages, and better working conditions.

COMPETENCY 7   UNDERSTAND THE MAJOR POLITICAL, SOCIAL, ECONOMIC, SCIENTIFIC, AND CULTURAL DEVELOPMENTS AND TURNING POINTS IN U.S. HISTORY SINCE 1900

Skill 7.1   Examine factors related to the rise of the Progressive Movement and assess the influence of Progressive reforms

The tremendous change that resulted from the Industrial Revolution led to a demand for reform that would control the power wielded by big corporations. The gap between the industrial moguls and the working people was growing. This disparity between rich and poor resulted in a public outcry for reform at the same time there was an outcry for governmental reform to end the political corruption and elitism of the day.

This fire was fueled by the writings of investigative journalists – the "muckrakers" – who published scathing exposes of political and business wrongdoing and corruption. The result was the rise of a group of politicians and reformers who supported a wide array of populist causes. The period 1900 to 1917 came to be known as the **Progressive Era**. Although these leaders came from many different backgrounds and were driven by different ideologies, they shared a common fundamental belief that government should be eradicating social ills and promoting the common good and the equality guaranteed by the Constitution.

The reforms initiated by these leaders and the spirit of **Progressivism** were far-reaching. Politically, many states enacted the initiative and the referendum. The adoption of the recall occurred in many states. Several states enacted legislation that would undermine the power of political machines. On a national level, the two most significant political changes were (1) the ratification of the 17th amendment, which required that all U.S. Senators be chosen by popular election, and (2) the ratification of the 19th Amendment, which granted women the right to vote.

Major economic reforms of the period included aggressive enforcement of the Sherman Antitrust Act; passage of the Elkins Act and the Hepburn Act, which gave the Interstate Commerce Commission greater power to regulate the railroads; the Pure Food and Drug Act, which prohibited the use of harmful chemicals in food; The Meat Inspection Act, which regulated the meat industry to protect the public against tainted meat; the prohibition of child labor in over two-thirds of the states; mandatory workmen's compensation; and the creation of the Department of Commerce and Labor.

Responding to concern over the environmental effects of the timber, ranching, and mining industries, Roosevelt set aside 238 million acres of federal lands to protect them from development. Wildlife preserves were established, the national park system was expanded, and the National Conservation Commission was created. The Newlands Reclamation Act also provided federal funding for the construction of irrigation projects and dams in semi-arid areas of the country. The Wilson Administration carried out additional reforms. The Federal Reserve Act created a national banking system, providing a stable money supply. The Sherman Act and the Clayton Antitrust Act defined unfair competition, made corporate officers liable for the illegal actions of employees, and exempted labor unions from antitrust lawsuits. The Federal Trade Commission was established to enforce these measures. Finally, the 16th amendment was ratified, establishing an income tax. This measure was designed to relieve the poor of a disproportionate burden in funding the federal government and make the wealthy pay a greater share of the nation's tax burden.

Skill 7.2   Demonstrate an understanding of developments in literature, the arts, and other fields during the 20th century

Music. The 20th century experienced a revolution in music. In keeping with the exceptionally high value of individuality and unique personal expression, there was a quest for new and unique forms of musical expression.

The major forms inspired by classical music have continued, though with certain modifications. The symphony has continued in form, but with greater dissonance and great experimentation in rhythm. Major symphonic composers of the century include: Gustav Mahler, Jean Sibelius, Dmitry Shostakovich, Serge Prokofiev, Sergey Rachmaninov, and Leonard Bernstein. Opera began to change after WWII as composers began to incorporate other musical forms that were emerging during the century. Notable operatic composers include Benjamin Britten, Karlheinz Stockhausen, Virgil Thomson, Douglas Moore, Philip Glass and John Adams. Ballet tended to focus on music written specifically for its needs. This trend included such composers as Claude Debussy, Maurice Ravel and R. Strauss. Igor Stravinsky's *The Rite of Spring*, however, was internationally recognized for its violent rhythms and dissonance. The second half of the century was marked by the tendency to re-stage ballets with existing music. The exceptions were Aaron Copland, Hans Werner Henze and Benjamin Britten.

Musical Theater was an evolution from the operettas of the Romantic Period and the traditions of the European music hall and American vaudeville. Most notable in this form are Leonard Bernstein and Steven Sondheim. Film Music also developed during this century. The soundtracks for films were either adaptations of classical music or new compositions from composers like Elmer Bernstein, Bernard Herrman, Max Steiner and Dmitri Tiomkin.

American Popular music evolved from folk music. This was the music of the first half of the century, characterized by a consistent structure of two verses, a chorus, and a repetition of the chorus. The songs were written to be sung by average persons, and the tunes were usually harmonized. Much of this music originated in New York's Tin Pan Alley. Particularly notable during this period were Irving Berlin, George and Ira Gershwin, and a host of others. After WWII, teen music began to dominate. New forms emerged from various ethnic and regional groups, including Blues, Rhythm and Blues and Rap from the African American community; Country music from the south and the southwest; folk music, jazz, and rock 'n' roll.

Art. The primary expression of the first half of the decade was Modernism. The avant garde perspective encouraged all types of innovation and experimentation. Key elements of this movement have been abstraction, cubism, surrealism, realism, and abstract expressionism. Notable among the artists of this period for the birth or perfection of particular styles are Henri Matisse, Pablo Picasso, George Rouault, Gustav Klimt, George Braque, Salvador Dali, Hans Arp, Rene Magrite, and Marcel Duchamp. In the U.S., realism tended to find regional expressions—as in the Ashcan School and Robert Henri, Midwestern Regionalism and Grant Wood. Other particularly notable painters are Edward Hopper and Georgia O'Keeffe. The New York School came to be known for a style known as Abstract Expressionism and included such artists as Jackson Pollock, Willem de Kooning, and Larry Rivers. Other painters of the period were Mark Rothko, Clement Greenberg, Ellsworth Kelly and the Op Art Movement.

In sculpture, many of the same patterns and trends were applied. Innovations included the exploration of empty space (Henry Moore), the effort to incorporate cubism in three dimensions (Marcel Duchamp), and the use of welded metal to create kinetic sculpture (Alexander Calder).

Postmodernism took over art since 1950. This art style includes Minimalism, Figurative Styles, Pop Art, Conceptual Art, and Installation Art. Photography has developed as an art form, as well, during the 20th century.

Literature. The writings of this period invite readers to ponder the nature and the cost of war, the meaning of the human struggle for freedom, and the possibility of everyone enjoying basic human and civil rights. Literature has cried out against change, as well as embraced it. By the beginning of the 20th century, literature was reflecting the struggle of the modern individual to find a place and a meaning in a new world that seemed like a jungle. Literature has reflected the observation that not only does the modern human not know how to find meaning, he/she does not actually know what he/she is seeking. It is this crisis of identity that has been the subject of most modern literature. This can be seen in the writings of Joseph Conrad, Sigmund Freud, James Joyce, Eugene O'Neill, Luigi Pirandello, Samuel Beckett, George Bernard Shaw, T.S. Eliot, Franz Kafka, Albert Camus, Boris Pasternak, Graham Greene, Tennessee Williams, and others.

Significant contributions in literature, music, art and other fields were made by African-Americans and women as well.

The historical record of African-Americans is known to all. Sold into slavery by rival tribes, they were brought against their will to the West Indies and southern America to slave on the plantations in a life-long condition of servitude and bondage. The 13th Constitutional Amendment abolished slavery; the 14th gave them U.S. citizenship; and the 15th gave them the right to vote. Efforts of well-known African-Americans resulted in some improvements although the struggle was continuous without let-up. Many were outspoken and urged and led protests against the continued onslaught of discrimination and inequality.

The leading black spokesman from 1890 to 1915 was educator **Booker T. Washington**. He recognized the need of vocational education for African-Americans, educating them for skills and training for such areas as domestic service, farming, the skilled trades, and small business enterprises. He founded and built in Alabama the famous Tuskegee Institute.

W.E.B. DuBois, another outstanding African-American leader and spokesman, believed that only continuous and vigorous protests against injustices and inequalities, coupled with appeals to black pride, would effect changes. The results of his efforts was the formation of the Urban League and the NAACP (the National Association for the Advancement of Colored People), which today continues to eliminate discrimination and secure equality and equal rights.

Others who made significant contributions were **Dr. George Washington Carver**, who helped improve agricultural techniques for both black and white farmers; the writers **William Wells Brown, Paul L. Dunbar, Langston Hughes**, and **Charles W. Chesnutt**; the musicians **Duke Ellington, W.C. Handy, Marion Anderson, Louis Armstrong, Leontyne Price, Jessye Norman, Ella Fitzgerald**; and many others.

Students of American history are familiar with the accomplishments and contributions of American women. Previous mention has been made of the accomplishments of such 19th century women as: writer **Louisa May Alcott**; abolitionist **Harriet Beecher Stowe**; women's rights activists **Elizabeth Cady Stanton** and **Lucretia Mott**; physician **Dr. Elizabeth Blackwell**; women's education activists **Mary Lyon, Catharine Esther Beecher**, and **Emma Hart Willard**; prison and asylum reform activist **Dorothea Dix**; social reformer, humanitarian, pursuer of peace **Jane Addams**; aviatrix **Amelia Earhart**; women's suffrage activists **Susan B. Anthony, Carrie Chapman Catt**, and **Anna Howard Shaw**; Supreme Court Associate Justices **Sandra Day O'Connor** and **Ruth Bader Ginsberg**; and many more who have made tremendous contributions in science, politics and government, music and the arts (such as **Jane Alexander** who was National Chairperson of the National Endowment for the Arts), education, athletics, law, etc.

Skill 7.3   Analyze the causes of the Great Depression and its effects on U.S. society, and the impact of the New Deal on American life

The 1929 Stock Market Crash was the powerful event that is generally interpreted as the beginning of the Great Depression in America. Although the crash of the Stock Market was unexpected, it was not without identifiable causes. The 1920s had been a decade of social and economic growth and hope. But the attitudes and actions of the 1920s regarding wealth, production, and investment created several trends that quietly set the stage for the 1929 disaster.

Uneven distribution of wealth: In the 1920s, the distribution of wealth between the rich and the middle class was grossly disproportionate. In 1929, the combined income of the top 0.1% of the population was equal to the combined income of the bottom 42%. The top 0.1% of the population controlled 34% of all savings, while 80% of Americans had no savings. Capitalism was making the wealthy richer at the expense of the workers. Between 1920 and 1929, the amount of disposable income per person rose 9%. The top 0.1% of the population, however, enjoyed an increase in disposable income of 75%. One reason for this disparity was increased manufacturing productivity during the 1920s. Average worker productivity in manufacturing increased 32% during this period. Yet, wages in manufacturing increased only 8%. The wages of the workers rose very slowly, failing to keep pace with increasing productivity. As production costs fell and prices remained constant, profits soared. But profits were retained by the companies and the owners.

The Legislative and Executive branches of the Coolidge administration tended to favor business and the wealthy. The Revenue Act of 1926 reduced income taxes for the wealthy significantly. This bill lowered taxes so that a person with a million-dollar income saw his/her taxes reduced from $600,000 to $200,000. Despite the rise of labor unions, even the Supreme Court ruled in ways that further widened the gap between the rich and the middle class. In the case of Adkins v. Children's Hospital (1923), the Court ruled that minimum wage legislation was unconstitutional.

This kind of disparity in the distribution of wealth weakened the economy. Demand was unable to equal supply. The surplus of manufactured goods was beyond the reach of the poor and the middle class. The wealthy, however, could purchase all they wanted with a smaller and smaller portion of their income. This meant that in order for the economy to remain stable, the wealthy had to invest their money and spend money on luxury items while others bought on credit.

The majority of the population did not have enough money to buy what was necessary to meet their needs. The concept of buying on credit caught on very quickly. Buying on credit, however, creates artificial demand for products people cannot ordinarily afford. This has two effects: First, at some point, there is less need to purchase products (because they have already been bought). Second, at some point, paying for previous purchases makes it impossible to purchase new products. This exacerbated the problem of a surplus of goods.

The economy also relied on investment and luxury spending by the rich in the 1920s. Luxury spending, however, only occurs when people are confident with regard to the economy and the future. Should these people lose confidence, that luxury spending would come to an abrupt halt. This is precisely what happened when the stock market crashed in 1929. Investing in business produces returns for the investor. During the 1920s, investing was very healthy. Investors, however, began to expect greater returns on their investments. This led many to make speculative investments in risky opportunities.

The disproportionate distribution of wealth between the rich and the middle class mirrors the uneven distribution of wealth between industries. In 1929, half of all corporate wealth was controlled by just 200 companies. The automotive industry was growing exceptionally quickly, but agriculture was steadily declining. In fact, in 1921 food prices dropped about 70% due to surplus. The average income in agriculture was only about one-third of the national average across all industries.

Two industries, automotive and radio, drove the economy in the 1920s. During this decade, the government tended to support new industries rather than agriculture. During WWI, the government had subsidized farms and paid ridiculously high prices for grains. Farmers had been encouraged to buy and farm more land and to use new technology to increase production. The nation was feeding much of Europe during and in the aftermath of the war. But when the war ended, these farm policies were cut off. Prices plummeted, farmers fell into debt, and farm prices declined. The agriculture industry was on the brink of ruin before the stock market crash.

The concentration of production and economic stability in the automotive industry and the production and sale of radios was expected to last forever. But there comes a point when the growth of an industry slows due to market saturation. When these two industries declined, due to decreased demand, they caused the collapse of other industries upon which they were dependent (e.g., rubber tires, glass, fuel, construction, etc.).

The other factor contributing to the Great Depression was the economic condition of Europe. The U.S. was lending money to European nations to rebuild. Many of these countries used this money to purchase U.S. food and manufactured goods. But they were not able to pay off their debts. While the U.S. was providing money, food, and goods to Europe, however, it was not willing to buy European goods. Trade barriers were enacted to maintain a favorable trade balance.

Risky speculative investments in the stock market was the second major factor contributing to the stock market crash of 1929 and the ensuing depression. Stock market speculation was spectacular throughout the 1920s. In 1929, shares traded on the New York Stock Exchange reached 1,124,800,410. In 1928 and 1929 stock prices doubled and tripled (RCA stock prices rose from 85 to 420 within one year). The opportunity to achieve such profits was irresistible. In much the same way that buying goods on credit became popular, buying stock on margin allowed people to invest a very small amount of money in the hope of receiving exceptional profit. This created an investing craze that drove the market higher and higher. But brokers were also charging higher interest rates on their margin loans (nearly 20%). If, however, the price of the stock dropped, the investor owed the broker the amount borrowed plus interest.

Several other factors are cited by some scholars as contributing to the Great Depression. First, in 1929, the Federal Reserve increased interest rates. Second, some believe that as interest rates rose and the stock market began to decline, people began to hoard money. This was certainly the case after the crash. There is a question that it was a cause of the crash.

In September 1929, stock prices began to slip somewhat, yet people remained optimistic. On Monday, October 21, prices began to fall quickly. The volume traded was so high that the tickers were unable to keep up. Investors were frightened, and they started selling very quickly. This caused further collapse. For the next two days prices stabilized somewhat. On **Black Thursday**, October 24, prices plummeted again. By this time investors had lost confidence. On Friday and Saturday an attempt to stop the crash was made by some leading bankers. But on Monday the 28th, prices began to fall again, declining by 13% in one day. The next day, **Black Tuesday, October 29**, saw 16.4 million shares traded. Stock prices fell so far, that at many times no one was willing to buy at any price.

Unemployment quickly reached 25% nationwide. People thrown out of their homes created makeshift domiciles of cardboard, scraps of wood and tents. With unmasked reference to President Hoover, who was quite obviously overwhelmed by the situation and incompetent to deal with it, these communities were called **"Hoovervilles."** Families stood in bread lines, rural workers left the dust bowl of the plains to search for work in California, and banks failed. More than 100,000 businesses failed between 1929 and 1932. The despair that swept the nation left an indelible scar on all who endured the Depression.

When the stock market crashed, businesses collapsed. Without demand for products other businesses and industries collapsed. This set in motion a domino effect, bringing down the businesses and industries that provided raw materials or components to these industries. Hundreds of thousands became jobless. Then the jobless often became homeless. Desperation prevailed. Little had been done to assess the toll hunger, inadequate nutrition, or starvation took on the health of those who were children during this time. Indeed, food was cheap, relatively speaking, but there was little money to buy it.

Everyone who lived through the Great Depression was permanently affected in some way. Many never trusted banks again. Many people of this generation later hoarded cash so they would not risk losing everything again. Some permanently rejected the use of credit.

In the immediate aftermath of the stock market crash, many urged President Herbert Hoover to provide government relief. Hoover responded by urging the nation to be patient. By the time he signed relief bills in 1932, it was too late.

Hoover's bid for re-election in 1932 failed. The new president, Franklin D. Roosevelt, won the White House on his promise to the American people of a "new deal." Upon assuming the office, Roosevelt and his advisers immediately launched a massive program of innovation and experimentation to try to bring the Depression to an end and get the nation back on track. Congress gave the president unprecedented power to act to save the nation. During the next eight years, the most extensive and broadly-based legislation in the nation's history was enacted. The legislation was intended to accomplish three goals: relief, recovery, and reform.

The first step in the "**New Deal"** was to relieve suffering. This was accomplished through a number of job-creation projects. The second step, the recovery aspect, was to stimulate the economy. The third step was to create social and economic change through innovative legislation.

The National Recovery Administration attempted to accomplish several goals:

- Restore employment
- Increase general purchasing power
- Provide character-building activity for unemployed youth
- Encourage decentralization of industry and thus divert population from crowded cities to rural or semi-rural communities
- Develop river resources in the interest of navigation and cheap power and light
- Complete flood control on a permanent basis
- Enlarge the national program of forest protection and develop forest resources
- Control farm production and improve farm prices
- Assist home builders and home owners
- Restore public faith in banking and trust operations
- Recapture the value of physical assets, whether in real property, securities, or other investments

These objectives and their accomplishment implied a restoration of public confidence and courage.

Among the "alphabet organizations" set up to work out the details of the recovery plan, the most prominent were:

- **Agricultural Adjustment Administration** (AAA), designed to readjust agricultural production and prices thereby boosting farm income
- **Civilian Conservation Corps** (CCC), designed to give wholesome, useful activity in the forestry service to unemployed young men
- **Civil Works Administration** (CWA) and the **Public Works Administration** (PWA), designed to give employment in the construction and repair of public buildings, parks, and highways
- **Works Progress Administration** (WPA), whose task was to move individuals from relief rolls to work projects or private employment

The **Tennessee Valley Authority** (TVA) was of a more permanent nature, designed to improve the navigability of the Tennessee River and increase productivity of the timber and farm lands in its valley. This program built 16 dams that provided water control and hydroelectric generation.

The **Public Works Administration** employed Americans on over 34,000 public works projects at a cost of more than $4 billion. Among these projects was the construction of a highway that linked the Florida Keys and Miami, the Boulder Dam (now the Hoover Dam), and numerous highway projects.

To provide economic stability and prevent another crash, Congress passed the **Glass-Steagall Act**, which separated banking and investing. The Securities and Exchange Commission was created to regulate dangerous speculative practices on Wall Street. The Wagner Act guaranteed a number of rights to workers and unions in an effort to improve worker-employer relations.

The **Social Security Act of 1935** established pensions for the aged and infirm as well as a system of unemployment insurance.

Much of the recovery program was to respond to an emergency, but certain permanent national policies emerged. The intention of the public was to employ their government in supervising and, to an extent, regulating business operations—from corporate activities to labor problems. This included protecting bank depositors and the credit system of the country, employing gold resources and currency adjustments to aid permanent restoration of normal living, and, if possible, establishing a line of subsistence below which no useful citizen would be permitted to sink.

Many of the steps taken by the Roosevelt administration have had far-reaching effects. They alleviated the economic disaster of the Great Depression, enacted controls that would mitigate the risk of another stock market crash, and provided greater security for workers. The nation's economy, however, did not fully recover until America entered World War II.

Skill 7.4   Recognize the impact on U.S. society and political life of ideological and political developments in Europe and Asia

The decade following World War II saw tremendous growth in **socialism**. Economic planning and the nationalization of industry were undertaken in many countries. This political balance leaves most industrialized countries with a mixed socialist-capitalist economy. So long as there is no major worldwide depression, this situation may remain relatively stable. The consequences of World War II, particularly the independence of former European colonies, had opened vast new areas for the attempted development of socialist forms. Most have tried to aspire to the democratic type but very few have succeeded except where democratic traditions were strong. Socialism, though concentrating on economic relationships, has always considered itself a complete approach to human society.

It was in London in 1864 that Karl Marx organized the first Socialist International. This radical leftist organization died off after limping along for twelve years, by which time its headquarters had moved to New York. After the passage of about another twelve years, the *Second Socialist International* met in Paris to celebrate the anniversary of the fall of the Bastille in the French Revolution. By this time, serious factions were developing. There were the Anarchists, who wanted to tear down everything, Communists who wanted to tear down the established order and build another in its place, and the Democratic-Socialist majority who favored peaceful political action.

Struggling for internal peace and cohesion right up to the First World War, socialism would remain largely ineffectual at this critical international time. Peace brought them all together again in Bern, Switzerland, but by this time the Soviet Union had been created, and the Russian Communists refused to attend the meeting on the ground that the Second Socialist International opposed the type of dictatorship it saw as necessary in order to achieve revolutions. Thus, the Communist International was created in direct opposition to the Socialist International. The socialists went on to advocate the "triumph of democracy, firmly rooted in the principles of liberty." The main objective of this new Socialist International was to maintain the peace, an ironic and very elusive goal in the period between the two world wars.

The Nazi attack on Poland in September,of 1939 completely shattered the organization. In 1946, however, a new Socialist Information and Liaison Office was set up to reestablish old contacts. Subsequently, in 1951, the Communist International was revived with a conference in Frankfurt, Germany, where it adopted a document entitled "Aims and Tasks of Democratic Socialism." A summary of these objectives gives a good picture of modern Democratic-Socialism as it exists on paper in its ideal form.

As always, the first principle is nationalized ownership of the major means of production and distribution. Usually, public ownership is deemed appropriate for strategically important services such as public utilities, banking, and resource industries involving coal, iron, lumber and oil. Farming has never been considered well adapted to public administration and has usually been excluded from nationalization. From this takeover of the free enterprise system, socialists expect a more perfect freedom to evolve—offering equal opportunity for all, minimizing class conflict, producing better products for less cost, and establishing security from physical want or need.

All socialism denies certain freedoms, sometimes hidden in what it considers favorable terms. It deprives the minority of special economic privileges for the benefit of the majority. The more left wing, communistic socialism may deny the democratic process entirely. Traditionally defined, democracy holds to the idea that the people, exercising their majority opinion at the polls, will arrive at the common good by electing representative individuals to govern them. Communists would interpret this to mean the tyranny of an uneducated majority obliged to decide between a politically selected group of would-be leaders.

While communism and socialism arose in response to the excesses of 19th-century capitalism, all three have matured in the past 100 years. Capitalism has mellowed, while a sibling rivalry may continue to exist between communism and socialism. Officially, communism clings to the idea of revolution and the seizing of capitalist property by the state without compensation. Socialism, on the other hand, accepts gradualism, feeling that a revolution, particularly in an industrial society would be ruinous. In fact, socialists—in some situations even communists—have come to realize that not all economic institutions function better in public hands. Private responsibility frequently offers benefits that go to the public good. This is particularly true in the agricultural sector, where personal ownership and cultivation of land have always been deeply valued.

Fascism – In general, fascism is the effort to create, by dictatorial means, a viable national society in which competing interests are to be adjusted to each other by being entirely subordinated to the service of the state. The following features have been characteristic of fascism in its various manifestations: (1) an origin at a time of serious economic disruption and of rapid and bewildering social change; (2) a philosophy that rejects democratic and humanitarian ideals and glorifies the absolute sovereignty of the state, the unity and destiny of the people, and their unquestioning loyalty and obedience to the dictator; (3) aggressive nationalism, which calls for the mobilization and regimentation of every aspect of national life and makes open use of violence and intimidation; (4) the simulation of mass popular support, accomplished by outlawing all but a single political party and by using suppression, censorship, and propaganda; and (5) a program of vigorous action including economic reconstruction, industrialization, pursuit of economic self-sufficiency, territorial expansion, and war that is dramatized as bold, adventurous, and promising a glorious future.

Fascist movements often had socialist origins. For example, in Italy, where fascism first arose in place of socialism, Benito Mussolini sought to impose what he called "**corporativism**." A fascist "corporate" state would, in theory, run the economy for the benefit of the whole country like a corporation. It would be centrally controlled and managed by an elite who would see that its benefits would go to everyone.

Fascism has always declared itself the uncompromising enemy of communism, with which, however, fascist actions have much in common. (In fact, many of the methods of organization and propaganda used by fascists were taken from the experience of the early Russian communists, along with the belief in a single strong political party, secret police, etc.) The propertied interests and the upper classes, fearful of revolution, often gave their support to fascism on the basis of promises by the fascist leaders to maintain the status quo and safeguard property.

Once established, a fascist regime ruthlessly crushes communist and socialist parties as well as all democratic opposition. It regiments the propertied interests to its national goals and wins the potentially revolutionary masses to fascist programs by substituting a rabid nationalism for class conflict. Thus fascism may be regarded as an extreme defensive expedient adopted by a nation faced with the sometimes-illusionary threat of communist subversion or revolution. Under fascism, capital is regulated as much as labor and fascist contempt for legal or constitutional guarantees effectively destroyed whatever security the capitalistic system had enjoyed under pre-fascist governments.

In addition, fascist or similar regimes are at times anti-Communist as evidenced by the Molotov-Ribbentrop Pact of 1939. During the period of alliance created by the treaty, Italy and Germany and their satellite countries ceased their anti-Communist propaganda. They emphasized their own revolutionary and proletarian origins and attacked the so-called plutocratic western democracies.

In theory at least, the chief distinction between fascism and communism is that fascism is nationalist, exalting the interests of the state and glorifying war between nations, whereas, communism is internationalist, exalting the interests of a specific economic class (the proletariat) and glorifying worldwide class warfare. In practice, however, this fundamental distinction loses some of its validity for, in its heyday, fascism was also an internationalist movement. It was a movement dedicated to world conquest (like communism), as evidenced by the events prior to and during the Second World War. At the same time, many elements in communism as it evolved came to be very nationalistic as well.

Skill 7.5   Evaluate the effects of World Wars I and II on U.S. politics and society and their impact on the role of the United States in world affairs

World War I, or as it was simply known then, the Great War, was an almost inevitable result of European alliances and nationalist sentiment and the assassination of the Archduke Ferdinand of Austria by a Serbian nationalist in June 1914. Though initially a conflict between the **Central Powers** (Germany, Austria-Hungary, and Turkey) and the **Allied Powers** (mainly France, Britain, Russia, Italy, and Japan), by 1917 the United States was forced to abandon its position of neutrality and enter the war on the side of the Allied Powers.

Although President Wilson had staked US neutrality on shipping with all belligerents equally, the British Navy's dominance of the Atlantic soon created a trade imbalance favoring the Allied Powers. To counter this, the Germans began using **u-boats** or submarines to sink ships carrying arms and munitions to the Allies. One such casualty was the HMS **Lusitania** in 1915. Ostensibly, when the passenger ship sank, among the casualties were 128 American passengers. When this was combined with a growing number of attacks on American merchant vessels, the US public was slowly but surely turning toward war.

Perhaps the final guarantor of US involvement was the Zimmerman Note, an intercepted telegram from Germany to Mexico. In this telegram, addressed to the German Foreign Minister, Germany promised to restore land that had once been Mexico's, if Mexico joined the Central Powers. When the note was finally made public, the US was at last ready to enter the war in 1917. For the first time ever, American troops would fight on European soil.

The war itself was brutal, considered the first modern war by historians and noted for its use of new techniques and technology. This included both the submarine and the airplane, as well as the use of poison gas and trench warfare. Those two factors combined to make the war a horrific experience for all involved, an experience that had lasting repercussions on international affairs.

The United States, however, was determined not to take part in those affairs. Ironically, it would be President Wilson's **Fourteen Points** which would become the primary basis for the peace treaty ending the war. A proponent of open agreements (unlike the secret alliances that had dragged Europe into the war in the first place), Wilson also made strong arguments for free trade, disarmament, and an end to colonialism. His most important point was the creation of a **League of Nations**, an international body created to provide a forum for nations to resolve their differences without resorting to armed conflict.

Wilson's fellow Americans did not share his enthusiasm for American involvement in international affairs, and certainly wanted no part of any league. Consequently, the US returned to its isolationist policies, preferring to deal with the problems at home and let Europe handle itself. This policy continued even as it became increasingly clearer in the latter half of the 1930's that war was again imminent. Germany had been treated harshly by the terms of the Treaty of Versailles, largely as a combined result of forced disarmament and the payment of reparations, or paying for war damages, an aspect of the Treaty insisted upon by the European members of the Allied Powers. Stinging from that, and under the leadership of Adolf Hitler, Germany began acquiring territory and quietly rearming.

Despite European attempts at **Appeasement**, or diplomatic solutions to Germany's wants, war again broke out after Germany invaded Poland in 1939. Once again, the United States declared its neutrality. And once again, that neutrality leaned heavily in favor of the **Allies** (Great Britain, France, and the Soviet Union) as they fought against the **Axis** (Germany, Italy, and Japan). American politicians were once again committed to the notion that this was a European conflict in which American troops should not get involved.

The American isolationist mood was given a shocking and lasting blow in 1941 with the Japanese attack on Pearl Harbor. The United States no longer had a choice about whether to take part in the war. Japan had made them a combatant with a single surprise attack. The nation arose and forcefully entered the international arena as never before. Declaring itself "the arsenal of democracy," it entered the Second World War and emerged not only victorious, but also as the *strongest power* on the Earth. It would now have a permanent and leading place in world affairs.

In the aftermath of the Second World War, with the Soviet Union having emerged as the *second* strongest power on Earth, the United States embarked on a policy known as "Containment" of the Communist menace. This involved what came to be known as the "Marshall Plan" and the "Truman Doctrine." The **Marshall Plan** involved the economic aid that was sent to Europe in the aftermath of the Second World War aimed at preventing the spread of communism. To that end, the US has devoted a larger and larger share of its foreign policy, diplomacy, and both economic and military might to combating it.

The **Truman Doctrine** offered military aid to those countries that were in danger of communist upheaval. This led to the era known as the Cold War in which the United States took the lead along with the Western European nations against the Soviet Union and the Eastern Bloc countries. It was also at this time that the United States finally gave up on George Washington's advice against "European entanglements" and joined the **North Atlantic Treaty Organization** or NATO. This was formed in 1949 and was comprised of the United States and several Western European nations for the purposes of opposing communist aggression.

The United Nations was also formed at this time (1945) to replace the defunct League of Nations for the purposes of ensuring world peace. Even with American involvement, the UN would prove largely ineffective in maintaining world peace.

In the 1950s, the United States embarked on what was called the "Eisenhower Doctrine," after the then President Eisenhower. This aimed at trying to maintain peace in a troubled area of the world, the Middle East. However, unlike the Truman Doctrine in Europe, it would have little success.

The United States also became involved in a number of world conflicts in the ensuing years. Each had at the core the struggle against communist expansion. Among these were the Korean Conflict (1950-1953), the Vietnam War (1965-1975), and various continuing entanglements in Central and South America and the Middle East. By the early 1970s under the leadership of then Secretary of State, Henry Kissinger, the United States and its allies embarked on the policy that came to be known as "Détente." This was aimed at the easing of tensions between the United States and its allies and the Soviet Union and its allies.

By the 1980s, the United States embarked on what some saw as a renewal of the Cold War. This owed to the fact that the United States was becoming more involved in trying to prevent communist insurgency in Central America. A massive expansion of its armed forces and the development of space-based weapons systems were undertaken at this time.   As this occurred, the Soviet Union, with a failing economic system and a foolhardy adventure in Afghanistan, found itself unable to compete. By 1989, events had come to a head. This ended with the breakdown of the Communist Bloc, the virtual end of the monolithic Soviet Union, and the collapse of the communist system by the early 1990s.

The United States remains active in world affairs in trying to promote peace and reconciliation, with a new specter rising to challenge it and the world, the specter of nationalism.

Skill 7.6 **Analyze the principal causes, key events, and major consequences of postwar struggles for social, legal, economic, and political equity**

The Cold War was, more than anything else, an ideological struggle between proponents of democracy and those of communism. The two major players were the United States and the Soviet Union, but other countries were involved as well. It was a "cold" war because no large-scale fighting took place directly between the two big protagonists.

It wasn't just form of government that was driving this war, either. Economics were a main concern as well. A concern in both countries was that the precious resources (such as oil and food) from other like-minded countries wouldn't be allowed to flow to "the other side." These resources didn't much flow between the U.S. and Soviet Union, either.

The Soviet Union kept a tight leash on its supporting countries, including all of Eastern Europe, which made up a military organization called the **Warsaw Pact**. The Western nations responded with a military organization of their own, NATO. Another prime battleground was Asia, where the Soviet Union had allies in China, North Korea, and North Vietnam and the U.S. had allies in Japan, South Korea, Taiwan, and South Vietnam. The Korean Conflict and Vietnam War were major conflicts in which both big protagonists played big roles but didn't directly fight each other. The main symbol of the Cold War was the arms race, a continual buildup of missiles, tanks, and other weapons that became ever more technologically advanced and increasingly more deadly. The ultimate weapon, which both sides had in abundance, was the nuclear bomb. Spending on weapons and defensive systems eventually occupied great percentages of the budgets of the U.S. and the USSR, and some historians argue that this high level of spending played a large part in the end of the latter.

The war was a cultural struggle as well. Adults brought up their children to hate "the Americans" or "the Communists." Cold War tensions spilled over into many parts of life in countries around the world. The ways of life in countries on either side of the divide were so different that they served entirely foreign to outside observers.

The Cold War continued in varying degrees from 1947 to 1991, when the Soviet Union collapsed. Other Eastern European countries had seen their communist governments overthrown by this time as well, marking the shredding of the "Iron Curtain."

Skill 7.7   Compare the effects of military and ideological conflicts on U.S. domestic policies and foreign relations

In America after World War I, President Wilson lost in his efforts to get the U.S. Senate to approve the peace treaty. The Senate at the time was a reflection of American public opinion and its rejection of the treaty was a rejection of Wilson. The approval of the treaty would have made the U.S. a member of the League of Nations but Americans had just come off a bloody war to ensure that democracy would exist throughout the world. Americans just did not want to accept any responsibility that resulted from its new position of power and were afraid that membership in the League of Nations would embroil the U.S. in future disputes in Europe.

Pre-war empires in Europe lost tremendous amounts of territories as well as the wealth of natural resources in them. New, independent nations were formed and some predominately ethnic areas came under control of nations of different cultural backgrounds. Some national boundary changes overlapped and created tensions and hard feelings as well as political and economic confusion. The wishes and desires of every national or cultural group could not possibly be realized and satisfied, resulting in disappointment for those who were victorious as well as those who were defeated. Germany received harsher terms than expected from the treaty, which weakened its post-war government and, along with the worldwide depression of the 1930s, set the stage for the rise of Adolf Hitler and his Nationalist Socialist Party and World War II.

The world after World War II was a complicated place. The Axis powers were defeated, but the Cold War had sprung up in its place. Many countries struggled to get out of the debt and devastation that their Nazi occupiers had wrought. The American **Marshall Plan** helped the nations of Western Europe get back on their feet. The Soviet Union helped the Eastern European nations return to greatness, with Communist governments at the helm. The nations of Asia were rebuilt as well, with Communism taking over China and Americanization taking over Japan and Taiwan. East and West struggled for control in this arena, especially in Korea and Southeast Asia. When Communism fell in the USSR and Eastern Europe, it remained in China, North Korea, and Vietnam; Vietnam's neighbors, however, set their own path to government.

The United Nations, a more successful successor to the League of Nations (which couldn't prevent World War II), began in the waning days of the war. It brought the nations of the world together to discuss their problems, rather than fight about them. Another successful method of keeping the peace since the war has been the atomic bomb. On a more pacific note, UNICEF, a worldwide children's fund has been able to achieve great things in just a few decades of existence. Other peace-based organizations like the Red Cross and Doctors Without Borders have seen their membership and their efficacy rise during this time as well.

The kind of nationalism that Europe saw in the 19th century spilled over into the mid-20th century, with former colonies of European powers declaring themselves independent, especially in Africa. India, a longtime British protectorate, also achieved independence at this time. With independence, these countries continued to grow. Some of these nations now experience severe overcrowding and dearth of precious resources.

The Middle East has been an especially violent part of the world since the war and the inception of the State of Israel. The struggle for supremacy in the Persian Gulf area has brought about a handful of wars as well. Oil, needed to power the world's devastatingly large transportation and manufacturing engines, is king of all resources.

COMPETENCY 8 UNDERSTAND THE MAJOR POLITICAL, SOCIAL, AND ECONOMIC DEVELOPMENTS AND THE KEY ERAS AND EVENTS IN NEW YORK STATE HISTORY

Skill 8.1 **Analyze the continuing contributions and influence of the Haudenosaunee (Iroquois) and Algonquin peoples in the economic, social, and political development of New York State and the nation**

The area now known as the State of New York was initially inhabited by several tribes that were part of one of two major Native American Nations. These were the Iroquois Nation and the Algonquian Nation.

The confederacy of Iroquois tribes was known as the **Haudenosaunee**, the League of Peace and Power. They are often called the people of the Long House. Their original homeland was in upstate New York between the Adirondack Mountains and Niagara Falls. As a result of migration and conquest, they controlled most of the northeastern United States and Eastern Canada by the time of the first European contact. The confederacy had a constitution prior to the arrival of Europeans. It was known as the Gayanashagowa ("Great Law of Peace"). This was recorded in memory using a device in the form of special beads called wampum. There is no consensus among historians about the date of the origin of this constitution. Dating has ranged from 1142 to the early 1600s. The confederacy consisted of five nations, later six.

The name "people of the longhouse" was derived from the traditional dwelling, the longhouse. Each longhouse was occupied by a matron, her daughters, and their husbands and children. The matrons controlled the clans, and the children belonged to their mother's clan.

The original five tribes or nations were:

1) The Mohawk, Keepers of the Eastern Door of the symbolic longhouse, also known as the People of Flint
2) The Oneida, the People of Stone
3) The Onondaga, the People on the Hill
4) The Cayuga, the People at the Mucky Land
5) The Seneca, the Great Hill People and the Keepers of the Western Door

After 1722, the Tuscarora were added to the confederation as a sixth, non-voting member. The confederation was ruled by a council of 50 chiefs. Each nation was assigned a set number of chiefships. The men were elected by the clan matrons.

At the time of initial European contact, the Iroquois practiced hunting and gathering, which supplemented agriculture or the main basis of their economy. It was primarily the women who practiced agriculture, while the men functioned as hunters and warriors. This agricultural basis of the economy encouraged permanent settlements into villages. These villages moved only after depleting the soil (about every 20 years) through continuous harvesting of maize, beans and squash. The Iroquois had a reputation as fierce warriors.

During the century prior to the American Revolution there were numerous wars with the Algonquin and other tribes of the **Algonquin Nation**. Their decision to oppose the colonists and support the British during the Revolutionary War was extremely unfortunate. As the American incursion into their territory gained pace after the Revolution, many of the Iroquois were driven into southern Ontario.

Much of the homeland of the Iroquois was ceded to New York land speculators through various treaties after the Revolutionary War. During the war, the confederation had been split in allegiance between support for the Americans and support for the British. In 1779, the alliance with Great Britain was defeated. In 1794, the Confederacy signed the Treaty of Canandaigua.

In many ways, the Iroquois were not significantly different from neighboring tribes. What made them unique was a sophisticated political system, with a system of checks, balances and supreme law. The central authority of the League was very limited. This left each tribe the autonomy to pursue its own interests. They were also quite skilled in diplomacy. There is great discussion about the influence the Iroquois government exerted upon the Framers of the Articles of Confederation and the U.S. Constitution.

The Dutch were the primary trading partners of the Iroquois peoples. They traded beaver and other furs for various European goods.

The Algonquian peoples were a group of tribes that were united to greater or lesser degrees by a shared language family. The Long Island Algonquians are generally Mohegan Indians; the New York Algonquians are generally Mahicans and Munsee Delawares. The Algonquin tribe called themselves Anishinabe.

Each of the individual tribes had unique cultural elements and traditions. Most of the tribes built and traveled in birch bark or dugout canoes. In the north, the tribes used snowshoes and dogsleds for winter travel. Hunters and warriors usually used bows and arrows, spears, and heavy wooden clubs. Each tribe also had its own form of government. Most tribes had some type of tribal council consisting of the leaders of each village. In most of the tribes, each band lived in a village of small round buildings called wigwams.

The Algonquin were semi-nomadic, moving as necessary to search for food. Most of their diet came from hunting, trapping, fishing, and gathering. Their social structure was patriarchal: the men were the leaders and heads of the family. Territorial hunting rights tended to be passed from father to son. Although the various tribes were not united (as were the Iroquois), they were among the first to create alliances with the French traders. The tribes that lived south of the Great Lakes were able to practice agriculture, at least to some extent. In addition to maize, beans and squash, they cultivated sunflowers and tobacco.

Algonquian territories and the Ottawa River were critical locations in trade routes. This facilitated cultural exchange, as well as commerce. They allied themselves with the French under Champlain in 1603. In 1632, after Sir David Kirke's occupation of New France, the French began to trade muskets with the Algonquins and other native peoples. As French settlements grew, French Jesuits began to convert the native people to Roman Catholicism. They were the traditional enemies of the Iroquois, a factor that encourage the Iroquois to side with the British.

Skill 8.2   Recognize key institutions and describe the structure of colonial New York

The first Europeans to arrive in New York were the Dutch led by Henry Hudson in 1609. Searching for a shortcut to India, and not finding one, they sailed on very quickly. Long Island was explored in 1614 by Adriaen Block, a Dutchman, who first mapped the island and gave it its name. The first settlements in New York were established in 1624 when the Dutch West India Company sent out a contingent of colonists. Most of these people settled in the northern Hudson Valley near what is now Albany. The next group of settlers arrived the next year and settled on the lower tip of Manhattan. This settlement came to be known as New Amsterdam. But in 1635, Charles I of England gave all of Long Island to the Earl of Sterling.

Peter Minuit, one of the early Dutch settlers and the first governor of New Amsterdam, purchased Manhattan Island from the local people for trinkets valued at about $24. The colony was then named New Netherland. It grew slowly because the Dutch West India Company was more interested in the West Indies than in the northern territories. They traded with the native peoples, primarily for furs. In 1629, the company offered its members large estates, which were called patroonships, if they would send new settlers to the region. There was little interest. In 1637, the company appointed Willem Kieft director-general of the colony. His efforts to rule as a dictator sparked a series of disputes and wars with the local Algonquian tribes. He was replaced in 1647 by Peter Stuyvesant, who also tried to rule as a dictator. His imposition of high taxes on imports was unpopular. In 1650 Stuyvesant was forced to cede all of Long Island east of Oyster Bay to Connecticut, which was a British colony.

In March of 1664, Charles II gave Long Island to the Duke of York. Within a matter of months, the English forced the Dutch to give up claims to New Amsterdam, which then became known as New York.

In 1664, King Charles II decided to claim the entire New York region on the basis of explorations made for England by John Cabot in 1497 and 1498. Charles granted his brother James, Duke of York and Albany, all the land between the Connecticut and Delaware rivers. The Dutch settlement near Fort Orange was renamed Albany.

In 1665, the first governor of the colony, refusing to create an assembly to govern the colony, drafted the "Duke's Laws." This permitted the people to elect their own town boards and constables. It also guaranteed freedom of religion. These rights were extended to the rest of the colony later.

In 1682, Thomas Dongan became governor. He created a representative assembly of settlers, which adopted the "Charter of Liberties and Privileges" the next year. This charter provided for an elected legislature which was empowered to levy taxes and make laws. It guaranteed trial by jury and religious freedom. New York and Albany were granted charters and allowed limited home rule and trading rights. He also created goodwill with the Iroquois. The next year, the Duke of York and Albany became king as James II. He incorporated New York within the New England colony, placing it within strict control of a royal governor. This new governor ruled from Boston, which enraged the colonists. The English governors gave huge land grants to their friends. The result was that most of the land was controlled by a very small number of landowners. Most were more interested in speculation than settlement. Particularly important was the establishment of the manors. This, in turn placed the control of colonial affairs in the hands of the small number of landowners and the wealthy merchants of New York City.

When news reached the colony that James II had been overthrown in the Glorious Revolution and the colonial governor had been captured by rebels in Boston, an uprising persuaded Jacob Leisler to take command of the colony. He was able to establish control of the entire colony and establish an assembly before a new British representative of the new King William III arrived. Leisler was immediately tried, convicted of treason and executed.

The population was comprised mostly of farmers and others who held jobs associated with agriculture. The growth of crafts and trades was determined by the needs of the community. These farmers grew crops and husbanded livestock. The economy was based on the barter system. The coastal areas developed a large fishing industry. Whaling was also a major part of the economy. The export of whale oil began in the 17th century, but did not become truly profitable until the 19th century.

Intellectually, two primary movements, the Scientific Revolution and the Enlightenment, promoted scientific knowledge, a skepticism toward beliefs that could not be verified by science or logic, and scientific explanation of many things about the natural world that were previously unexplained. Enlightenment thinking fostered several attacks on traditional religious beliefs. Partially in response to these attacks, the American colonies experienced a rebirth of religious fervor known as The First Great Awakening. Revival ministers during the 1730s and 1740s preached against the emptiness of materialism, talked about the corruption of human nature, and called for immediate repentance and a renewal of inner religious consciousness. Two of the leading revivalists were George Whitfield and Jonathan Edwards. This resulted in a polarization of Christians along the lines of "enthusiasm" and created a number of new churches, denominations and sects, as well as schools and universities that would teach according to their principles.

Colonial economy developed around the European policy of mercantilism. This theory is based upon the idea that a nation must export more than it imports in order to build a strong and stable economy. As a result, Great Britain implemented a number of measures aimed at achieving this favorable trade balance, particularly the four Navigation Acts.

Skill 8.3   Examine the role of New York State in the American Revolution and analyze major issues, events, and developments in New York during the Revolutionary Era

The earliest signs of the American Revolution became evident over the issue of trade and taxation. In 1765, the British Parliament passed the Stamp Act, which directly taxed trade in the American colonies. As primary colonial harbors, New York City and Boston would have felt the sting from this tax most severely. In 1765, New York was the site of the Stamp Act Congress, a collection of representatives from the colonies that united in opposition to the Stamp Act, claiming that only colonial governments had the right to pass taxes on the colonial trade. New York merchants led a boycott on British goods in protest, and were later joined by Boston merchants. On November 1, 1765, when the Stamp Act was to have gone into effect, violence erupted in New York City and an effigy of the colonial governor was burned. The New York assembly also refused a direct request from the British military to enforce the Quartering Act, which required colonists to house and feed British troops.

Fearing revolution, King George III repealed the Stamp Act in 1766. At the same time, however, Parliament passed a series of acts designed to give Britain even more power over colonial affairs. New York continued to refuse to enforce the Quartering Act as tensions grew and revolution sparked.

New York was a principal battleground of the Revolutionary War, with nearly one third of the battles of the war fought within its boundaries. The British recognized its importance as both a major harbor and its strategic location between New England and the rest of the colonies. The **Battle of Long Island** in 1776 resulted in Washington's defeat by Howe, and established a British foothold that would endure throughout the Revolution. Washington retreated to Brooklyn Heights, then to Manhattan.

Earlier in the hostilities, Ethan Allen had led a successful attack on **Fort Ticonderoga** on Lake Champlain, securing much needed military supplies, including cannons, which were removed to Boston. Now the British retook the fort and marched toward Albany to drive a wedge through the center of the colonies. Having been driven across the Delaware River to Pennsylvania, Washington and the main army began to move back north, winning key victories in New Jersey.

The **Battle of Saratoga**, New York, between the British under **General Burgoyne** and the American troops led by **Benedict Arnold,** was a critical turning point in the War. In two battles, the American forces weakened the British troops to the point of surrender, thereby foiling the British strategy to use New York as a dividing wedge. The decisive victory at Saratoga convinced France to enter the fray on the side of the American colonies. This alliance with France was crucial in the eventual American victory.

Skill 8.4   Evaluate the role of New York City in the development of the state and national economies

New York City has played a critical role in the development of the State of New York and the nation in many capacities. The huge harbor made the city an important port in colonial times. The construction of the wooden wall that was intended to keep out aggressors became both an actual and a symbolic center of economy and commerce. The tree at the end of the street where traders and dealers gathered informally later became the site of the New York Stock Exchange. This marked the beginning of New York's importance in the state's economy and the national economy. In time, it made the city a central point in international economy.

Two principal waterways, one natural, one man-made, helped contribute to New York City's prominence. The first of these is the **Hudson River**. First explored by Henry Hudson for the Dutch in 1609, it played a key role in the settlement of the Hudson Valley, which began in 1623. During the Revolutionary War, it was the sight of several battles because of its importance as a key logistical asset. Later, it was linked by a series of canals to the Great Lakes, the Delaware River, and the St Lawrence River Valley, making it a vital link for commerce.

Perhaps the greatest of those canals was the **Erie Canal**. The greatest public works project in the United States prior to the Civil War, it was first built by the State of New York between 1817 and 1825, and then later enlarged between 1836 and 1862. Spanning 363 miles between the Great Lakes and the Hudson River, for a time it was the principal commercial route from the Atlantic to the Great Lakes and Midwest regions of the United States. An astonishing technical marvel for the time, the canal had lasting effect on the development of upstate New York as well as New York City itself.

The construction of the Erie Canal further enhanced the importance of the port of New York. Parts of it were incorporated into its successor, the Barge Canal, in 1918. This system of waterways was later expanded even more with the construction of the St. Lawrence Seaway. Transportation on land developed very quickly after the construction of a system of turnpikes, beginning in the 1880s. By 1853, railroads crossed the state and connected to those that crossed the nation, and the Erie Canal's importance began to diminish. But the effects it had wrought upon the status of New York City would be lasting.

New York City now has one of the largest regional economies in the nation. It is a global center for business and commerce. With London, Hong Kong, Paris and Tokyo, New York City is one of the main cities that control world finance. Many consider it the financial capital of the world. In addition to finance and commerce, New York City is critical to the insurance and real estate industries. It is also the single most important center for publishing, mass media and journalism in the country. In addition, it is critical in medical research, technology, fashion and the arts. More Fortune 500 companies are based in New York City than any other city in the nation. Many international companies are also headquartered in the city.

New York City has historically been the point of entry into the U.S. for millions of immigrants. This made the city a major haven for oppressed people throughout the world and the point of entry that made the nation a "melting pot." The decision to locate the headquarters of the United Nations in New York has also made it a critical center of international politics and democracy.

Skill 8.5 **Recognize the role of immigration and migration in the evolution of New York politics and society and analyze the continuing impact of immigration and migration on the development of New York State**

As one of the first colonized areas in the nation, New York was a major point of entry for immigrants. The melding of the Dutch, French and British settlers into a unified colony was the first step along the way to becoming the melting pot that New York has been to this day. The large harbor, along with the state's growing reputation for business, industry, and commerce, made New York a place of special opportunity for immigrants seeking freedom and opportunity.

The development of Ellis Island as an immigrant processing center made it the point of entry for millions who came to America in search of political or religious freedom, safe haven from political oppression, and the quest for the American dream. The gift of the Statue of Liberty and its placement in New York harbor made New York the symbol of American opportunity and freedom.

Throughout the history of America, New York has welcomed people from all parts of the world and created within the state a truly international and unique cultural mecca. To be sure, some groups of immigrants created their own sub-cultures within the state. Many of those continue today. Through the port of New York and the city's ability to acclimate and absorb immigrants and provide them a living, the nation has welcomed a population that has been repeatedly enriched by the cultural mix.

Skill 8.6 **Understand the experiences and contributions of various ethnic, racial, religious, and cultural groups in historical and contemporary New York State**

The Dutch settlers of the early colonial period introduced many goods to North America that profoundly affected the nature of the development of both the state and the nation. The trade of the Dutch West India Company provided the foundation for an economy based on trade and commerce.

As African Americans left the rural South and migrated to the North in search of opportunity, many settled in Harlem in New York City. By the 1920s Harlem had become a center of life and activity for persons of color. The music, art, and literature of this community gave birth to a cultural movement known as **the Harlem Renaissance**. The artistic expressions that emerged from this community in the 1920s and 1930s celebrated the black experience, black traditions, and the voices of black America.

Major writers and works of this movement include:
- Langston Hughes – *The Weary Blues*
- Nella Larsen – *Passing*
- Zora Neale Hurston – *Their Eyes Were Watching God*
- Claude McKay
- Countee Cullen
- Jean Toomer

Although Puerto Rico became a territory of the U.S. at the end of the Spanish American War, there was little immigration during the first half of the century. The transition from Spanish colony to U.S. possession was not easy for the people of Puerto Rico. Residents have been U.S. citizens since 1917, but they have no representation in the Congress. Technically, moving from the island to the U.S. mainland is considered internal migration rather than immigration. This does not, however, recognize that leaving an island with a distinct culture and identity involves the same cultural conflicts and intellectual, language and other adjustments as those faced by most immigrants. A severe economic depression created widespread poverty in the early part of the 20th century. Few Puerto Ricans were able to afford the fare to travel by boat to the mainland. In 1910, there were only about 2,000 Puerto Ricans living on the mainland; most created small enclaves in New York City. By 1945, there were 13,000 Puerto Ricans in New York City. But by 1946, there were more than 50,000. And for each of the next 10 years, over 25,000 more would immigrate each year. By the mid-1960s, there were more than a million Puerto Ricans on the mainland.

The primary factors that account for the sudden migration are:

- Continuing economic depression in Puerto Rico
- Recruitment for workers from Puerto Rico by U.S. factory owners and employment agencies
- The return of thousands of war veterans to Puerto Rico who wanted more than the island could offer
- Most important, the sudden availability of air travel at an affordable cost

Many of the immigrant Puerto Ricans established communities in major east coast cities and mid-Atlantic farming regions, and also in the mill towns of New England. A very large number of these immigrants settled in the northeastern part of Manhattan that came to be known as **Spanish Harlem**. They quickly became an important factor in the city's political and cultural life. Although the first generation of migrants faced prejudice, unemployment, discrimination, and poverty, most remained and learned to thrive.

Today, Puerto Rican immigrants and their descendants have developed several means of preserving and teaching their heritage. Their communities are strong and integrated into the mainstream of the society. They have contributed to the growth of the nation and the inclusion within every area of American life from politics to education to sports and the arts.

COMPETENCY 9   UNDERSTAND THE STRUGGLE FOR FUNDAMENTAL HUMAN RIGHTS AND THE EFFORTS OF NATIONS, INDIVIDUALS, AND INTERNATIONAL ORGANIZATIONS TO ESTABLISH AND PROTECT THOSE RIGHTS

Skill 9.1   Examine fundamental statements of human rights and evaluate their role in establishing and extending the concept of human rights

The cause of human rights has been advanced significantly since the 18th century, both in theory and in fact. Several fundamental statements of human rights have extended and established human rights throughout the world.

The U.S. Declaration of Independence declared that certain truths are self-evident: All men are created equal and they are inherently endowed with certain unalienable rights that no government should ever violate. These rights include the right to life, liberty and the pursuit of happiness. When a government infringes upon those rights or fails to protect those rights, it is both the right and the duty of the people to overthrow that government and to establish in its place a new government that will protect those rights.

The Declaration of the Rights of Man and of the Citizen is a document created by the French National Assembly and issued in 1789. It sets forth the "natural, inalienable and sacred rights of man." It proclaims the following rights:
- Men are born and remain free and equal in rights. Social distinctions may only be founded upon the general good.
- The aim of all political association is the preservation of the natural and imprescriptible rights of man: liberty, property, security and resistance to oppression.
- All sovereignty resides essentially in the nation. No body or individual may exercise any authority which does not proceed directly from the nation.
- Liberty is the freedom to do everything which injures no one else; hence the exercise of these rights has no limits except those which assure to the other members of the society the enjoyment of the same rights. These limits can only be determined by law.
- Law can only prohibit such actions as are hurtful to society.
- Law is the expression of the general will. Every citizen has a right to participate in the formation of law. It must be the same for all. All citizens, being equal in the eyes of the law, are equally eligible to all dignities and to all public positions and occupations, according to their abilities.
- No person shall be accused, arrested or imprisoned except in the cases and according to the forms prescribed by law.
- The law shall provide for such punishments only as are strictly and obviously necessary.

- All persons are held innocent until they have been declared guilty. If it is necessary to arrest a person, all harshness not essential to the securing of the prisoner's person shall be severely repressed by law.
- No one shall be disquieted on account of his opinions, including religious views, provided their manifestation does not disturb the peace.
- The free communication of ideas and opinions is one of the most precious of the rights of man.
- The security of the rights of man and of the citizen requires public military force. These forces are, therefore, established for the good of all and not for the personal advantage of those to whom they shall be entrusted.
- A common contribution is essential for the maintenance of the public forces and for the cost of administration. This should be equitably distributed among all the citizens in proportion to their means.
- All the citizens have a right to decide, either personally or by their representatives, as to the necessity of the public contribution.
- Society has the right to require of every public agent an account of his administration.
- A society in which the observance of the law is not assured, nor the separation of powers defined, has no constitution at all.
- Since property is an inviolable and sacred right, no one shall be deprived thereof except where public necessity, legally determined, shall clearly demand it, and then only on condition that the owner shall have been previously and equitably indemnified.

The United Nations Declaration of Universal Human Rights (1948). The declaration opens with these words: "Whereas recognition of the inherent dignity and of the equal and inalienable rights of all members of the human family is the foundation of freedom, justice and peace in the world. Whereas disregard and contempt for human rights have resulted in barbarous acts which have outraged the conscience of mankind, and the advent of a world in which human beings shall enjoy freedom of speech and belief and freedom from fear and want has been proclaimed as the highest aspiration of the common people."

1. All human beings are born free and equal in dignity and rights. They are endowed with reason and conscience and should act towards one another in a spirit of brotherhood.
2. Everyone is entitled to all the rights and freedoms set forth in this Declaration, without distinction of any kind.
3. Everyone has the right to life, liberty and security of person.
4. No one shall be held in slavery or servitude.
5. No one shall be subjected to torture or to cruel, inhuman or degrading treatment or punishment.
6. Everyone has the right to recognition everywhere as a person before the law.
7. All are equal before the law and are entitled without any discrimination to equal protection of the law.

8. Everyone has the right to an effective remedy by the competent national tribunals for acts violating the fundamental rights granted him by the constitution of by law.
9. No one shall be subjected to arbitrary arrest, detention or exile.
10. Everyone is entitled in full equality to a fair and public hearing by an independent and impartial tribunal, in the determination of his rights and obligations and of any criminal charge against him.
11. Everyone charged with a penal offence has the right to be presumed innocent until proved guilty according to law in a public trial at which he has had all the guarantees necessary for his defence. No one shall be held guilty of any penal offence on account of any act or omission which did not constitute a penal offence, under national or international law, at the time when it was committed
12. No one shall be subjected to arbitrary interference with his privacy, family, home or correspondence, nor to attacks upon his honour and reputation.
13. Everyone has the right to freedom of movement and residence within the borders of each state. Everyone has the right to leave any country, including his own, and to return to his country.
14. Everyone has the right to seek and to enjoy in other countries asylum from persecution. This right may not be invoked in the case of prosecutions genuinely arising from non-political crimes or from acts contrary to the purposes and principles of the United Nations.
15. Everyone has the right to a nationality. No one shall be arbitrarily deprived of his nationality nor denied the right to change his nationality.
16. Men and women of full age have the right to marry and to found a family. They are entitled to equal rights as to marriage, during marriage and at its dissolution. Marriage shall be entered into only with the free and full consent of the intending spouses. The family is the natural and fundamental group unit of society and is entitled to protection by society and the State.
17. Everyone has the right to own property alone or in association with others. No one shall be arbitrarily deprived of his property.
18. Everyone has the right to freedom of thought, conscience and religion, including the right to change his religion or belief, and freedom to manifest his religion or belief in teaching, practice, worship and observance.
19. Everyone has the right to freedom of opinion and expression.
20. Everyone has the fight to freedom of peaceful assembly and association. No one may be compelled to belong to an association
21. Everyone has the right to take part in the government of his country, directly or through freely chosen representatives. Everyone has the right of equal access to public service in his country. The will of the people shall be the basis of the authority of government.
22. Everyone has the right to social security and is entitled to realization of the economic, social and cultural rights indispensable for his dignity and the free development of his personality.

23. Everyone has the right to work. Everyone, without any discrimination, has the right to equal pay for equal work. Everyone who works has the right to just and favourable remuneration. Everyone has the right to form and to join trade unions for the protection of his interests.

24. Everyone has the right to rest and leisure, including reasonable limitation of working hours and periodic holidays with pay.

25. Everyone has the right to a standard of living adequate for the health and well-being of himself and his family, and the right to security in the event of unemployment, sickness, disability, widowhood, old age or other lack of livelihood in circumstances beyond his control. Motherhood and childhood are entitled to special care and assistance. All children shall enjoy the same social protection.

26. Everyone has the right to education. Education shall be directed to the full development of the human personality and to the strengthening of respect for human rights and fundamental freedoms. Parents have a prior right to choose the kind of education that shall be given to their children.

27. Everyone has the right freely to participate in the cultural life of the community. Everyone has the right to the protection of the moral and materials interests resulting from any scientific, literary or artistic production of which he is the author.

28. Everyone is entitled to a social and international order in which the rights and freedoms set forth in this Declaration can be fully realized.

The United Nations Convention on the Rights of the Child brings together the rights of children as they are enumerated in other international documents. In this document, those rights are clearly and completely stated, along with the explanation of the guiding principals that define the way society views children. The goal of the document is to clarify the environment that is necessary to enable every human being to develop to their full potential. The Convention calls for resources and contributions to be made to ensure the full development and survival of all children. The document also requires the establishment of appropriate means to protect children from neglect, exploitation and abuse. The document also recognizes that parents have the most important role in raising children.

Skill 9.2   Recognize arguments used to justify systematic violations of human rights and analyze the use of such arguments to discriminate against, oppress, or annihilate targeted groups

Nativism is the fear that certain new immigrants will introduce foreign political, economic or cultural values and behaviors that threaten the prevailing norms and values of a nation or a society. It usually involves restrictions on immigrants and sometimes includes policies that favor the interests of established residents (i.e. "natives") over those of immigrants.

During the reign of Louis XIV in France, the **Huguenots**, French Protestants, were persecuted by the government, which was closely allied with the Roman Catholic Church. Louis was attempting to limit the role of the Roman Catholic Church in France and determine its affairs. The Huguenots were severely oppressed until they finally left the country.

The **Chinese Exclusion Act**, approved by the U.S. Congress in 1882 was the ultimate expression of anti-Chinese feeling. It prohibited Chinese immigration for ten years. In 1892, it was extended for another ten years. In 1902, it became permanent. It was not repealed until China and the U.S. became allies against the Japanese during World War II. This law also produced further difficulties for the Chinese, including boycotts of Chinese-produced goods.

Internment of people of Japanese ancestry. From the turn of the 20th century, there was tension between Caucasians and Japanese in California. A series of laws had been passed discouraging Japanese immigration and prohibiting land ownership by Japanese. The Alien Registration Act of 1940 (the Smith Act) required the fingerprinting and registration of all aliens over the age of 14. Aliens were also required to report any change of address within 5 days. Almost 5 million aliens registered under the provisions of this act. The Japanese attack on Pearl Harbor (December 7, 1941) raised suspicion that Japan was planning a full-scale attack on the West Coast. Many believed that American citizenship did not necessarily imply loyalty. Some authorities feared sabotage of both civilian and military facilities within the country. By February 1942, Presidential Executive Orders had authorized the arrest of all aliens suspected of subversive activities and the creation of exclusion zones where people could be isolated from the remainder of the population and kept where they could not damage national infrastructure. These War Relocation Camps were used to isolate about 120,000 Japanese and Japanese Americans (62% were citizens) during World War II.

The **Bataan Death March** occurred in the Philippines during World War II. In 1942 the Japanese army overran an American outpost of Bataan. About 75,000 American and Filipino prisoners were captured. They were forcibly marched to a prison camp. Many died during the course of the march. Those that survived the march were eventually rescued by a combined Filipino and American effort. The few survivors had been badly treated, starved, and had received little or no medical treatment.

The **Massacre at Tianamen Square** occurred when a student-led democratic movement demonstrated in Tiananmen Square in Beijing in 1989. The month-long protest captured international media attention and was one of the largest protests in recent Chinese history with estimates of up to four million people taking part. Conflicting demands by various students groups, coupled with resistance to the ideals of the movement by hard-line government officials, eventually led to a military enforced crackdown involving the use of tanks. Many of the leaders were imprisoned, and though there may well have been hundreds of casualties official numbers have been repressed.

Skill 9.3   Demonstrate an understanding of the concept of genocide and analyze how specific instances of genocide have occurred

Genocide is defined by the <u>**Convention on the Prevention and Punishment of the Crime of Genocide**</u> (CPPCG) Article 2 as "any of the following acts committed with intent to destroy, in whole or in part, a **national, ethnic, racial** or **religious** group, as such: Killing members of the group; Causing serious bodily or mental harm to members of the group; Deliberately inflicting on the group conditions of life calculated to bring about its physical destruction in whole or in part; Imposing measures intended to prevent births within the group; and forcibly transferring children of the group to another group."

Notable instances of genocide have occurred throughout history and throughout the world.

In the United States, efforts to claim and expand the territory of the new nation and its perceived rights to settle the nation led to the attempted extermination of the Native American peoples. To be sure, many died from diseases introduced by European settlers against which the Native Americans had no acquired or natural resistance. The Native Peoples were, however, systematically pushed west, where they were out of the way of progress and national development. The Native Peoples were relocated to undesirable lands where many starved. The most systematic efforts, however, occurred in the Indian Wars when entire villages and tribes were wantonly slaughtered. The massacre at **Wounded Knee** is a memorable example of this policy.

During the reign of the Ottoman Empire, the government of the Young Turks, 1915-1917 forced the mass evacuation of over one million Armenians. Many died or were executed in the process. This is referred to as the **Armenian Genocide**, and indeed the term was coined to describe the event. The Armenians were Christians in a Muslim empire. When the Russians defeated the Ottoman Empire in 1915, the Young Turks placed the blame on the Armenians.

Perhaps one of the most well-known examples of genocide was the **Holocaust.** This systematic effort to eradicate the Jews and other "undesireables" from Nazi Germany is as frightening for the number of victims and the means in which they were slaughtered, as it is for the ruthless and bureaucratic efficiency with which it was carried out. It's important to note in any discussion of the Holocaust that this was not the first time Europe had seen policies aimed at eradicating the Jewish population. Numerous **pogroms** had occurred throughout European history, all aimed at ridding European society of Jewish influence. The difference between those earlier efforts and what happened under the Nazis lies chiefly in the scope and scale with which it happened, but those are significant enough to set it apart from its historical precedents.

It should also be noted that this was not an overnight program. The decision to implement organized mass murder came after 1 million Jews had already been killed. Prior to the **Final Solution**, as it was officially termed, the Jews had been systematically stripped of their property, their posessions, and their rights. On Novbember 9, 1938, the Nazis coordinated an attack on Jewish-owned businesses and synagogues. The event became known as **kristallnacht** or "cyrstal night" after all the broken glass left in the streets. The Jews were herded into ghetto neighborhoods under strict control, and eventually the decision was made to relocate them to **Concentration Camp**s scattered throughout Nazi territory. Although it is a common misconception, not all Concentration Camps were **Death Camps**. Although many died at both, mass extermination was the official policy only at the latter camps, which included the most notorious camps of **Auschwitz, Buchenwald**, and **Dachau**.

At all camps, however, prisoners were tortured, malnourished, and literally worked to death. Methods of mass execution in the death camps varied, but the use of poison gas is perhaps the most well known. Jewish prisoners would be rounded up and escorted to showers that dispensed poison gas instead of water, their bodies later disposed of in either mass graves or through mass cremation.

Although the Jews were the primary target of the Holocaust, many othert groups suffered as well. Gypsies were also despised by the Nazis, and subject to persecution and execution in a manner similar to the Jews. Likewise, other "undesirable" elements, such as homosexuals, were rounded up and sent to the camps. The Jews represent the largest single group of victims of the Holocaust, and it has become forever linked with their history.

There is some dispute in the historical record as to just how much was known about the Holocaust while it was happening, even inside Nazi Germany. As official policy, little effort was made to keep it secret. At the same time, the camps were generally in less populated areas and the Nazi government did not encourage open discussion concerning its actions. Reports that did emerge before the end of the war were met with skepticism that such a thing was even possible, let alone a reality, and it wasn't until the first of these camps were liberated by the Allies that the true scope of the horrors which had taken place were finally revealed.

Nor has genocide been relegated soley to the past. In 1994, ethnic conflict between the **Tutsis** and the **Hutus** in the African nation of **Rwanda** escalated into a full-scale genocide. In the span of a single year, at least 500,000 people were killed as extremist militant Hutu groups slaughtered bothTutsis and moderate Hutus. Although conlfict between warring tribes in post-Colonial African nations is, unfortunately, not all that unusual, what made the Rwandan genocide different was the swifteness and the ferocity with which it was carried out.

As shocking as the violence was, the situation took an even more tragic turn when the international community largely ignored the violence. This was not a case where people were being massacred out of sight. Quite the contrary, the violence and destruction were well-documented by the international media and other aid groups. This time, there were almost nightly news stories featuring horrific pictures and video accompanied by equally horrific events. Countries like the United States failed to speak up against the genocide even as it unfolded on their nightly news broadcasts. A UN peacekeeping force was led by Canada, but the UN Security council failed to give them the authority to use force to prevent or halt the killings.

The slaughter only abated when the Tutsis managed to sieze control of the government. Fearing reprisals, a mass exodus of many of the remaining Hutus followed, pouring into neighboring countries. These refugees in turn helped fuel conflict in the Democratic Republic of Congo, leading to even more deaths.

In Europe in the 1990s, officially sanctioned genocide was given a new term, **Ethnic Cleansing**. This term was used to describe the treatment of Bosnian Muslims, ethnic Serbs in a region of Coratia, and particularly ethnic Albanians in the Serbian province of Kosovo. These ethnically oriented conflicts erupted as the nation of Yuoglsavia broke apart in the wake of the collapse of the Soviet Union. Conflicts became common between the new nations—particularly conflcit led by the Serbian leader **Slobodan Milosevic**, as he sought to undu Kosovo's historical autonomy. Eventually, the atrocities being committed gained the attention of both Russia and the Western nations, leading to the intervention of NATO air and ground troops as well as poltitical pressure to end the conflcit. Milosevic was eventually arrested and tried for crimes against humanity, though he died before completion of his trial.

Skill 9.4   **Demonstrate an understanding of the transatlantic slave trade of the 17th and 18th centuries; the economic, social, political, and religious support of slavery; and the consequences of slavery as a social and economic institution in the United States and elsewhere**

The transatlantic slave trade refers to the purchase and transportation of people from West and Central Africa to the New World for slavery and other forms of bondage. The slaves were the middle element of a very prosperous three-part trade cycle. The trade in slaves began in response to a labor shortage in the New World. There was a great need for cheap labor in mining and in agriculture. Particularly in the predominantly agricultural South, harvesting of many of the major cash crops – sugar, rice, tobacco, cotton – were labor-intensive.

Europeans bought slaves who were generally captured in wars between African kingdoms. In some cases, Europeans even tried to instigate wars to create a supply of slaves. The prices were modest. African labor came to be considered to be in abundant supply and not very valuable. The slaves were then transported to the coast and sold at European trading posts in exchange for muskets and manufactured goods. Slaves were generally war captives or criminals.

Most estimates place the number of Africans involved in the slave trade in the area of 30 million. Half of them died in Africa from combat wounds. They were loaded into ships as tightly as they could be "packed in" and they were given minimal food and water. Most estimate the number who died on the ships from torture, disease and malnutrition at about three million. The ships delivered them to "seasoning camps" in the Caribbean where they were tortured into submission. Approximately two million more died there.

The slave trade was the second leg in the triangular Atlantic trade route. Ships would leave Europe with manufactured goods that were sold or traded in Africa for slaves. The slaves would be sold in the Americas for agricultural products, which would be delivered back to Europe.

Although some religious leaders decried slavery from the beginning, most supported the slave trade by church teaching and by introducing the idea of the black man's and the white man's separate roles. Some taught that blacks should labor in exchange for the blessings of European civilization, including Christianity.

Seventy percent of the slaves brought to the U.S. were used in the production of sugar, which was the most labor-intensive crop. Others were used to harvest coffee, cotton, tobacco and other crop.

The economy of the Southern states was almost entirely dependent upon slave labor to plant, tend and harvest the crops that were in demand throughout the rest of the world.

Skill 9.5 **Demonstrate an understanding of how social philosophy, economic forces, geography, and politics contributed to the existence and continuation of the Irish Famine**

The Irish Famine of 1845-1849 is alternately referred to as the Irish Potato Famine, The Great Famine or the Great Hunger. The immediate cause of the famine was the appearance of "the blight." This was the destruction of the potato crops due to a fungus. The potato was the primary food source for much of the population of Ireland at the time. Deaths were not officially recorded, but are believed to be in the 500,000- to one-million range during the five years from 1846 to 1851. Although estimates vary, the number of people who emigrated from Ireland is in the neighborhood of two million.

The famine was more than potato blight. It was the culmination of a biological, political, social and economic catastrophe that can be attributed to contributing factors on the parts of both the British and the Irish. The famine essentially changed Irish culture and tradition forever.

The food value of the potato made it the single staple in the Irish food system. British laws (the Popery Act) prohibited Irish Catholics from passing family landholdings to a single son. This meant that land was subdivided among the male descendents in the family. The number of surviving male heirs was increasing, combining with the opportunity to own land, this led to sons marrying earlier and producing large families. With the legal restrictions on inheritance of land, this eventually meant that at the time when family size was increasing, the size of the land available to them was decreasing.

Ireland's economic/social vehicle for assistance to the poor was inadequate to meet the needs of the starving thousands. The program was funded by taxes charged to landholders on the basis of the number of tenants on the estate. As poverty and starvation increased, so did the financial need. This resulted in increasing tax rates on the landholders. To remain solvent, many landowners evicted tenants in an effort to reduce the tax bill. But this left more people poor and in need of assistance, which led to another increase in tax rates. In an effort to find an escape route from this vicious circle, some landowners paid passage to other countries rather than evict tenants. The ships on which they took passage came to be called "coffin ships." Many of these emigrants died during the voyage to North America. Many of the landowners who attempted to care for their tenants went bankrupt in the process. Ten percent of the estates were bankrupt by 1850. There were many charitable donations from around the world, but they were not adequate to solve such a large problem.

The responses of those leading the government of the United Kingdom were completely inadequate. It is believed that in 1851 the actual population of Ireland was 6.6 million. By 1911, it was only 4.4 million.

The Irish who emigrated to the U.S. for the most part became residents of cities. With no money, they were forced to remain in the port cities at which they arrived. By 1850, the Irish accounted for one-fourth of the population of Boston, New York City, Philadelphia and Baltimore.

Skill 9.6 **Recognize the work of individuals who have fought for and advanced the cause of universal human rights**

Margaret Fuller – Perhaps the first women's rights activist in the first half of the 19th century, Fuller was also a journalist. She was the first female journalist to work on the staff of a major newspaper. She had strong connections with Transcendentalism.

Frederick Douglass – A 19th century African American abolitionist. Douglass was an escaped slave and a particularly captivating public speaker. His autobiography, *Narrative of the Life of Frederick Douglass*, relates, in particular, the violence that was turned upon him because of his beliefs. In his later years, he was active in efforts to overturn Jim Crow laws.

Jane Addams – A late 19th and early 20th century social reformer who founded Hull House in Chicago (a settlement house) and worked for women's rights and for peace. She was awarded the Nobel Peace Prize in 1931.

Mohandas Gandhi – A leading political figure of the 20th century in India, and leader of India's drive for independence from Great Britain. Gandhi used and taught methods of passive resistance and nonviolent disobedience, including hunger strikes and boycotts, to influence British leaders. He was assassinated in 1948, just after India won its independence.

Margaret Sanger – The founder of the birth control movement in the 1910s and 1920s. She, in fact, coined the term. She struggled against the hostility of the medical profession and fought for the repeal of laws which existed in most states that prohibited contraception. Later in life, she led the Planned Parenthood Federation.

Eleanor Roosevelt – The wife of President Franklin D. Roosevelt was well known and respected throughout the world for her humanitarian and diplomatic efforts. She represented the U.S. in the U.N General Assembly from 1949-1952.

Martin Luther King, Jr. – An African American clergyman and leader of the American Civil Rights Movement. He advocated nonviolent opposition to segregation and to force people to notice injustice. He received the Nobel Peace Prize in 1964. He was assassinated in 1968.

Cesar Chavez – An American labor leader, who organized food harvesters in California in the 1960s into the United Farm Workers. Many of the members were Mexican Americans, like Chavez. The union led nationwide boycotts against the table grape industry and the lettuce industry. He is known for his commitment to non-violence.

Elie Wiesel – A 20th century Jewish novelist, philosopher and humanitarian who has written more than 40 works of fiction. He is a Holocaust survivor, whose experiences are related in *Night*. Wiesel was awarded the Nobel Peace Prize in 1986. The Nobel selection committee called him a "messenger to mankind," noting that through his struggle to come to terms with "his own personal experience of total humiliation and of the utter contempt for humanity shown in the Nazi death camps," as well as his "practical work in the cause of peace," Wiesel has delivered a powerful message "of peace, atonement and human dignity" to humanity.

Nelson Mandela – A major figure and leader in the struggle against apartheid by South African blacks. In the 1960s he was sentenced to life imprisonment for sabotage and conspiracy by the white government. In 1990, he was released as part of an effort to reach a compromise with South African blacks. He became the leading spokesperson for the anti-apartheid movement and the dismantling of racist policies in South Africa.

Skill 9.7   Identify historical and contemporary efforts to overcome exploitation and ensure the human rights of groups and individuals, and analyze the successes and limitations of these efforts

The rise of the abolitionist movement in the North, the publication of *Uncle Tom's Cabin*, and issues of trade and efforts by the national government to control trade for the regions coalesced around the issue of slavery in a nation that was founded on the principle of the inalienable right of every person to be free. As the South defended its lifestyle and its economy and the right of the states to be self-determining, the North became stronger in its criticism of slavery. The result was a growing sectionalism.

The Supreme Court in 1857 handed down a decision guaranteed to cause explosions throughout the country. **Dred Scott** was a slave whose owner had taken him from slave state Missouri, then to free state Illinois, into Minnesota Territory, free under the provisions of the Missouri Compromise, then finally back to slave state Missouri. Abolitionists pursued the dilemma by presenting a court case, stating that since Scott had lived in a free state and free territory, he was in actuality a free man. Two lower courts had ruled before the Supreme Court became involved, one ruling in favor and one against. The Supreme Court decided that residing in a free state and free territory did not make Scott a free man because Scott (and all other slaves) was not an U.S. citizen or a state citizen of Missouri. Therefore, he did not have the right to sue in state or federal courts. The Court went a step further and ruled that the old Missouri Compromise was now unconstitutional because Congress did not have the power to prohibit slavery in the Territories.

Anti-slavery supporters were stunned. They had just recently formed the new Republican Party and one of its platforms was keeping slavery out of the Territories. Now, according to the decision in the Dred Scott case, this basic party principle was unconstitutional. The only way to ban slavery in new areas was by a Constitutional amendment, requiring ratification by three-fourths of all states. At this time, this was out of the question because the supporters would be unable to get a majority due to Southern opposition.

In 1859, abolitionist John Brown and his followers seized the federal arsenal at Harper's Ferry in what is now West Virginia. His purpose was to take the guns stored in the arsenal, give them to slaves nearby, and lead them in a widespread rebellion. He and his men were captured by Colonel Robert E. Lee of the United States Army. After a trial with a guilty verdict, he was hanged. Most Southerners felt that the majority of Northerners approved of Brown's actions; in actuality, most of them were stunned and shocked. Southern newspapers took great pains to quote a small but well-known minority of abolitionists who applauded and supported Brown's actions. This merely served to widen the gap between the two sections.

The phrase "the civil rights movement" generally refers to the nationwide effort made by black people and those who supported them to gain equal rights to whites and to eliminate segregation. Discussion of this movement is generally understood in terms of the period of the 1950s and 1960s.

The **key people** in the civil rights movement are:

Rosa Parks -- a black seamstress from Montgomery Alabama who, in 1955, refused to give up her seat on the bus to a white man. This event is generally understood as the spark that lit the fire of the Civil Rights Movement. She has been generally regarded as the "mother of the Civil Rights Movement."

Martin Luther King, Jr.-- the most prominent member of the Civil Rights movement. King promoted nonviolent methods of opposition to segregation. The "Letter from Birmingham Jail" explained the purpose of nonviolent action as a way to make people notice injustice. He led the march on Washington in 1963, at which he delivered the "I Have a Dream" speech. He received the 1968 Nobel Prize for Peace.

James Meredith – the first African American to enroll at the University of Mississippi.

Emmett Till – a teenage boy who was murdered in Mississippi while visiting from Chicago. The crime of which he was accused was "whistling at a white woman in a store." He was beaten and murdered, and his body was dumped in a river. His two white abductors were apprehended and tried. They were acquitted by an all-white jury. After the acquittal, they admitted their guilt, but remained free because of double jeopardy laws.

Ralph Abernathy – a major figure in the Civil Rights Movement who succeeded Martin Luther King, Jr. as head of the Southern Christian Leadership Conference.

Malcolm X – born Malcolm Little, he was a political leader and part of the Civil Rights Movement. He was a prominent Black Muslim who advocated the use of all methods, including violence where necessary, to achieve equality.

Stokeley Carmichael – one of the leaders of the Black Power movement that called for independent development of political and social institutions for blacks. Carmichael called for black pride and maintenance of black culture. He was head of the Student Nonviolent Coordinating Committee.

Key events of the Civil Rights Movement include:

Brown vs. Board of Education, 1954

The murder of Emmett Till, 1955

Rosa Parks and the Montgomery Bus Boycott, 1955-56 – After refusing to give up her seat on a bus in Montgomery, Alabama, Parks was arrested, tried, and convicted of disorderly conduct and violating a local ordinance. When word reached the black community a bus boycott was organized to protest the segregation of blacks and whites on public buses. The boycott lasted 381 days, until the ordinance was lifted.

Strategy shift to "direct action" – nonviolent resistance and civil disobedience, 1955 – 1965. This action consisted mostly of bus boycotts, sit-ins, freedom rides.

Formation of the Southern Christian Leadership Conference, 1957 -- This group was formed by Martin Luther King, Jr., John Duffy, Rev. C. D. Steele, Rev. T. J. Jemison, Rev. Fred Shuttlesworth, Ella Baker, A. Philip Randolph, Bayard Rustin and Stanley Levison. The group provided training and assistance to local efforts to fight segregation. Nonviolence was its central doctrine and its major method of fighting segregation and racism.

The Desegregation of Little Rock, 1957 -- Following up on the decision of the Supreme Court in Brown vs. Board of Education, the Arkansas school board voted to integrate the school system. The NAACP chose Arkansas as the place to push integration because it was considered a relatively progressive Southern state. However, the governor called up the National Guard to prevent nine black students from attending Little Rock's Central High School.

Sit-ins – In 1960, students began to stage "sit-ins" at local lunch counters and stores as a means of protesting the refusal of those businesses to desegregate. The first was in Greensboro, NC. This led to a rash of similar campaigns throughout the South. Demonstrators began to protest parks, beaches, theaters, museums, and libraries. When arrested, the protesters made "jail-no-bail" pledges. This called attention to their cause and put the financial burden of providing jail space and food on the cities.

Freedom Rides – Activists traveled by bus throughout the Deep South to desegregate bus terminals (required by federal law). These protesters undertook extremely dangerous protests. Many buses were firebombed, attacked by the KKK, and beaten. They were crammed into small, airless jail cells and mistreated in many ways. Key figures in this effort included John Lewis, James Lawson, Diane Nash, Bob Moses, James Bevel, Charles McDew, Bernard Lafayette, Charles Jones, Lonnie King, Julian Bond, Hosea Williams, and Stokeley Carmichael.

The Birmingham Campaign, 1963-64 -- A campaign was planned to use sit-in, kneel-ins in churches, and a march to the county building to launch a voter registration campaign. The City obtained an injunction forbidding all such protests. The protesters, including Martin Luther King, Jr., believed the injunction was unconstitutional, and defied it. They were arrested. While in jail, King wrote his famous Letter from Birmingham Jail. When the campaign began to falter, the "Children's Crusade" called students to leave school and join the protests. The events became news when more than 600 students were jailed. The next day more students joined the protest. The media was present and broadcast to the nation, vivid pictures of fire hoses being used to knock down children and dogs attacking some of them. The resulting public outrage led the Kennedy administration to intervene. About a month later, a committee was formed to end hiring discrimination, arrange for the release of jailed protesters, and establish normative communication between blacks and whites. Four months later, the KKK bombed the Sixteenth Street Baptist Church, killing four girls.

The March on Washington, 1963 -- This was a march on Washington for jobs and freedom. It was a combined effort of all major civil rights organizations. The goals of the march were: meaningful civil rights laws, a massive federal works program, full and fair employment, decent housing, the right to vote, and adequate integrated education. It was at this march that Martin Luther King, Jr. made the famous "I Have a Dream" speech.

Mississippi Freedom Summer, 1964 -- Students were brought from other states to Mississippi to assist local activists in registering voters, teaching in "Freedom Schools" and in forming the Mississippi Freedom Democratic Party. Three of the workers disappeared – murdered by the KKK. It took six weeks to find their bodies. The national uproar forced President Johnson to send in the FBI. Johnson was able to use public sentiment to effect passage in Congress of the Civil Rights Act of 1964.

Selma to Montgomery marches, 1965 -- Attempts to obtain voter registration in Selma, Alabama had been largely unsuccessful due to opposition from the city's sheriff. M.L. King came to the city to lead a series of marches. He and over 200 demonstrators were arrested and jailed. Each successive march was met with violent resistance by police. In March, a group of over 600 intended to walk from Selma to Montgomery (54 miles). News media were on hand when, six blocks into the march, state and local law enforcement officials attacked the marchers with billy clubs, tear gas, rubber tubes wrapped in barbed wire and bull whips. They were driven back to Selma. National broadcast of the footage provoked a nation-wide response. President Johnson again used public sentiment to achieve passage of the Voting Rights Act of 1965. This law changed the political landscape of the South irrevocably.

Key policies, legislation and court cases included the following:

Brown v. Board of Education, 1954 – the Supreme Court declared that Plessy v. Ferguson was unconstitutional. This was the ruling that had established "Separate but Equal" as the basis for segregation. With this decision, the Court ordered immediate desegregation.

Civil Rights Act of 1964 – bars discrimination in public accommodations, employment and education

Voting Rights Act of 1965 – suspended poll taxes, literacy tests and other voter tests for voter registration

Since 1941, a number of anti-discrimination laws have been passed by the Congress. These acts have protected the civil rights of several groups of Americans. These laws include:

- Fair Employment Act of 1941
- Civil Rights Act of 1964
- Immigration and Nationality Services Act of 1965
- Voting Rights Act of 1965
- Civil Rights Act of 1968
- Age Discrimination in Employment Act of 1967
- Age Discrimination Act of 1975
- Pregnancy Discrimination Act of 1978
- Americans with Disabilities Act of 1990
- Civil Rights Act of 1991
- Employment Non-Discrimination Act

Numerous groups have used various forms of protest, attempts to sway public opinion, legal action, and congressional lobbying to obtain full protection of their civil rights under the Constitution.

"**Minority rights**" encompasses two ideas: the first is the normal individual rights of members of ethnic, racial, class, religious or sexual minorities; the second is collective rights of minority groups. Various civil rights movements have sought to guarantee that the individual rights of persons are not denied on the basis of being part of a minority group. The effects of these movements may be seen in guarantees of minority representation, affirmative action quotas, etc.

The **disability rights** movement was a successful effort to guarantee access to public buildings and transportation, equal access to education and employment, and equal protection under the law in terms of access to insurance, and other basic rights of American citizens. As a result of these efforts, public buildings and public transportation must be accessible to persons with disabilities; discrimination in hiring or housing on the basis of disability is also illegal. A "prisoners' rights" movement has been working for many years to ensure the basic human rights of persons incarcerated for crimes. Immigrant rights movements have provided for employment and housing rights, as well as prevented abuse of immigrants through hate crimes. In some states, immigrant rights movements have led to bilingual education and public information access. Another group movement to obtain equal rights is the lesbian, gay, bisexual and transgender social movement. This movement seeks equal housing, freedom from social and employment discrimination, and equal recognition of relationships under the law.

The women's rights movement is concerned with the freedoms of women as differentiated from broader ideas of human rights. These issues are generally different from those that affect men and boys because of biological conditions or social constructs. The rights the movement has sought to protect throughout history include:

- The right to vote
- The right to work
- The right to fair wages
- The right to bodily integrity and autonomy
- The right to own property
- The right to an education
- The right to hold public office
- Marital rights
- Parental rights
- Religious rights
- The right to serve in the military
- The right to enter into legal contracts

The movement for women's rights has resulted in many social and political changes. Many of the ideas that seemed very radical merely 100 years ago are now normative.

Some of the most famous leaders in the women's movement throughout American history are:

- Abigail Adams
- Susan B. Anthony
- Gloria E. Anzaldua
- Betty Friedan
- Olympe de Gouges
- Gloria Steinem
- Harriet Tubman
- Mary Wollstonecraft
- Virginia Woolf
- Germaine Greer

Many within the women's movement are primarily committed to justice and the natural rights of all people. This has led many members of the women's movement to be involved in the Black Civil Rights Movement, the gay rights movement, and the recent social movement to protect the rights of fathers.

After WWII, women were expected to return to the life of homebound docility of the pre-war years. But during the war they were actively recruited into the workplace, indeed into traditionally male jobs in heavy industry. The freedoms they enjoyed and the opportunity to explore their full potential were not things they were willing to give up so easily. The post-war years were a time of hope and great prosperity. Women, like minorities, began to demand their legal rights and freedoms. The women's movement, like the Civil Rights Movement and other efforts to accomplish social reform and human rights, grew from the opportunities that arose from the same periods of struggle and hardship that led others to demand their rights and freedoms.

Skill 9.8   Recognize the role of governments and international organizations in establishing human rights standards, and analyze barriers to enforcing human rights legislation and voluntary compacts

Individuals and societies have divided the earth's surface through conflict for a number of reasons:

- The domination of peoples or societies, e.g., colonialism
- The control of valuable resources, e.g., oil
- The control of strategic routes, e.g., the Panama Canal

Religion, political ideology, national origin, language, and race can spur conflicts. Conflicts can result from disagreement over how land, ocean or natural resources will be developed, shared, and used. Conflicts have resulted from trade, migration, and settlement rights. Conflicts can occur between small groups of people, between cities, between nations, between religious groups, and between multinational alliances.

Today, the world is primarily divided by political/administrative interests into state sovereignties. A particular region is recognized to be controlled by a particular government, including its territory, population and natural resources. The only area of the earth's surface that today is not defined by state or national sovereignty is Antarctica.

Alliances are developed among nations on the basis of political philosophy, economic concerns, cultural similarities, religious interests, or for military defense. Some of the most notable alliances today are:
- The United Nations
- The North Atlantic Treaty Organization
- The Caribbean Community
- The Common Market
- The Council of Arab Economic Unity
- The European Union

Throughout human history, there have been conflicts on virtually every scale over the right to divide the Earth according to differing perceptions, needs and values. These conflicts have ranged from tribal conflicts to urban riots, to civil wars, to regional wars, to world wars. While these conflicts have traditionally centered on control of land surfaces, new disputes are beginning to arise over the resources of the oceans and space. International organizations such as the UN and the World Bank have programs to assist developing nations with loans and education so they might join the international economy. Many countries are taking steps to regulate immigration. **(Also refer to Skill 9.1)**

DOMAIN II.   GEOGRAPHY

COMPETENCY 10   UNDERSTAND FUNDAMENTAL GEOGRAPHIC
                  CONCEPTS, THEMES, AND TERMS AND APPLY THAT
                  KNOWLEDGE TO DESCRIBE AND ANALYZE
                  GEOGRAPHIC PHENOMENA

Skill 10.1   Use geographic terms, concepts, and models to examine
               general geographic developments and specific geographic
               problems

GEOGRAPHY involves studying location and how living things and earth's
features are distributed throughout the earth. It includes where animals, people,
and plants live and the effects of their relationship with earth's physical features.
Geographers also explore the locations of earth's features, how they got there,
and why it is so important.

What geographers study can be broken down into four areas:

Location: being able to find the exact site of anything on the earth
Spatial relations: the relationships of earth's features, places, and groups of
people with one another due to their location
Regional characteristics: characteristics of a place, such as landform and
climate, types of plants and animals, and kinds of people who live there and how
they use the land
Forces that change the earth: such as human activities and natural forces

Geographical studies are divided into:

Regional: elements and characteristics of a place or region
Topical: one earth feature or one human activity occurring throughout the entire
world
Physical: earth's physical features—what creates and changes them, and their
relationships to each other and to human activities
Human: human activity patterns and how they relate to the environment,
including political, cultural, historical, urban, social, and geographical fields of
study

Special research methods used by geographers include mapping, interviewing,
field studies, mathematics, statistics, and scientific instruments.

Eratosthenes was an ancient Greek mathematician who calculated the
circumference of the earth.

Strabo wrote a geographical depiction of the known ancient world in 17 volumes.

Ptolemy contributed his skills in mapping and theories from studies in astronomy to geographic knowledge.

Christopher Columbus became known for his famous first voyage, sailing west to find the riches of the east and finding the Western Hemisphere instead.

Marco Polo, Vasco da Gama, and Magellan were three of many explorers and colonizers who contributed to geographic knowledge.

National Geographic Society is publisher of the *National Geographic* magazine and funds expeditions and other activities furthering geographic education.

Geography is the study of the earth, its people, and how people adapt to life on earth and how they use its resources. It is undeniably connected to history, economics, political science, sociology, anthropology, and even a bit of archaeology. Geography not only deals with people and the earth today but also with:

How did it all begin?
What is the background of the people of an area?
What kind of government or political system do they have?
How does that affect their ways of producing goods and the distribution of them?
What kind of relationships do these people have with other groups?
How is the way they live their lives affected by their physical environment?
In what ways do they effect change in their way of living?
All of this is tied in with their physical environment, the earth and its people.

Skill 10.2   Demonstrate an understanding of absolute and relative location on the earth's surface

Two of the most important terms in the study of geography are *absolute* and *relative* location. Both technically describe the same thing, but both are also, in many respects, as different as day and night.

First, what is **location**? We want to know this in order to determine where something is and where we can find it. We want to point to a spot on a map and say, "that is where we are" or "that is where we want to be." In another way, we want to know where something is as compared to other things. It is very difficult for many people to describe something without referring to something else. Associative reasoning is a powerful way to think.

Absolute location is the exact whereabouts of a person, place, or thing, according to any kind of geographical indicators you want to name. You could be talking about latitude and longitude or GPS or any kind of indicators at all. For example, Paris is at 48 degrees north longitude and 2 degrees east latitude. You can't get much more exact than that. If you had a map that showed every degree of latitude and longitude, you could pinpoint exactly where Paris was and have absolutely no doubt that your geographical depiction was accurate.

Many geographers prefer to use absolute location because of its precision. If you have access to maps and compasses and GPS indicators, why not describe the absolute location of something? It's much more accurate than other means of describing where something is. An absolute location can also be much simpler. Someone might ask you where the nearest post office is and you might say, "It's at the southeast corner of First Avenue and Main Street." That's about as absolute as you can get.

Relative location, on the other hand, is *always* a description that involves more than one thing. When you describe a relative location, you tell where something is by describing what is around it. The same description of where the nearest post office is in terms of absolute location might be this: "It's down the street from the supermarket, on the right side of the street, next to the dentist's office."

We use relative location to be not necessarily less precise but to be more in tune with the real world. Very few people carry exact maps or GPS locators around with them. Nearly everyone, though, can find a location if they have it described to them in terms of what is nearby.

Absolute location can be a bit more map-like and direction-oriented as well. You might say that Chicago is east of Seattle or that St. Louis is north of New Orleans. This is not nearly as involved as the post office location description. In the same way, you might say that Chicago is on Lake Michigan.

Skill 10.3   **Analyze the spatial organization of peoples, places and environments on the earth's surface**

Spatial organization is a description of how things are grouped in a given space. In geographical terms, this can describe people, places, and environments anywhere and everywhere on Earth.

The most basic form of spatial organization for people is where they live. Majority of people live near other people, in villages, towns, cities and settlements. These people live near others in order to take advantage of the goods and services that naturally arise from cooperation. These villages, towns, cities and settlements are, to varying degrees, near bodies of water. Water is a staple of survival for every person on the planet and is also a good source of energy for factories and other industries, as well as a form of transportation for people and goods.

Another way to describe where people live is by the **geography** and **topography** around them. The vast majority of people on the planet live in areas that are very hospitable. Yes, people live in the Himalayas and in the Sahara, but the populations in those areas are small indeed when compared to the plains of China, India, Europe, and the United States. People naturally want to live where they won't have to work really hard just to survive, and world population patterns reflect this.

We can examine the spatial organization of the places where people live. For example, in a city, where are the factories and heavy industry buildings? Are they near airports or train stations? Are they on the edge of town, near major roads? What about housing developments? Are they near these industries, or are they far away? Where are the other industry buildings? Where are the schools and hospitals and parks? What about the police and fire stations? How close are homes to each of these things? Towns and especially cities are routinely organized into neighborhoods, so that each house or home is near to most things that its residents might need on a regular basis. This means that large cities have multiple schools, hospitals, grocery stores, fire stations, etc.

Related to this is the distance between cities, towns, villages, or settlements. In certain parts of the United States and definitely in many countries in Europe, the population settlement patterns achieve megalopolis standards, with no clear boundaries from one town to the next. Other, more sparsely populated areas have towns that are few and far between and have relatively few people in them. Some exceptions to this exist, of course, like oases in the deserts; for the most part, however, population centers tend to be relatively near one another or at least near smaller towns.

Most places in the world are in some manner close to agricultural land as well. Food makes the world go round and some cities are more agriculturally inclined than others. Rare is the city, however, that grows absolutely no crops. The kind of food grown is almost entirely dependent on the kind of land available and the climate surrounding that land. Rice doesn't grow well in the desert, for instance, nor do bananas grow well in snowy lands. Certain crops are easier to transport than others and the ones that aren't are usually grown near ports or other areas of export.

The one thing that changes all of these is the airplane. Flight has made possible global commerce and goods exchange on a level never before seen. Foods from all around the world can be flown literally around the world and, with the aid of refrigeration techniques, be kept fresh enough to sell in markets nearly everywhere. The same is true of medicine and, unfortunately, weapons.

Skill 10.4   Formulate geographic questions to address problems and issues in other disciplines

Geography can lend itself to many other disciplines. The versatility and breadth of geographical discussions contain many elements that can translate and have a bearing on problems and solutions in other fields of study.

One of the foremost examples of this is geography's application to economics. People looking to locate manufacturing plants will naturally consider **geographic factors** when making their final decision. Will the plant depend on hydroelectric power? If so, then should the plant be located near a natural water source, like a river or lake or dam? Will the plant be exporting or importing a large amount of products? If so, then where is the nearest airport and how far away are the nearest highways and residential areas? If the plant owners will depend heavily on land-based transportation, what is the surrounding terrain like? Can heavy trucks easily connect from plant to highway, and vice versa? Is privacy a concern? How will what the company is doing affect the local community? Strip mining of local hills and mountains could be a source of much friction. If the plant is manufacturing secret products, then the owners will want to situate that plant as far away from the rest of civilization as possible, within the guidelines already mentioned.

Simpler decisions take place when a group of people is looking to open a new business or shopping mall. Practical considerations such as the locations of nearby homes and possible competitors factor into the decision of where to locate that new business or shopping mall. Is the city an urban hub, with shoppers already coming from nearby towns? If so, the new business can count on more than just the local population for business. If the business is a grocery store, can the owners count on a steady supply of varied foods and liquids to keep customers keeping back? If the business is a niche market, then is the local population large enough to sustain such a niche?

Armed conflict and the strategies involved also take lessons from geography. Until the advent of airpower as a military device, whichever army held the high ground on a battlefield was in a superior position. This still holds true today, to a large extent, even with the presence of fighter jets and bomber planes in the sky, unless one side of a war has such an overwhelming air force that the sorties are constant. (The First Iraq War was a good example of this.) Rivers and mountains still can form formidable barriers to land-based invasions. The seas and oceans of the world are now hotspots for battles as well, with the advent of fighting ships and, especially, submarines and aircraft carriers, each of which in its own way changed naval warfare profoundly.

Geography can even extend to politics. The way an industry or set of industries or a large group of people treat the land around them can be the source of political debate. So can the treatment of nearby wildlife. Some of the most caustic debates nowadays are between **animal rights activists** and proponents of technological growth at all costs. On a more traditional note, the closer a city or town is to a major airport and the more population that city has, the more times political candidates will be visiting that city in search of support from voters who live there.

COMPETENCY 11 **UNDERSTAND THE MAJOR PHYSICAL FEATURES OF THE WORLD AND THE INTERCONNECTIONS BETWEEN PHYSICAL PROCESSES AND HUMAN ACTIVITY**

Skill 11.1 **Recognize the characteristics and spatial distribution of major land masses, landforms, and ecosystems on the earth's surface**

A landform comprises a geomorphological unit. Landforms are categorized by characteristics such as elevation, slope, orientation, stratification, rock exposure, and soil type. Landforms by name include berms, mounds, hills, cliffs, valleys, and others. Oceans and continents exemplify highest-order landforms. Landform elements are parts of a landform that can be further identified. The generic landform elements are: pits, peaks, channels, ridges, passes, pools, planes etc, and can be often extracted from a digital elevation model using some automated or semi-automated techniques.

Elementary landforms (segments, facets, relief units) are the smallest homogeneous divisions of the land surface, at the given scale/resolution. A plateau or a hill can be observed at various scales ranging from few hundred meters to hundreds of kilometers. Hence, the spatial distribution of landforms is often fuzzy and scale-dependent as is the case for soils and geological strata. A number of factors, ranging from plate tectonics to erosion and deposition can generate and affect landforms. Biological factors can also influence landforms—see for example the role of plants in the development of dune systems and salt marshes, and the work of corals and algae in the formation of coral reefs. Weather is the condition of the air which surrounds the day-to-day atmospheric conditions including temperature, air pressure, wind and moisture or precipitation which includes rain, snow, hail, or sleet.

Climate is average weather or daily weather conditions for a specific region or location over a long or extended period of time. Studying the climate of an area includes information gathered on the area's monthly and yearly temperatures and its monthly and yearly amounts of precipitation. In addition, a characteristic of an area's climate is the length of its growing season.

In northern and central United States, northern China, south central and southeastern Canada, and the western and southeastern parts of the former Soviet Union is found the "climate of four seasons," the humid continental climate--spring, summer, fall, and winter. Cold winters, hot summers, and enough rainfall to grow a variety of crops are the major characteristics of this climate. In areas where the humid continental climate is found are some of the world's best farmlands as well as important activities such as trading and mining. Differences in temperatures throughout the year are determined by the distance a place is inland, away from the coasts.

The **steppe** or **prairie** climate is located in the interiors of the large continents like Asia and North America. These dry flatlands are far from ocean breezes and are called prairies or the Great Plains in Canada and the United States and steppes in Asia. Although the summers are hot and the winters are cold, the big difference is rainfall. In the steppe climate, rainfall is light and uncertain, 10 to 20 inches a year. Where rain is more plentiful, grass grows; in areas of less, the steppes or prairies gradually become deserts. These are found in the Gobi Desert of Asia, central and western Australia, southwestern United States, and in the smaller deserts found in Pakistan, Argentina, and Africa south of the Equator.

The two major climates found in the high latitudes are **tundra** and **taiga**. The word tundra meaning marshy plain is a Russian word and aptly describes the climatic conditions in the northern areas of Russia, Europe, and Canada. Winters are extremely cold and very long. Most of the year, the ground is frozen but becomes rather mushy during the very short summer months. Surprisingly less snow falls in the area of the tundra than in the eastern part of the United States. However, due to the harshness of the extreme cold, very few people live there and no crops can be raised. Despite having a small human population, many plants and animals are found there.

The taiga is the northern forest region and is located south of the tundra. The world's largest forestlands are found here along with vast mineral wealth and fur-bearing animals. The climate is so extreme that very few people live here, not being able to raise crops due to the extremely short growing season. The winter temperatures are colder and the summer temperatures are hotter than those in the tundra because the taiga climate region is farther from the waters of the Arctic Ocean. The taiga is found in the northern parts of Russia, Sweden, Norway, Finland, Canada, and Alaska with most of their lands covered with marshes and swamps.

The humid **subtropical climate** is found north and south of the tropics and is moist indeed. The areas having this type of climate are found on the eastern side of their continents and include Japan, mainland China, Australia, Africa, South America, and the United States--the southeastern coasts of these areas. An interesting feature of their locations is that warm ocean currents are found there. The winds that blow across these currents bring in warm moist air all year round. Long, warm summers; short, mild winters; a long growing season allow for different crops to be grown several times a year. All contribute to the productivity of this climate type that supports more people than any of the other climates.

The **marine climate** is found in Western Europe, the British Isles, the U.S. Pacific Northwest, the western coast of Canada and southern Chile, southern New Zealand and southeastern Australia. A common characteristic of these lands is that they are either near water or surrounded by it. The ocean winds are wet and warm, bringing a mild rainy climate to these areas. In the summer, the daily temperatures average at or below 70 degrees F. During the winter, because of the warming effect of the ocean waters, the temperatures rarely fall below freezing.

In northern and central United States, northern China, south central and southeastern Canada, and the western and southeastern parts of the former Soviet Union is found the **"climate of four seasons,"** the **humid continental climate**--spring, summer, fall, and winter. Cold winters, hot summers, and enough rainfall to grow a variety of crops are the major characteristics of this climate. In areas where the humid continental climate is found are some of the world's best farmlands as well as important activities such as trading and mining. Differences in temperatures throughout the year are determined by the distance a place is inland.

In certain areas of the earth there exists a type of climate unique to areas with high mountains, usually different from their surroundings. This type of climate is called a "vertical climate" because the temperatures, crops, vegetation, and human activities change and become different as one ascends the different levels of elevation. At the foot of the mountain, a hot and rainy climate is found with the cultivation of many lowland crops. As one climbs higher, the air becomes cooler, the climate changes sharply, and different economic activities change, such as grazing sheep and growing corn. At the top of many mountains, snow is found year round.

Skill 11.2   Forces that have shaped the earth's surface

Plate tectonics is a geological theory that explains **continental drift**, which is the large movement of the solid portions of the Earth's crust floating on the molten mantle. There are ten major tectonic plates, with several smaller plates. The surface of the earth can be drastically affected at the boundaries of these plates.

There are three types of plate boundaries, convergent, divergent and transform. Convergent boundaries are where plates are moving toward one another. When this happens, the two plates collide and fold up against one another, called **continental collision**, or one plate slides under the other, called **subduction**. Continental collision can create high mountain ranges, such as the Andes and Himalayas. Subduction often results in volcanic activity along the boundary, as in the "Ring of Fire" along the northern coasts of the Pacific Ocean.

Divergent boundaries occur where plates are moving away from one another, creating **rifts** in the surface. The Mid-Atlantic Ridge on the floor of the Atlantic Ocean, and the Great Rift Valley in east Africa are examples of rifts at divergent plate boundaries. Transform boundaries are where plates are moving in opposite directions along their boundary, grinding against one another. The tremendous pressures that build along these types of boundaries often lead to earthquake activity when this pressure is released. The San Andreas Fault along the West Coast of North America is an example of a transform boundary.

Erosion is the displacement of solid earth surfaces such as rock and soil. Erosion is often a result of wind, water or ice acting on surfaces with loose particles, such as sand, loose soils, or decomposing rock. Gravity can also cause erosion on loose surfaces. Factors such as slope, soil and rock composition, plant cover, and human activity all affect erosion.

Weathering is the natural decomposition of the Earth's surface from contact with the atmosphere. It is not the same as erosion, but can be a factor in erosion. Heat, water, ice and pressure are all factors that can lead to weathering. Chemicals in the atmosphere can also contribute to weathering

Transportation is the movement of eroded material from one place to another by wind, water or ice. Examples of transportation include pebbles rolling down a streambed and boulders being carried by moving glaciers.

Deposition is the result of transportation, and occurs when the material being carried settles on the surface and is deposited. Sand dunes and moraines are formed by transportation and deposition of glacial material.

Skill 11.3   Evaluate the impact of population growth and change on the physical environment

By nature, people are social creatures. They generally live in communities or settlements of some kind and size. Settlements are the cradles of culture, political structure, education, and the management of resources. The relative placement of these settlements or communities is shaped by the proximity to natural resources, the movement of raw materials, the production of finished products, the availability of a workforce, and the delivery of finished products. Shared values, language, culture, religion, and subsistence will, at least to some extent, determine the composition of communities.

Settlements begin in areas that offer the natural resources to support life – food and water. With the ability to manage the environment, one finds a concentration of populations. With the ability to transport raw materials and finished products comes mobility. With increasing technology and the rise of industrial centers comes a migration of the workforce.

Cities are the major hubs of human settlement. Almost half of the population of the world now lives in cities. These percentages are much higher in developed regions. Established cities continue to grow. The fastest growth, however, is occurring in developing areas. In some regions there are "metropolitan areas" made up of urban and suburban areas. In some places, cities and urban areas have become interconnected into "megalopoli" (e.g., Tokyo-Kawasaki-Yokohama).

The concentrations of populations and the divisions of these areas among various groups that constitute the cities can differ significantly. North American cities are different from European cities in terms of shape, size, population density, and modes of transportation. While in North America, the wealthiest economic groups tend to live outside the cities, the opposite is true in Latin American cities.

There are significant differences among the cities of the world in terms of connectedness to other cities. While European and North American cities tend to be well linked both by transportation and communication connections, there are other places in the world in which communication between the cities of the country may be inferior to communication with the rest of the world.

Rural areas tend to be less densely populated due to the needs of agriculture. More land is needed to produce crops or for animal husbandry than for manufacturing, especially in a city in which the buildings tend to be taller. Rural areas, however, must be connected via communication and transportation in order to provide food and raw materials to urban areas. Social policy addresses basic human needs for the sustainability of the individual and the society. The concerns of social policy, then, include food, clean water, shelter, clothing, education, health, and social security. Social policy is part of public policy, determined by the city, the state, the nation, responsible for human welfare in a particular region.

Skill 11.4 Analyze how urbanization, industrialization, and economic development affect landforms and water systems

In recent years, the depletion of natural capital and attempts to move to sustainable development has been a major focus of development agencies. This is of particular concern in rainforest regions, which hold most of the Earth's natural biodiversity -- irreplaceable genetic natural capital. Conservation of natural resources is the major focus of Natural Capitalism, environmentalism, the ecology movement, and Green Parties. Some view this depletion as a major source of social unrest and conflicts in developing nations.

Environmental policy is concerned with the sustainability of the earth, the region under the administration of the governing group or individual or a local habitat. Environmental policy tries to preserve the region, habitat or ecosystem.

Because humans, both individually and in community, rely upon the environment to sustain human life, social and environmental policy must be mutually supportable. Because humans, both individually and in community, live upon the earth, draw upon the natural resources of the earth, and affect the environment in many ways, environmental and social policy must be mutually supportive.

If modern societies have no understanding of the limitations of natural resources or how their actions affect the environment, and they act without regard for the sustainability of the earth, it will become impossible for the earth to sustain human existence. At the same time, the resources of the earth are necessary to support human welfare. Environmental policies must recognize that the planet is the home of humans and other species.

For centuries, social policies, economic policies, and political policies have ignored the impact of human existence and human civilization upon the environment. Human civilization has disrupted the ecological balance, contributed to the extinction of animal and plant species, and destroyed ecosystems through uncontrolled harvesting.

In an age of global warming, unprecedented demand upon natural resources, and a shrinking planet, social and environmental policies must become increasingly interdependent if the planet is to continue to support life and human civilization.

Skill 11.5 Analyze how physical factors influence and are influenced by patterns of human settlement and cultural development

Human communities subsisted initially as gatherers – gathering berries, leaves, etc. With the invention of tools it became possible to dig for roots, hunt small animals, and catch fish from rivers and oceans. Humans observed their environments and soon learned to plant seeds and harvest crops. As people migrated to areas in which game and fertile soil were abundant, communities began to develop. When people had the knowledge to grow crops and the skills to hunt game, they began to understand division of labor. Some of the people in the community tended to agricultural needs while others hunted game.

As habitats attracted larger numbers of people, environments became crowded and there was competition. The concept of division of labor and sharing of food soon came, in more heavily populated areas, to be managed. Groups of people focused on growing crops while others concentrated on hunting. Experience led to the development of skills and of knowledge that make the work easier. Farmers began to develop new plant species and hunters began to protect animal species from other predators for their own use. This ability to manage the environment led people to settle down, to guard their resources, and to manage them.

Camps soon became villages. Villages became year-round settlements. Animals were domesticated and gathered into herds that met the needs of the village. With the settled life it was no longer necessary to "travel light." Pottery was developed for storing and cooking food.

By 8000 BCE, culture was beginning to evolve in these villages. Agriculture was developed for the production of grain crops, which led to a decreased reliance on wild plants. Domesticating animals for various purposes decreased the need to hunt wild game. Life became more settled. It was then possible to turn attention to such matters as managing water supplies, producing tools, making cloth, etc. There was both the social interaction and the opportunity to reflect upon existence. Mythologies arose and various kinds of belief systems. Rituals arose that re-enacted the mythologies that gave meaning to life.

As farming and animal husbandry skills increased, the dependence upon wild game and food gathering declined. With this change came the realization that a larger number of people could be supported on the produce of farming and animal husbandry.

Two things seem to have come together to produce cultures and civilizations: a society and culture based on agriculture and the development of centers of the community with literate social and religious structures. The members of these hierarchies then managed water supply and irrigation, ritual and religious life, and exerted their own right to use a portion of the goods produced by the community for their own subsistence in return for their management.

Sharpened skills, development of more sophisticated tools, commerce with other communities, and increasing knowledge of their environment, the resources available to them, and responses to the needs to share good, order community life, and protect their possessions from outsiders led to further division of labor and community development.

As trade routes developed and travel between cities became easier, trade led to specialization. Trade enables a people to obtain the goods they desire in exchange for the goods they are able to produce. This, in turn, leads to increased attention to refinements of technique and the sharing of ideas. The knowledge of a new discovery or invention provides knowledge and technology that increases the ability to produce goods for trade.

As each community learns the value of the goods it produces and improves its ability to produce the goods in greater quantity, industry is born.

COMPETENCY 12   UNDERSTAND THE MAJOR PHYSICAL AND
                CULTURAL REGIONS OF THE WORLD, RECOGNIZE
                GEOGRAPHIC RELATIONSHIPS AND INTERACTIONS
                AMONG REGIONS, AND DEMONSTRATE AN
                APPRECIATION OF THE DIVERSE PERSPECTIVES OF
                DIFFERENT HUMAN GROUPS AND CULTURES BOTH
                PAST AND PRESENT

**Skill 12.1   Demonstrate a familiarity with the major cultural groups
            associated with particular regions and the nature and extent of
            their interactions**

Social scientists use the term **culture** to describe the way of life of a group of
people. This would include not only art, music, and literature but also beliefs,
customs, languages, traditions, inventions--in short, any way of life whether
complex or simple. The term **geography** is defined as the study of earth's
features and living things as to their location, relationship with each other, how
they came to be there, and why it is so important.

Physical geography is concerned with the locations of such earth features as
climate, water, and land; how these relate to and affect each other and human
activities; and what forces shaped and changed them. All three of these earth
features affect the lives of all humans having a direct influence on what is made
and produced, where it occurs, how it occurs, and what makes it possible. The
combination of the different climate conditions and types of landforms and other
surface features work together all around the earth to give the many varied
cultures their unique characteristics and distinctions.

Cultural geography studies the location, characteristics, and influence of the
physical environment on different cultures around the earth. Also included in
these studies are comparisons and influences of the many varied cultures. Ease
of travel and up-to-the-minute, state-of-the-art communication techniques ease
the difficulties of understanding cultural differences making it easier to come in
contact with them.

**Skill 12.2   Evaluate the economic, environmental, political, and cultural
            factors contributing to the distribution and migration of human
            populations**

Physical locations of the earth's surface features include the four major
hemispheres and the parts of the earth's continents in them. Political locations
are the political divisions, if any, within each continent. Both physical and political
locations are precisely determined in two ways: (1) Surveying is done to
determine boundary lines and distance from other features. (2) Exact locations
are precisely determined by imaginary lines of latitude (parallels) and longitude
(meridians). The intersection of these lines at right angles forms a grid, making it
impossible to pinpoint an exact location of any place using any two grip
coordinates.

SOCIAL STUDIES   173

The **Eastern Hemisphere**, located between the North and South Poles and between the Prime Meridian (0 degrees longitude) east to the International Date Line at 180 degrees longitude, consists of most of Europe, all of Australia, most of Africa, and all of Asia, except for a tiny piece of the easternmost part of Russia that extends east of 180 degrees longitude.

The Western Hemisphere, located between the North and South Poles and between the Prime Meridian (0 degrees longitude) west to the International Date Line at 180 degrees longitude, consists of all of North and South America, a tiny part of the easternmost part of Russia that extends east of 180 degrees longitude, and a part of Europe that extends west of the Prime Meridian (0 degrees longitude).

The **Northern Hemisphere**, located between the North Pole and the Equator, contains all of the continents of Europe and North America and parts of South America, Africa, and most of Asia.

The **Southern Hemisphere**, located between the South Pole and the Equator, contains all of Australia, a small part of Asia, about one-third of Africa, most of South America, and all of Antarctica.

Of the seven continents, only one contains just one entire country and is the only island continent, Australia. Its political divisions consist of six states and one territory: Western Australia, South Australia, Tasmania, Victoria, New South Wales, Queensland, and Northern Territory.

Africa is made up of 54 separate countries, the major ones being Egypt, Nigeria, South Africa, Zaire, Kenya, Algeria, Morocco, and the large island of Madagascar.

Asia consists of 49 separate countries, some of which include China, Japan, India, Turkey, Israel, Iraq, Iran, Indonesia, Jordan, Vietnam, Thailand, and the Philippines.

Europe's 43 separate nations include France, Russia, Malta, Denmark, Hungary, Greece, Bosnia and Herzegovina.

North America consists of Canada and the United States of America and the island nations of the West Indies and the "land bridge" of Middle America, including Cuba, Jamaica, Mexico, Panama, and others.

Thirteen separate nations together occupy the continent of South America, among them such nations as Brazil, Paraguay, Ecuador, and Suriname.

The continent of Antarctica has no political boundaries or divisions but is the location of a number of science and research stations managed by nations such as Russia, Japan, France, Australia, and India.

Skill 12.3   Examine the development and interrelationship of belief systems in different regions of the world

Belief systems, like other cultural elements or institutions, spread through human interaction. It is thus natural that religions and belief systems may have regional or cultural markers that are transmitted across regions. Religions and belief systems general originate in a particular region, with elements that are culturally or regionally defined or influenced. As belief systems are introduced to new groups or societies, some of those regional and cultural markers will also penetrate the new society. By the same token, as interaction between the originating society and the new society continues and the belief system finds new expression, some regional or cultural elements introduced by the new society will be carried back to the originating culture.

Belief systems are introduced to new societies in a variety of ways. One method is military and political conquest. As the originating society conquers a new territory and incorporates it into the political entity, belief systems are frequently either peaceably spread to the conquered people or forced upon them in the name of cultural unity. This has occurred frequently in human history. The rise and spread of the Islamic Empire both converted and forced the conversion of conquered peoples to Islam. Another example may be seen in the conversion of the Emperor Constantine to Christianity and his imposition of Christianity upon Rome as the national religion.

Belief systems are also introduced through other types of human interaction. This occurs through commercial interaction, the identification of common or similar primitive mythologies (for example, similar creation and great flood myths). Educational interaction and cultural sharing between cultures also frequently carries religious belief systems, as well.

Skill 12.4   Analyze the changes that occur in the use and distribution of natural resources and how resource use influences economic and cultural development

Natural resources are features of the earth's surface or substances that occur naturally and are considered to have value in their original form. Natural resources that are extracted or purified become commodities. Thus, mining, oil extraction, fishing and forestry are generally considered natural resource industries.

Natural resources are classified into renewable and non-renewable resources. Renewable resources are living resources that can renew themselves if they are not over-harvested. These include fish, coffee, forests, etc. Non-living renewable natural resources include water, wind, soil, tides and solar radiation.

The natural resources of a nation often determine its economy and its wealth. This, in turn, contributes to the nation's political influence. A nation with significant resources in raw metallic ores, petroleum deposits, coal, etc. will develop an economy and a culture based, at least to some degree, on the extraction and refinement of those raw materials. Such natural resources as rain forests provide the raw materials for the development of medicines and other products.

Civilizations require supplies of water and food products. Agricultural communities will develop in regions with arable land that can produce crops for its own needs and for other regions. The ability to move water to high-demand areas and to harness the power of water and wind to provide energy is another use of natural resources.

Societies that support their economy by managing, harvesting, extracting, and utilizing natural resources develop cultural identities that reflect the means of subsistence. These societies and cultures will develop the means of sustaining and protecting both the resources and the ecosystems.

COMPETENCY 13   UNDERSTAND THE MAJOR PHYSICAL AND CULTURAL REGIONS OF NEW YORK STATE AND THE UNITED STATES; ANALYZE GEOGRAPHIC RELATIONSHIPS WITHIN AND BETWEEN REGIONS; AND DEMONSTRATE AN UNDERSTANDING OF THE INFLUENCE OF GEOGRAPHY ON THE GROWTH AND EVOLUTION OF U.S. SOCIETY

Skill 13.1   **Recognize the geological, climatic, and biological factors that have determined the location of major state and national resources**

The northern and eastern sections of New York are mountainous, while the remainder of the state is a region of low plateaus and rolling plains. Excluding Long Island, the surface of which is low and level, New York can be divided into several well-marked physical regions.

Eastern Mountain Belt. This is a region of rugged hills and low mountains, the continuation of the Green Mountains and of the Berkshire Hills of New England. It occupies the entire portion east of the Hudson River ("River of Steep Hills").

The Plateau Region and the Catskill Mountains. West of the Hudson River is the plateau region, which extends through Southern and Central New York almost to Lake Erie. This region is the northern extension of the Allegheny plateau, which skirts the western base of the Appalachian Mountains. The eastern limit of this plateau is formed by the Catskill Mountains. The Catskills cover an area of about 500 square miles, and are in the form of a group rather than a range. Many of their slopes are wooded, and the intervening valleys are fertile. The highest peak, Slide Mountain, has an altitude of 4,205 feet, and there are several peaks between 3,000 and 4,000 feet high. This entire extensive plateau region is divided by many deep and wide valleys, which have a general direction from north to south.

The Adirondacks. The most notable feature of New York's surface is the roughly circular mountain region believed to have been the first mountains of the western world to emerge from the ocean, and known as the Adirondacks. This region has an area of over 5,000 square miles and covers the northeastern portion of the state, extending south to the Mohawk Valley. The region is noted for its rugged peaks, primeval forests, and its hundreds of lakes and mountain streams. It contains many peaks between 3,000 and 4,000 feet high. Mount Marcy, at 5,344 feed, is the highest point of the state.

To the west of the Adirondacks and north of the plateau region extends the lake-shore plain, which has a slightly undulating surface, sloping gently toward Lake Erie and Lake Ontario. The soil of this plain is very fertile, and the region is particularly suited to fruit-raising.

The Mohawk Valley extends from the Hudson River near Albany and west to Utica, is the low, narrow valley of the Mohawk River, dividing the Adirondacks from the Catskills. The Hudson-Mohawk Valley forms the only great break in the Appalachian system and the best access to the interior of the continent. It provided the only natural trade route between the Atlantic and the Great Lakes prior to the construction of the Erie Canal; the Hudson-Lake Champlain route was very important in the early years of the colonies.

Rivers. All parts of the state are well supplied with rivers, which find their way into the Atlantic Ocean by five different drainage basins. These navigable waters and the open valleys which lead out in all directions have been among the main factors which have contributed to give New York its leading commercial position. Foremost among them are the Hudson and the Mohawk. The rivers in the northern part of the state flow into Lakes Erie and Ontario and are drained through the Saint Lawrence River into the Atlantic Ocean. Among these rivers are the Genesee, which completely traverses the state from south to north, and the Oswego and its tributary the Seneca, which gather the waters of the Finger Lakes. The southern part of the state is drained by the Delaware, the Susquehanna, and the Allegheny.

Waterfalls. Many of these rivers flow through wide and fertile valleys during the greater part of their course, but at some points pass through deep gorges and form notable waterfalls. These falls are sources of water power, a fact that has caused the establishment of large industrial plants in their neighborhood.

Lakes. New York contains a large number of lakes, either wholly or partly within its boundaries. Most notable are Lake George and Lake Champlain. In the plateau region directly south of Lake Ontario there is a group of long, narrow, navigable lakes, nearly parallel to each other, with their greatest length extending from north to south. These are known as the Finger Lakes. Northeast of these is Lake Oneida. In the extreme southwestern part of the state is Lake Chautauqua.

During the glacial epoch, ice sheets covered most of the northern part of the continent, extending about as far south as New York Bay and the Ohio, Missouri and Columbia Rivers. There was also extensive glaciation in the Rocky Mountains and in the Sierra Nevadas. The ice accumulated around several centers of dispersion. As it reached a significant thickness, it moved outward from the center in all directions, but primarily southward. At their greatest extent they covered hundreds of thousands of square miles and were several thousand feet thick, so that mountains such as the Adirondacks were completely buried in ice. As the ice advanced, it removed the soil and loose material down to the bedrock, into which it gouged deeply in places. Hilltops were ground down and valleys were deepened, and a large amount of rock material was removed and transported by the ice, sometimes for hundreds of miles.

In time, the ice sheets spread to a point where their southern margins could no longer extend, beyond which the ice melted as fast as it advanced. The transported material was deposited at the margin of the ice in an irregular, hummocky ridge called the *terminal moraine*, or was borne away by water flowing from the melting ice. When the glaciers' advance had stopped, they began to melt away from the area they had occupied, leaving behind them great drift sheets formed of the transported material. In areas of little relief, such as the prairies of the North Central states, the thick blanket of drift obliterated the former topography and gave a new surface to the region. On this surface a new system of drainage developed which in many regions is characterized by the abundance of lakes and swamps. As the ice disappeared, many temporary lakes were formed in low places along the ice margin. When these lakes melted and drained through the opening of lower outlets, the silt deposited on their former beds became the fertile soil.

Skill 13.2 Analyze basic types of land use and development in New York State and the United States

Land use is the function of the land – what use is made of it. Land use and development models attempt to explain the layout of urban areas, primarily in "more economically developed countries" or in "less economically developed countries."

Two primary land use models are generally applied to urban regions. These are: (1) **The Burgess Model** (also called the Concentric Model), in which cities are seen to develop in a series of concentric circles with the central business district at the center, ringed by the factories and industrial usage area, ringed by the low class residential area, then the middle class residential area, and finally the high class residential area (often suburbs); and (2) **The Hoyt Model** (also called the Sector Model), in which the central business district occupies a central area of a circle, with factories and industry occupying an elongated area that abuts the city center, and with the low class residential area surrounding the industrial area, and the middle class residential area forming a semi-circle toward the other side of the city center, and a small upper class residential sector extending from the city center out through the middle of the middle-class residential area.

In rural areas, land use will probably include agriculture, forestry, and possibly fishing. **The Von Thunen Model** observes a city as the center of a state or region, from which a series of concentric circles emanates, each devoted to particular rural land usage patterns: The first ring from the city would be devoted to dairy farming and intensive farming, which allows produce to reach the market quickly. The second zone would focus on timber and firewood for fuel and building materials, which, because of its weight, needs to be relatively close to the city. The third zone would be dedicated to extensive field crops such as grains. The fourth zone would be dedicated to ranching and/or animal husbandry. Beyond this, unoccupied wilderness would remain.

Skill 13.3   Demonstrate an understanding of the origins of place names in the United States

Place names throughout the world tend to reflect similar sources. The primary sources of place names are: (1) geographic features, (2) the names of founders, (3) place names that repeat place names in the home countries of origin, (4) names of rivers, (5) names based on important events that occurred at the site, (6) names of famous persons who were born near the site, (7) names taken over or continued from previous civilizations and cultures that inhabited the area.

A city may be named "Portsmouth" because it is located at the mouth of rivers emptying into a larger body of water that forms a significant port. The use of "bourne" for a place near a stream reflects Saxon origins, as does "burg" for a large village, or "stoc" for a pasture, or "stow" for a holy place, or "worth" or "worthy" for a fenced or enclosed area.

In the U.S., many place names are adopted from the names used by the Native Americans who first populated them. The Hudson River is named for Henry Hudson, the Dutch explorer who first explored it. Many mountains and rivers are named for the person who first identified them or crossed them (Pike's Peak, for example). Cities are named for honored leaders (Lincoln, Washington, etc.). Many U.S. place names are taken over from places in Great Britain, the Netherlands, France, or other countries from which large groups immigrated.

Skill 13.4   Identify factors affecting the pattern and infrastructure of urban areas in New York State and the United States and describe the consequences of these patterns for various population segments

Environmental and geographic factors have affected the pattern of urban development in New York and the rest of the US. In turn, urban infrastructure and development patterns are interrelated factors, which affect one another.

The growth of urban areas is often linked to the advantages provided by its geographic location. Before the advent of efficient overland routes of commerce such as railroads and highways, water provided the primary means of transportation of commercial goods. Most large American cities are situated along bodies of water. New York's major cities include Buffalo, on Lake Erie, Albany, on the Hudson River, and of course New York City, situated on a large harbor where two major rivers meet the Atlantic Ocean. Where water traffic was not provided for naturally, New Yorkers built a series of canals, including the Erie Canal, which sparked the growth of inland cities.

As transportation technology advanced, the supporting infrastructure was built to connect cities with one another and to connect remote areas to larger communities. The railroad, for example, allowed for the quick transport of agricultural products from rural areas to urban centers. This newfound efficiency not only further fueled the growth of urban centers, it changed the economy of rural America. Where once farmers had practiced only subsistence farming – growing enough to support one's own family – the new infrastructure meant that one could convert agricultural products into cash by selling them at market.

For urban dwellers, improvements in building technology and advances in transportation allowed for larger cities. Growth brought with it a new set of problems unique to each location. The bodies of water that had made the development of cities possible in their early days also formed natural barriers to growth. Further infrastructure in the form of bridges, tunnels and ferry routes were needed to connect central urban areas with outlying communities.

As cities grew in population, living conditions became more crowded. As roads and bridges became better, and transportation technology improved, many people began to look outside the city for living space. Along with the development of these new suburbs came the infrastructure to connect them to the city in the form of commuter railroads and highways. In the case of New York City, which is situated mainly on islands, a mass transit system became crucial early on to bring essential workers from outlying areas into the commercial centers.

The growth of suburbs had the effect in many cities of creating a type of economic segregation. Working class people who could not afford new suburban homes and perhaps an automobile to carry them to and from work were relegated to closer, more densely populated areas. Frequently, these areas had to be passed through by those on their way to the suburbs, and rail lines and freeways sometimes bisected these urban communities.

In the modern age, advancements in telecommunications infrastructure may have an impact on urban growth patterns as information can pass instantly and freely between almost any two points on the globe, allowing access to some aspects of urban life to those in remote areas.

Skill 13.5   **Examine the role of demographic processes in U.S. society and the impact of migration on individuals, groups, and the nation**

A **population** is a group of people living within a certain geographic area. Populations are usually measured on a regular basis by census, which also measures age, economic, ethnic and other data. Populations change over time due to many factors, and these changes can have significant impact on cultures.

When a population grows in size, it becomes necessary for it to either expand its geographic boundaries to make room for new people or to increase its density. Population density is simply the number of people in a population divided by the geographic area in which they live. Cultures with a high population density are likely to have different ways of interacting with one another than those with low density, as people live in closer to proximity to one another.

As a population grows, its economic needs change. More basic needs are required, and more workers are needed to produce them. If a population's production or purchasing power does not keep pace with its growth, its economy can be adversely affected. The age distribution of a population can impact the economy as well, if the number of young and old people who are not working is disproportionate to those who are.

Growth in some areas may spur migration to other parts of a population's geographic region that are less densely populated. This redistribution of population also places demands on the economy, as infrastructure is needed to connect these new areas to older population centers, and land is put to new use.

Populations can grow naturally, when the rate of birth is higher than the rate of death, or by adding new people from other populations through **immigration**. Immigration is often a source of societal change as people from other cultures bring their institutions and language to a new area. Immigration also impacts a population's educational and economic institutions as immigrants enter the workforce and place their children in schools.

Populations can also decline in number, when the death rate exceeds the birth rate or when people migrate to another area. War, famine, disease and natural disasters can also dramatically reduce a population. The economic problems from population decline can be similar to those from over population because economic demands may be higher than can be met. In extreme cases, a population may decline to the point where it can no longer perpetuate itself and its members and their culture either disappear or are absorbed into another population.

Demography is the branch of science of statistics most concerned with the social well being of people. **Demographic tables** may include: (1) analysis of the population on the basis of age, parentage, physical condition, race, occupation and civil position, giving the actual size and the density of each separate area; (2) changes in the population as a result of birth, marriage, and death; (3) statistics on population movements and their effects and their relations to given economic, social and political conditions; (4) statistics of crime, illegitimacy and suicide; and (5) levels of education and economic and social statistics.

Such information is also similar to that area of science known as **vital statistics** and as such is indispensable in studying social trends and making important legislative, economic, and social decisions. Such demographic information is gathered from census, and registrar reports and the like, and by state laws such information, especially the vital kind, is kept by physicians, attorneys, funeral directors, members of the clergy, and similar professional people. In the United States, such demographic information is compiled, kept and published by the Public Health Service of the United States Department of Health, Education, and Welfare.

The most important element of this information is the so-called **rate**, which customarily represents the average of births and deaths for a unit of 1000 population over a given calendar year. These general rates are called **crude rates**, which are then subdivided into *sex, color, age, occupation, locality, etc.* They are then known as **refined rates**.

In examining **statistics** and the sources of statistical data one must also be aware of the methods of statistical information gathering. For instance, there are many good sources of raw statistical data. Books such as *The Statistical Abstract of the United States,* published by the United States Chamber of Commerce, *The World Fact Book,* published by the Central Intelligence Agency, or *The Monthly Labor Review* published by the United States Department of Labor are excellent examples that contain much raw data. Many such yearbooks and the like on various topics are readily available from any library, or from the government itself. However, knowing how that data and information was gathered is at least as important as the figures themselves. Only by having knowledge of statistical language and methodology can one really gauge the usefulness of any given piece of data presented. Thus, we must first understand just what statistics are and what they can and cannot tell us. Simply put, statistics is the mathematical science that deals with the collection, organization, presentation, and analysis of various forms of numerical data and with the problems such as interpreting and understanding such data. The raw materials of statistics are sets of numbers obtained from enumerations or measurements collected by various methods of extrapolation, such as census taking, interviews, and observations.

In collecting any such statistical information and data, care and adequate precautions must always be taken in order to ensure that the knowledge obtained is complete and accurate. It is also important to be aware of just how much data is necessary to collect in order to establish the idea that is to be formulated. One important idea to understand is that statistics usually deal with a specific **model**, **hypothesis**, or **theory** that is to be proven—though one should be aware that a theory can never actually be proved correct, it can only really be corroborated. (**Corroboration** means that the data presented is more consistent with this theory than with any other theory, so it makes sense to use this theory.) One should also be aware that **correlation** (the joint movement of various data points) does not infer **causation** (the change in one of those data points caused the other data points to change). It is important that one take these aspects into account so that one can be in a better position to appreciate what the collected data is really saying.

Once collected, data must then be arranged, tabulated, and presented to permit ready and meaningful analysis and interpretation. Often, tables, charts or graphs will be used to present the information in a concise easy-to-see manner, with the information sometimes presented in raw numerical order as well. **Tests of reliability** are used, bearing in mind the manner in which the data has been collected and the inherent biases of any artificially created model to be used to explain real world events. Indeed, the methods used and the inherent biases and actual reasons for doing the study must never be discounted.

Skill 13.6   Analyze cross-cultural exchanges and the efforts of various groups to maintain their individual cultural identities

Cultural identity is the identification of individuals or groups as they are influenced by their belonging to a particular group or culture. This refers to the sense of who one is, what values are important, and what racial or ethnic characteristics are important in one's self-understanding and manner of interacting with the world and with others. In a nation with a well-deserved reputation as a "melting pot," the attachment to cultural identities can become a divisive factor in communities and societies. Cosmopolitanism, its alternative, tends to blur those cultural differences in the creation of a shared new culture.

Throughout the history of the nation, groups have defined themselves and/or assimilated into the larger population to varying degrees. In order for a society to function as a cohesive and unifying force, there must be some degree of enculturation of all groups. The alternative is a competing, and often conflicting, collection of subgroups that are not able to cohere into a society. This failure to assimilate will often result in culture wars as values and lifestyles come into conflict.

Cross-cultural exchanges, however, can enrich every involved group of persons with the discovery of shared values and needs, as well as an appreciation for unique cultural characteristics of each. For the most part, the history of the nation has been the story of successful enculturation and cultural enrichment. The notable failures, often resulting from one sort of prejudice and intolerance or another, are well known. For example, cultural biases have led to the oppression of the Irish or the Chinese immigrants in various parts of the country. Racial biases have led to various kinds of disenfranchisement and oppression of other groups of immigrants. Perhaps most notably, the bias of the European settlers against the civilization and culture of the Native peoples of North America has caused mass extermination, relocation, and isolation.

Skill 13.7 Evaluate relationships between human activity and the natural environment and analyze how technological change has affected human communities and natural systems in New York State and the United States

Since the dawn of agriculture, humans have modified their environment to suit their needs and to provide food and shelter. These changes always affect the environment, sometimes adversely, from a human perspective.

Agriculture, for instance, often involves loosening topsoil by plowing before planting. This in turn affects how water and wind act on the soil, and can lead to erosion. In extreme cases, erosion can leave a plot of agricultural land unsuitable for use. Technological advances have led to a modern method of farming that relies less on plowing the soil before planting, but more on chemical fertilizers, pesticides and herbicides. These chemicals can find their way into groundwater, affecting the environment.

Cities are large examples of how technological change has allowed humans to modify their environment to suit their needs. At the end of the 18th century, advances made in England in the construction of canals were brought to New York and an ambitious project to connect Lake Erie with the Hudson River by canal was planned. The Erie Canal was built through miles of virgin wilderness, opening natural areas to settlement and commerce. Towns along the canal grew and thrived, including Buffalo, Rochester and Albany. The canal also opened westward expansion beyond the borders of New York by opening a route between the Midwest and the East Coast.

Further advances in transportation and building methods allow for larger and denser communities, which themselves affect the environment in many ways. Concentrated consumption of fuels by automobiles and home-heating systems affect the quality of the air in and around cities. The lack of exposed ground means that rainwater runs off of roads and rooftops into sewer systems instead of seeping into the ground, and often makes its way into nearby streams or rivers, carrying urban debris with it.

New York City, the nation's largest city, has had considerable impact on its island environment and is making extensive use of new technology to reduce its energy use. New York City has the world's largest mass transit system, for instance, including hybrid buses that reduce emissions. New "clean" methods of energy production are being explored, such as underwater turbines that are run by tidal forces, and wind power. Cities like New York also have an impact on the surrounding areas that supply resources such as water. A large portion of the Catskill Mountains in New York is restricted from development because the watershed supplies water to New York City.

Ecology is the study of how living organisms interact with the physical aspects of their surroundings (their environment), including soil, water, air, and other living things. **Biogeography** is the study of how the surface features of the earth – form, movement, and climate – affect living things.

Three levels of environmental understanding are critical:

1. An **ecosystem** is a community (of any size) consisting of a physical environment and the organisms that live within it.

2. A **biome** is a large area of land with characteristic climate, soil, and mixture of plants and animals. Biomes are made up of groups of ecosystems. Major biomes are: desert, chaparral, savanna, tropical rainforest, temperate grassland, temperate deciduous forest, taiga, and tundra.

3. A **habitat** is the set of surroundings within which members of a species normally live. Elements of the habitat include soil, water, predators, and competitors.

Within habitats, interactions between members of the species occur. These interactions occur between members of the same species and between members of different species. Interaction tends to be of three types:

1. **Competition**. Competition occurs between members of the same species or between members of different species for resources required to continue life, to grow, or to reproduce. For example, competition for acorns can occur between squirrels or it can occur between squirrels and woodpeckers. One species can either push out or cause the demise of another species if it is better adapted to obtain the resource. When a new species is introduced into a habitat, the result can be a loss of the native species and/or significant change to the habitat. For example, the introduction of the Asian plant Kudzu into the American South has resulted in the destruction of several species because Kudzu grows and spreads very quickly and smothers everything in its path.

2. **Predation**. Predators are organisms that live by hunting and eating other organisms. The species best suited for hunting other species in the habitat will be the species that survives. Larger species that have better hunting skills reduce the amount of prey available for smaller and/or weaker species. This affects both the amount of available prey and the diversity of species that are able to survive in the habitat.

3. **Symbiosis** is a condition in which two organisms of different species are able to live in the same environment over an extended period of time without harming one another. In some cases one species may benefit without harming the other. In other cases both species benefit.

Different organisms are by nature best suited for existence in particular environments. When an organism is displaced to a different environment or when the environment changes for some reason, its ability to survive is determined by its ability to *adapt* to the new environment. Adaptation can take the form of structural change, physiological change, or behavioral modification.

Biodiversity refers to the variety of species and organisms, as well as the variety of habitats available on the earth. Biodiversity provides the life-support system for the various habitats and species. The greater the degree of biodiversity, the more species and habitats will continue to survive.

When human and other population and migration changes, climate changes, or natural disasters disrupt the delicate balance of a habitat or an ecosystem, species either adapt or become extinct.

Natural changes can occur that alter habitats – floods, volcanoes, storms, earthquakes. These changes can affect the species that exist within the habitat, either by causing extinction or by changing the environment in a way that will no longer support the life systems. Climate changes can have similar effects. Inhabiting species, however, can also alter habitats, particularly through migration. Human civilization, population growth, and efforts to control the environment can have many negative effects on various habitats. Humans change their environments to suit their particular needs and interests. This can result in changes that result in the extinction of species or changes to the habitat itself. For example, deforestation damages the stability of mountain surfaces. One particularly devastating example is in the removal of the grasses of the Great Plains for agriculture. Tilling the ground and planting crops left the soil unprotected. Sustained drought dried out the soil into dust. When windstorms occurred, the topsoil was stripped away and blown all the way to the Atlantic Ocean.

DOMAIN III.   ECONOMICS

COMPETENCY 14   UNDERSTAND IMPORTANT ECONOMIC CONCEPTS,
                 TERMS, AND THEORIES, AND APPLY THAT
                 KNOWLEDGE TO ANALYZE BASIC ECONOMIC
                 PHENOMENA

Skill 14.1   Recognize basic economic questions and apply fundamental
              economic concepts to analyze general economic phenomena
              and specific economic problems

Economics is the study of how a society allocates its scarce **resources** to satisfy
essentially unlimited and competing **wants**. A fundamental fact of economics is
that resources are scarce and wants are infinite. That scarce resources have to
satisfy unlimited wants means that choices have to be made. If society uses its
resources to produce good A, then it doesn't have those resources to produce
good B. More of good A means less of good B. This trade-off is referred to as the
opportunity cost, or the value of the sacrificed alternative.

Economic systems refer to the arrangements a society has devised to answer
what are known as the Three Questions: what goods to produce; how to produce
the goods; and for whom are the goods being produced, or how is the allocation
of the output determined. Different "isms" exist to define the method of resource
and output allocation. A market economy answers these questions in terms of
demand and supply and the use of markets. Demand is based on consumer
preferences and satisfaction, and refers to the quantities of a good or service that
buyers are willing and able to buy at different prices during a given period of time.
Supply is based on costs of production and refers to the quantities that sellers
are willing and able to sell at different prices during a given period of time. The
market equilibrium price is determined where the decisions of buyers coincide
with the decisions of sellers.

Consumers vote for the products they want with their dollar spending. Goods
acquiring enough dollar votes are profitable, signaling to the producers that
society wants their scarce resources used in this way. This is how the "What"
question is answered. The producer then hires inputs in accordance with the
goods consumers want, looking for the most efficient or lowest cost method of
production. The lower the firm's **costs** for any given level of revenue, the higher
the firm's **profits**. This is the way in which the "How" question is answered in a
market economy. The "For Whom" question is answered in the marketplace by
the determination of the equilibrium price. **Price** serves to ration the good to
those that can and will transact at the market price of better. Those who can't or
won't are excluded from the market. This mechanism results in market efficiency
or obtaining the most output from the available inputs that are consistent with the
preferences of consumers. Society's scarce resources are being used the way
society wants them to be used.

Skill 14.2   Compare the different perspectives of macro and microeconomics

Microeconomics studies the behavior and decision-making of individual economic units, like consumers and firms. Macroeconomics is a study of the national economy or the aggregate units that comprise the economy. In microeconomics, the firm's cost structure is studied and then put together with the firm's revenue structure to determine the kind of market the firm functions in: **perfect competition, monopoly, oligopoly** or **monopolistic competition**. Each of these market structures has the same cost structures with the differences being determined on the demand side of the market.

There are four kinds of market structures in the output market: perfect competition, monopoly, monopolistic competition and oligopoly. For the most part, perfect competition is a theoretical extreme, most closely approximated by agriculture. The numerous firms sell a product identical to that sold by all other firms in the industry and have no control over the price. The price is a given to the firm. Buyers and sellers have full market information and there are no barriers to entry. A **barrier to entry** is anything that makes it difficult for firms to enter or leave the industry. The opposite of a perfectly competitive firm is a monopolist. Monopoly is a market structure in which there is only one seller who can control his price. The firm is equal to the industry. A monopolist becomes a monopolist and remains a monopolist because of barriers to entry, which are very high. These barriers to entry, like a very high fixed cost structure, function to keep new firms from entering the industry. Monopoly is illegal in the U.S. economy. In between the two extremes are the two market structures that all U.S. firms fall into. Oligopoly is a market structure in which there are a few sellers of products that may be either homogeneous, like steel, or heterogeneous, like automobiles. There are high barriers to entry, which is why there are only a few firms in each industry. Monopolistic competition is the situation you see in shopping centers. There are numerous firms, each selling products that are similar, but not identical, like brand name shoes or clothing. Barriers to entry are not as high as in oligopoly, which is why there are more firms.

From a macro view, the firm is a part of the business sector and contributes to **Gross Domestic Product** through the investment component. The GDP is equal to the consumption expenditures of consumers plus the investment expenditures of businesses plus spending of all three levels of government plus the net export spending in the foreign sector.

$$GDP = C + I + G + (X-M)$$

The firm is not distinguished as an individual entity but is a part of the aggregate.

Skill 14.3   Recognize the economic theories of Adam Smith, Thomas Malthus, and David Ricardo, and analyze the characteristics of laissez-faire economics

Laissez-faire economics or pure capitalism is based on free markets without government interference in the marketplace. The role for government was to establish the framework for the functioning of the economy, determining things like standards of weights and measures, providing public goods, etc. **Adam Smith**, author of *The Wealth of Nations*, believed that free markets should exist without government interference because any interference interfered with the rights and liberties of the market participants even though laissez-faire economics results in an unequal distribution of income. The economy, if left alone, would function as if an invisible hand guided it to an efficient allocation of resources.

Parson Malthus was an economist whose theories led to economics being called the dismal science. His theory can best be summed as saying that the population growth would exceed the growth of the food supply. This would result in the lower classes experiencing increasing poverty.

David Ricardo is the classical economist who developed the theory of economic rent and the theory of comparative advantage. These are his two biggest contributions. His theory of economic rent is based on the fact that land is fixed in supply. As such, its supply curve is perfectly inelastic and the price of land then is determined solely by the demand. Ricardo's theory of comparative advantage is the basis for international trade theory which states that nations should specialize in the production of the good which they can produce at a relatively lower opportunity cost that their trading partner can. They should use all of their resources to produce the good in which they have the comparative advantage and then trade for goods in which other nations have a comparative advantage. Trade based on comparative advantage results in greater levels of output, income and employment for all trading partners. All nations benefit from free trade.

Skill 14.4   Examine economic practices from the perspective of differing economic theories

Demand-side economics is the traditional macroeconomic approach to the economy and is based on Keynesian economics. This school of thought explains the levels of output, income and employment in terms of the level of aggregate spending in the economy. A recession occurs when there is a deficiency in aggregate spending. There is not sufficient demand in the economy to cause the labor force to be employed. The government needs to stimulate the economy by monetary and/or fiscal policy to stimulate a higher level of spending. This will cause a rightward shift of the aggregate demand curve. The increase in demand will cause suppliers to hire more workers to produce the additional output they are producing. Keynes believed that only fiscal policy was effective. Inflation was caused by the opposite situation. There is excess aggregate demand in the economy. Since producers can't produce any more output (assumption of full employment), the only effect is inflation. Here, the role for government is to slow down an economy that is expanding too quickly. The way to do this is to use contractionary monetary and/or fiscal policy. In the Keynesian model, unemployment and inflation are mutually exclusive; they can't both occur at the same time.

Supply side economics came into being in the 1980s to address the issue of **stagflation**. This was a situation where the economy experienced rising inflation and unemployment, something that the demand side model couldn't explain or solve. The economy's problems were caused by a shifting aggregate supply curve, not the aggregate demand curve. Therefore the solution was to implement policies aimed at causing an increase in aggregate supply. These policies became known as supply side economics. They included tax incentives to induce people to work, programs aimed at improving the quality of the labor force, deregulation and improvement of the infrastructure. These were the policies of the Reagan administration.

Skill 14.5   Apply fundamental concepts of international economics to specific economic situations

The theory of comparative advantage says that trade should be based on the comparative opportunity costs between two nations. The nation that can produce a good more cheaply should specialize in the production of that good and trade for the good in which it has the comparative disadvantage. In this way both nations will experience gains from trade. A basis for trade exists if there are differing comparative costs in each country. Suppose country A can produce 10 units of good X or 10 units of good Y with its resources. Country B can produce 30 units of X or 10 units of Y with its resources. What are the relative costs in each country? In country A, one X costs one unit of Y and in country B one X costs three units of Y. Good Y is cheaper in country B than it is in country A, 1/3X = 1 Y in country B versus 1Y = 1X in country A. Country B has the comparative advantage in the production of Y and country A has the comparative advantage in the production of good X. According to trade theory, each country should specialize in the production of the good in which it has the comparative advantage. Country B will devote all of its resources to the production of good Y and country A will devote its resources to the production of good X. Each country will trade for the good in which it has the comparative disadvantage.

When nations engage in trade, the traded items have to be paid for. This involves **exchange rate** and international currency markets. Today, the exchange rates for most currencies float. This means the exchange rate is determined by supply and demand, just like the price of any good. Governments are not required to intervene in the market, as they were when exchange rates were fixed. Under the Bretton Woods system, the U.S. dollar was quoted in terms of gold and all other major currencies were quoted in terms of the dollar. This meant that nations were required to buy and sell currencies to maintain the par value of their currency.

Situations of disequilibrium resulted from imbalances in the nation's Balance of Payments, which was an accounting statement of all of a nation's inflows and outflows. If a nation's inflows did not equal its outflows, its currency would come under pressure. A surplus in the Balance of Payments put upward pressure on the currency and the country would have to sell its currency against the dollar to increase the supply and take the upward pressure off of the exchange rate. If there was a deficit in the Balance of Payment, there would be downward pressure on the exchange rate and the nation would have to buy its currency against the dollar.

The continued Payments imbalances resulted in one crisis after another in the world currency markets until the Bretton Woods system was ended. Currencies have been floating since 1973. This means they adjust to trade imbalances with their values appreciating or depreciating automatically without any form of intervention. There have been no crises in the currency markets since currencies have been floating.

COMPETENCY 15   UNDERSTAND ECONOMIC SYSTEMS

Skill 15.1   Identify the characteristics of traditional, command, market, and mixed economies

The **traditional economy** is one based on custom and usually exists in less developed countries. The people do things the way their ancestors did so they are not too technologically advanced. Technology and equipment are viewed as a threat to the old way of doing things and to their tradition. There is very little upward mobility for the same reason. The model of capitalism is based on private ownership of the means of production and operates on the basis of free markets, on both the input and output side. The free markets function to coordinate market activity and to achieve an efficient allocation of resources. **Laissez-faire capitalism** is based on the premise of no government intervention in the economy. The **market** will eliminate any unemployment or inflation that occurs. Government needs only to provide the framework for the functioning of the economy and to protect private property. A **command economy** is almost the exact opposite of a market economy. A command economy is based on government ownership of the means of production and the use of planning to take the place of the market. Instead of the market determining the output mix and the allocation of resources, the bureaucracy fulfills this role by determining the output mix and establishing production target for the enterprises, which are publicly owned. The result is inefficiency. A **mixed economy** uses a combination of markets and planning, with the degree of each varying according to country. The real world can be described as mixed economies.

Skill 15.2   Analyze how different types of economic systems address basic questions concerning resource allocation, production, distribution, and consumption

Economic systems refer to the arrangements a society has devised to answer what are known as the Three Questions: What goods to produce, How to produce the goods, and For Whom are the goods being produced, or how is the allocation of the output determined. Different economic systems answer these questions in different ways. These are the different "isms" that exist that define the method of resource and output allocation.

A market economy answers these questions in terms of demand and supply and the use of markets. Consumers vote for the products they want with their dollar spending. Goods acquiring enough dollar votes are profitable, signaling to the producers that society wants their scarce resources used in this way. This is how the "What" question is answered. The producer then hires inputs in accordance with the goods consumers want, looking for the most efficient or lowest cost method of production. The lower the firm's costs for any given level of revenue, the higher the firm's profits. This is the way in which the "How" question is answered in a market economy. The "For Whom" question is answered in the marketplace by the determination of the equilibrium price. Price serves to ration the good to those that can and will transact at the market price of better. Those who can't or won't are excluded from the market. The United States has a market economy.

The opposite of the market economy is called the centrally planned economy. This used to be called Communism, even though the term in not correct in a strict Marxian sense. In a planned economy, the means of production are publicly owned with little, if any public ownership. Instead of the Three Questions being solved by markets, they have a planning authority that makes the decisions in place of markets. The planning authority decides what will be produced and how. Since most planned economies directed resources into the production of capital and military goods, there was little remaining for consumer goods and the result was chronic shortages. Price functioned as an accounting measure and did not reflect scarcity. The former Soviet Union and most of the Eastern Bloc countries were planned economies of this sort.

In between the two extremes is market socialism. This is a mixed economic system that uses both markets and planning. Planning is usually used to direct resources at the upper levels of the economy, with markets being used to determine prices of consumer goods and wages. This kind of economic system answers the three questions with planning and markets. The former Yugoslavia was a market socialist economy.

You can put each nation of the world on a continuum in terms of these characteristics and rank them from most capitalistic to the most planned. The United States would probably rank as the most capitalistic and North Korea would probably rank as the most planned, but this doesn't mean that the United States doesn't engage in planning or that economies like mainland China don't use markets.

Skill 15.3   Apply procedures used in measuring and compare national production and standards of living for various types of contemporary economic systems

Macroeconomics is concerned with a study of the economy's overall economic performance, or what is called the Gross Domestic Product or GDP. The GDP is a monetary measure of the economy's output during a specified time period and is used by all nations to measure and compare national production. Tabulating the economy's output can be measured in two ways, both of which give the same result: the expenditures approach and the incomes approach. Basically, what is spent on the national output by each sector of the economy is equal to what is earned producing the national output by each of the factors of production. The two methods have to be equal.

The macro economy consists of four broad sectors: **consumers, businesses, government** and the **foreign sector**. In the expenditures approach, GDP is determined by the amount of spending in each sector. GDP is equal to the consumption expenditures of consumers plus the investment expenditures of businesses plus spending of all three levels of government plus the net export spending in the foreign sector.

$$GDP = C + I + G + (X-M)$$

The above formula is called the GDP identity. The computation of GDP includes only final goods and services, not the value of intermediate goods. An intermediate good is a good that is used in the production of other goods. It is an input and its value is included in the price of the final good. If the value of intermediate goods is included, there would be double counting and GDP would be overstated.

Assessing and comparing standards of living between nations is not easy. GDP itself is not an indicator of living conditions. If a nation's GDP figure is divided by its population to obtain per capita GDP, this can function somewhat as a basis for comparison between countries. But it doesn't provide information about work-leisure time or if the composition of output is right for the particular society.

Skill 15.4   Analyze ways in which different types of economic systems influence social structure

The social structure of a society is definitely affected by the type of economic system. A traditional economy where they do things the way they always have, based on tradition is not receptive to change. The social structure is the same as it was generations ago. Incentives are there to improve or get ahead because of tradition. They don't have much of a tax base to raise revenues and implement social welfare programs. A planned economy with government ownership of the means of production was supposed to be a classless society, but the upper levels of government and the military were a notch above the population. Individual and entrepreneurial incentives were lacking since there was no private ownership of business or possibility of profit. In a mixed economy and in a market economy, the individual is allowed the financial rewards for his entrepreneurial ventures. More people are willing to take the risk for the chance of succeeding. Therefore, the resulting social structure is a spectrum from very poor to very rich.

Skill 15.5   Recognize and compare various strategies of economic growth and development

There is more than one strategy of economic growth and development and the strategy that a country selects must be consistent with its situation. The strategy chosen by the United States may not be well suited for less developed countries (LDC). Most of the developing countries are producers of agricultural products. Many of these countries need agricultural growth in order to feed their own population. For many this requires investment in equipment and machinery that they can't afford. In some cases, they need land reform so people have workable plots of land. Hand in hand with the problem of agricultural growth is the problem of population growth. Many LDCs have large populations and a labor force that suffers from unemployment or underemployment. They need some method of controlling the growth of the population and giving the labor force the necessary training it requires. An increase in a resource, like labor, should be a factor contributing to economic growth, but that labor force must be productive and employed.

One method of growth is through commodity. Most LDCs are producers of primary products like minerals and ore and other natural resources. Many developed countries are dependent on the LDCs for these commodities. LDCs complain of price instability in the markets for these products. When a nation's economy is dependent on two or three primary commodities, any change in demand or supply results in big changes in the economies of the producers. This is why they have developed buffer stocks as a form of price stabilization to try to insulate the economies from market instability. The oil producing countries went a step further and formed a **cartel**. Cartelization is a form of collusion. It is when all of the producers act together and function as a monopolist.

The purpose of the cartel is to raise price by restricting supply. This only works if all of the members adhere to the production controls. The big problem with cartels is cheating. This occurs when one or more cartel member doesn't follow the production controls. In spite of this, OPEC has been a very successful cartel.

Import substitution and export development are two other growth strategies. Import substitution is a strategy of protecting the domestic industry with trade barriers so the population buys the domestically produced product. Sheltering the domestic industry allows it to grow to a point where it will hopefully be competitive in world markets. It also leads to higher employment levels in the domestic country. The problem is they may be sheltering an industry that will never be competitive, especially if the industry isn't consistent with the resource base and technology of the domestic country. They will require imports of those products. Export development is closer to the principle of comparative advantage. The country exports the goods that its resources are suited for and imports those goods that its resources are not suited for. Export development as a growth strategy has been more successful than import substitution.

Skill 15.6 Analyze the interdependence of economic systems and the role of multinational corporations in the global economy

In today's world, markets are international. Nations are all part of a global economy. No nation exists in isolationism or is totally independent of other nations. **Isolationism** is referred to as autarky or a closed economy. No one nation has all of the resources needed to be totally self-sufficient in everything it produces and consumes. Even a nation with such a well diversified resource base like the United States has to import items like coffee, tea and other items. The United States is not as dependent on trade as are other nations but we still need to trade for goods and items that we either can't produce domestically or that we can't produce as cheaply as other nations can.

Membership in a **global economy** means that what one nation does affects other nations because economies are linked through international trade, commerce and finance. They all have open economies and they are all interdependent. International transactions affect the levels of income, employment and prices in each of the trading economies. The relative importance of trade is based on what percentage of Gross Domestic Product trade constitutes. In a country like the United States, trade represents only a few percent points of GDP. In other nations, trade may represent over 50 percent of GDP. For those countries, changes in international transactions can cause many economic fluctuations and problems.

Trade barriers are a way in which economic problems are caused in other countries. Suppose the domestic government is confronted with rising unemployment in the domestic industry due to cheaper foreign imports. Consumers are buying the cheaper foreign import instead of the higher priced domestic good. In order to protect domestic labor, government imposes a **tariff**, thus raising the price of the more efficiently produced foreign good. The result of the tariff is that consumers buy more of the domestic good and less of the foreign good. The problem is that the foreign good is the product of the foreign nation's labor. A decrease in the demand for the foreign good means foreign producers don't need as much labor, so they lay-off workers in the foreign country. The result of the trade barrier is that unemployment has been exported from the domestic country to the foreign country. What one nation does affects other nations.

The exact same thing can happen through the exchange rate and other capital markets. Capital goes where it receives the highest rate of return, regardless of national borders. Nations can affect their exchange rate values by buying and selling foreign exchange in the currency markets. Suppose the United States decides that a lower-valued dollar will stimulate its exports leading to higher employment levels in the United States. The United States, in effect, sells dollars on the open market, thus increasing the supply of dollars on the world market. The effect is a depreciation of the dollar. The lower-valued dollar makes U.S. exports more attractive to foreigners who buy the relatively cheaper U.S. exports instead of the now relatively higher priced domestic goods. The increased demand for U.S. exports leads to higher employment levels in the export industries in the U.S. The lower demand for domestic products in the foreign country leads to unemployment in their domestic industries. Again, what one nation does affects other nations.

The existence of multinational corporations means that plants also go where the lowest cost deal is because it leads to higher levels of profits for them. Membership in a global economy adds another dimension to economics, in terms of aiding developing countries and in terms of national policies that are implemented.

COMPETENCY 16   UNDERSTAND THE COMPONENTS, STRUCTURE, ORGANIZATION, AND OPERATION OF THE U.S. ECONOMY

Skill 16.1   Recognize basic values and principles of the U.S. economic system

Free enterprise, individual entrepreneurship, competitive markets and consumer sovereignty are all parts of a **market economy**. Individuals have the right to make their own decisions as to what they want to do as a career. The financial incentives are there for individuals who are willing to take the risk. A successful venture earns profit. It is these financial incentives that serve to motivate inventors and small businesses. The same is true for businesses. They are free to determine what production technique they want to use and what output they want to produce within the confines of the legal system. They can make investments based on their own decisions. Nobody is telling them what to do. Competitive markets, relatively free from government interference are also a manifestation of the freedom that the U.S. economic system is based on. These markets function on the basis of supply and demand to determine output mix and resource allocation. There is no commissar dictating what is produced and how. Since consumers buy the goods and services that give them satisfaction, this means that, for the most part, they don't buy the goods and services that they don't want that don't give them satisfaction. **Consumers** are, in effect, voting for the goods and services that they want with the dollars or what is called dollar voting. Consumers are basically signaling firms as to how they want society's scarce resources used with their dollar votes. A good that society wants acquires enough dollar votes for the producer to experience profits – a situation where the firm's revenues exceed the firm's costs. The existence of profits indicate to the firm that it is producing the goods and services that consumers want and that society's scarce resources are being used in accordance with consumer preferences. When a firm does not have a profitable product, it is because that product is not tabulating enough dollar votes of consumers. Consumers don't want the good or service and they don't want society's scarce resources being used in its production.

This process where consumers vote with their dollars is called **consumer sovereignty**. Consumers are basically directing the allocation of scarce resources in the economy with the dollar spending. Firms, who are in business to earn profit, then hire resources, or inputs, in accordance with consumer preferences. This is the way in which resources are allocated in a market economy. This is the manner in which society achieves the output mix that it desires.

Skill 16.2   Analyze relationships among profit, capital, and competition in the U.S. economic system

Profit, capital and competition all go together in the U.S. economic system. Competition is determined by market structure. Since the cost curves are the same for all the firms, the only difference comes from the revenue side. The most competitive of all market structures is perfect competition, characterized by numerous buyers and sellers, all with perfect knowledge. No one seller is big enough to influence price so the firm is a price taker. Products are homogenous so buyers are indifferent as to whom they buy from.

The absence of barriers to entry makes it easy for firms to enter and leave the industry. At the other end of the spectrum is monopoly, the only seller of a unique product. Barriers to entry are significant enough to keep firms from entering or leaving the industry. In monopolistic competition firms sell similar products in an industry with low barriers to entry, making it easy for firms to enter and leave the industry. Oligopoly is a market structure with a few large firms selling heterogeneous or homogeneous product in a market structure with the strength of barriers to entry varying. Each firm maximizes profit by producing at the point where marginal cost equals marginal revenue.

The existence of economic profits, an above normal rate of return, attracts capital to an industry and results in expansion. Whether or not new firms can enter depends on barriers to entry. Firms can enter easily in perfect competition and the expansion will continue until economic profits are eliminated and firms earn a normal rate of return. The significant barriers to entry in monopoly serve to keep firms out so the monopolist continues to earn an above normal rate of return. Some firms will be able to enter in monopolistic competition but won't have a monopoly over the existing firm's brand name. The competitiveness of the market structure determines whether new firms or capital can enter in response to profits.

Skill 16.3   Identify the functions of, and evaluate relationships among, basic components of the U.S. economic system

Households, businesses and government are related through the circular flow diagram. There are two markets. The **input market** is where factor owners sell their factors and employers hire their inputs. The **output market** is where firms sell the output they produce with their inputs It's where factors owners spend their incomes on goods and services. There are two sectors, households and businesses. **Households** sell their factors in the input market and use their income to purchase goods and services in the output market. So wages, interest, rent and profit flow from the business sectors to the household sector. Households that earn their factor incomes in the factor market spend their incomes on goods and services produced by businesses and sold in the output market. Receipts for goods and services flow from households to businesses.

Government receives tax payments from households and businesses and provides services to businesses and households. Each of the three is a component of the aggregate sectors of the economy and as such makes a contribution to the GDP.

Skill 16.4   Examine the impact of organized labor on the U.S. economy

Labor unions in America arose when employees who had no say concerning deplorable working conditions began to join forces to try to change this. Viewed in this perspective, the history of the labor movement can be traced back to the colonial period as workers banded together amongst themselves and with other organizations in support of different goals. The workers that engaged in these activities were subject to actions from dismissal to blacklisting. It wasn't until 1881 that the first permanent union structure was founded on the principles of Samuel Gompers. This became known as the **American Federation of Labor** and was based on three principles.

The first principle is practical business unionism, which is the belief that unions should only concern themselves with the problems of their members: working conditions, hours, wages, job security, etc. The second principle is political neutrality. Unions should stay out of politics, and the government should stay out of the union movement and the collective bargaining process. The third principle is trade autonomy, the belief that unions should be organized on the basis of trade. There should be one union for each craft or trade; there should not be unions consisting of members from all trades. The AFL organized only craft or trade workers, and not industrial workers. The large pool of industrial workers was eventually organized by the Congress of Industrial Organization, and in 1955 the two merged to become the AFL-CIO.

The unions have various methods they can use to obtain benefits for their members. They have supported the enactment of various kinds of labor law legislation that eventually regulated both sides of the labor market, union and employer from various unfair labor and union practices, like yellow-dog contracts, boycotts, featherbedding, and hot cargo clauses. They have also supported legislation that resulted in minimum wage and unemployment insurance. Supporting and opposing legislation isn't the only way of obtaining benefits for members. The most direct way of obtaining benefits is through the collective bargaining process.

Collective bargaining refers to the negotiating of a labor agreement or the settling of a grievance under an existing contract. When the union and the employee can't come to terms, there is always the weapon of the **strike**. During a strike, the union members withhold their labor services in order to put financial pressure on the employer. The employer can respond with a **lockout**, which puts pressure on the union and the workers. Eventually an agreement is reached, with or without a strike or lockout.

Unions have benefited their members tremendously over the years in terms of gaining wage and benefit concessions from employers. The existence of organized labor has benefited non-union labor by raising the level of wages and benefits since non-union firms had to raise wages to keep their employees.

Skill 16.5   Analyze factors affecting the formulation of U.S. economic policy and apply this knowledge to the analysis of specific economic issues and problems

U.S. economic policy is based on promoting full employment and stable prices in the economy. The economy needs a stable environment in which to function. With this end in mind, monetary policy and/or fiscal policy is used to fine-tune the economy and to steer it toward its goals. Contractionary monetary and/or fiscal policies are used to slow an economy that is expanding too quickly. Expansionary monetary and/or fiscal policies are used to stimulate a sluggish economy to eliminate unemployment. The Fed has been raising interest rates until just recently to keep the economy from entering periods of inflation. Hurricane Katrina and the Iraqi War contributed to rising energy prices which had a rippling effect through the economy. The latest figures released showed an increase in unemployment and a slow down in the growth of GDP. This indicates that growth is slowing down and that the economy might be entering a period of recession. The Iraq War, the rise in oil prices, the situation in Lebanon are all factors that influence the U.S. economy. Did the Fed raise interest rates too much trying to fend off inflation and caused a recession? Only time will tell. If the unemployment and growth figures continue to rise, the Fed may have to lower interest rates to stimulate the economy. However, this will only work for a demand-side problem.

Skill 16.6   Evaluate economic mobility and inequality with the U.S. economic system

Economic mobility and inequality exist within the U.S. economic system. **Economic mobility** refers to the ability of factors, particularly labor, to move around the country in response to employment opportunities. The U.S. economy is so big that there can be unemployment in one part of the country while there are labor shortages in other parts of the country. In many cases, there are institutional rigidities, like lack of information, that prevent workers from migrating in response to employment opportunities. State job services exist to provide information about available job opportunities, even though many workers are reluctant to migrate due to family situations.

Inequality exists within the U.S. economic system. An unequal distribution of income is a part of market economies. Wages are based on contributions which are partly dependent on education and training. The more highly specialized the labor skill provided, the higher the income. So no matter what kind of policies there are, there will also be an unequal distribution of income.

DOMAIN IV.   CIVICS, CITIZENSHIP, AND GOVERNMENT

COMPETENCY 17   UNDERSTAND IMPORTANT POLITICAL SCIENCE
CONCEPTS, TERMS AND THEORIES, AND APPLY
THAT KNOWLEDGE TO ANALYZE CONTEMPORARY
POLITICAL ISSUES

Skill 17.1   Analyze the origins and the purposes of government and the
impact of government and human activity at the local, state,
national and international levels

Government ultimately began as a form of protection. A strong person, usually
one of the best warriors or someone who had the support of many strong men,
assumed command of a people or a city or a land. The power to rule those
people rested in his hands. (The vast majority of rulers throughout history have
been male.) Laws existed insofar as the pronouncements and decision of the
ruler and were not, in practice, written down, leading to inconsistency. Religious
leaders had a strong hand in governing the lives of people, and in many
instances the political leader was also the primary religious figure.

First in Greece and then in Rome and then in other places throughout the world,
the idea of government by more than one person or more than just a handful
came to the fore. Even though more people were involved, the purpose of
government hadn't changed. These governments still existed to keep the peace
and protect their people from encroachments by both inside and outside forces.

Through the Middle Ages and on into even the 20th century, many countries still
had **monarchs** as their heads of state. These monarchs made laws (or, later,
upheld laws), but the laws were still designed to protect the welfare of the
people—and the state.

In the modern day, people are subject to **laws** made by many levels of
government. Local governments such as city and county bodies are allowed to
pass ordinances covering certain local matters, such as property taxation, school
districting, civil infractions and business licensing. These local bodies have
perhaps the least political power in the governmental hierarchy, but being small
and relatively accessible, they are often the level at which many citizens become
directly involved with government. Funding for local governments often comes
from property and sales taxes.

State governments in the United States are mainly patterned after the federal
government, with an elected legislative body, a judicial system, and a governor
who oversees the executive branch. Like the federal government, state
governments derive their authority from **constitutions**. State legislation applies
to all residents of that state, and local laws must conform. State government
funding is frequently from state income tax and sales taxes.

The national or federal government of the United States derives its power from the US Constitution and has three branches, the legislative, executive and judicial. The federal government exists to make national policy and to legislate matters that affect the residents of all states, and to settle matters between states. National income tax is the primary source for federal funding.

The US Constitution also provides the federal government with the authority to make treaties and enter agreements with foreign countries, creating a body of international law. While there is no authoritative international government, organizations such as the United Nations, the European Union and other smaller groups exist to promote economic and political cooperation between nations.

Skill 17.2   Apply basic concepts of political science to analyze general political phenomena and specific political issues

Political science examines the theory of politics and how it behaves in countries and in international situations. Political science has certain varied aspects, including political history, political philosophy, economics, and international relations. All of these aspects can be used to examine both general and specific political issues today.

For example, a general issue in the United States is the preponderance of the two-party system. American politics is full of political parties, but only the Democrats and Republicans get major funding and large slates of candidates for elections across the country.

- This is due in large part to the political history of the country, which has tended to discourage any other participation. The Reform Party was a major force in America until a few years ago, but it now seems to be fading into irrelevance.
- Political philosophy speaks to this issue in that the ideologies of the Democratic and Republican Parties are generally wide enough to cover the views of most Americans. Extreme left- or right-wing parties have their adherents, but they (the adherents and the parties) are few and far between.
- Economics speaks to this in that it is very difficult for parties other than the two big ones to afford any kind of parity-achieving efforts. The two big parties are so much a dichotomous part of American political thinking that any outside forces face an inherently uphill battle just to get dollars and cents to conduct campaigns.
- In international relations as well, the Democratic and Republican Parties are familiar to leaders of and observers from other countries. Again we see the ideologies of these parties, which encompass a wide range of political beliefs, many of which can be found in the leaders of other countries as well.

A specific issue that can be examined in these terms is capital punishment.

- The political history of the United States includes a long history of capital punishment, by both the federal and state governments. (Theoretically, local governments have no such power.) This tradition was handed down from the European countries that spawned the settlers who eventually became the forerunners of Americans today. The Supreme Court has, from time to time, found elements of capital punishment unconstitutional because of the Eighth Amendment prohibition of cruel and unusual punishment; but the general practices of lethal injection remain on the legal books of many state governments.

- Political philosophy on this issue generally falls into the two camps of Yes or No. Those in favor of capital punishment usually have their beliefs for a reason, as do those who oppose it. In many cases, those who favor it have been victims of crimes. This is the case for many who oppose it, however, so this issue cannot be classified in just one camp. The U.S. Government doesn't make a habit of executing people. Certain states, however, do.

- Economics is definitely a factor in this debate. Those who favor capital punishment point to how much money the state saves by avoiding the expensive legal alternative, life imprisonment. Those who oppose capital punishment, however, point to the legal system in America, which requires exhaustive appeals and seemingly endless amounts of time, to make sure not only that an innocent person is not executed but also that that person is not treated inhumanely in the process.

- International relations can be examined as well. The U.S. is one of a handful of First World countries that have laws providing for capital punishment. This subject is sometimes a sore spot for American diplomats when dealing with countries whose people expressly detest executing criminals.

Skill 17.3 **Demonstrate an understanding of various governmental systems and apply that knowledge to the analysis of historical and contemporary societies**

The most familiar form of government throughout history was the monarchy. We can include dictatorships or authoritarian governments in this description because the basic idea—that one person was in charge of the government—applies to all. In this kind of government, the head of state was responsible for governing his or her subjects. Written laws have increasingly been the standard as the centuries have progressed. Monarchies and one-person governments still exist today, although they are rare. In these states, the emphasis is on keeping the monarch in power, and many laws of the country have been written with that purpose in mind.

Authoritarian governments still exist today, mostly in the form of communist societies, like China. In this form of government, all the members of the government belong to one political party; in China's case, it is the Communist Party. Not all members of the government believe the same on small issues, but significant issues require party unity. Organization of alternative political parties is widely and strongly discouraged. This was the case in the Soviet Union, the best-known communist state, which disappeared in 1991. Also in many authoritarian governments, industries exist to produce revenues for the state. The flip side of this is that the government is responsible for the upkeep and outlays for these industries. This was more the case in the Soviet Union than it is in China, but certain elements of authoritarianism pervade Chinese society.

The most familiar form of government to most Westerners is **representative government**, commonly called a republic or democracy. The idea behind this form of government is that the people in a society are ultimately responsible for their government and the laws that it passes, enforces, and interprets in that they, the people, elect many of the members of that government. The members of a representative government are much more aware of public opinion than their authoritarian-government counterparts.

Representative government began, in Western tradition, in Greece, with **direct democracy**, then progressed to the republic in Rome and on into other democracies and republics, most famously the United States and many other countries around the world. These governments are termed democracies by many, but they are more properly called republics. A democracy involves *everyone* in a society having a say in who is elected to that society's government. This is certainly not the case in the U.S., in which not only does everyone not vote but also not everyone *can* vote. Another main difference between a true democracy and the kind of democracy that the U.S. and other countries are called these days is that in a true democracy, a vote on anything can be called at any time.

Skill 17.4 Evaluate domestic and global political issues from various ideological perspectives

Ideology is a comprehensive set of ideas or a way of looking at things, like the world or, more specifically, like politics. Someone who views the world in conservative terms is likely also to have conservative political views. The opposite of conservatism is usually referred to as liberalism. These two ideologies are generally referred to as "the Right" and "the Left."

In general, conservatives and liberals are on opposite sides of issues. A prime example of this is abortion. Generally speaking, liberals support a woman's right to choose to have an abortion and conservatives oppose that right. Liberals see that right as a personal issue, one protected by the constitutional right to privacy. This right is guaranteed under a famous Supreme Court case known as *Roe* v. *Wade* (1973). For conservatives, abortion is more a moral or religious issue, with abortion opponents viewing the practice as killing unborn children. At the center of this divisive issue is the debate over when life begins. Abortion opponents believe that life begins at conception; liberals aren't so sure.

If we take a step back, we can see how this issue is a reflection of the overall division in ideologies of the two camps. Conservatives tend to see the world as a dangerous place, one in which religion and morality are large parts of society and their political thinking. These thinkers are reluctant to embrace radical change or other things that go against their way of thinking developed over time and contemplation. Liberals, on the other hand, tend to be more open-minded on issues, being more willing to change their minds or accept ideas or policies that aren't exactly traditional or "safe." The abortion issue represents a deep divide along the lines of religious thinking, with liberals willing to take matters of the body into their own hands and conservatives reserving such rights for religious debates.

A global issue that demonstrates ideological differences of liberals and conservatives is environmentalism. In general, conservatives are more willing to desecrate the environment in the name of human progress, whereas liberals are more inclined to curtail any practices that will harm the environment. This is one example of ideological reversal, since conservatives are generally the ones who are averse to change and liberals are the ones who often seek to embrace change and new ideas. Environmentalism is certainly a global issue, especially in the areas of petroleum consumption and global warming. On both of these issues, conservatives are currently the ones pursuing policies that favor more of both and liberals are working toward curtailing such policies. Extending that thinking further, both liberals and conservatives will look more favorably on people in other countries who embrace the policies that they favor. Such political embraces shape the international debates of many countries.

COMPETENCY 18   UNDERSTAND THE PRINCIPLES OF DEMOCRATIC GOVERNMENT IN THE UNITES STATES; THE ROLES, RIGHTS, AND RESPONSIBILITIES OF INDIVIDUAL CITIZENS IN A DEMOCRATIC SOCIETY; AND THE STRUCTURE, ORGANIZATION, AND OPERATION OF GOVERNMENT AT THE FEDERAL, STATE, AND LOCAL LEVELS

Skill 18.1   Recognize the ideals and issues expressed in the Declaration of Independence

The terms "**civil liberties**" and "**civil rights**" are often used interchangeably, but there are some fine distinctions between the two terms. The term "civil liberties" is more often used to imply that the state has a positive role to play in assuring that all its' citizens will have equal protection and justice under the law with equal opportunities to exercise their privileges of citizenship and to participate fully in the life of the nation, regardless of race, religion, sex, color or creed. The term "civil rights" is used more often to refer to rights that may be described as guarantees that are specified as against the state authority implying limitations on the actions of the state to interfere with citizens' liberties. Although the term "civil rights" has thus been identified with the ideal of equality and the term "civil liberties" with the idea of freedom, the two concepts are really inseparable and interacting. Equality implies the proper ordering of liberty in a society so that one individual's freedom does not infringe on the rights of others.

The beginnings of civil liberties and the idea of civil rights in the United States go back to the ideas of the ancient Greeks. This was illustrated by the early struggle for civil rights against the British and the very philosophies that led people to come to the New World in the first place. Religious freedom, political freedom, and the right to live one's life as one sees fit are basic to the American ideal. These were embodied in the ideas expressed in the Declaration of Independence and the Constitution.

The three most basic rights guaranteed by the Declaration of Independence are "life, liberty, and the pursuit of happiness." The first one is self-explanatory: Americans are guaranteed the right to live their lives in America. The second one is basic as well: Americans are guaranteed the right to live their lives *free* in America. The last basic right is more esoteric but no less important: Americans are guaranteed the right to pursue a happy life. First and foremost, they are allowed the ability to make a life for themselves in America. That happiness also extends to the pursuit of life free from oppression or discrimination, two things African-Americans, women, and non-white Americans have suffered to varying degrees throughout the history of the country.

The Declaration of Independence is an outgrowth of both ancient Greek ideas of democracy and individual rights and the ideas of the European Enlightenment and the Renaissance, especially the ideology of the political thinker **John Locke**. Thomas Jefferson (1743-1826) the principle author of the Declaration borrowed much from Locke's theories and writings. John Locke was one of the most influential political writers of the 17th century who put great emphasis on human rights and put forth the belief that when governments violate those rights people should rebel. He wrote the book "Two Treatises of Government" in 1690, which had tremendous influence on political thought in the American colonies and helped shape the U.S. Constitution and Declaration of Independence.

Essentially, Jefferson applied Locke's principles to the contemporary American situation. Jefferson argued that the currently reigning King George III had repeatedly violated the rights of the colonists as subjects of the British Crown. Disdaining the colonial petition for redress of grievances (a right guaranteed by the Declaration of Rights of 1689), the King seemed bent upon establishing an "absolute tyranny" over the colonies. Such disgraceful behavior itself violated the reasons for which government had been instituted. The American colonists were left with no choice, *"it is their right, it is their duty, to throw off such a government, and to provide new guards for their future security,"* so wrote Thomas Jefferson.

Though his fundamental principles were derived from Locke's, Jefferson was bolder than his intellectual mentor. He went further in that his view of natural rights was much broader than Locke's and less tied to the idea of property rights.

For instance, though both Jefferson and Locke believed very strongly in property rights, especially as a guard for individual liberty, the famous line in the Declaration about people being endowed with the inalienable right to "life, liberty and the pursuit of happiness", was originally Locke's idea. It was "life, liberty, and *private property"*. Jefferson didn't want to tie the idea of rights to any one particular circumstance. However, he changed Locke's original specific reliance on property and substituted the more general idea of human happiness as being a fundamental right that is the duty of a government to protect.

Locke and Jefferson both stressed that the individual citizen's rights are prior to and more important than any obligation to the state. Government is the servant of the people. The officials of government hold their positions at the sufferance of the people. Their job is to ensure that the rights of the people are preserved and protected by that government. The citizens come first, the government comes second. The Declaration thus turned out to be one of the most important and historic documents that expounded the inherent rights of all peoples—a document still looked up to as an ideal and an example.

The Declaration of Independence was the founding document of the United States of America. The Articles of Confederation were the first attempt of the newly independent states to reach a new understanding amongst themselves. The Declaration was intended to demonstrate the reasons that the colonies were seeking separation from Great Britain. Conceived by and written for the most part by Thomas Jefferson, it is not only important for what it says, but also for how it says it. The Declaration is in many respects a poetic document. Instead of a simple recitation of the colonists' grievances, it set out clearly the reasons why the colonists were seeking their freedom from Great Britain. They had tried all means to resolve the dispute peacefully. It was the right of a people, when all other methods of addressing their grievances have been tried and failed, to separate themselves from that power that was keeping them from fully expressing their rights to "**life, liberty, and the pursuit of happiness.**"

By 1776, the colonists and their representatives in the Second Continental Congress realized that things were past the point of no return. The Declaration of Independence was drafted and declared July 4, 1776. George Washington labored against tremendous odds to wage a victorious war. The turning point in the Americans' favor occurred in 1777 with the American victory at Saratoga. This victory decided for the French to align themselves with the Americans against the British. With the aid of Admiral deGrasse and French warships blocking the entrance to Chesapeake Bay, British General Cornwallis trapped at Yorktown, Virginia, surrendered in 1781 and the war was over. The Treaty of Paris, officially ending the war, was signed in 1783.

Skill 18.2 Analyze the fundamental ideas and purposes of the U.S. Constitution and the Constitution of the State of New York

Within a few months from the adoption of the Articles of Confederation, it became apparent that there were serious defects in the system of government established for the new republic. There was a need for change that would create a national government with adequate powers to replace the Confederation, which was actually only a league of sovereign states. In 1786, an effort to regulate interstate commerce ended in what is known as the **Annapolis Convention**. Because only five states were represented, this Convention was not able to accomplish definitive results. The debates, however, made it clear that a government with as little authority could not regulate foreign and interstate commerce as the government established by the Confederation. Congress was, therefore, asked to call a convention to provide a constitution that would address the emerging needs of the new nation. The convention met under the presidency of George Washington, with 55 of the 65 appointed members present. A constitution was written in four months.

The Constitution of the United States is the fundamental law of the republic. It is a precise, formal, written document, often looked up to as extraordinary and supreme. The founders of the Union established it as the highest governmental authority. There is no national power superior to it. The foundations were so broadly laid as to provide for the expansion of national life and to make it an instrument which would last for all time. To maintain its stability, the framers created a difficult process for making any changes to it. No amendment can become valid until it is ratified by three fourths of all of the states. The British system of government was part of the basis of the final document. But significant changes were necessary to meet the needs of a partnership of states that were tied together as a single federation, yet sovereign in their own local affairs. This constitution established a system of government that was unique and advanced far beyond other systems of its day.

There were, to be sure, differences of opinion. The compromises that resolved these conflicts are reflected in the final document. The first point of disagreement and compromise was related to the presidency. Some wanted a strong, centralized, individual authority. Others feared autocracy or the growth of monarchy. The compromise was to give the President broad powers but to limit the amount of time, through term of office, that any individual could exercise that power. The power to make appointments and to conclude treaties was controlled by the requirement of the consent of the Senate.

The second conflict was between large and small states. The large states wanted power proportionate to their voting strength; the small states opposed this plan. The compromise was that all states should have equal voting power in the Senate, but to make the membership of the House of Representatives determined in proportion to population.

The third conflict was about slavery. The compromise was that (a) fugitive slaves should be returned by states to which they might flee for refuge, and (b) that no law would be passed for 20 years prohibiting the importation of slaves.

The fourth major area of conflict was how the President would be chosen. One side of the disagreement argued for election by direct vote of the people. The other side thought Congress should choose the President. One group feared the ignorance of the people; the other feared the power of a small group of people. The Compromise was the **Electoral College**.

The constitution binds the states in a governmental unity in everything that affects the welfare of all. At the same time, it recognizes the right of the people of each state to independence of action in matters that relate only to them. Since the Federal Constitution is the law of the land, all other laws must conform to it.

The debates conducted during the Constitutional Congress represent the issues and the arguments that led to the compromises in the final document. The debates also reflect the concerns of the Founding Fathers that the rights of the people be protected from abrogation by the government itself and the determination that no branch of government should have enough power to continually dominate the others. There is, therefore, a system of checks and balances.

The New York Constitution was adopted on April 20, 1777 and included New York's statement of independence from Britain. Drafted by **John Jay**, it was based on the colonial charter and created three sections of government, as the US Constitution would later do. Powers were combined in the three branches in the New York constitution, however, with the legislature able to appoint executive positions and the courts having power to revise legislation. The governor had no direct veto power.

The New York constitution created the public university system and allowed for the assistance of the indigent. It remained in effect until it was superseded in 1821 by a new constitution. That constitution contained an enumerated bill of rights, and has been extensively revised and amended. The powers and limitations of the three branches of government have been more clearly defined, and brought closer in line with the federal system. Like most state constitutions, the New York Constitution has been extensively amended.

Skill 18.3   **Identify the political, legal, and personal rights guaranteed by the Constitution of the State of New York and the U.S. Constitution and demonstrate an understanding of how those rights have been denied and achieved throughout U.S. history**

Bill Of Rights - The first ten amendments to the United States Constitution deal with civil liberties and civil rights. James Madison was credited with writing a majority of them. They are in brief:

1. **Freedom of Religion, Freedom of Speech, Freedom of the Press, the Right to Peaceful Assembly**
2. **Right to Bear Arms**
3. **Security from the quartering of troops in homes**
4. **Right against unreasonable search and seizures**
5. **Right against self-incrimination**
6. **Right to trial by jury, right to legal council**
7. **Right to jury trial for civil actions**
8. **No cruel or unusual punishment allowed**
9. **These rights shall not deny other rights the people enjoy**
10. **Powers not mentioned in the Constitution shall be retained by the states or the people**

The Magna Carta - This charter has been considered the basis of English constitution liberties. It was granted to a representative group of English barons and nobles on *June 15, 1215* by the British King John, after they had forced it on him. The English barons and nobles sought to limit what they had come to perceive as the overwhelming power of the Monarchy in public affairs. The Magna Carta is considered to be the first modern document that sought to try to limit the powers of the given state authority. It guaranteed feudal rights, regulated the justice system, and abolished many abuses of the King's power to tax and regulates trade. It said that the king could not raise new taxes without first consulting a Great Council, made up of nobles, barons, and Church people. Significantly the Magna Carta only dealt with the rights of the upper classes of the nobility and all of its provisions excluded the rights of the common people. However, gradually the rights won by the nobles were given to other English people.

The Great Council grew into a representative assembly called the Parliament. By the 1600s, Parliament was divided into the House of Lords, made up of nobles and the House of Commons. Members of the House of Commons were elected to office. In the beginning, only a few wealthy men could vote. Still, English people firmly believed that the ruler must consult Parliament on money matters and obey the law. Thus, it did set a precedent that there was a limit to the allowed power of the state. A precedent, which would have no small effect on the history of political revolution, is notably the American Revolution.

The Petition of Right - In English history, it was the title of a petition that was addressed to the King of England *Charles I,* by the British parliament in *1628*. The Parliament demanded that the king stop proclaiming new taxes without its' consent. Parliament demanded that he cease housing soldiers and sailors in the homes of private citizens, proclaiming martial law in times of peace, and that no subject should be imprisoned without a good cause being shown. After some attempts to circumvent these demands, Charles finally agreed to them. They later had an important effect on the demands of the revolutionary colonists, as these were some of the rights that, as Englishmen, they felt were being denied to them. The Petition of Right was also the basis of specific protections that the designers of the Constitution made a point of inserting in the document.

British Bill of Rights - Also known as the *Declaration of Rights,* it spelled out the rights that were considered to belong to Englishmen and was granted by *King William III* in 1869. It had previously been passed by a convention of the Parliament and it came out of the struggle for power that took place in Great Britain and at that time was known as *The Glorious Revolution*. It was known as a revolution that was accomplished with virtually no bloodshed and led to King William III and Queen Mary II becoming joint sovereigns.

The Declaration itself was very similar in style to the later American Bill of Rights. It protected the rights of individuals and gave anyone accused of a crime the right to trial by jury. It outlawed cruel punishments; also, it stated that a ruler could not raise taxes or an army without the consent of Parliament. The colonists as Englishmen were protected by these provisions. The colonists considered abridgments of these rights that helped to contribute to the revolutionary spirit of the times.

All of these events and the principles that arose from them are of the utmost importance in understanding the process that eventually led to the ideals that are inherent in the Constitution of the United States. In addition, the fact is that all of these ideals are universal in nature and have become the basis for the idea of human freedoms throughout the world.

Skill 18.4   Examine the civic values and responsibilities of citizens in a democratic society

A citizen in a democratic society is expected to do certain things in order to remain such a citizen. First and foremost, that person is expected to follow the laws of that society. The vast majority of the laws of a democratic society have been enacted to facilitate the continuance of that society. Many of these laws also have the rights of the citizens in mind. It is certainly easier to follow some of these laws than others. Throughout the history of democratic societies, however, laws have been passed that seem to violate the very spirit of the rights of those citizens. In such cases, people have worked to overturn such laws, either directly or by means of pursuing judicial solutions or indirectly by way of making sure that the lawmakers who created such laws are not re-elected. This reinforces the idea that citizens have a responsibility to themselves as well and that if government is infringing on their basic rights, they have a natural right to speak up and do something about it. Related to this is the idea that the government of a democratic society exists in part to protect the rights of its citizens. People expect such protection, in both real and virtual terms. Real terms include civil and countrywide defense, and virtual terms include laws and the people who make them. If such protection standards are not being met, then the citizens have the right and even the duty to demand such protection and work to see that it is maintained or restored.

Citizens of a democratic society are also expected to participate in the political process, either directly or indirectly. In theory, anyone who is a citizen of a democratic society can get himself or herself elected to *something*, be it at the local, state, or federal level. Other ways to participate in the political process include donating time and/or money to the political campaigns of others and speaking out on behalf of or against certain issues. The most basic level of participation in the political process is to vote.

A democratic society is built on the theory of participatory government. Citizens of such a society expect that political debates on important issues will be public and ongoing, so that they can keep themselves informed on how their representatives view such issues. Information is meant to be shared, especially in a democratic society. If major political meetings begin to take place in private, without witnesses or records, then the citizens have the right to demand that such proceedings be made current, for only then can they know whether their government is acting on their behalf.

Skill 18.5   Analyze the concept of federalism and recognize its evolution in American political thought and practice

Federalism in colonial America meant belief in a strong central government. The Articles of Confederation provided for a weak central government, and lawmakers and citizens alike saw the unlikelihood of such an idea. One of the debates that shaped the ratification of the Constitution was the idea that the national government would be superior in status to state and local governments. Indeed, the national government is often called the *federal* government as well. In this historical political debate, those who favored a strong federal government were called Federalists and those opposed styled themselves anti-Federalists.

Beginning with opinions written by Chief Justice John Marshall (including *Gibbons* v. *Ogden* and *McCulloch* v. *Maryland*), a series of Supreme Court decisions affirmed the supremacy of the federal government over that of the states. After all, if a state could tax the federal government, as was argued in *McCulloch*, then the federal government could theoretically yield its authority to that state, giving it supremacy over every other state; and *that* would undermine the authority of the federal government, not only in the minds of the judges of the federal and state courts but also in the hearts and minds of the people, of both the United States and other countries. This tradition has continued to the present day, with states being unable to sue the federal government, disputes between states being settled by federal courts, and foreign threats being answered by a national defense force. In today's political discussions, the idea of states' superseding the federal government seems foreign indeed.

In the present day, however, the word *federalism* refers to the idea of democracy or republic itself, not necessarily the idea that the national government is superior to state and local governments. More to the point, federalism describes a government whose powers are divided between entities, so that no one part of that government is totally supreme over others. This is to be found in the famous "checks and balances" ideas of the Constitution itself. The three top branches of the U.S. Government have their various duties and responsibilities, and each can "check" or "balance" the other two, with the result being a three-headed whole that exists to protect and further the rights and defense of its citizens.

Federalism is also used to describe the idea that power and authority is divided, not only between the three top branches of the federal government but also between the federal government as a whole and state and local governments. Citizens of such a society are expected to be sovereign to governments on all three levels, and the governments of those three levels are expected to legislate accordingly.

Skill 18.6   Analyze the factors that have expanded or limited the role of the individual in U.S. political life during the 20th century

During the 20th century, participation in American politics has risen to an all-time high. This is because of both an increase in population and an increase in ease in participation in the political process. During the period 1900–1999, laws at all levels of government have made it easier for the average American to participate in politics, be that running for office or simply voting.

Poll taxes and literacy tests have been outlawed through laws passed in both the 19th and 20th centuries; as a result, more people than ever before can express themselves politically by voting. Another recent enhancement of the voter registration is the so-called "Motor-Voter" practice, which allows new citizens to register to vote when they register for a driver's license. This practice made it easier for people to register, and study after study has shown that awareness is key to increasing registration and, subsequently, voting.

Also in the 20th century, the idea of the impenetrability of government has largely and gradually receded. At the turn of the century and for much of the time before World War II, it was generally believed that only the rich and extremely powerful and popular could run for elective office. The "common man" didn't know enough or have the requisite desire to attempt to be elected, an idea that went back as far as and continues to be embodied in the philosophy of the Electoral College. However, especially with the passage of the 19th Amendment, which guaranteed women the right to vote in all American elections, the idea that *anyone* could run for office began to be accepted more and more. Civil rights laws of the second half of the 20th century also encouraged minorities to participate in the political process, largely by removing barriers to such participation.

COMPETENCY 19   **UNDERSTAND THE U.S. ELECTION PROCESS AND THE ROLES OF POLITICAL PARTIES, PRESSURE GROUPS, AND SPECIAL INTERESTS IN THE U.S. POLITICAL SYSTEM**

Skill 19.1   Identify and describe the components of the U.S. electoral process

The U.S. electoral process has many and varied elements, from simple voting to complex campaigning for office. Everything in between is complex and detailed. First of all, American citizens vote. They vote for laws and statues and referenda and elected officials. They have to register in order to vote, and at that time they can declare their intended membership in a political party. America has a large list of political parties, which have varying degrees of membership. The Democratic and Republican Parties are the two with the most money and power, but other political parties abound. In some cases, people who are registered members of a political party are allowed to vote for only members of that political party. This takes place in many cases in primary elections, when, for example, a number of people are running to secure the nomination of one political party for a general election. If you are a registered Democrat, then in the primary election, you will be able to vote for only Democratic candidates; this restriction will be lifted for the general election, in which the Democratic Party will expect you to vote for that party's candidate but in which you can also vote for whomever you want. A potential voter need not register for a political party, however.

Candidates affiliate themselves with political parties, and then go about the business of campaigning, which includes getting the word out on their candidacy, what they believe in, and what they will do if elected. Candidates sometimes get together for debates to showcase their views on important issues of the day and how those views differ from those of their opponents. Candidates give public speeches, attend public functions, and explain their views to reporters, for coverage in the mass media. The results of elections are made known very quickly, sometimes instantly, thanks to computerized vote tallying. Once results are finalized, winning candidates give victory speeches and losing candidates give concession speeches. Losing candidates go back to the lives they were leading, and winning candidates get ready to take their places in the local, state, or national government.

Elections take place regularly, so voters know just how long it will be before the next election. Some candidates begin planning their next campaign the day after their victory or loss. Some voters have the option to **recall** elected candidates; such a measure, however, is drastic and requires extensive effort to get the motion on the ballot. As such, recalls of elected candidates are relatively rare. One widely publicized recall in recent years was that of California Governor Gray Davis, who was replaced by movie star Arnold Schwarzenegger.

Another method of removing public officials from office is **impeachment**. This is also rare but still a possibility. Both houses of the state or federal government get involved, and both houses have to approve the impeachment measures by a large margin. In the case of the federal government, the House of Representatives votes to impeach a federal official and the Senate votes to convict or acquit. Conviction means that the official must leave office immediately; acquittal results in no penalties or fines.

The College of Electors—or the Electoral College, as it is more commonly known—has a long and distinguished history of mirroring the political will of the American voters. On some occasions, the results have not been entirely consonant with the popular vote. Article II of the Constitution lists the specifics of the Electoral College. The Founding Fathers included the Electoral College as one of the famous "checks and balances" for two reasons: 1) to give states with small populations more of an equal weight in the presidential election, and 2) they didn't trust the common man (women couldn't vote then) to be able to make an informed decision on which candidate would make the best president. Each state had just one vote, regardless of how many members of the House represented that state. So, the one vote that the state of New York cast would be decided by an initial vote of New York's Representatives. (If that initial vote was a tie, then that deadlock would have to be broken.)

In addition, when the Constitution was being written, not many people knew much about government, politics, or presidential elections. A large number of people were farmers or lived in rural areas, where they were far more concerned with making a living and providing for their families than they were with who was running for which office. Many of these "common people" could not read or write, either, and wouldn't be able to read a ballot in any case. Like it or not, the Founding Fathers thought that even if these "common people" could vote, they wouldn't necessarily make the best decision for who would make the best president. So, the Electoral College was born.

Technically, the electors do not have to vote for anyone. The Constitution does not require them to do so. And throughout the history of presidential elections, some have indeed voted for someone else. But tradition holds that the electors vote for the candidate chosen by their state, and so the vast majority of electors do just that. The Electoral College meets a few weeks after the presidential election. Mostly, their meeting is a formality. When all the electoral votes are counted, the president with the most votes wins. In most cases, the candidate who wins the popular vote also wins in the Electoral College. However, this has not always been the case.

The most recent example of this was the 2000 Presidential Election. The Democratic Party's nominee was Vice President Al Gore. A presidential candidate himself back in 1988, Gore had served as vice president for both of President Bill Clinton's terms. The Republican Party's nominee was George W. Bush, governor of Texas and son of former President George Bush. The election was hotly contested, and many states went down to the wire, being decided by only a handful of votes. The one state that seemed to be flip-flopping as Election Day turned into Election Night was Florida. In the end, Gore won the popular vote, by nearly 540,000 votes. But he didn't win the electoral vote. The vote was so close in Florida that a recount was necessary under federal law. Eventually, the Supreme Court weighed in and stopped all the recounts. The last count had Bush winning by less than a thousand votes. That gave him Florida and the White House.

Because of these irregularities, many have taken up the cry to eliminate the Electoral College, which they see as archaic and capable of distorting the will of the people. After all, they argue, elections these days come down to one or two key states, as if the votes of the people in all the other states don't matter. Proponents of the Electoral College point to the tradition of the entity and all of the other elections in which the electoral vote mirrored the popular vote. Eliminating the Electoral College would require a constitutional amendment. The debate crops up every four years; in the past decade, though, the debate has lasted longer between elections **(See also Section 6.1).**

Skill 19.2   Evaluate the role of lobbyists in the modern legislative process

Lobbyists are a very visible and time-honored part of the political process. They wield power to varying degrees, depending on the issues involved and how much the parties they represent want to maintain the status quo or effect change.

A lobbyist is someone who works for a political cause by attempting to influence lawmakers to vote a certain way on issues of the day. For example, a lobbyist for an oil production company would urge lawmakers not to increase existing or create new taxes on oil. This urging takes many forms, among them direct communication and letter-writing or phone-in campaigns designed to stir up public sentiment for or against an issue or set of issues. Another common form of lobbying is gifts, including meals and entertainment "given" to lawmakers and paid for by lobbyists. Such "gifts" are not illegal and are intended to make the lawmakers who receive them more inclined to vote in favor of the lobbyists' interests. In the past, lobbyists would threaten physical violence if lawmakers didn't vote their way. Nowadays, these threats take the form of removal of funding, refusal to support the candidate's future campaigns, and revelations of compromising information about the lawmaker.

Lobbyists also serve to make lawmakers aware of information that they might not have, including how other lawmakers view the important issues of the day. Few and far between is the lawmaker who wants to stand up for impossible causes or suggest a radical change in policy; more prevalent is the lawmaker who wants to be a part of a coalition or be a part of the status quo. Lobbyists can make available information useful to both of these kinds of lawmakers, thus furthering their chances of success. Such information usually comes with a price, however, a price that routinely is an impassioned plea or even demand to vote a certain way on a certain bill.

Not all lobbyists work for high-powered organizations. Some work for themselves or for smaller companies. These lobbyists have the same intentions and the same purposes as their more visible and well-financed colleagues, even though they might not have the same resources at their disposal.

Lobbyists also attempt to influence one another. Some issues create strange bedfellows, and lobbyists who work for different employers might find themselves on the same side of an issue and end up working together for a larger cause, to achieve a common goal.

Skill 19.3   Examine ways in which U.S. citizens participate in and influence the political process

The most basic way for citizens to participate in the political process is to **vote**. Since the passing of the 23rd Amendment in 1965, US citizens who are at least 18 years old are eligible to vote. Elections are held at regular intervals at all levels of government, allowing citizens to weigh in on local matters as well as those of national scope.

Citizens wishing to engage in the political process to a greater degree have several paths open, such as participating in local government. Counties, states, and sometimes neighborhoods are governed by locally elected boards or councils that meet publicly. Citizens are usually able to address these boards, bringing their concerns and expressing their opinions on matters being considered. Citizens may even wish to stand for local election and join a governing board, or seek support for higher office.

Supporting a political party is another means by which citizens can participate in the political process. Political parties endorse certain platforms that express general social and political goals, and support member candidates in election campaigns. Political parties make use of much volunteer labor, with supporters making telephone calls, distributing printed material and campaigning for the party's causes and candidates. Political parties solicit donations to support their efforts as well. Contributing money to a political party is another form of participation citizens can undertake.

Another form of political activity is to support an issue-related political group. Several political groups work actively to sway public opinion on various issues or on behalf of a segment of American society. These groups may have representatives who meet with state and federal legislators to "lobby" them—to provide them with information on an issue and persuade them to take favorable action.

Skill 19.4 Analyze factors that influence political elections at the local, state, and national levels

If there's one thing that drives American politics more than any other, it's **money**. More often than not, the candidate who has the most money at his or her disposal has the best chance of getting or keeping political office. Money can buy so many things that are necessary to a successful campaign that it is entirely indispensable. Money drives the utilization of every other factor in the running of a campaign.

First and foremost, money is needed to pay the people who will run a candidate's campaign. A candidate cannot expect people to give up, in some cases, years of their lives without monetary compensation. Volunteers on a political campaign are plentiful, but they are not at the top levels. The faithful lieutenants of a campaign are paid performers.

Money is also needed to buy or rent all of the tangible and intangible *things* that are needed to power a political campaign: office supplies, meeting places, transportation vehicles, and many more. The inventory of these items can add up frighteningly quickly, and money can appear to disappear like water down a drain.

Of course, the expense that gets the most exposure these days is **media** advertising, specifically television advertising. This is the most expensive kind of advertising, but it also has the potential to reach the widest audience. TV ad prices can run into the hundreds of thousands of dollars, depending on when they run; but they have the potential to reach perhaps millions of viewers. Here, too, money can disappear quickly. A political campaign is also a fashion show and candidates cannot afford to go without showing their friendly faces to as wide an audience as possible on a regular basis. Other forms of advertising include radio and Web ads, signs and billboards, and good old-fashioned flyers.

The sources of all this money that is needed to run a successful political campaign are varied. A candidate might have a significant amount of money in his or her own personal coffers. In rare cases, the candidate finances the entire campaign. However, the most prevalent source of money is outside donations. A candidate's friends and family might donate funds to the campaign, as well as the campaign workers themselves. State and federal governments will also contribute to most regional or national campaigns, provided that the candidate can prove that he or she can raise a certain amount of money first. The largest source of campaign finance money, however, comes from so-called "special interests." A large company such as an oil company or a manufacturer of electronic goods will want to keep prices or tariffs down and so will want to make sure that laws lifting those prices or tariffs aren't passed.

To this end, the company will contribute money to the campaigns of candidates who are likely to vote to keep those prices or tariffs down. A candidate is not obligated to accept such a donation, of course, and further is not obligated to vote in favor of the interests of the special interest; however, doing the former might create a shortage of money and doing the latter might ensure that no further donations come from that or any other special interest. An oil company wants to protect its interests, and its leaders don't very much care which political candidate is doing that for them as long as it is being done.

Another powerful source of support for a political campaign is **special interest groups** of a political nature. These are not necessarily economic powers but rather groups whose people want to effect political change (or make sure that such change doesn't take place, depending on the status of the laws at the time). A good example of a special interest group is an anti-abortion group or a pro-choice group. The abortion issue is still a divisive one in American politics, and many groups will want to protect or defend or ban—depending on which side they're on—certain rights and practices. An anti-abortion group, for example, might pay big money to candidates who pledge to work against laws that protect the right for women to have abortions. As long as these candidates continue to assure their supporters that they will keep on fighting the fight, the money will continue to flow. This kind of social group usually has a large number of dedicated individuals who do much more than vote: They organize themselves into political action committees, attend meetings and rallies, and work to make sure that their message gets out to a wide audience. Methods of spreading the word often include media advertising on behalf of their chosen candidates. This kind of expenditure is no doubt welcomed by the candidates, who will get the benefit of the exposure but won't have to spend that money because someone else is signing the checks.

COMPETENCY 20 UNDERSTAND INTERNATIONAL RELATIONS, THE FORMATION AND EXECUTION OF U.S. FOREIGN POLICY, AND THE PURPOSES AND FUNCTIONS OF INTERNATIONAL ORGANIZATIONS

Skill 20.1 Recognize the administrative components of U.S. foreign-policy making and their roles and responsibilities

The elements of the U.S. Government that pursue and conduct foreign policy are large and varied. Some are in the Legislative Branch; others are in the Executive Branch.

The most well known foreign policy advocate is the **Secretary of State**, who resides in the Executive Branch and is appointed by the President and confirmed by Congress. The Secretary of State is the country's primary ambassador to other countries, having prime responsibilities in this regard for attending international meetings, brokering peace deals, and negotiating treaties. The Secretary of State often acts as the "voice of the country," speaking for the interests of the United States to the rest of the world. A political element exists in this scenario as well: Since the Secretary of State is appointed by the president, he or she is expected to follow the policy directives of the president. It is usually the case that the two people are of the same political party and share political views on important issues. The result of this is that, in some cases, the views and actions of the Secretary of State are in line with a few or a great many people but not with all U.S. citizens. Such is the nature of politics.

The Executive Branch also has a **National Security Council**, which advises the president on matters of foreign policy. Members of this group are not nearly as visible or well traveled as the Secretary of State, but they do provide the president and other members of the government with valuable information on goings-on elsewhere in the world.

The most numerous of the Executive Branch members involved in foreign policy are the **ambassadors**. Most countries throughout the world have ambassadors, people who reside in other countries in order to be lobbyists for their home countries' interests. The United States has ambassadors to most countries in the world; by the same token, most countries in the world have embassies, buildings and organizations that contain offices for these ambassadors. These ambassadors attend official functions in their "adopted" countries and speak for their countries in international meetings.

The Legislative Branch plays an important role in U.S. foreign policy as well. The Senate in particular is responsible for approving treaties and ambassadorial appointments. Both houses of Congress have committees of lawmakers who specialize in foreign policy. These lawmakers make a habit of keeping abreast of happenings elsewhere in the world and advising their fellow lawmakers on foreign businesses, issues, and conflicts. These foreign-policy-focused lawmakers often tour other countries and attend state functions, but they don't have the voice or responsibility of ambassadors.

Increasingly, state and local governments practice foreign policy as well. Governors and lawmakers of many states have trade agreements with other countries; these agreements are not on the order of national agreements, but they do deal with foreign relations all the same, mainly with economics. Local governments, too, get involved with things overseas. A good example of this is the growing practice of implementing a "sister city," whereby a city in the U.S. "adopts" a city in another country and exchanges ideas, goods, services, and technology and other resources with its new "companion."

Skill 20.2 Analyze the cultural and ideological influences that have shaped U.S. foreign policy since World War II

In 1946, Josef Stalin stated publicly that the presence of capitalism and its development of the world's economy made international peace impossible. This led an American diplomat in Moscow, George F. Kennan, to propose, as a response to Stalin and as a statement of U.S. foreign policy, the idea and goal of the U.S. to be to contain or limit the extension or expansion of Soviet Communist policies and activities. After Soviet efforts in Iran, Greece, and Turkey, U.S. President Harry Truman stated what is known as the Truman Doctrine which committed the U.S. to a policy of intervention in order to contain or stop the spread of communism throughout the world.

After 1945, social and economic chaos continued in Western Europe, especially in Germany. Secretary of State George C. Marshall came to realize that the U.S. had serious problems and to assist in the recovery, he proposed a program known as the European Recovery Program or **the Marshall Plan**. Although the Soviet Union withdrew from any participation, the U.S. continued the work of assisting Europe in regaining economic stability. In Germany, the situation was critical with the American Army shouldering the staggering burden of relieving the serious problems of the German economy. In February 1948, Britain and the U.S. combined their two zones, with France joining in June.

The Cold War was, more than anything else, an ideological struggle between proponents of democracy and those of communism. The two major players were the United States and the Soviet Union, but other countries were involved as well. It was a "cold" war because no large-scale fighting took place directly between the two big protagonists, though both governments engaged in **proxy wars** around the globe by supporting a particular government or insurgency, often with money, arms, or even troops, in defense of the values of the supporting power.

It wasn't just form of government that was driving this war, either. Economics were a main concern as well. A concern in both countries was that the precious resources (such as oil and food) from other like-minded countries wouldn't be allowed to flow to "the other side." These resources didn't much flow between the U.S. and Soviet Union, either.

The Soviet Union kept much more of a tight leash on its supporting countries, including all of Eastern Europe, which made up a military organization called the Warsaw Pact. The Western nations responded with a military organization of their own, NATO. Another prime battleground was Asia, where the Soviet Union had allies in China, North Korea, and North Vietnam and the U.S. had allies in Japan, South Korea, Taiwan, and South Vietnam. The Korean War and Vietnam War were major conflicts in which both big protagonists played big roles but didn't directly fight each other.

The main symbol of the Cold War was the arms race, a continual buildup of missiles, tanks, and other weapons that became ever more technologically advanced and increasingly more deadly. The ultimate weapon, which both sides had in abundance, was the **nuclear bomb**. Spending on weapons and defensive systems eventually occupied great percentages of the budgets of the U.S. and the USSR, and some historians argue that this high level of spending played a large part in the end of the latter.

The war was a cultural struggle as well. Adults brought up their children to hate "the Americans" or "the Communists." Cold War tensions spilled over into many parts of life in countries around the world. The ways of life in countries on either side of the divide were so different that they served entirely foreign to outside observers. The Cold War continued to varying degrees from 1947 to 1991, when the Soviet Union collapsed. Other Eastern European countries had seen their communist governments overthrown by this time as well, marking the shredding of the "Iron Curtain."

The major thrust of U.S. foreign policy from the end of World War II to 1990 was the post-war struggle between non-Communist nations, led by the United States, and the Soviet Union and the Communist nations who were its allies. It was referred to as a "Cold War" because its conflicts did not lead to a major war of fighting, or a "hot war." Both the Soviet Union and the United States embarked on a buildup of various types of nuclear weapons. Both nations had the capability of destroying each other but because of the continuous threat of nuclear war and accidents, extreme caution was practiced on both sides. The efforts of both sides to serve and protect their political philosophies and to support and assist their allies resulted in a number of events during this 45-year period.

Skill 20.3   Consider ways in which the United States has influenced other nations and how other nations have influenced U.S. political and social life

The United States has influenced other nations in many ways in the more than 200 years of its existence. The areas of this influence include political, economic, and cultural elements.

The democratic government familiar to most Americans is not an American invention but is certainly an American export. American envoys have trumpeted the virtues of representative government throughout the world. This has encouraged many countries to embrace the ideals of democracy and has also inspired distrust and even hatred in other countries that have authoritarian governments.

The market economy of the United States has been a model of efficiency and openness for other countries as well. The spirit of free enterprise that drives the American economy has been a major export to burgeoning democracies as well as a source of scorn for those living in command economies.

Perhaps the most recognizable American export, though, is American culture. Some of the more visible elements of American culture seen nearly everywhere in the world are Coca-Cola and McDonald's. Other popular products are everywhere as well, including other fast-food chains and soft drinks and the eponymous iPod. American music and films are popular in other countries as well, as are the people who make them.

Another popular element of American life that has been successfully exported, nearly from the moment of the country's inception, is "the American Dream," the idea that anyone from anywhere else can come to America and find the freedom to pursue the job and lifestyle that they want. The United States was built on the backs of immigrants and immigration continues to be popular today.

The main way that other countries have influenced America and Americans is perhaps economically. Goods from other countries—most notably, Japan, China, Taiwan, India, and a few European nations—have taken over many areas of the American economy. Main examples of this are cars, computers, and mobile phones.

In political terms, the main outside influence on the U.S. was by the Soviet Union during the Cold War. Obsession with Communism and the possible spread of it dominated political discussions in America for nearly 50 years, until the fall of the Soviet Union, in 1991. The Korean War and the Vietnam War were direct results of this political tension, as was the Cuban Missile Crisis. This political tension led the U.S. to pursue a vigorous foreign policy of "containment" and preventing the "Domino Theory" from coming true and all manner of other anti-Communist efforts. China is a Communist country as well, but the relationship between the U.S. and that country has been far less contentious than that of the U.S. and the USSR, except for the 1950s, when American and Chinese armed forces met on the battlefields in Korea.

The contentiousness surrounding the current Iraq War have been a major influence on how other countries currently view the U.S., although no countries have been successful in ending the war.

Skill 20.4 Identify the goals, structures, and functions of the United Nations

The **United Nations** (U.N.) is an international organization headquartered in New York City. The U.N. was founded in 1945. Representatives of 51 countries signed the original agreement. More and more countries have joined since then, and membership now includes 192 countries.

At the top of the U.N. hierarchy is the Security Council, a group that has 15 members. Five of these are permanent members and can veto any U.N. resolution. The permanent members are the United States, United Kingdom, France, China, and Russia. The other ten members are elected for two-year terms, with five being elected each year.

The General Assembly is the only organization that has every member nation represented. Each country sends one person to officially represent it in the General Assembly, which meets regularly at U.N. Headquarters in New York. Special sessions of the General Assembly are rare but not unheard of.

Perhaps the most well known U.N. figure is the **Secretary General** who acts as the administrative head of the entire U.N. He or she is the spokesperson for the U.N. The Secretary General serves a five-year term and can be re-elected, by the General Assembly. By tradition, the Secretary General is not from a nation that is a permanent member of the Security Council. The Secretary General is the head of the Secretariat, another important U.N. body that exists mainly to support the inner workings of the General Assembly.

Another of the major organizations within the U.N. is the International Court of Justice, which has its headquarters in The Hague, the Netherlands. This court is responsible for trying people suspected of international crimes.

One of the prime functions of the United Nations is to keep peace throughout the world. Member nations send a large number of armed forces on a rotating basis to the U.N. Peacekeeping Force, which sends troops to armed conflicts or violent situations. This peacekeeping extends to elections, and U.N. peacekeepers have both observed and enforced free practices for elections across the globe.

Related to the peacekeeping mission of the U.N. is its pursuit of human rights. Genocide and other examples of inhumanity are not tolerated, and U.N. members work tirelessly to discourage such efforts, including sending armed troops to stop them. The U.N. has a Universal Declaration of Human Rights to support this and several other high-profile organizations, including the United Nations Children's Fund (UNICEF) and the World Health Organization (WHO). U.N. workers have led humanitarian efforts around the world, delivering food and liquids to famine-stricken areas.

COMPETENCY 21   UNDERSTAND HOW TO LOCATE, GATHER, AND ORGANIZE PRIMARY AND SECONDARY INFORMATION USING SOCIAL SCIENCE RESOURCES AND RESEARCH METHODOLOGIES

Skill 21.1   Recognize the characteristics and uses of historical, geographic, and social science reference materials

Historical data can come from a wide range of sources beginning with libraries. Records and guides are almost universally digitally organized and available for instant searching by era, topic, event, personality, or area. The **Internet** offers possibilities for finding even the most obscure information. However, even with all these resources available, nothing is more valuable than a visit to the site being researched including a visit to historical societies, local libraries, sometimes even local schools. A historian was searching for an answer to the question as to why her great-great-grandfather had enlisted in the Union army even though he lived in the Deep South, so she went to the site where he grew up and found the answer in the historical records stored in the local school house for lack of a formal historical society. The residents of the little town were also able to answer her question. She would never have found that historical information if she hadn't visited the site.

The same things could be said about geographical data. It's possible to find a map of almost any area online; however, the best maps will be available locally as will knowledge and information about the development of the area. For example, a court house had been moved from one small town to another in a county in Tennessee for no apparent reason. However, the local old-timers can tell you. The railroad wanted to come through town, and the farmers in the area surrounding the previous court house didn't want to raise the $100,000 it would take; they were also concerned that the trains would scare their cows. This information is not in a history book, yet it would be very important to a study of the geography of the area.

Skill 21.2   Identify the characteristics and uses of various social science resources and compare the advantages and disadvantages of primary and secondary sources

The world of social science research has never been so open to new possibilities. Where our predecessors were unable to tread for fear of exceeding the limits of the available data, data access and data transfer, analytic routines, or computing power, today's social scientists can advance with confidence. Where once social scientists of empirical bent struggled with punch cards, chattering computer terminals, and jobs disappearing into the black hole of remote mainframe processors, often never reappearing, we now enjoy massive arrays of data, powerful personal computers on our desks, online access to data, and suites of sophisticated analytic packages. Never before has the social scientist come so well armed. Advances in technology can free social scientists from the tyranny of simplification that has often hampered attempts to grasp the complexity of the world.

Refer to the content under **Skill 23.3** for a thorough discussion of primary and secondary sources. Primary sources for a study in social sciences may be obtained one-on-one: the children in the school where you are a teacher or via electronic means. For example, government sources contain much data for social sciences research such as census statistics, employment statistics, health statistics, etc., that can be readily accessed and manipulated.

Secondary sources may also be obtained in a hands-on fashion: interviews of people with first-hand knowledge; books, journals, etc., that record primary statistics or analyses of primary statistics. However, the best source for obtaining that information is the Internet. For example, a potential resource for social science information is MOST (Management of Social Transformations), which maintains a website filled with information on what they do and how they do it.

Skill 21.3 Apply procedures for retrieving and using information from traditional sources and new technologies

Libraries of all sorts are valuable when conducting research and nowadays almost all have digitized search systems to assist in finding information on almost any subject. Even so, the Internet with powerful search engines like Google readily available can retrieve information that doesn't exist in libraries or if it does exist, is much more difficult to retrieve.

Conducting a research project once involved the use of punch cards, microfiche and other manual means of storing the data in a retrievable fashion. No more. With high-powered computers available to anyone who chooses to conduct research, the organizing of the data in a retrievable fashion has been revolutionized. Creating multi-level folders, copying and pasting into the folders, making ongoing additions to the bibliography at the very time that a source is consulted, and using search-and-find functions make this stage of the research process go much faster with less frustration and a decrease in the likelihood that important data might be overlooked.

Serious research requires high-level analytical skills when it comes to processing and interpreting data. A degree in statistics or at least a graduate-level concentration is very useful. However, a team approach to a research project will include a statistician in addition to those members who are knowledgeable in the social sciences.

Skill 21.4 Demonstrate an understanding of appropriate methods and techniques for collecting information in the social sciences and applying basic research procedures

The scientific method is the process by which researchers over time endeavor to construct an accurate (that is, reliable, consistent and non-arbitrary) representation of the world. Recognizing that personal and cultural beliefs influence both our perceptions and our interpretations of natural phenomena, standard procedures and criteria minimize those influences when developing a theory.

The scientific method has four steps:

1. Observation and description of a phenomenon or group of phenomena
2. Formulation of a hypothesis to explain the phenomena
3. Use of the hypothesis to predict the existence of other phenomena or to predict quantitatively the results of new observations
4. Performance of experimental tests of the predictions by several independent experimenters and properly performed experiments

While the researcher may bring certain biases to the study, it's important that bias not be permitted to enter into the interpretation. It's also important that data that doesn't fit the hypothesis not be ruled out. This is unlikely to happen if the researcher is open to the possibility that the hypothesis might turn out to be null. Another important caution is to be certain that the methods for analyzing and interpreting are flawless. Abiding by these mandates is important if the discovery is to make a contribution to human understanding.

Skill 21.5   Summarize data and organize information related to the social sciences into logical and coherent outlines

The phenomena that interest social scientists are usually complex. Capturing that complexity more fully requires the assessment of simultaneous co-variations along the following dimensions: the units of observation, their characteristics, and time. This is how behavior occurs. For example, obtaining a richer and more accurate picture of the progress of school children means measuring changes in their knowledge attainment over time together with changes in the school over time. This acknowledges that changes in one area of behavior are usually contingent on changes in other areas. Models used for research in the past were inadequate to handle the complexities suggested by multiple co-variations. However, the evolution of computerized data processing has taken away that constraint.

While descriptions of the research project and presentation of outcomes along with analysis must be a part of every report, graphs, charts, and sometimes maps are necessary to make the results clearly understandable.

COMPETENCY 22 UNDERSTAND AND APPLY METHODS FOR INTERPRETING AND COMMUNICATING VISUAL SOURCES OF SOCIAL STUDIES INFORMATION

Skill 22.1 Interpret graphic and quantitative data

Maps are a quick way of gaining information that, otherwise, might take hundreds of words to explain. Maps reflect the great variety of knowledge covered by social sciences. To show such a variety of information, maps are made in many different ways. Because of this variety, maps must be understood in order to make the best sense of them. Once they are understood, maps provide a solid foundation for social science studies.

To apply information obtained from **graphs** one must understand the two major reasons why graphs are used:

1. To present a model or theory visually in order to show how two or more variables interrelate
2. To present real world data visually in order to show how two or more variables interrelate

Most often used are those known as **bar graphs** and **line graphs**. (Charts are often used for similar reasons and are explained in the next section.)

Graphs themselves are most useful when one wishes to demonstrate the sequential increase or decrease of a variable, or to show specific correlations between two or more variables in a given circumstance.

Most common is the **bar graph** because it is an easy way of visually showing the difference in a given set of variables. However, it is limited in that it cannot really show the actual proportional increase, or decrease, of each given variable in terms of the other. (In order to show a decrease, a bar graph must show the "bar" under the starting line, thus removing the ability to really show how the different variables would relate to each other.)

Thus, in order to accomplish this one must use a **line graph**. Line graphs can be of two types: a **linear** or **non-linear** graph. A linear line graph uses a series of straight lines; a non-linear line graph uses a curved line. Though the lines can be either straight or curved, all of the lines are called **curves**.

A line graph uses a number line or **axis**. The numbers are generally placed in order, equal distances from one another. The number line is used to represent a number, degree or some such other variable at an appropriate point on the line. Two lines are used, intersecting at a specific point. They are referred to as the X-axis and the Y-axis.

The Y-axis is a vertical line the X-axis is a horizontal line. Together they form a **coordinate system**. The difference between a point on the line of the X-axis and the Y-axis is called the **slope** of the line, or the change in the value on the vertical axis divided by the change in the value on the horizontal axis. The Y-axis number is called the **rise** and the X-axis number is called the **run**, thus the equation for slope is:

SLOPE = RISE - (Change in value on the vertical axis)
RUN - (Change in value on the horizontal axis)

The slope tells the amount of increase or decrease of a given **specific** variable. When using two or more variables one can plot the amount of difference between them in any given situation. This makes presenting information on a line graph more involved. It also makes it more informative and accurate than a simple bar graph. Knowledge of the term slope and what it is and how it is measured helps us to describe verbally the pictures we are seeing visually. For example, if a curve is said to have a slope of "zero", you should picture a flat line. If a curve has a slope of "one", you should picture a rising line that makes a 45-degree angle with the horizontal and vertical axis lines.

The preceding examples are of **linear** (straight line) curves. With **non-linear** curves (the ones that really do curve) the slope of the curve is constantly changing, so as a result, we must then understand that the slope of the non-linear curved line will be at a specific point. How is this done? The slope of a non-linear curve is determined by the slope of a straight line that intersects the curve at that specific point.

In all graphs, an upward sloping line represents a direct relationship between the two variables. A downward slope represents an inverse relationship between the two variables. In reading any graph, one must always be very careful to understand what is being measured, what can be deduced and what cannot be deduced from the given graph.

To use **charts** correctly, one should remember the reasons one uses graphs. The general ideas are similar. It is usually a question as to which, a graph or chart, is more capable of adequately portraying the information one wants to illustrate. One can see the difference between them and realize that in many ways graphs and charts are interrelated. One of the most common types, because it is easiest to read and understand, even for the lay person, is the **pie-chart**.

You can see pie-charts used often, especially when one is trying to illustrate the differences in percentages among various items, or when one is demonstrating the divisions of a whole.

Skill 22.2   Identify the purpose, message, and/or historical context of a political poster or editorial cartoon

Posters. The power of the political poster in the 21st century seems trivial considering the barrage of electronic campaigning, mudslinging, and reporting that seems to have taken over the video and audio media in election season. Even so, the political poster has been a powerful propaganda tool, and it has been around for a long time. For example, in the 1st century AD, a poster that calls for the election of a Satrius as quinquennial has survived to this day. Nowhere have political posters been used more powerfully or effectively than in Russia in the 1920s in the campaign to promote communism. Many of the greatest Russian writers of that era were the poster writers. Those posters would not be understood at all except in the light of what was going on in the country at the time.

However, today we see them primarily at rallies and protests where they are usually hand-lettered and hand-drawn. The message is rarely subtle. Understanding the messages of posters requires little thought as a rule. However, they are usually meaningless unless the context is clearly understood. For example, a poster reading "Camp Democracy" can only be understood in the context of the protests of the Iraq War near President George W. Bush's home near Crawford, Texas. "Impeach" posters are understood in 2006 to be directed at President Bush, not a local mayor or representative.

Cartoons. The political cartoon (aka editorial) presents a message or point of view concerning people, events, or situations using caricature and symbolism to convey the cartoonist's ideas, sometimes subtly, sometimes brashly, but always quickly. A good political cartoon will have wit and humor, which is usually obtained by exaggeration that is slick and not used merely for comic effect. It will also have a foundation in truth; that is, the characters must be recognizable to the viewer and the point of the drawing must have some basis in fact even if it has a philosophical bias. The third requirement is a moral purpose.

Using political cartoons as a teaching tool enlivens lectures, prompts classroom discussion, promotes critical thinking, develops multiple talents and learning styles, and helps prepare students for standardized tests. It also provides humor. However, it may be the most difficult form of literature to teach. Many teachers who choose to include them in their social studies curricula caution that, while students may enjoy them, it's doubtful whether they are actually getting the cartoonists' messages.

The best strategy for teaching such a unit is through a subskills approach that leads students step-by-step to higher orders of critical thinking. For example, the teacher can introduce caricature and use cartoons to illustrate the principles. Students are able to identify and interpret symbols if they are given the principles for doing so and get plenty of practice, and cartoons are excellent for this. It can cut down the time it takes for students to develop these skills, and many of the students who might lose the struggle to learn to identify symbols may overcome the roadblocks through the analysis of political cartoons. Many political cartoons exist for the teacher to use in the classroom and they are more readily available than ever before.

A popular example of an editorial cartoon that provides a way to analyze current events in politics is the popular comic strip "Doonesbury" by Gary Trudeau. For example, in the time period prior to the 2004 presidential election, Alex, the media savvy teenager does her best for political participation. In January she rallies her middle school classmates to the phones for a Deanathon and by August she is luring Ralph Nader supporters into discussions on Internet chat rooms. Knowledgeable about government, active in the political process, and willing to enlist others, Alex has many traits sought by the proponents of civics education.

Skill 22.3   Use information derived from visual sources to analyze historical, geographic, economic, or political science issues and phenomena

Suppose you are preparing for a presentation on the Civil War and you intend to focus on causes, an issue that has often been debated. If you are examining the matter of slavery as a cause, a graph of the increase in the number of slaves by area of the country for the previous 100 years would be very useful in the discussion. If you are focusing on the economic conditions that were driving the politics of the age, graphs of GDP, distribution of wealth geographically and individually, and relationship of wealth to ownership of slaves would be useful.

If you are discussing the war in Iraq, detailed maps with geopolitical elements would help clarify not only the day-to-day happenings but also the historical features that led up to it. A map showing the number of oil fields and where they are situated with regard to the various political factions and charts showing output of those fields historically would be useful.

If you are teaching the history of space travel, photos of the most famous astronauts will add interest to the discussion. Graphs showing the growth of the industry and charts showing discoveries and their relationship to the lives of everyday Americans would be helpful.

Geography and history classes are notoriously labeled by students as dull. With all the visual resources available nowadays, those classes have the potential for being the most exciting courses in the curriculum.

Skill 22.4 Recognize the problem of cartographic distortion and analyze the advantages and disadvantages of various standard map projections

We use **illustrations** of various sorts because it is often easier to demonstrate a given idea visually instead of orally. Sometimes it is even easier to do so with an illustration than a description. This is especially true in the areas of education and research because humans are visually stimulated. It is a fact that any idea presented visually in some manner is always easier to understand and to comprehend than simply getting an idea across verbally, by hearing it or reading it. Among the more common illustrations used in political and social sciences are various types of **maps, graphs and charts.**

Photographs and **globes** are useful as well, but as they are limited in what kind of information that they can show, they are rarely used. Unless, as in the case of a photograph, it is of a particular political figure or a time that one wishes to visualize.

Although maps have advantages over globes and photographs, they do have a major disadvantage. This problem must be considered as well. The major problem of all maps comes about because most maps are flat and the Earth is a sphere. It is impossible to reproduce exactly on a flat surface an object shaped like a sphere. In order to put the earth's features onto a map they must be stretched in some way. This stretching is called **distortion.**

Distortion does not mean that maps are wrong it simply means that they are not perfect representations of the Earth or its parts. **Cartographers,** or mapmakers, understand the problems of distortion. They try to design them so that there is as little distortion as possible in the maps.

The process of putting the features of the Earth onto a flat surface is called **projection**. All maps are really map projections. There are many different types. Each one deals in a different way with the problem of distortion. Map projections are made in a number of ways. Some are done using complicated mathematics. However, the basic ideas behind map projections can be understood by looking at the three most common types:

(1) **Cylindrical Projections** - These are done by taking a cylinder of paper and wrapping it around a globe. A light is used to project the globe's features onto the paper. Distortion is least where the paper touches the globe. For example, suppose that the paper was wrapped so that it touched the globe at the equator, the map from this projection would have just a little distortion near the equator. However, in moving north or south of the equator, the distortion would increase as you moved further away from the equator. The best known and most widely used cylindrical projection is the **Mercator Projection.** Gerard's Mercator, a Flemish mapmaker, first developed it in 1569.

(2) **Conical Projections** - The name for these maps comes from the fact that the projection is made onto a cone of paper. The cone is made so that it touches a globe at the base of the cone only. It can also be made so that it cuts through part of the globe in two different places. Again, there is the least distortion where the paper touches the globe. If the cone touches at two different points, there is some distortion at both of them. Conical projections are most often used to map areas in the **middle latitudes**. Maps of the United States are most often conical projections. This is because most of the country lies within these latitudes.

(3) **Flat-Plane Projections** - These are made with a flat piece of paper. It touches the globe at one point only. Areas near this point show little distortion. Flat-plane projections are often used to show the areas of the north and south poles. One such flat projection is called a **Gnomonic Projection**. On this kind of map all meridians appear as straight lines, Gnomonic projections are useful because any straight line drawn between points on it forms a **Great-Circle Route**.

Great-Circle Routes can best be described by thinking of a globe and when using the globe the shortest route between two points on it can be found by simply stretching a string from one point to the other. However, if the string was extended in reality, so that it took into effect the globe's curvature, it would then make a great-circle. A great-circle is any circle that cuts a sphere, such as the globe, into two equal parts. Because of distortion, most maps do not show great-circle routes as straight lines, Gnomonic projections, however, do show the shortest distance between the two places as a straight line, because of this they are valuable for navigation. They are called **Great-Circle Sailing Maps.**

Skill 22.5   Evaluate the appropriateness of alternative written and graph formats for conveying a specific body of information

In other words, how do you choose when to use words, when to use charts, when to use graphs, and when to use maps and/or illustrations (photos, etc.)? This is sometimes a difficult choice to make. To a large extent, it depends on the audience. A picture is worth a thousand words to most audiences; however, for children they are vital, as they are sometimes for older people. Also, if some members of the audience are speakers of English as a second language, graphics are extremely useful in increasing understanding of principles and events.

Another factor that is important in such a choice is how complicated the information is. Charts can go a long way in simplifying even complex ideas. Maps can defog a discussion of a geographical area that is not familiar to the audience. Photographs of people, places, or happenings can bring ideas to life. Something else to consider is retention. If an idea is reinforced by a visual, it will be remembered longer because the listener has had access to it through more than one sense.

COMPETENCY 23 UNDERSTAND HOW TO ANALYZE, EVALUATE, AND SYNTHESIZE SOCIAL STUDIES INFORMATION, MAKE GENERALIZATIONS, AND REACH SUPPORTABLE JUDGMENTS AND CONCLUSIONS

Skill 23.1 Identify central questions in public policy debates

The struggle over what is to be the fair method to ensure equal political representation for all different groups in the United States continues to dominate the national debate. This has revolved around the problems of trying to ensure proper racial and minority representation. Various civil rights acts, notably the Voting Rights Act of 1965, sought to eliminate the remaining features of unequal suffrage in the United States.

Most recently, the question has revolved around the issue of what is called "**gerrymandering,**" which involves the adjustment of various electoral districts in order to achieve a predetermined goal. Usually this is used in regards to the problem of minority political representation. The fact that gerrymandering sometimes creates odd and unusual looking districts (this is where the practice gets its name) and most often the sole basis of the adjustments is racial. This has led to the questioning of this practice being a fair, let alone a constitutional, way for society to achieve its desired goals. This promises to be the major issue in national electoral politics for some time to come. The debate has centered on those of the "left" (Liberals), who favor such methods, and the "right" (Conservatives), who oppose them. Overall, most Americans would consider themselves in the "middle" (Moderates).

How best to move forward with ensuring civil liberties and civil rights for all continues to dominate the national debate. In recent times, issues seem to revolve not around individual rights, but what has been called "group rights" has been raised. At the forefront of the debate is whether some specific remedies like affirmative action, quotas, gerrymandering and various other forms of preferential treatment are actually fair or just as bad as the ills they are supposed to cure. At present, no easy answers seem to be forthcoming. It is a testament to the American system that it has shown itself able to enter into these debates, to find solutions and tended to come out stronger.

Skill 23.2   Distinguish between fact and opinion in conflicting historical narratives

"The sky is blue." "The sky looks like rain." One of those statements is a fact and the other is an opinion. This is because one is **readily provable by objective empirical data**, while the other is a **subjective evaluation based upon personal bias**. This means that facts are things that can be proved by the usual means of study and experimentation. We can look and see the color of the sky. Since the shade we are observing is expressed as the color blue and is an accepted norm, the observation that the sky is blue is therefore a fact. (Of course, this depends on other external factors such as time and weather conditions, but in general this is a factual statement.)

This brings us to our next idea: that it looks like rain. This is a subjective observation in that an individual's perception will differ from another. What looks like rain to one person will not necessarily look like that to another.

This is an important concept to understand since much of what actually is studied in political science is, in reality, simply the opinions of various political theorists and philosophers. The truth of their individual philosophies is demonstrated by how well they, (when they have been tried), work in the so called "real world."

The question thus remains as to how to differentiate fact from opinion. The best and only way is to ask oneself if what is being stated can be proved from other sources, by other methods, or by the simple process of **reasoning**.

Historians use primary sources from the actual time they are studying whenever possible. Ancient Greek records of interaction with Egypt, letters from an Egyptian ruler to regional governors, and inscriptions from the Fourteenth Egyptian Dynasty are all primary sources created at or near the actual time being studied. Letters from a nineteenth century Egyptologist would not be considered primary sources, as they were created thousands of years after the fact and may not actually be about the subject being studied.

The resources used in the study of history can be divided into two major groups: **primary sources** and **secondary sources**.

Primary sources are works, records, etc. that were created during the period being studied or immediately after it. Secondary sources are works written significantly after the period being studied and based upon primary sources. "Primary sources are the basic materials that provide the raw data and information for the historian. Secondary sources are the works that contain the explications of, and judgments on, this primary material." [Source: Norman F Cantor & Richard I. Schneider. "HOW TO STUDY HISTORY," Harlan Davidson, Inc., 1967, pp. 23-24.]

Skill 23.3 Analyze factors affecting the reliability of source materials

Primary sources include the following kinds of materials:

- Documents that reflect the immediate, everyday concerns of people: memoranda, bills, deeds, charters, newspaper reports, pamphlets, graffiti, popular writings, journals or diaries, records of decision-making bodies, letters, receipts, snapshots, etc.
- Theoretical writings which reflect care and consideration in composition and an attempt to convince or persuade. The topic will generally be deeper and have more persuasive value than is the case with "immediate" documents. These may include newspaper or magazine editorials, sermons, political speeches, philosophical writings, etc.
- Narrative accounts of events, ideas, trends, etc. written with intention by someone contemporary with the events described.
- Statistical data, although statistics may be misleading.
- Literature and nonverbal materials, novels, stories, poetry and essays from the period, as well as coins, archaeological artifacts, and art produced during the period.

Guidelines for the use of primary resources:

1. Be certain that you understand how language was used at the time of writing and that you understand the context in which it was produced.
2. Do not read history blindly; but be certain that you understand both explicit and implicit referenced in the material.
3. Read the entire text you are reviewing; do not simply extract a few sentences to read.
4. Although anthologies of materials may help you identify primary source materials, the full original text should be consulted.

Secondary sources include the following kinds of materials:

- Books written on the basis of primary materials about the period of time
- Books written on the basis of primary materials about persons who played a major role in the events under consideration
- Books and articles written on the basis of primary materials about the culture, the social norms, the language, and the values of the period
- Quotations from primary sources
- Statistical data on the period
- The conclusions and inferences of other historians
- Multiple interpretations of the ethos of the time

Guidelines for the use of secondary sources:

1. Do not rely upon only a single secondary source.
2. Check facts and interpretations against primary sources whenever possible.
3. Do not accept the conclusions of other historians uncritically.
4. Place greatest reliance on secondary sources created by the best and most respected scholars.
5. Do not use the inferences of other scholars as if they were facts.
6. Ensure that you recognize any bias the writer brings to his/her interpretation of history.
7. Understand the primary point of the book as a basis for evaluating the value of the material presented in it to your questions.

Skill 23.4   Synthesize social studies information from multiple sources

A synthesis of information from multiple sources requires an understanding of the content chosen for the synthesis, first of all. The writer of the synthesis will, no doubt, wish to incorporate his/her own ideas, particularly in any conclusions that are drawn, and show relationships to those of the chosen sources. That can only happen if the writer has a firm grip on what others have said or written. The focus is not so much on documentary methods but on techniques of critically examining and evaluating the ideas of others. Even so, careful documentation is extremely important in this type of presentation, particularly with regard to which particular edition is being read in the case of written sources; and date, location, etc., of online sources. The phrase "downloaded from such-and-such a website on such-and-such a date" is useful. If the conversation, interview, or speech is live, date, circumstances, and location must be indicated.

The purpose of a synthesis is to understand the works of others and to use that work in shaping a conclusion. The writer or speaker must clearly differentiate between the ideas that come from a source and his/her own.

Skill 23.5 Determine whether specific conclusions or generalizations are supported by verifiable evidence

Helping students become critical thinkers is an important objective of the social studies curriculum. The history, geography, and political science classes provide many opportunities to teach students to recognize and understand reasoning errors. Errors tend to fall into two categories: a) inadequate reasons and b) misleading reasoning.

Inadequate reasons:

1. Faulty analogies: The two things being compared must be similar in all significant aspects if the reasoning is to be relied upon. If there is a major difference between the two, then the argument falls apart.
2. False cause *(Post Hoc Ergo Propter Hoc)*: after this, therefore because of this. There must be a factual tie between the effect and its declared cause.
3. *Ad Hominen*: Attacking the person instead of addressing the issues.
4. Slippery Slope: The domino effect. This is usually prophetic in nature—predicting what will follow if a certain event occurs. This is only reliable when it is used in hindsight—not in predicting the future because no one is wise enough to know the future.
5. Hasty Conclusions: Leaping to conclusions when not enough evidence has been collected. A good example is the accusations made in the 1996 bombing at the summer Olympics in Atlanta. Not enough evidence had been collected and the wrong man was arrested.

Misleading reasoning:

1. The Red Herring: comes from a smoked fish being dragged across a trail to distract hunting dogs. Often used in politics—getting your opponent on the defensive about a different issue than the one under discussion.
2. *Ad Populum* or Jumping on the Bandwagon: "Everybody's doing it, so it must be right." Biggest is not necessarily best when it comes to following a crowd.
3. Appeal to Tradition: "We've always done it this way." Often used to squelch innovation.
4. The False Dilemma or the Either/Or Fallacy: No other alternative is possible except the extremes at each end. Used in politics a lot. The creative statesman finds other alternatives.

<u>DOMAIN VI.</u>   HISTORY: CONSTRUCTED RESPONSE ASSIGNMENT

This assignment will be to write a response of about 150 -300 words on the assigned topic. The response will be evaluated on the basis of three criteria:

- PURPOSE: Fulfill the charge of the assignment.
- APPLICATION OF CONTENT: Accurately and effectively apply the relevant knowledge and skills.
- SUPPORT: Support the response with appropriate examples and/or sound reasoning reflecting an understanding of the relevant knowledge and skills.

Assigned Topic: Describe the rivalry between England and France

Although geographically located on opposite sides of the English Channel, historically, France and England have been on opposite sides of conflicts for the last few centuries.

One historical event was the Hundred Years' War that lasted 116 years. The Hundred Years' War was not the beginning of this conflict; it was a continuation of one that had existed since the time of the first Norman Kings of England. Every king from Henry II to Edward II had engaged in warfare against French Kings on the continent since the English laid claim to the French throne. However, by 1214, the Kings of England had lost a substantial portion of their lands in France including Normandy.

The ongoing rivalry over the years forced the Native Americans in the New World to take sides against each other in the ensuing conflicts and battles. The French and Indian War fought in North America pitted England and the young colonists against the French explorers who were laying claim to the vast lands of the Ohio Country.

When the colonists revolted against the English King in 1776, the French were willing to help the colonists fight the English.

During the War of 1812, the Americans battled Great Britain, then the world's greatest military power, especially on the high seas, while Great Britain was fighting France during the Napoleonic Wars that ultimately brought great change to Europe.

In recent history, the two countries continue to oppose each other in the latest War in Iraq, where the United Kingdom supports the United States' efforts to fight the war on terror in the Middle East and France has provided little to no support to the United States. It would seem that if there is a conflict or global issue to be had, you will find England on one side of the table and France on the other.

Bibliography

Adams, James Truslow. (2006). "The March of Democracy," Vol 1. "The Rise of the Union". New York: Charles Scribner's Sons, Publisher.

Barbini, John & Warshaw, Steven. (2006). "The World Past and Present." New York: Harcourt, Brace, Jovanovich, Publishers.

Berthon, Simon & Robinson, Andrew. (2006. "The Shape of the World." Chicago: Rand McNally, Publisher.

Bram, Leon (Vice-President and Editorial Director). (2006). "Funk and Wagnalls New Encyclopedia." United States of America.

Burns, Edward McNall & Ralph, Philip Lee. (2006. "World Civilizations Their History and Culture" (5th ed.). New York: W.W. Norton & Company, Inc., Publishers.

Dauben, Joseph W. (2006). "The World Book Encyclopedia." Chicago: World Book Inc. A Scott Fetzer Company, Publisher.

De Blij, H.J. & Muller, Peter O. (2006). "Geography Regions and Concepts" (Sixth
Edition). New York: John Wiley & Sons, Inc., Publisher.

Encyclopedia Americana. (2006). Danbury, Connecticut: Grolier Incorporated, Publisher.

Heigh, Christopher (Editor). (2006). "The Cambridge Historical Encyclopedia of Great Britain and Ireland." Cambridge: Cambridge University Press, Publisher.

Hunkins, Francis P. & Armstrong, David G. (2006). "World Geography People and Places." Columbus, Ohio: Charles E. Merrill Publishing Co. A Bell & Howell Company, Publishers.

Jarolimek, John; Anderson, J. Hubert & Durand, Loyal, Jr. (2006). "World Neighbors." New York: Macmillan Publishing Company. London: Collier Macmillan Publishers.

McConnell, Campbell R. (2006). "Economics-Principles, Problems, and Policies" (Tenth Edition). New York: McGraw-Hill Book Company, Publisher.

Millard, Dr. Anne & Vanags, Patricia. (2006). "The Usborne Book of World History." London: Usborne Publishing Ltd., Publisher.

Novosad, Charles (Executive Editor). (2006). "The Nystrom Desk Atlas." Chicago: Nystrom Division of Herff Jones, Inc., Publisher.

Patton, Clyde P.; Rengert, Arlene C.; Saveland, Robert N.; Cooper, Kenneth S. & Cam, Patricia T. (2006). "A World View." Morristown, N.J.: Silver Burdette Companion, Publisher.

Schwartz, Melvin & O'Connor, John R. (2006). "Exploring A Changing World." New York: Globe Book Company, Publisher.

"The Annals of America: Selected Readings on Great Issues in American History 1620-1968." (2006). United States of America: William Benton, Publisher.

Tindall, George Brown & Shi, David E. (2006). "America-A Narrative History" (Fourth Edition). New York: W.W. Norton & Company, Publisher.

Todd, Lewis Paul & Curti, Merle. (2006). "Rise of the American Nation" (Third Edition). New York: Harcourt, Brace, Jovanovich, Inc., Publishers.

Tyler, Jenny; Watts, Lisa; Bowyer, Carol; Trundle, Roma & Warrender, Annabelle (2006) 'The Usbome Book of World Geography." London: Usbome Publishing Ltd., Publisher.

Willson, David H. (2006). "A History of England." Hinsdale, Illinois: The Dryder Press, inc., Publisher

Sample Test

1. **Divisions of time in history (periodizations) may be determined by all but which of the following?** *(Easy) (Skill 1.1)*

    A. Date

    B. Geography

    C. Cultural Advances

    D. Individual Historians

2. **The "father of history" is considered to be:** *(Easy) (Skill 1.1)*

    A. Aristotle

    B. Thucydides

    C. Plato

    D. Herodotus

3. **Which of the following would not be considered a primary source?** *(Rigorous) (Skill 1.3)*

    A. An 1863 newspaper account of the Gettysburg address

    B. The text of the Gettysburg Address

    C. A historical analysis of the Gettysburg Address

    D. A narrative account of the Gettysburg Address from a spectator in the crowd

4. **The study of social behavior of minority groups would be in the area of:** *(Average Rigor) (Skill 1.4)*

    A. Psychohistory

    B. Psychology

    C. Sociology

    D. Cultural Geography

5. "Participant observation" is a method of study most closely associated with and used in: *(Rigorous) (Skill 1.4)*

   A. Anthropology

   B. Archaeology

   C. Sociology

   D. Political Science

6. The study of a people's language and writing would be part of all of the following except: *(Rigorous) (Skill 1.4)*

   A. Sociology

   B. Archaeology

   C. History

   D. Geography

7. The study of past human cultures based on physical artifacts is: *(Average Rigor)(Skill 1.4)*

   A. History

   B. Anthropology

   C. Cultural Geography

   D. Archaeology

8. Which of the following is not one of the schools of narrative history? *(Rigorous) (Skill 1.5)*

   A. Comparative Sociological

   B. Economic

   C. Intellectual

   D. Political-Institutional

9. The early ancient civilizations developed systems of government: *(Rigorous) (Skill 2.1)*

   A. To provide for defense against attack

   B. To regulate trade

   C. To regulate and direct the economic activities of the people as they worked together in groups

   D. To decide on the boundaries of the different fields during planting seasons

10. The principle of zero in mathematics is the discovery of which ancient civilization? *(Average Rigor) (Skill 2.1)*

A. Egypt

B. Persia

C. India

D. Babylon

11. Which ancient civilization is credited with being the first to develop irrigation techniques through the use of canals, dikes, and devices for raising water? *(Average Rigor) (Skill 2.1)*

A. The Sumerians

B. The Egyptians

C. The Babylonians

D.The Akkadians

12. Bathtubs, hot and cold running water, and sewage systems with flush toilets were developed by the: *(Average Rigor) (Skill 2.1)*

A. Minoans

B. Mycenaeans

C. Phoenicians

D. Greeks

13. An early cultural group was so skillful in navigating on the seas that they were able to sail at night guided by stars. They were the: *(Average Rigor) (Skill 2.1)*

A. Greeks

B. Persians

C. Minoans

D. Phoenicians

14. Of the legacies of the Roman Empire listed below, the most influential, effective and lasting is: *(Rigorous) (Skill 2.2)*

A. The language of Latin

B. Roman law, justice, and political system

C. Engineering and building

D. The writings of its poets and historians

15. **Which of the following areas would NOT be a primary area of hog production?** *(Rigorous) (Skill 2.3)*

   A. Midland England

   B. The Mekong delta of Vietnam

   C. Central Syria

   D. Northeast Iowa

16. **The first ancient civilization to introduce and practice monotheism was the:** *(Average Rigor) (Skill 2.3)*

   A. Sumerians

   Minoans

   Phoenicians

   Hebrews

17. **Much of the history of Sub-Saharan Africa was recorded by _____ historians.** *(Average Rigor) (Skill 2.4)*

   A. Islamic

   B. Christian

   C. Buddhist

   D. Hindu

18. **India's greatest ruler is considered to be:** *(Average Rigor) (Skill 2.5)*

   A. Akbar

   B. Ashoka

   C. Babur

   D. Jahangeer

19. **Which one of the following is not an important legacy of the Byzantine Empire?** *(Rigorous) (Skill 2.5)*

   A. It protected Western Europe from various attacks from the East by such groups as the Persians, Ottoman Turks, and Barbarians

   B. It played a part in preserving the literature, philosophy, and language of ancient Greece

   C. Its military organization was the foundation for modern armies

   D. It kept the legal traditions of Roman government, collecting and organizing many ancient Roman laws

20. **Which one of the following did not contribute to the early medieval European civilization?** *(Rigorous) (Skill 2.6)*

   A. The heritage from the classical cultures

   B. The Christian religion

   C. The influence of the German Barbarians

   D. The spread of ideas through trade and commerce

21. **The Lords of feudal Japan were known as**: *(Easy) (Skill 2.6)*

   A. Daimyo

   B. Samurai

   C. Ronin

   D. Bushido

22. **All of the following were accomplishments of the Renaissance except:** *(Rigorous) (Skill 3.1)*

   A. Invention of the printing press

   B. A rekindling of interest in the learning of classical Greece and Rome

   C. Growth in literature, philosophy and art

   D. Better military tactics

23. **The results of the Renaissance, Enlightenment, Commercial and Industrial Revolutions were more unfortunate for the people of:** *(Rigorous) (Skill 3.1)*

   A. Asia

   B. Latin America

   C. Africa

   D. Middle East

24. The ideas and innovations of the period of the Renaissance were spread throughout Europe mainly because of: *(Rigorous)* *(Skill 3.1)*

    A. Extensive exploration

    B. Craft workers and their guilds

    C. The invention of the printing press

    D. Increased travel and trade

25. The "divine right" of kings was the key political characteristic of: *(Easy)* *(Skill 3.2)*

    A. The Age of Absolutism

    B. The Age of Reason

    C. The Age of Feudalism

    D. The Age of Despotism

26. The English explorer who gave England its claim to North American was: **(Easy)** *(Skill 3.3)*

    A. Raleigh

    B. Hawkins

    C. Drake

    D. Cabot

27. Colonial expansion by Western European powers in the 18th and 19th centuries was due primarily to: *(Rigorous)* *(Skill 3.3)*

    A. Building and opening the Suez Canal

    B. The Industrial Revolution

    C. Marked improvements in transportation

    D. Complete independence of all the Americas and loss of European domination and influence

28. Nineteenth century imperialism by Western European nations had important and far-reaching effects on the colonial peoples they ruled. All four of the following are the result of this. Which one was most important and had lasting effects on key 20th century events? *(Rigorous)* *(Skill 3.3)*

    A. Local wars were ended

    B. Living standards were raised

    C. Demands for self government and feelings of nationalism surfaced

    D. Economic developments occurred

29. **The Age of Exploration begun in the 1400s was led by:** *(Easy) (Skill 3.3)*

   A. The Portuguese

   B. The Spanish

   C. The English

   D. The Dutch

30. **Which scientist introduced a radical approach to the study of motion, examining not why but how objects moved?** *(Average Rigor) (Skill 3.4)*

   A. Kepler

   B. Pascal

   C. Galileo

   D. Newton

31. **Great Britain became the center of technological and industrial development during the 19th century chiefly on the basis of:** *(Rigorous) (Skill 3.4)*

   A. Central location relative to the population centers of Europe

   B. Colonial conquests and military victories over European powers

   C. Reliance on exterior sources of financing

   D. Resources of coal and production of steel

32. **Which Enlightenment philosopher pioneered the doctrine of empiricism?** *(Average Rigor) (Skill 3.5)*

   A. David Hume

   B. John Locke

   C. Jean-Jacques Rousseau

   D. Immanuel Kant

33. **Which country was not one of the principal nations in the Vietnam War?** *(Easy) (Skill 4.1)*

   A. United States

   B. Australia

   C. New Zealand

   D. France

34. **Which of the following most closely characterizes the geopolitical events of the USSR in 1991-92:** *(Rigorous) (Skill 4.1)*

   A. The USSR established greater military and economic control over the 15 Soviet republics

   B. The Baltic states (Estonia, Latvia, Lithuania) declared independence, while the remainder of the USSR remained intact

   C. Fourteen of 15 Soviet republics declared some degree of autonomy, the USSR was officially dissolved, and the Supreme Soviet rescinded the Soviet Treaty of 1922

   D. All 15 Soviet republics simultaneously declared immediate and full independence from the USSR with no provisions for a transitional form of government

35. **Starting in the 19th century, Europe entered into a 100-year period of relative peace following the defeat of which person?** *(Average Rigor) (Skill 4.2)*

   A. Napoleon

   B. Bismarck

   C. Franco

   D. Cromwell

36. **Which one of the following would not be considered a result of World War II?** *(Rigorous) (Skill 4.3)*

   A. Economic depressions and slow resumption of trade and financial aid

   B. Western Europe was no longer the center of world power

   C. The beginnings of new power struggles not only in Europe but in Asia as well

   D. Territorial and boundary changes for many nations, especially in Europe

37. China's last imperial ruling dynasty was one of its most stable and successful and, under its rule, Chinese culture made an outstanding impression on Western nations. This dynasty was: *(Easy)* *(Skill 4.4)*

A. Min

B. Manchu

C. Han

D. Chou

38. Which of the following is most responsible for making electronic goods affordable to most people? *(Rigorous)* *(Skill 4.5)*

A. Capitalism

B. Mass Production

C. Outsourcing

D. The Internet

39. The crisis of ___ marked the beginning of the end for the First Era of Globalization. *(Average Rigor)* *(Skill 4.6)*

A. The Gold Standard

B. Ethnic Conflicts

C. The Socialist Revolution

D. The Rise of Facism

40. An extensive knowledge of surgery and medicine as well as principles of irrigation, fertilization and terrace farming was unique to: *(Average Rigor)* *(Skill 5.1)*

A. The Mayans

B. The Atacamas

C. The Incas

D. The Tarapacas

41. What was a major source of contention between American settlers in Texas and the Mexican government in the 1830s and 1840s? (Rigorous) *(Skill 6.2)*

A. The Americans wished to retain slavery which had been outlawed in Mexico

B. The Americans had agreed to learn Spanish and become Roman Catholic, but failed to do so

C. The Americans retained ties to the United States, and Santa Ana feared the power of the U.S.

D. All of the above were contentious issues between American settlers and the Mexican government

42. Which one of the following is not a reason why Europeans came to the New World? (Rigorous) *(Skill 5.2)*

A. To find resources in order to increase wealth

B. To establish trade

C. To increase a ruler's power and importance

D. To spread Christianity

43. The year 1619 was memorable for the colony of Virginia. Three events occurred resulting in lasting effects on US history. Which one of the following is not one of the events? (Rigorous) *(Skill 5.2)*

A. Twenty African slaves arrived

B. The London Company granted the colony a charter making it independent

C. The colonists were given the right by the London Company to govern themselves through representative government in the Virginia House of Burgesses

D. The London Company sent to the colony 60 women who were quickly married, establishing families and stability in the colony

44. **The Boston Tea Party happened as a result of the passage of which act by Parliament?** *(Easy) (Skill 5.3)*

    A. Stamp Act

    B. Quartering Act

    C. Sugar Act

    D. Townshend Act

45. **Under the brand new Constitution, the most urgent of the many problems facing the new federal government was that of:** *(Rigorous) (Skill 5.4)*

    A. Maintaining a strong army and navy

    B. Establishing a strong foreign policy

    C. Raising money to pay salaries and war debts

    D. Setting up courts, passing Federal laws, and providing for law enforcement officers

46. **The US Constitution was a vast improvement over the weak Articles of Confederation. Which one of the four statements below is not a description of the Constitution?** *(Rigorous) (Skill 5.4)*

    A. The establishment of a strong central government in no way lessened or weakened the individual states

    B. Individual rights were protected and secured

    C. The Constitution demands unquestioned respect and subservience to the federal government by all states and citizens

    D. Its flexibility and adaptation to change gives it a sense of timelessness

47. US foreign minister Robert R. Livingstone said, "From this day the United States takes their place among the greatest powers." He was referring to the action taken by President Thomas Jefferson: *(Rigorous) (Skill 5.5)*

A. Who had authorized the purchase of the Louisiana Purchase

B. Who sent the US Marines and naval ships to fight the Barbary pirates

C. Who had commissioned the Lewis and Clark Expedition

D. Who repealed the Embargo Act

48. "Marbury vs Madison (1803)" was an important Supreme Court case, which set the precedent for: *(Average Rigor) (Skill 5.5)*

A. The elastic clause

B. Judicial review

C. The supreme law of the land

D. Popular sovereignty in the territories

49. Which of the following was not a reason for the War of 1812? *(Rigorous) (Skill 5.6)*

A. Resentment by Spain over the sale, exploration, and settlement of the Louisiana Territory

B. The westward movement of farmers because of the need for more land

C. Canadian fur traders were agitating the northwestern Indians to fight American expansion

D. Britain continued to seize American ships on the high seas and force American seamen to serve aboard British ships

50. Which party later evolved into the modern Democrats? *(Easy) (Skill 6.1)*

A. Nationalists

B. Whigs

C. Anti-Federalists

D. Liberty

51. After the War of 1812, Henry Clay and others proposed economic measures, including raising tariffs to protect American farmers and manufacturers from foreign competition. These measures were proposed in the period known as: *(Average Rigor)* *(Skill 6.2)*

A. Era of Nationalism

B. American Expansion

C. Era of Good Feeling

D. American System

52. It can be reasonably stated that the change in the United States from primarily an agricultural country into a industrial power was due to all of the following except: *(Rigorous)* *(Skill 6.2)*

A. Tariffs on foreign imports

B. Millions of hardworking immigrants

C. An increase in technological developments

D. The change from steam to electricity for powering industrial machinery

53. The Social Gospel Movement arose during which of the Great Awakenings? *(Easy)* *(Skill 6.3)*

A. First

B. Second

C. Third

D. Fourth

54. Historians state that the West helped to speed up the Industrial Revolution. Which one of the following statements was not a reason for this? *(Rigorous)* *(Skill 6.4)*

A. Food supplies for the ever increasing urban populations came from farms in the West

B. A tremendous supply of gold and silver from western mines provided the capital needed to built industries

C. Descendants of western settlers, educated as engineers, geologists, and metallurgists in the East, returned to the West to mine the mineral resources needed for industry

D. Iron, copper, and other minerals from western mines were important resources in manufacturing products

55. The belief that the United States should control all of North America was called: *(Easy) (Skill 6.4)*

A. Westward Expansion

B. Pan Americanism

C. Manifest Destiny

D. Nationalism

56. Which ethnic group is most responsible for helping to construct the trans-national railroad? *(Average Rigor) (Skill 6.5)*

A. Asians

B. Hispanics

C. Native Americans

D. African Americans

57. The three day Battle of Gettysburg was the turning point of the Civil War for the North, leading to ultimate victory. The battle in the West, reinforcing the North's victory and sealing the South's defeat, was the day after Gettysburg at: *(Easy) (Skill 6.6)*

A. Perryville

B. Vicksburg

C. Stones River

D. Shiloh

58. The Radical Republicans who pushed the harsh Reconstruction measures through Congress after Lincoln's death lost public and moderate Republican support when they went too far: *(Rigorous) (Skill 6.6)*

A. In their efforts to impeach the President

B. By dividing 10 southern states into military-controlled districts

C. By making the 10 southern states give freed African Americans the right to vote

D. Sending carpetbaggers into the South to build up support for Congressional

59. The principle of "popular sovereignty" or allowing people in any territory to make their own decision concerning slavery was stated by: *(Average Rigor) (Skill 6.6)*

    A. Henry Clay

    B. Daniel Webster

    C. John C. Calhoun

    D. Stephen A. Douglas

60. The post-Civil War years were a time of low public morality, a time of greed, graft, and dishonesty. Which one of the reasons listed would not be accurate? *(Rigorous) (Skill 6.6)*

    A. The war itself because of the money and materials needed to carry on the War

    B. The very rapid growth of industry and big business after the War

    C. The personal example set by President Grant

    D. Unscrupulous heads of large impersonal corporations

61. The defeat of which European nation marked the United States' emergence as a world power? *(Average Rigor) (Skill 6.7)*

    A. England

    B. France

    C. Spain

    D. Germany

62. During the 1920s, the United States almost completely stopped all immigration. One of the reasons was: *(Rigorous) (Skill 7.1)*

    A. Plentiful cheap unskilled labor was no longer needed by industrialists

    B. War debts from World War I made it difficult to render financial assistance

    C. European nations were reluctant to allow people to leave since there was need to rebuild populations and economic stability

    D. The United States did not become a member of the League of Nations

63. Which figure was the leading spokesperson for African Americans of his era and the founder of the Tuskegee Institute? *(Easy) (Skill 7.2)*

A. Booker T. Washington

B. W.E.B. DuBois

C. George Washington Carver

D. Langston Hughes

64. Which two industries drove the economy of the 1920's? *(Average Rigor) (Skill 7.3)*

A. Automotive and Avionics

B. Textiles and Refining

C. Refining and Railroads

D. Automotive and Radio

65. Fascism is said to have often begun in socialist countries. Which was the first such country to go from socialism to fascism? *(Easy) (Skill 7.4)*

A. Spain

B. Italy

C. Russia

D. Germany

66. Of all the major causes of both World Wars I and II, the most significant one is considered to be: *(Rigorous) (Skill 7.5)*

A. Extreme nationalism

B. Military buildup and aggression

C. Political unrest

D. Agreements and alliances

67. A well-known World War II figure who said that democracy was like a rotting corpse that had to be replaced by a superior way of life and more efficient government was: *(Easy) (Skill 7.5)*

A. Hitler

B. Stalin

C. Tojo

D. Mussolini

68. President Truman suspended Gen. Douglas MacArthur from command of Allied forces in Korea because of: *(Rigorous)* *(Skill 7.5)*

    A. MacArthur's inability to make any progress against North Koreans

    B. MacArthur's criticism of Truman claiming that the president would not allow him to pursue aggressive tactics against communists

    C. The harsh treatment MacArthur exhibited toward the Japanese after World War II

    D. The ability of the U.S. Navy to continue the conflict without the presence of MacArthur

69. After World War II, the United States: *(Rigorous)* *(Skill 7.5)*

    A. Limited its involvement in European affairs

    B. Shifted foreign policy from Europe to Asia

    C. Passed legislation setting tariffs on imports and aiding farmers

    D. Entered the greatest period of economic growth in its history

70. The Soviet Union's military alliance with Eastern Europe was known as: *(Easy)* *(Skill 7.6)*

    A. NATO

    B. KGB

    C. The Iron Curtain

    D. The Warsaw Pact

71. Which of the following was the unsuccessful predecessor to the United Nations? *(Easy)* *(Skill 7.7)*

    A. League of Nations

    B. World Council

    C. World Court

    D. League of Five Nations

72. Native peoples in early New York consisted of a confederacy of Iroquois tribes known as the Haudenosaunee, the League of Peace and Power. How many tribes were there originally? *(Easy)* *(Skill 8.1)*

    A. 4

    B. 5

    C. 6

    D. 7

73. **New York was initially inhabited by what two native peoples?** *(Easy) (Skill 8.1)*

    A. Sioux and Pawnee

    B. Micmac and Wampanoag

    C. Iroquois and Algonquin

    D. Nez Perce and Cherokee

74. **Government regulation of economic activities for favorable balance of trade was the first major economic theory. It was called:** *(Rigorous) (Skill 8.2)*

    A. Laissez-faire

    B. Globalism

    C. Mercantilism

    D. Syndicalism

75. **Who was the governor of colonial New York known for buying present-day Manhattan for about $24 in trinkets?** *(Easy) (Skill 8.2)*

    A. Willem Kieft

    B. Duke of York

    C. Henry Hudson

    D. Peter Minuit

76. **France decided in 1777 to help the American colonies in their war against Britain. This decision was based on:** *(Rigorous) (Skill 8.3)*

    A. The naval victory of John Paul Jones over the British ship "Serapes"

    B. The survival of the terrible winter at Valley Forge

    C. The success of colonial guerilla fighters in the South

    D. The defeat of the British at Saratoga

77. **The tree at the end of the street where traders and dealers gathered informally later became the site of:** *(Easy) (Skill 8.4)*

    A. Broadway and 44th

    B. Main Street

    C. Avenue of the Americas

    D. New York Stock Exchange

78. **Which island was used as an immigrant processing center?** *(Easy) (Skill 8.5)*

    A. Ellis

    B. Staten

    C. Manhattan

    D. Liberty

79. **What was the name of the cultural revival after the Civil War that took place in New York?** *(Average Rigor) (Skill 8.6)*

    A. The Revolutionary War

    B. The Second Great Awakening

    C. The Harlem Renaissance

    D. The Gilded Age

80. **The idea that everyone has the right to education was expressed in which document?** *(Average Rigor) (Skill 9.1)*

    A. Declaration of the Rights of Man and Citizens

    B. Declaration of Independence

    C. UN Convention on the Rights of Children

    D. UN Declaration of Universal Human Rights

81. **Which group was interned in "War Relocation Camps" by the United Sates during WWII?** *(Easy) (Skill 9.2)*

    A. Japanese

    B. Germans

    C. Chinese

    D. Italians

82. **"Genocide" was first used to describe the deaths of:** *(Average Rigor) (Skill 9.3)*

    A. Native Americans at Wounded Knee

    B. The Holocaust

    C. Armenians at the hands of the Turks in WWI

    D. Warring tribes in Rwanda

83. **Slavery arose in the southern colonies partly as a perceived economical way to:** *(Rigorous) (Skill 9.4)*

   A. Increase the owner's wealth through human beings used as a source of exchange

   B. Cultivate large plantations of cotton, tobacco, rice, indigo, and other crops

   C. Provide Africans with humanitarian aid, such as health care, Christianity, and literacy

   D. Keep ships' holds full of cargo on two out of three legs of the "triangular trade" voyage

84. **Europeans generally bought slaves who had been captured by:** *(Average Rigor) (Skill 9.4)*

   A. Americans

   B. Europeans

   C. Asians

   D. Africans

85. **The Irish Famine resulted in part from a failure of what crop?** *(Easy) (Skill 9.5)*

   A. Potatoes

   B. Corn

   C. Rice

   D. Cabbage

86. **The founder of the birth control movement was:** *(Easy) (Skill 9.6)*

   A. Margaret Sanger

   B. Eleanor Roosevelt

   C. Jane Addams

   D. Elie Wiesel

87. **Which of the following most closely characterizes the Supreme Court's decision in Brown v. Board of Education?** *(Rigorous) (Skill 9.7)*

   A. Chief Justice Warren had to cast the deciding vote in a sharply divided the Supreme Court

   B. The decision was rendered along sectional lines, with northerners voting for integration and southerners voting for continued segregation

   C. The decision was 7-2 with dissenting justices not even preparing a written dissent

   D. Chief Justice Warren was able to persuade the Supreme Court to render a unanimous decision

88. **A geographer wishes to study the effects of a flood on subsequent settlement patterns. Which might he or she find most useful?** *(Rigorous) (Skill 10.1)*

   A. A film clip of the floodwaters

   B. An aerial photograph of the river's source

   C. Census data taken after the floo

   D. A soil map of the A and B horizons beneath the flood area

89. **Which location may be found in Canada?** *(Rigorous) (Skill 10.2)*

   A. 27 N 93 W

   B. 41 N 93 E

   C. 50 N 111 W

   D. 18 N 120 W

90. **Geography was first studied in an organized manner by:** *(Average Rigor) (Skill 10.1)*

    A. The Egyptians

    B. The Greeks

    C. The Romans

    D. The Arabs

91. **Meridians, or lines of longitude, not only help in pinpointing locations but are also used for:** *(Average Rigor) (Skill 10.2)*

    A. Measuring distance from the Poles

    B. Determining direction of ocean currents

    C. Determining the time around the world

    D. Measuring distance on the equator

92. **Which of the following is an example of relative location?** *(Rigorous) (Skill 10.2)*

    A. The Post Office is at the NW corner of 1st and Main

    B. The Post Office is down the street from the courthouse

    C. The Post Office is at 422 Elm

    D. The Post Office is at 48☐N 2☐E

93. **A description of how things are grouped in a given area is known as:** *(Average Rigor) (Skill 10.3)*
    A. Geography

    B. Spatial Organization

    C. Geometry

    D. Topography

94.	One of the foremost areas to which geography applies is: *(Average Rigor) (Skill 10.4)*

A.	Sociology

B.	Mathematics

C.	Economics

D.	Politics

95.	Which one of the following does not affect climate? *(Average Rigor) (Skill 11.1)*

A.	Elevation or altitude

B.	Ocean currents

C.	Latitude

D.	Longitude

96.	Soil erosion is most likely to occur in large amounts in: *(Average Rigor) (Skill 11.2)*

A.	Mountain ranges

B.	Deserts

C.	Tropical rainforests

D.	River valleys

97.	Almost half of the world's population lives in which areas? *(Average Rigor) (Skill 11.3)*

A.	Rural Areas

B.	Cities

C.	Suburbs

D.	Megalopolises

98.	Which one of the following is not a use for a region's wetlands? *(Rigorous) (Skill 11.4)*

A.	Produces fresh clean water

B.	Provides habitat for wildlife

C.	Provides water for hydroelectric power

D.	Controls floods

99. The end of hunting, gathering, and fishing among prehistoric people was due to: *(Rigorous)* *(Skill 11.5)*

    A. Domestication of animals

    B. Building crude huts and houses

    C. Development of agriculture

    D. Organized government in villages

100. Which branch of geography is concerned with the location of features and how they affect human activity? *(Average Rigor)* *(Skill 12.1)*

    A. Physical

    B. Cultural

    C. Sociological

    D. Historical

101. Which continent contains just one country? *(Easy)* *(Skill 12.2)*

    A. Asia

    B. Austria

    C. Antarctica

    D. Australia

102. The conversion of Constantine to Christianity is an example of the spreading of a belief system through: *(Rigorous)* *(Skill 12.3)*

    A. Conquest

    B. Commercial Exchange

    C. Education

    D. Cultural Exchange

103. Which of the following is not a natural resource industry? *(Rigorous) (Skill 12.4)*

    A. Fishing

    B. Farming

    C. Forestry

    D. Mining

104. The ___ model envisions cities in concentric circles. *(Average Rigor) (Skill 13.2)*

    A. Sector

    B. Von Thunen

    C. Burgess

    D. Hoyt

105. The Hudson River is named for Henry Hudson, an Englishman who was known for exploring the _____. *(Easy) (Skill 13.3)*

    A. Dutch

    B. English

    C. French

    D. Spanish

106. The growth of the suburbs often creates which type of segregation in cities? *(Average Rigor) (Skill 13.4)*

    A. Political

    B. Economic

    C. Ethnic

    D. Racial

107. Which branch of statistics is most concerned with people's social well-being? *(Average Rigor) (Skill 13.5)*

    A. Demography

    B. Paleography

    C. Causation

    D. Graphology

108. The designation of individuals or groups as they are influenced by their belonging to a particular group is known as: *(Average Rigor) (Skill 13.6)*

    A. Cosmopolitanism

    B. Cultural Identity

    C. Melting Pot

    D. Ethnography

109. **Which canal was built to link Lake Erie with the Hudson River?** *(Easy) (Skill 13.7)*

    A. Erie Canal

    B. Suez Canal

    C. Hudson Canal

    D. St Lawrence Seaway

110. **Potential customers for any product or service are not only called consumers but can also be called a:** *(Average Rigor) (Skill 14.1)*

    A. Resource

    B. Base

    C. Commodity

    D. Market

111. **Shopping centers represent which economic model?** *(Rigorous) (Skill 14.2)*

    A. Perfect Competition

    B. Oligopoly

    C. Monopoly

    D. Monopolistic Competition

112. **The economic system promoting individual ownership of land, capital, and businesses with minimal governmental regulations is called:** *(Rigorous) (Skill 14.3)*

    A. Macro-economy

    B. Micro-economy

    C. Laissez-faire

    D. Free enterprise

113. **The "father" of modern economics is considered by most economists to be:** *(Average Rigor) (Skill 14.3)*

    A. Thomas Robert Malthus

    B. John Stuart Mill

    C. Adam Smith

    D. John Maynard Keynes

114. The idea that continued population growth would, in future years, seriously affect a nation's productive capabilities was stated by: *(Average Rigor) (Skill 14.3)*

    A. Keynes

    B. Mill

    C. Malthus

    D. Friedman

115. The idea or proposal for more equal division of profits among employers and workers was put forth by: *(Average Rigor) (Skill 14.4)*

    A. Karl Marx

    B. Thomas Malthus

    C. Adam Smith

    D. John Stuart Mill

116. One method of trade restriction used by some nations is: *(Rigorous) (Skill 14.5)*

    A. Limited treaties

    B. Floating exchange rate

    C. Bill of exchange

    D. Import Quotas

117. If the price of Good G increases, what is likely to happen with regard to comparable Good H? *(Rigorous) (Skill 15.1)*

    A. The demand for Good G will stay the same

    B. The demand for Good G will increase

    C. The demand for Good H will increase

    D. The demand for Good H will decrease

118. The study of the ways in which different societies around the world deal with the problems of limited resources and unlimited needs and wants is in the area of: *(Rigorous) (Skill 15.2)*

   A. Economics

   B. Sociology

   C. Anthropology

   D. Political Science

119. The macro-economy consists of all but which of the following sectors? *(Rigorous) (Skill 15.3)*

   A. Consumer

   B. Business

   C. Foreign

   D. Private

120. Which of the following is an example of why the United States does not operate as a closed economy? *(Rigorous) (Skill 15.6)*

   A. Coffee

   B. Rice

   C. Cotton

   D. Oil

121. In the United States government, the power of taxation and borrowing is: *(Rigorous) (Skill 16.1)*

   A. Implied or suggested

   B. Concurrent or shared

   C. Delegated or expressed

   D. Reserved

122. The US economic system combines all but which of the following? *(Rigorous) (Skill 16.2)*

   A. Capital

   B. Cost

   C. Profit

   D. Competition

123. In the US government, the power of coining money is: *(Rigorous) (Skill 16.3)*

   A. Implied or suggested

   B. Concurrent or shared

   C. Delegated or expressed

   D. Reserved

124. In the United States, federal investigations into business activities are handled by the: *(Average Rigor) (Skill 16.3)*

    A. Department of Treasury

    B. Security & Exchange Commission

    C. Government Accounting Office

    D. Federal Trade Commission

125. The American labor union movement started gaining new momentum: *(Average Rigor) (Skill 16.4)*

    A. During the building of the railroads

    B. After 1865 with the growth of cities

    C. With the rise of industrial giants such as Carnegie and Vanderbilt

    D. During the war years of 1861-1865

126. The Fed will ___ interest rates to avoid inflation and ___ interest rates to stimulate the economy. *(Average Rigor) (Skill 16.5)*

    A. lower … raise

    B. raise … lower

    C. raise … also raise

    D. lower … also lower

127. Economic mobility refers particularly to what factor's ability to move? *(Rigorous) (Skill 16.6)*

    A. Resources

    B. Money

    C. Labor

    D. Management

128. The study of the exercise of power and political behavior in human society today would be conducted by experts in: *(Average Rigor) (Skill 17.2)*

   A. History

   B. Sociology

   C. Political Science

   D. Anthropology

129. Which of the following is an example of a direct democracy? *(Average Rigor) (Skill 17.3)*

   A. Elected representatives

   B. Greek city-states

   C. The United States Senate

   D. The United States House of Representative

130. The programs such as unemployment insurance and health insurance for the elderly are the responsibility of: *(Average Rigor) (Skill 17.4)*

   A. Federal government

   B. Local government

   C. State government

   D. Communal government

131. A political philosophy favoring or supporting rapid social changes in order to correct social and economic inequalities is called: *(Rigorous) (Skill 17.4)*

   A. Nationalism

   B. Liberalism

   C. Conservatism

   D. Federalism

132. The principle of "life, liberty, and the pursuit of happiness" was borrowed from the ideas expressed by which figure? *(Average Rigor) (Skill 18.1)*

    A. Locke

    B. Rousseau

    C. Aristotle

    D. Montesquieu

133. The foundation of modern constitutionalism is embodied in the idea that government is limited by law. This was stated by: *(Average Rigor) (Skill 18.2)*

    A. John Locke

    B. Rousseau

    C. St. Thomas Aquinas

    D. Montesquieu

134. To be eligible to be elected president, one must: *(Easy) (Skill 18.2)*

    A. Be a citizen for at least five years

    B. Be a citizen for seven years

    C. Have been born a citizen

    D. Be a naturalized citizen

135. After ratification of the new Constitution, the most urgent of the many problems facing the new federal government was that of: *(Rigorous) (Skill 18.2)*

    A. Maintaining a strong army and navy

    B. Establishing a strong foreign policy

    C. Raising money to pay salaries and war debts

    D. Setting up courts, passing federal laws, and providing for law enforcement officers

136. Which of the following is considered the basis of English constitutional liberties? *(Average Rigor)* *(Skill 18.3)*

A. Bill of Rights

B. Petition of Rights

C. Declaration of Rights

D. Magna Carta

137. The term that best describes how the Supreme Court can block laws that may be unconstitutional from being enacted is: *(Average Rigor)* *(Skill 18.3)*

A. Jurisprudence

B. Judicial Review

C. Exclusionary Rule

D. Right of Petition

138. The most basic level of participation in the political process is: *(Average Rigor)* *(Skill 18.4)*

A. Obeying laws

B. Donating time or money

C. Voting

D. Running for office

139. The source of authority for national, state, and local governments in the US is: *(Average Rigor)* *(Skill 18.5)*

A. The will of the people

B. The US Constitution

C. Written laws

D. The Bill of Rights

140. Which of the following is a recent attempt to encourage voter registration? *(Average Rigor)* *(Skill 18.6)*

A. Motor-Voter acts

B. Poll Taxes

C. Exit Polls

D. Literacy Tests

141. On the spectrum of American politics, the label that most accurately describes voters to the "right of center" is: *(Average Rigor)* *(Skill 19.1)*

A. Moderates

B. Liberals

C. Conservatives

D. Socialists

142. **Which of the following lobbying tactics is illegal?** *(Rigorous) (Skill 19.2)*

    A. Paying for Congress members to travel

    B. Direct communications with Congress members

    C. Paying for meals or other entertainment for Congress members

    D. Paying cash to Congress members

143. **Which one of the following is not a function or responsibility of the US political parties?** *(Rigorous) (Skill 19.3)*

    A. Conducting elections or the voting process

    B. Obtaining funds needed for election campaigns

    C. Choosing candidates to run for public office

    D. Making voters aware of issues and other public affairs information

144. **What is the one thing that drives American politics more than any other?** *(Average Rigor) (Skill 19.4)*

    A. Money

    B. Race

    C. Issues

    D. Party Lines

145. **Which group in the Executive Branch advises the President on foreign policy? (Average Rigor) (Skill 20.1)**

    A. NSC

    B. NSA

    C. CIA

    D. FBI

146. **Which program was established to aid Europe's economic recovery after World War II?** *(Easy) (Skill 20.2)*

    A. The Kennan Plan

    B. The Marshall Plan

    C. The Truman Doctrine

    D. The Cold War

147. **The United Nations Security Council has __ members, of which ___ are permanent members.** *(Average Rigor) (Skill 20.4)*

    A. 10 … 3

    B. 10 … 5

    C. 15 … 5

    D. 20 … 7

148. **The best place to find historical data is most often**: *(Average Rigor) (Skill 21.1)*

    A. The library

    B. The locale where the event happened

    C. The internet

    D. Public Records

149. **For the historian studying ancient Egypt, which of the following would be least useful?** *(Rigorous) (Skill 21.2)*

    A. The record of an ancient Greek historian on Greek-Egyptian interaction

    B. Letters from an Egyptian ruler to his/her regional governors

    C. Inscriptions on stele of the Fourteenth Egyptian Dynasty

    D. Letters from a nineteenth century Egyptologist to his wife

150. **A team approach to a research project should include which position?** *(Average Rigor) (Skill 21.3)*

    A. Statistician

    B. Dietician

    C. Mortician

    D. Mathematician

151. **Which is not part of the scientific method?** *(Average Rigor) (Skill 21.4)*

    A. Formulation

    B. Testing

    C. Observation

    D. Interpretation

152. **A project looking at the progress of school children must also take into account changes for which of the following?** *(Rigorous) (Skill 21.5)*

    A. The school

    B. The teachers

    C. The home

    D. The Society

153. **What are used to show how either theoretical or real world data interrelate using two or more variables?** *(Average Rigor) (Skill 22.1)*

    A. Graphs

    B. Charts

    C. Maps

    D. Diagram

154. **A good political cartoon will have all but which of the following?** *(Average Rigor) (Skill 22.2)*

    A. Wit and humor

    B. Foundation in truth

    C. Moral Purpose

    D. Party Affiliation

155. **A map of oil fields in the Middle East might be useful for discussing which of the following?** *(Rigorous) (Skill 22.3)*

    A. OPEC

    B. NATO

    C. ASEAN

    D. NAFTA

156. **Maps based on gnomonic projections are also known as what kind of maps?** *(Easy) (Skill 22.4)*

    A. Great Square

    B. Great Circle

    C. Great Sailing

    D. Great Route

157. For which age group would pictures be most vital in a presentation? *(Average Rigor) (Skill 22.5)*

    A. Elementary School

    B. Middle School

    C. High School

    D. University

158. The adjustment of various electoral districts in order to achieve a predetermined goal is referred to as: *(Average Rigor) (Skill 23.1)*

    A. Racial Quotas

    B. Salamandering

    C. Gerrymandering

    D. Mercator Projections

159. Which of the following is a fact? *(Average Rigor) (Skill 23.2)*

    A. That cloud looks dark.

    B. It looks like rain.

    C. It looks like snow.

    D. It looks like a rabbit.

160. Which of the following would best apply to both primary and secondary sources with regard to careful usage? *(Rigorous) (Skill 23.3)*

    A. Understanding the use of period language

    B. Consulting the original text

    C. Check bias

    D. Do not rely on one source

161. The purpose of ___ is to understand the works of others and to use that work in shaping a conclusion. *(Rigorous) (Skill 23.4)*

    A. Synergy

    B. Synthesis

    C. Synchronicity

    D. Syllogism

162. Which of the following is an example of an inadequate (as opposed to a misleading) reason? *(Rigorous) (Skill 23.5)*

    A. Ad hominem

    B. Ad populum

    C. Red Herring

    D. False Dilemma

Answer Key

1.	D	41.	D	81.	A	121.	B	161.	B
2.	D	42.	B	82.	C	122.	C	162.	A
3.	C	43.	B	83.	B	123.	C		
4.	C	44.	D	84.	D	124.	D		
5.	A	45.	C	85.	A	125.	B		
6.	A	46.	C	86.	A	126.	B		
7.	D	47.	A	87.	D	127.	C		
8.	A	48.	B	88.	C	128.	C		
9.	C	49.	A	89.	C	129.	B		
10.	C	50.	C	90.	B	130.	C		
11.	A	51.	D	91.	C	131.	B		
12.	A	52.	A	92.	B	132.	A		
13.	D	53.	C	93.	B	133.	C		
14.	B	54.	C	94.	C	134.	C		
15.	C	55.	C	95.	D	135.	C		
16.	D	56.	A	96.	C	136.	D		
17.	A	57.	B	97.	B	137.	B		
18.	A	58.	A	98.	C	138.	C		
19.	C	59.	D	99.	C	139.	A		
20.	D	60.	C	100.	A	140.	A		
21.	A	61.	C	101.	D	141.	C		
22.	D	62.	A	102.	A	142.	D		
23.	C	63.	A	103.	B	143.	A		
24.	C	64.	D	104.	C	144.	A		
25.	A	65.	C	105.	A	145.	A		
26.	D	66.	A	106.	B	146.	B		
27.	B	67.	D	107.	A	147.	C		
28.	C	68.	B	108.	B	148.	B		
29.	A	69.	D	109.	A	149.	D		
30.	C	70.	D	110.	D	150.	A		
31.	D	71.	A	111.	D	151.	D		
32.	A	72.	B	112.	D	152.	A		
33.	D	73.	C	113.	C	153.	A		
34.	C	74.	C	114.	C	154.	D		
35.	A	75.	D	115.	D	155.	A		
36.	A	76.	D	116.	D	156.	B		
37.	B	77.	D	117.	C	157.	A		
38.	B	78.	A	118.	A	158.	C		
39.	A	79.	C	119.	D	159.	A		
40.	C	80.	D	120.	A	160.	D		

Rigor Table

	Easy 20%	Average Rigor 40%	Rigorous 40%
Question #	1,2,21,25,26,29,33,37,44,50, 53, 55, 57, 63,65,67,70,71, 72,73,75,77,78,81,85,86,101,105,109,134,146,156	4,7,10,11,12,13,16,17,18,30,32,35, 39,40,48,51,56,59 61,64,79,80,82,84 ,90,91,93,94,95,96,97,100,104,106, 107,108,110,113, 114,115,124,125, 126,128,129,130, 132,133,136,137, 138,139,140,141, 144,145,147,148, 150,151,153,154, 157,158,159,	3,5,6,8,9,14,15,19 20,22,23,24,27,28 31,34,36,38,41,42 43,45,46,47,49,52 54,58,60,62,66,68 69,74,76,83,87,88 89,92,98,99,102, 103,111,112,116, 117,118,119,120, 121,122,123,127, 131,135,142,143, 149,155,160,161, 162

Rationales with Sample Questions

1. **Divisions of time in history (periodizations) may be determined by all but which of the following: (Easy) (Skill 1.1)**

    A. Date

    B. Geography

    C. Cultural Advances

    D. Individual Historians

Answer: D. Individual Historians

While there are obvious examples for the first three answers (1500's, Roman Era, Renaissance), historians themselves, no matter how much they may contribute to our understanding of an era, did not generally live in it nor are representative of it. Consequently, though some eras are named for individuals (Victorian Era), these are not historians.

2. **The "father of history" is considered to be:** *(Easy) (Skill 1.1)*

    A. Aristotle

    B. Thucydides

    C. Plato

    D. Herodotus

Answer: D. Herodotus

Aristotle (A) and Plato (C) both contributed to the field of political science. Thucydides (B) wrote an authentic account of the war between Athens and Sparta titled "History of the Peloponnesian War". So it is Herodotus, (D), who was the first major Greek historian who wrote the account of the wars between the Greeks and Persians; often called the "Father of History".

3.   **Which of the following would not be considered a primary source? (Rigorous) (Skill 1.3)**

A. An 1863 newspaper account of the Gettysburg Address

B. The text of the Gettysburg Address

C. A historical analysis of the Gettysburg Address

D. A narrative account of the Gettysburg Address from a spectator in the crowd.

Answer: C. A historical analysis of the Gettysburg Address

All of the other answers are considered first-hand accounts of Lincoln's speech, or the speech itself. Therefore only (C), the second-hand analysis, is not a primary source.

4.   **The study of the social behavior of minority groups would be in the area of: (Average Rigor) (Skill 1.4)**

A. Anthropology

B. Psychology

C. Sociology

D. Cultural Geography

Answer: C. Sociology

The study of social behavior in minority groups would be primarily in the area of Sociology, as it is the discipline most concerned with social interaction and being. However, it could be argued that Anthropology, Psychology, and Cultural Geography could have some interest in the study as well.

5. **"Participant observation" is a method of study most closely associated with and used in:** *(Rigorous) (Skill 1.4)*

    A. Anthropology

    B. Archaeology

    C. Sociology

    D. Political science

Answer: A. Anthropology

"Participant observation" is a method of study most closely associated with and used in (A) anthropology or the study of current human cultures. (B) Archaeologists typically the study of the remains of people, animals or other physical things. (C) Sociology is the study of human society and usually consists of surveys, controlled experiments, and field studies. (D) Political science is the study of political life including justice, freedom, power and equality in a variety of methods.

6. **The study of a people's language and writing would be part of all of the following except:** *(Rigorous) (Skill 1.4)*

    A. Sociology

    B. Archaeology

    C. History

    D. Geography

Answer: A. Sociology

The study of a people's language and writing would be a part of studies in the disciplines of sociology (study of social interaction and organization), archaeology, (study of ancient artifacts including written works), and history (the study of the past). Language and writing would be less important to geography that tends to focus more on locations and spatial relations than on the people in those regions and their languages or writings.

7. **The study of past human cultures based on physical artifacts is:**
    (Average Rigor)(Skill 1.4)

    A. History

    B. Anthropology

    C. Cultural Geography

    D. Archaeology

Answer: D. Archaeology

Archaeology is the study of past human cultures based on physical artifacts such as fossils, carvings, paintings, and engraved writings.

8. **Which of the following is not one of the schools of narrative history?**
    (Rigorous) (Skill 1.5)

    A. Comparative Sociological

    B. Economic

    C. Intellectual

    D. Political-Institutional

Answer: A. Comparative Sociological

The narrative history approach attempts to provide a general account of the most important things people have said, done, written, etc. in the past. Some scholars feel that what happened in economic terms (B), or the ideas (C) or the politics and laws (D) of a period are most important. Sociology is generally concerned with contemporary society and in any event would be more interested in people's interactions than trying to form a narrative from past sources.

9. **The early ancient civilizations developed systems of government:** *(Rigorous) (Skill 2.1)*

    A. To provide for defense against attack

    B. To regulate trade

    C. To regulate and direct the economic activities of the people as they worked together in groups

    D. To decide on the boundaries of the different fields during planting seasons

Answer: C. To regulate and direct the economic activities of the people as they worked together in groups

Although ancient civilizations were concerned with defense, trade regulation and the maintenance of boundaries in their fields, they could not have done any of them without first regulating and directing the economic activities of the people as they worked in groups. This provided for a stable economic base from which they could trade and actually had something worth providing defense for.

10. **The principle of zero in mathematics is the discovery of the ancient civilization found in:** *(Average Rigor) (Skill 2.1)*

    A. Egypt

    B. Persia

    C. India

    D. Babylon

Answer: C. India

Although the Egyptians practiced algebra and geometry, the Persians developed an alphabet, and the Babylonians developed Hammurabi's Code, which would come to be considered among the most important contributions of the Mesopotamian civilization, it was the Indians that created the idea of zero in mathematics changing drastically our ideas about numbers.

11. **Which ancient civilization is credited with being the first to develop irrigation techniques through the use of canals, dikes, and devices for raising water?** *(Average Rigor) (Skill 2.1)*

   A. The Sumerians

   B. The Egyptians

   C. The Babylonians

   D. The Akkadians

Answer: A. The Sumerians

The ancient (A) Sumerians of the Fertile Crescent of Mesopotamia are credited with being the first to develop irrigation techniques through the use of canals, dikes, and devices for raising water. The (B) Egyptians also practiced controlled irrigation but that was primarily through the use of the Nile's predictable flooding schedule. The (C) Babylonians were more noted for their revolutionary systems of law than their irrigation systems.

12. **Bathtubs, hot and cold running water, and sewage systems wit flush toilets were developed by the:** *(Average Rigor) (Skill 2.1)*

   A. Minoans

   B. Mycenaeans

   C. Phoenicians

   D. Greeks

Answer: A. Minoans

The (A) Minoans on the island of Crete are best known for their advanced ancient civilization in which such advances as bathtubs, hot and cold running water, sewage systems and flush toilets were developed. At the same time, the (B) Mycenaeans were flourishing on the mainland of what is now Greece. The (C) Phoenicians also flourished around 1250 B.C., however, their primary development was in language and arts. The great developments off the (D) Greeks were primarily in the fields of philosophy, political science, and early ideas of democracy.

13. **An early cultural group was so skillful in navigating on the sea that they were able to sail at night guided by stars. They were the:** *(Average Rigor) (Skill 2.1)*

    A. Greeks

    B. Persians

    C. Minoans

    D. Phoenicians

Answer: D. Phoenicians

Although the Greeks were quite able sailors and developed a strong navy in their defeat of the Persians at sea in the Battle of Marathon, it was the Eastern Mediterranean culture of the Phoenicians that had first developed the astronomical skill of sailing at night with the starts as their guide. The Minoans were an advanced early civilization off the Greek coast on Crete more noted for their innovations in terms of sewage systems, toilets, and running water.

14. **Of the legacies of the Roman Empire listed below, the most influential, effective and lasting is:** *(Rigorous) (Skill 2.2)*

    A. The language of Latin

    B. Roman law, justice, and political system

    C. Engineering and building

    D. The writings of its poets and historians

Answer: B. Roman law, justice, and political system

Of the lasting legacies of the Roman Empire, it is their law, justice, and political system (B) that has been the most effective and influential on our Western world today. English, Spanish, Italian, French, and others are all based on Latin (A), although that Roman language has itself has died out. The Roman engineering and building (C) and their writings and poetry (D) have also been influential but not nearly to the degree that their governmental and justice systems have been.

15. Which of the following areas would NOT be a primary area of hog production? *(Rigorous) (Skill 2.3)*

A. Midland England

B. The Mekong delta of Vietnam

C. Central Syria

D. Northeast Iowa

Answer: C. Central Syria

Pork is a common ingredient in the American, English, and Vietnamese cuisine, so one would reasonably expect to find hog production in (A) Midland England, (B) The Mekong Delta of Vietnam, and (D) Northeast Iowa. The population of Syria is predominantly Islamic, and Islam prohibits the eating of pork. Therefore, one would be unlikely to find extensive hog production in (C) Central Syria.

16. The first ancient civilization to introduce and practice monotheism was the: *(Average Rigor) (Skill 2.3)*

A. Sumerians

B. Minoans

C. Phoenicians

D. Hebrews

Answer: D. Hebrews

The (A) Sumerians and (C) Phoenicians both practiced religions in which many gods and goddesses were worshipped. Often these Gods/Goddesses were based on a feature of nature such as a sun, moon, weather, rocks, water, etc. The (B) Minoan culture shared many religious practices with the Ancient Egyptians. It seems that the king was somewhat of a god figure and the queen, a goddess. Much of the Minoan art point to worship of multiple gods. Therefore, only the (D) Hebrews introduced and fully practiced monotheism, or the belief in one god.

17. **Much of the history for Sub-Saharan Africa was recorded by ___ historians.** *(Average Rigor) (Skill 2.4)*

   A. Islamic

   B. Christian

   C. Buddhist

   D. Hindu

Answer: A. Islamic

As Islam became the predominant religion for Sub-Saharan Africa, it follows that much of the history of the nations in this region became written by Islamic (A) scholars. Christian (B) scholars would be more prominent in Europe, Buddhist (C) scholars in Asia, and Hindu (D) scholars on the Indian sub-continent.

18. **India's greatest ruler is considered to be:** *(Average Rigor) (Skill 2.5)*

   A. Akbar

   B. Asoka

   C. Babur

   D. Jahan

Answer: A. Akbar

Akbar (1556-1605) is considered to be India's greatest ruler. He combined a drive for conquest with a magnetic personality and went so far as to invent his own religion, Dinillahi, a combination of Islam, Christianity, Zoroastrianism, and Hinduism. Asoka (273 B.C.-232 B.C.) was also an important ruler as he was the first to bring together a fully united India. Babur (1483-1540) was both considered to be a failure as he struggled to maintain any power early in his reign, but later to be somewhat successful in his quest to reunite Northern India. Jahan's (1592-1666) rule of India is considered to be the golden age of art and literature in the region.

19. Which one of the following is not an important legacy of the Byzantine Empire? *(Rigorous) (Skill 2.5)*

  A. It protected Western Europe from various attacks from the East by such groups as the Persians, Ottoman Turks, and Barbarians

  B. It played a part in preserving the literature, philosophy, and language of ancient Greece

  C. Its military organization was the foundation for modern armies

  D. It kept the legal traditions of Roman government, collecting and organizing many ancient Roman laws.

Answer: C. Its military organization was the foundation for modern armies

The Byzantine Empire (1353-1453) was the successor to the Roman Empire in the East and protected Western Europe from invaders such as the Persians and Ottomans. It was a Christian incorporation of Greek philosophy, language, and literature along with Roman government and law. Though regarded as having a strong military, the Byzantine Empire is not particularly considered a foundation for modern armies.

20. Which one of the following did not contribute to the early medieval European civilization? *(Rigorous) (Skill 2.6)*

  A. The heritage from the classical cultures

  B. The Christian religion

  C. The influence of the German Barbarians

  D. The spread of ideas through trade and commerce

Answer: D. The spread of ideas through trade and commerce

The first three answers were all contributions to early medieval Europe and its plunge into feudalism. During this period, lives were often difficult and lived out on one single manor, with very little travel or spread of ideas through trade or commerce. Civilization seems to have halted progress during these years.

21. The lords of feudal Japan were known as: *(Easy) (Skill 2.6)*

   A. Daimyo

   B. Samurai

   C. Ronin

   D. Bushido

Answer: A. Daimyo

The lords of feudal Japan were known as Daimyo (A). They had warriors, known as Samurai (B) who served them. Samurai without masters were referred to as Ronin (C). Bushido (D) was the code of conduct of the Samurai.

22. All of the following were accomplishments of the Renaissance except: *(Rigorous) (Skill 3.1)*

   A. Invention of the printing press

   B. A rekindling of interest in the learning of classical Greece & Rome

   C. Growth in literature, philosophy, and art

   D. Better military tactics

Answer: D. Better military tactics

The Renaissance in Western Europe produced many important achievements that helped push immense progress among European civilization. Some of the most important developments during the Renaissance were Gutenberg's invention of the printing press in Germany and a reexamination of the ideas and philosophies of classical Greece and Rome that eventually helped Renaissance thinkers to approach more modern ideas. Also important during the Renaissance was the growth in literature (Petrarch, Boccaccio, Erasmus), philosophy (Machiavelli, More, Bacon) and art (Van Eyck, Giotto, da Vinci). Therefore, improved military tactics is the only possible answer as it was clearly not a characteristic of the Renaissance in Western Europe.

23. **The results of the Renaissance, Enlightenment, Commercial and the Industrial Revolutions were more unfortunate for the people of:** *(Rigorous) (Skill 3.1)*

   A. Asia

   B. Latin America

   C. Africa

   D. Middle East

Answer: C. Africa

The results of the Renaissance, Enlightenment, Commercial and Industrial Revolutions were quite beneficial for many people in much of the world. New ideas of humanism, religious tolerance, and secularism were spreading. Increased trade and manufacturing were surging economies in much of the world. The people of Africa, however, suffered during these times as they became largely left out of the developments. Also, the people of Africa were stolen, traded, and sold into slavery to provide a cheap labor force for the growing industries of Europe and the New World.

24. **The ideas and innovations of the period of the Renaissance were spread throughout Europe mainly because of:** *(Rigorous) (Skill 3.1)*

   A. Extensive exploration

   B. Craft workers and their guilds

   C. The invention of the printing press

   D. Increased travel and trade

Answer: C. The invention of the printing press

The ideas and innovations of the Renaissance were spread throughout Europe for a number of reasons. While exploration, increased travel, and spread of craft may have aided the spread of the Renaissance to small degrees, nothing was as important to the spread of ideas as Gutenberg's invention of the printing press in Germany.

25. The "divine right" of kings was the key political characteristic of: *(Easy)* *(Skill 3.2)*

   A. The Age of Absolutism

   B. The Age of Reason

   C. The Age of Feudalism

   D. The Age of Despotism

Answer: A. The Age of Absolutism

The "divine right" of kings was the key political characteristic of The Age of Absolutism and was most visible in the reign of King Louis XIV of France, as well as during the times of King James I and his son, Charles I. The divine right doctrine claims that kings and absolute leaders derive their right to rule by virtue of their birth alone. They see this both as a law of God and of nature.

26. The English explorer who gave England its claim to North America was: *(Easy)* *(Skill 3.3)*

   A. Raleigh

   B. Hawkins

   C. Drake

   D. Cabot

Answer: D. Cabot

Sir Walter Raleigh (1554-1618) was an English explorer and navigator, who was sent to the New World in search of riches. He founded the lost colony at Roanoke, Virginia, and was later imprisoned for a supposed plot to kill the King for which he was later released. Sir John Hawkins (1532-1595) and Sir Francis Drake (1540-1596) were both navigators who worked in the slave trade, made some voyages to the New World, and commanded ships against and defeated the Spanish Armada in 1588. John Cabot (1450-1498) was the English explorer who gave England claim to North America.

27. **Colonial expansion by Western European powers in the 18th and 19th centuries was due primarily to:** *(Rigorous) (Skill 3.3)*

   A. Building and opening the Suez Canal

   B. The Industrial Revolution

   C. Marked improvements in transportation

   D. Complete independence of all the Americas and loss of European domination and influence

Answer: B. The Industrial Revolution

Colonial expansion by Western European powers in the late 18th and 19th centuries was due primarily to the Industrial Revolution in Great Britain that spread across Europe and needed new natural resources and therefore, new locations from which to extract the raw materials needed to feed the new industries.

28. **Nineteenth century imperialism by Western Europe nations had important and far-reaching effects on the colonial peoples they ruled. All four of the following are the results of this. Which one was the most important and had lasting effects on key 20th century events?** *(Rigorous) (Skill 3.3)*

   A. Local wars were ended

   B. Living standards were raised

   C. Demands for self-government and feelings of nationalism surfaced

   D. Economic developments occurred

Answer: C. Demands for self-government and feelings of nationalism surfaced

The most important and lasting effect on events of the 20th century is the demands for self-government and the rise of nationalism. Both World Wars were caused to a large degree by the rise of nationalist sentiment across Europe and Asia. Nationalism has also fueled numerous liberation movements and revolutionary movements across the globe from Central and South America to the South Pacific to Africa and Asia.

29. **The Age of Exploration begun in the 1400s was led by:** *(Easy) (Skill 3.3)*

   A. The Portuguese

   B. The Spanish

   C. The English

   D. The Dutch

Answer: A. The Portuguese

Although the Age of Exploration had many important players among them, the Dutch, Spanish and English, it was the Portuguese who sent the first explorers to the New World.

30. **Which scientist introduced a radical approach to the study of motion, examining not why but how objects moved?** *(Average Rigor) (Skill 3.4)*

   A. Kepler

   B. Pascal

   C. Galileo

   D. Newton

Answer: C. Galileo

While all four men were scientists who made outstanding contributions to science, it was Galileo Galilei (C) who, near the end of the 16th century, introduced a radical approach to the study of motion. He moved from attempts to explain why objects move the way they do and began to use experiments to describe precisely how they move.

31. **Great Britain became the center of technological and industrial development during the nineteenth century chiefly on the basis of: *(Rigorous) (Skill 3.4)***

    A. Central location relative to the population centers of Europe

    B. Colonial conquests and military victories over European powers

    C. Reliance on exterior sources of financing

    D. Resources of coal and production of steel

Answer: D.   Resources of coal and production of steel

Great Britain possessed a unique set of advantages in the 18th and 19th century making it the perfect candidate for the technological advances of the industrial revolutions. (A) Relative isolation from the population centers in Europe meant little to Great Britain, which benefited from its own relatively unified and large domestic market and enabled it avoid the tariffs and inefficiencies of trading on the diverse (and complicated) continent. (B) Colonial conquests and military victories over European powers were fueled by Great Britain's industrial advances in transportation and weaponry, rather than being causes of them. (C) Reliance of exterior sources of funding – while Great Britain would enjoy an increasing influx of goods and capital from its colonies, the efficiency of its own domestic market consistently generated an impressive amount of capital for investment in the new technologies and industries of the age. (D) Great Britain's rich natural resources of coal and ore enabled steel production and, set alongside new factories in a Britain's landscape, allowed the production of goods quickly and efficiently.

32. **Which Enlightenment philosopher pioneered the doctrine of empiricism (believe it when you see it)?** *(Average Rigor) (Skill 3.5)*

   A. David Hume

   B. John Locke

   C. Jean-Jacques Rousseau

   D. Immanuel Kant

Answer: A. David Hume

England's David Hume (A) was a pioneer of the doctrine of empiricism (believing things only when you've seen the proof for yourself). He was naturally suspicious of things other people told him and constantly set out to discover the truth for himself. These two related ideas influenced great many thinkers after Hume and his writings.

33. **Which country was not one of the principle nations in the Vietnam War?** *(Easy) (Skill 4.1)*

   A. The United States

   B. Australia

   C. New Zealand

   D. France

Answer: D. France

Though originally part of the French Empire, by the time of the Vietnam War France (A) had pulled out of Vietnam, leaving it to the United States (A) to fight the war alongside troops from Australia (B) and New Zealand (C).

34. **Which of the following most closely characterizes the geopolitical events of the USSR in 1991-92:** *(Rigorous) (Skill 4.1)*

   A. The USSR established greater military and economic control over the fifteen Soviet republics

   B. The Baltic States (Estonia, Latvia, and Lithuania) declared independence, while the remainder of the USSR remained intact.

   C. Fourteen of fifteen Soviet republics declared some degree of autonomy; the USSR was officially dissolved; and the Supreme Soviet rescinded the Soviet Treaty of 1922

   D. All fifteen Soviet republics simultaneously declared immediate and full independence from the USSR with no provisions for a transitional form of government

Answer: C. Fourteen of fifteen Soviet republics declared some degree of autonomy; the USSR was officially dissolved; and the Supreme Soviet rescinded the Soviet Treaty of 1922

The unraveling of the USSR in 1991-92 and the establishment of independent republics in its wake was a complex, if relatively peaceful, end to its existence. After a succession of declarations of autonomy by constituent states forced the dissolution of the central government, the Baltic States of Latvia, Lithuania, and Estonia immediately declared their independence. Other republics took longer to reconfigure their relationships to one another. There was no serious attempt by the central government to resist these changes militarily or economically.

35. **Starting in the 19th Century, Europe entered into a 100 year period of relative peace following the defeat of which person?** *(Average Rigor) (Skill 4.2)*

    A. Napoleon

    B. Bismarck

    C. Franco

    D. Cromwell

Answer: A. Napoleon

Napoleon's defeat in 1815 would mark the end of major wars in Europe until the start of World War I. Bismarck (B) unified Germany, leading in part to WWI. Franco (C) was the 20th Century dictator of Spain, and Cromwell (D) was defeated in the 1600's.

36. **Which one of the following would not be considered a result of World War II?** *(Rigorous) (Skill 4.3)*

    A. Economic depressions and slow resumption of trade and financial aid

    B. Western Europe was no longer the center of world power

    C. The beginnings of new power struggles not only in Europe but in Asia as well

    D. Territorial and boundary changes for many nations, especially in Europe

Answer: A. Economic depressions and slow resumption of trade and financial aid

Following World War II, the economy was vibrant and flourished from the stimulant of war and an increased dependence of the world on United States industries. Therefore, World War II didn't result in economic depressions and slow resumption of trade and financial aid. All the rest are true.

37. **China's last imperial ruling dynasty was one of its most stable and successful and under its rule, Chinese culture made an outstanding impression on Western nations. This dynasty was:** *(Easy) (Skill 4.4)*

   A. Ming

   B. Manchu

   C. Han

   D. Chou

Answer: B. Manchu

Although the (A) Ming Dynasty lasted from 1368-1644 and was among the more successful dynasties, it was the (B) Manchu Dynasty, the last imperial ruling dynasty, which came to power in the 1600s and expanded China's power in Asia greatly that was and still is considered to be among the most important, most stable, and most successful of the Chinese dynasties. The (C) Han and (D) Chou Dynasties were part of the "ancient" dynasties of China.

38. **Which of the following is most responsible for making electronic goods affordable to most people?** *(Rigorous) (Skill 4.5)*

   A. Capitalism

   B. Mass Production

   C. Outsourcing

   D. The Internet

Answer: B. Mass production

The ability to make multiple quantities of cheaply produced items – such as cell phones – has allowed electronics to become so ubiquitous worldwide. This is true even in nations where capitalism (A) and outsourcing (C) are not as prevalent, such as China, which still has millions of citizens with cell phones. The internet (D) would not be of use to anyone who did not already have access to affordable electronics.

39. **The crisis of ___ marked the beginning of the end for the First Era of Globalization.** *(Average Rigor) (Skill 4.6)*

   A. The Gold Standard

   B. Ethnic Conflicts

   C. The Socialist Revolution

   D. The Rise of Facism

Answer: A. The Gold Standard

The First Era of Globalization started with the defeat of Napoleon and only began to disintegrate with the crisis of the gold standard (A) in the late 1920s and early 1930s. The other three answers led to other problems, but had little effect on the First Era, as they did not come into full force until after the era was over.

40. **An extensive knowledge of surgery and medicine as well as principles of irrigation, fertilization and terrace farming was unique to:** *(Average Rigor) (Skill 5.1)*

   A. The Mayans

   B. The Atacamas

   C. The Incas

   D. The Tarapacas

Answer: C. The Incas

The Incas of Peru had an extensive knowledge of surgery and medicine as well as principles of irrigation, fertilization, and terrace farming. These were unique achievements for an ancient civilization.

41. **What was a major source of contention between American settlers in Texas and the Mexican government in the 1830s and 1840s?** *(Rigorous) (Skill 6.2)*

    A. The Americans wished to retain slavery which had been outlawed in Mexico

    B. The Americans had agreed to learn Spanish and become Roman Catholic, but failed to do so

    C. The Americans retained ties to the United States, and Santa Anna feared the power of the U.S.

    D. All of the above were contentious issues between American settlers and the Mexican government

Answer: D. All of the above were contentious issues between American settlers and the Mexican government

The American settlers simply were not willing to assimilate into Mexican society but maintained their prior commitments to slave holding, the English language, Protestantism, and the United States government.

42. **Which one of the following is not a reason why Europeans came to the New World?** *(Rigorous) (Skill 5.2)*

    A. To find resources in order to increase wealth

    B. To establish trade

    C. To increase a ruler's power and importance

    D. To spread Christianity

Answer: B. To establish trade

The Europeans came to the New World for a number of reasons; they came to find new natural resources to extract for manufacturing. The Portuguese, Spanish and English were sent over to increase the monarch's power and spread influences such as religion (Christianity) and culture. Therefore, the only reason given that Europeans didn't come to the New World was to establish trade.

43. **The year 1619 was a memorable year for the colony of Virginia. Three important events occurred resulting in lasting effects on US history. Which one of the following was not one of the events?** *(Rigorous)* *(Skill 5.2)*

   A. Twenty African slaves arrived.

   B. The London Company granted the colony a charter making it independent.

   C. The colonists were given the right by the London Company to overn themselves through representative government in the Virginia House of Burgesses.

   D. The London Company sent to the colony 60 women who were quickly married, establishing families and stability in the colony.

Answer: B. The London Company granted the colony a charter making it independent.

In the year 1619, the Southern colony of Virginia had an eventful year during which answers (A), (C), and (D) all happened. The London Company did not, however, grant the colony a charter in 1619.

44. **The Boston Tea Party happened as a result of the passage of which act by Parliament?** *(Easy)* *(Skill 5.3)*

   A. Stamp Act

   B. Quartering Act

   C. Sugar Act

   D. Townshend Act

Answer: D. Townshend Act

The Stamp Act (A) applied to papers, the Quartering Act (B) concerned the housing of British soldiers, and the Sugar Act (C) placed a tax on molasses. The tax on tea, which led to the Boston Tea Party, was part of the Townshend Act.

45. **Under the brand new Constitution, the most urgent of the many problems facing the new federal government were that of:** *(Rigorous)* *(Skill 5.4)*

    A. Maintaining a strong army and navy

    B. Establishing a strong foreign policy

    C. Raising money to pay salaries and war debts

    D. Setting up courts, passing federal laws, and providing for law enforcement officers

Answer: C. Raising money to pay salaries and war debts

Maintaining strong military forces, establishment of a strong foreign policy, and setting up a justice system were important problems facing the United States under the newly ratified Constitution. However, the most important and pressing issue was how to raise money to pay salaries and war debts from the Revolutionary War. Alexander Hamilton (1755-1804) then Secretary of the Treasury proposed increased tariffs and taxes on products such as liquor. This money would be used to pay off war debts and to pay for internal programs. Hamilton also proposed the idea of a National Bank.

46. **The US Constitution was a vast improvement over the weak Articles of Confederation. Which one of the four statements below are not a description of the Constitution?** *(Rigorous) (Skill 5.4)*

   A. The establishment of a strong central government in no way lessened or weakened the individual states

   B. Individual rights were protected and secured

   C. The Constitution demands unquestioned respect and subservience to the federal government by all states and citizens

   D. Its flexibility and adaptation to change gives it a sense of timelessness

Answer: C. The Constitution demands unquestioned respect and subservience to the federal government by all states and citizens.

The U.S. Constitution was indeed a vast improvement over the Articles of Confederation and the authors of the document took great care to assure longevity. It clearly stated that the establishment of a strong central government in no way lessened or weakened the individual states. In the Bill of Rights, citizens were assured that individual rights were protected and secured. Possibly the most important feature of the new Constitution was its flexibility and adaptation to change which assured longevity.

Therefore, the only statement made that doesn't describe some facet of the Constitution is "The Constitution demands unquestioned respect and subservience to the federal government by all states and citizens". On the contrary, the Constitution made sure that citizens could critique and make changes to their government and encourages such critiques and changes as necessary for the preservation of democracy.

47. **U.S. foreign minister Robert R. Livingstone said, "From this day the United States take their place among the greatest powers." He was referring to the action taken by President Thomas Jefferson:** *(Rigorous)* *(Skill 5.5)*

   A. Who had authorized the purchase of the Louisiana Territory

   B. Who sent the US Marines and naval ships to fight the Barbary pirates

   C. Who had commissioned the Lewis and Clark expedition

   D. Who repealed the Embargo Act

Answer: A. Who had authorized the purchase of the Louisiana Territory

Livingstone's claim that "from this day, the United States takes their place among the greatest powers" was a reference to Jefferson's authorization and acquisition of the Louisiana Territory. What he meant was that now the United States was beginning to fulfill what would later become known as "Manifest Destiny", and it would be this growth of physical size and political power that put the United States on course to be a world super power.

48. **"Marbury vs Madison (1803)" was an important Supreme Court case which set the precedent for:** *(Average Rigor)* *(Skill 5.5)*

   A. The elastic clause

   B. Judicial review

   C. The supreme law of the land

   D. Popular sovereignty in the territories

Answer: B. Judicial review

Marbury vs Madison (1803) was an important case for the Supreme Court as it established judicial review. In that case, the Supreme Court set precedence to declare laws passed by Congress as unconstitutional. Popular sovereignty in the territories was a failed plan pushed by Stephen Davis to allow states to decide the slavery question themselves. (This was his attempt to appeal to the masses in the pre-Civil War elections.) The supreme law of the land is just that, the law that rules. The elastic clause is not a real term.

49. **Which of the following was not a reason for the War of 1812?** *(Rigorous) (Skill 5.6)*

    A. Resentment by Spain over the sale, exploration, and settlement of the Louisiana Territory

    B. The westward movement of farmers because of the need for more land

    C. Canadian fur traders were agitating the northwestern Indians to fight American expansion

    D. Britain continued to seize American ships on the high seas and force American seamen to serve aboard British ships

Answer: A. Resentment by Spain over the sale, exploration, and settlement of the Louisiana Territory

Reasons for the War of 1812 between the US and Great Britain included conflicts over expansion, farming, and shipping. Spain, however, had few problems with activity in the Louisiana Territory, and furthermore was not involved in the War of 1812.

50. **Which party later evolved into the modern Democrats?** *(Easy) (Skill 6.1)*

    A. Nationalists

    B. Whigs

    C. Anti-Federalists

    D. Liberty

Answer: C. Anti-Federalists

The first real party organization in the United States developed soon after the inauguration of Washington as President. His cabinet included people of both factions. Alexander Hamilton was the leader of the Nationalists (A) – the Federalist Party – and Jefferson was the spokesman for the Anti-Federalists (C), later known as Republicans, Democratic-Republicans, and finally Democrats. The Whigs (B) were primarily a party during the Articles of Confederation, while the Liberty party (D) was a short-lived abolitionist party.

51. **After the War of 1812, Henry Clay and others proposed economic measures, including raising tariffs to protect American farmers and manufacturers from foreign competition. These measures were proposed in the period known as:** *(Average Rigor) (Skill 6.2*

    A. Era of Nationalism

    B. American Expansion

    C. Era of Good Feeling

    D. American System

Answer: D. American System

The proposed economic measures were known as the American System (D). American Expansion (B) describes the movement of American settlers across the frontier towards the West. The "Era of Good Feeling" (C) followed the War of 1812 but doesn't describe the policies proposed by Clay. There is no "Era of Nationalism" (A).

52. **It can be reasonably stated that the change in the United States from primarily an agricultural country into an industrial power was due to all of the following except:** *(Rigorous) (Skill 6.2)*

    A. Tariffs on foreign imports

    B. Millions of hardworking immigrants

    C. An increase in technological developments

    D. The change from steam to electricity for powering industrial machinery

Answer: A. Tariffs on foreign imports

The change in the United States from primarily an agricultural country into an industrial power was a combination of millions of hard-working immigrants, an increase in technological developments, and the change from steam to electricity for powering industrial machinery. The only reason given that really had little effect was the tariffs on foreign imports.

53. **The Social Gospel Movement arose during which of the Great Awakenings?** *(Easy)* *(Skill 6.3)*

   A. First

   B. Second

   C. Third

   D. Fourth

Answer: C. Third

The First Great Awakening (A) was a religious movement within American Protestantism in the 1730s and 1740s. The Second Great Awakening (B) (the Great Revival) was a broad movement starting in the 1820's within American Protestantism that led to several kinds of activities that were distinguished by region and denominational tradition. The Third Great Awakening (the Missionary Awakening) (C) gave rise to the Social Gospel Movement. This period (1858 to 1908) resulted in a massive growth in membership of all major Protestant denominations through their missionary activities. There was no Fourth Great Awakening. (D)

54. **Historians state that the West helped to speed up the Industrial Revolution. Which one of the following statements was not a reason for this?** *(Rigorous) (Skill 6.4)*

   A. Food supplies for the ever-increasing urban populations came from farms in the West.

   B. A tremendous supply of gold and silver from western mines provided the capital needed to build industries.

   C. Descendants of western settlers, educated as engineers, geologists, and metallurgists in the East, returned to the West to mine the mineral resources needed for industry.

   D. Iron, copper, and other minerals from western mines were important resources in manufacturing products.

Answer: C. Descendants of western settlers, educated as engineers, geologists, and metallurgists in the East, returned to the West to mine the mineral resources needed for industry.

The West helped to speed up the Industrial Revolution in a number of important and significant ways. First, the land yielded crops for the growing urban populations. Second, the gold and silver supplies coming out of the Western mines provided the capital needed to build industries. Also, resources such as iron and copper were extracted from the mines in the West and provided natural resources for manufacturing. The descendants of western settlers typically didn't become educated and then returned to the West as miners. The miners were typically working class with little or no education.

55. **The belief that the United States should control all of North America was called:** *(Easy) (Skill 6.4)*

    A. Westward Expansion

    B. Pan Americanism

    C. Manifest Destiny

    D. Nationalism

Answer: C. Manifest Destiny

The belief that the United States should control all of North America was called (B) Manifest Destiny. This idea fueled much of the violence and aggression towards those already occupying the lands such as the Native Americans. Manifest Destiny was certainly driven by sentiments of (D) nationalism and gave rise to (A) westward expansion.

56. **Which group is most responsible for helping to construct the trans-national railroad?** *(Average Rigor) (Skill 6.5)*

    A. Asians

    B. Hispanics

    C. Native Americans

    D. African Americans

Answer: A. Asians

A mass influx of Chinese laborers provided much of the workforce for the trans-continental railroad, especially along the western end. Indeed, this influx was also responsible for the later number of Chinese settlers in the western portion of the United States.

57. **The three-day Battle of Gettysburg was the turning point of the Civil War for the North leading to ultimate victory. The battle in the West reinforcing the North's victory and sealing the South's defeat was the day after Gettysburg at:** *(Easy)* *(Skill 6.6)*

A. Perryville

B. Vicksburg

C. Stones River

D. Shiloh

Answer: B. Vicksburg

The Battle of Vicksburg was crucial in reinforcing the North's victory and sealing the south's defeat for a couple of reasons. First, the Battle of Vicksburg potentially gave the Union full control of the Mississippi River. More importantly, the battle split the Confederate Army and allowed General Grant to reach his goal of restoring commerce to the important northwest area.

58. **The Radical Republicans who pushed the harsh Reconstruction measures through Congress after Lincoln's death lost public and moderate Republican support when they went too far:** *(Rigorous) (Skill 6.6)*

   A. In their efforts to impeach the President

   B. By dividing ten southern states into military-controlled districts

   C. By making the ten southern states give freed African Americans the right to vote

   D. Sending carpetbaggers into the South to build up support for Congressional legislation

Answer: A. In their efforts to impeach the President

The public support and the moderate Republicans were actually being drawn towards the more radical end of the Republican spectrum following Lincoln's death during Reconstruction. Because many felt as though Andrew Johnson's policies towards the South were too soft and were running the risk of rebuilding the old system of white power and slavery. Even moderate Republicans in the North felt as though it was essential to rebuild the South but with the understanding that they must be abide by the Fourteenth and Fifteenth Amendment assuring Blacks freedom and the right to vote. The radical Republicans were so frustrated that the President would make concessions to the old Southerners that they attempted to impeach him. This turned back the support that they had received from the public and from moderates.

59. **The principle of "popular sovereignty", allowing people in any Territory to make their own decision concerning slavery was stated by:** *(Average Rigor) (Skill 6.6)*

A. Henry Clay

B. Daniel Webster

C. John C. Calhoun

D. Stephen A. Douglas

Answer: D. Stephen A. Douglas

(A) Henry Clay (1777-1852) and (B) Daniel Webster (1782-1852) were prominent Whigs in favor of promoting what Clay called "the American System". (C) John C. Calhoun (1782-1850) was very pro-slavery and a champion of states' rights. The principle of "popular sovereignty", in which people in each territory could make their own decisions concerning slavery, was the doctrine of (D) Stephen A. Douglas (1813-1861).

60. **The post-Civil War years were a time of low public morality, a time of greed, graft, and dishonesty. Which one of the reasons listed would not be accurate?** *(Rigorous) (Skill 6.6)*

    A. The war itself because of the money and materials needed to carry on war

    B. The very rapid growth of industry and big business after the war

    C. The personal example set by President Grant

    D. Unscrupulous heads of large impersonal corporations

Answer: C. The personal example set by President Grant

The Civil War had plunged the country into debt and ultimately into a recession by the 1890s. The rapid growth of industry and big business caused a polarization of rich and poor, workers and owners. Jobs were typically low-wage, long hours, and in poor working conditions. The heads of large impersonal corporations often treated their workers inhumanely and let morale drop to a record low, as well as trying to prevent and disband labor unions.

61. **The defeat of which European nation marked the United States' emergence as a world power.** *(Average Rigor) (Skill 6.7)*

    A. England

    B. France

    C. Spain

    D. Germany

Answer: C. Spain

After the US defeated England (A) - twice - it entered a period of isolationism. Although on the decline as a colonial power, the US defeat of Spain in 1898 marked a turning point in the US's world renown. By World War I, the US was already a world power (and did not defeat Germany (D) alone).The US has never been to war against France (B).

62. **During the 1920s, the United States almost completely stopped all immigration. One of the reasons was:** *(Rigorous) (Skill 7.1)*

    A. Plentiful cheap, unskilled labor was no longer needed by industrialists

    B. War debts from World War I made it difficult to render financial assistance

    C. European nations were reluctant to allow people to leave since there was a need to rebuild populations and economic stability

    D. The United States did not become a member of the League of Nations

Answer: A. Plentiful cheap, unskilled labor was no longer needed by industrialists

he primary reason that the United States almost completely stopped all immigration during the 1920s was because their once, much needed, cheap, unskilled labor jobs, made available by the once booming industrial economy, were no longer needed. This has much to do with the increased use of machines to do the work once done by cheap, unskilled laborers.

63. **Which figure was the leading spokesperson for African Americans of his era and the founder of the Tuskegee Institute?** *(Easy) (Skill 7.2)*

    A. Booker T Washington

    B. W.E.B. DuBois

    C. George Washington Carver

    D. Langston Hughes

Answer: A. Booker T Washington

While both Booker T Washington and W.E.B DuBois (B) were active spokespersons, only Booker T Washington (A) founded the Tuskegee Institute. George Washington Carver (C) was a scientist and Langston Hughes (D) a writer.

64. **Which two industries drove the economy of the 1920's?** *(Average Rigor)* *(Skill 7.3)*

   A. Automotive and Avionics

   B. Textiles and Refining

   C. Refining and Railroads

   D. Automotive and Radio

Answer: D. Automotive and Radio

Both the car and the radio were relatively new inventions, and their popularity with the American populace helped fuel a sizable demand for these commodities, which in turn drove the economy of the 1920's.

65. **Fascism is said to have often begun in socialist countries. Which was the first such country to go from socialism to fascism?** (Skill 7.4) *(Easy)* *(Skill 7.4*

   A. Spain

   B. Italy

   C. Russia

   D. Germany

Answer: C. Italy

Russia (C) never had a fascist government, in Germany (D) Hitler was elected chancellor in a republic, and in Spain (A) Franco defeated republican forces to gain power. It was in Italy (B), that Mussolini took power after a socialist government.

66. **Of all the major causes of both World Wars I and II, the most significant one is considered to be:** *(Rigorous)* *(Skill 7.5)*

    A. Extreme nationalism

    B. Military buildup and aggression

    C. Political unrest

    D. Agreements and alliances

Answer: A. Extreme nationalism

Although military buildup and aggression, political unrest, and agreements and alliances were all characteristic of the world climate before and during World War I and World War II, the most significant cause of both wars was extreme nationalism. Nationalism is the idea that the interests and needs of a particular nation are of the utmost and primary importance above all else. The nationalism that sparked WWI culminated in the assassination of Archduke Ferdinand by a Serb nationalist in 1914. Following WWI and the Treaty of Versailles, a new form of extreme nationalism began led by Adolf Hitler and the Nazi regime. Hitler's ideas were an example of extreme, oppressive nationalism combined with political, social and economic scapegoating and were the primary cause of WWII.

67. **A well known World War II figure who said that democracy was like a rotting corpse that had to be replaced by a superior way of life and more efficient government was:** *(Easy) (Skill 7.5)*

A. Hitler

B. Stalin

C. Tojo

D. Mussolini

Answer: D. Mussolini

(A) Adolf Hitler (1889-1945), the Nazi leader of Germany, and (C) Hideki Tojo (1884-1948), the Japanese General and Prime Minister, were well known World War II figures. (B) Joseph Stalin (1879-1953) was the Communist Russian head of state during World War II. Although all three were repressive in their actions, the quote came from (D) Benito Mussolini (1883-1945), the Fascist and leader of Italy during World War II.

68. **President Truman suspended Gen. Douglas MacArthur from command of Allied forces in Korea because of:** *(Rigorous) (Skill 7.5)*

   A. MacArthur's inability to make any progress against North Koreans

   B. MacArthur's criticism of Truman claiming that the president would not allow him to pursue aggressive tactics against communists

   C. The harsh treatment MacArthur exhibited toward the Japanese after World War II

   D. The ability of the U.S. Navy to continue the conflict without the presence of MacArthur

Answer: B. MacArthur's criticism of Truman, claiming that the president would not allow him to pursue aggressive tactics against communists

Truman suspended MacArthur because of clear insubordination: MacArthur had publicly criticized the president, his Commander in Chief, and had openly undermined his policy of negotiating a settlement with the communists. MacArthur was a general of proven effectiveness; so, (A) cannot be correct. MacArthur was actually rather lenient to the Japanese after World War II, and he was a general, not an admiral of the Navy.

69. **After World War II, the United States:** *(Rigorous) (Skill 7.5)*

A. Limited its involvement in European affairs

B. Shifted foreign policy emphasis from Europe to Asia

C. Passed significant legislation pertaining to aid to farmers and tariffs on imports

D. Entered the greatest period of economic growth in its history

Answer: D. Entered the greatest period of economic growth in its history

After World War II, the United States did not limit or shift its involvement in European affairs. In fact, it escalated the Cold War with the Soviet Union and attempted to contain Communism in Europe. There was no significant legislation pertaining to aid to farmers and tariffs on imports. In fact, since World War II, trade has become more liberal than ever. Due to this, the United States after World War II entered the greatest period of economic growth in its history and remains a world superpower.

70. **The Soviet Union's military alliance with Eastern Europe was known as:** *(Easy) (Skill 7.6)*

A. NATO

B. KGB

C. The Iron Curtain

D. The Warsaw Pact

Answer: D. The Warsaw Pact

In part as a response to the formation of NATO (A) by the Western powers, the Soviet Union created the Warsaw Pact (D) with the nations of Eastern Europe. The KGB (B) was the USSR's intelligence agency, while the Iron Curtain (C) was a term used by the West to describe the Soviet control of Eastern Europe.

71. **Which of the following was the unsuccessful predecessor to the United Nations?** *(Easy) (Skill 7.7)*

    A. League of Nations

    B. World Council

    C. World Court

    D. League of Five Nations

Answer: A. League of Nations

Following WWI, Woodrow Wilson proposed the creation of a League of Nations (A) to help govern world affairs. Congress would not approve of the US joining the League, and this, along with other problems, led to the League's collapse. There are a number of different groups that refer to themselves as a World Council (B), the World Court (C) is a legal institution, and the League of Five Nations (D) was an organization of five Iroquois tribes.

72. **Native peoples in early New York consisted of a confederacy of Iroquois tribes known as the Haudenosaunee, the League of Peace and Power. How many tribes were there originally?** *(Easy) (Skill 8.1)*

    A. 4

    B. 5

    C. 6

    D. 7

Answer: B. 5

The answer is 5 (B). The name "people of the longhouse" was derived from the traditional dwelling, the longhouse. The original five tribes or nations were Mohawk, Keepers of the Eastern Door of the symbolic longhouse, also known as the People of Flint; The Oneida, the People of Stone; The Onondaga, the People on the Hill; The Cayuga, the People at the Mucky Land, The Seneca were the Great Hill People and the Keepers of the Western Door. After 1722 the Tuscarora were added to the confederation as a sixth, non-voting member.

73. **New York was initially inhabited by what two native peoples?** *(Easy)* *(Skill 8.1)*

   A. Sioux and Pawnee

   B. Micmac and Wampanoag

   C. Iroquois and Algonquin

   D. Nez Perce and Cherokee

Answer: C. Iroquois and Algonquin

The area now known as the State of New York was initially inhabited by several tribes that were part of one of two major Native American Nations. These were the Iroquois Nation and the Algonquian Nation. (A) Sioux and Pawnee tribal lands were found primarily in Minnesota and Nebraska respectively. (B) Micmac and Wampanoag are tribes primarily found in New England and Canada. (D) Nez Perce and Cherokee were found in the Pacific Northwest and the Eastern parts of the United States respectively.

74. **Government regulation of economic activities for favorable balance of trade was the first major economic theory. It was called:** *(Rigorous)* *(Skill 8.2)*

   A. Laissez-faire

   B. Globalism

   C. Mercantilism

   D. Syndicalism

Answer: C. Mercantilism

(A) Laissez-faire calls for no government interference in economic and political policy. (B) Globalism is not an economic or political theory, though globalization is the idea that we are all increasingly connected in a worldwide system. (D) Syndicalism is similar to anarchism claiming that workers should control and govern economic policies and regulations as opposed to state control. Therefore, (C) mercantilism is the best regulation of economic activities for a favorable balance of trade.

75. **Who was the governor of colonial New York known for buying present day Manhattan for about $24 in trinkets?** *(Easy) (Skill 8.2)*

    A. Willem Kieft

    B. Duke of York

    C. Henry Hudson

    D. Peter Minuit

Answer: D.   Peter Minuit

Peter Minuit (D) was one of the early Dutch settlers and the first governor of New Amsterdam who purchased Manhattan Island from the local people for trinkets valued at about $24. Willem Kieft (A) was appointed director-general of the colony. His efforts to rule as a dictator sparked a series of disputes and wars with the local Algonquian tribes. (C) Duke of York was given present day Long Island in March of 1664 by King Charles II. (D) Henry Hudson was the first Dutchman to sail up the river that bears his name to discover New York.

76. **France decided in 1777 to help the American colonies in their war against Britain. This decision was based on:** *(Rigorous) (Skill 8.3)*

    A. The naval victory of John Paul Jones over the British ship "Serapis"

    B. The survival of the terrible winter at Valley Forge

    C. The success of colonial guerilla fighters in the South

    D. The defeat of the British at Saratoga

Answer: D. The defeat of the British at Saratoga

The defeat of the British at Saratoga was the overwhelming factor in the Franco-American alliance of 1777 that helped the American colonies defeat the British. Some historians believe that without the Franco-American alliance, the American Colonies would not have been able to defeat the British and American would have remained a British colony.

77. **The tree at the end of the street where traders and dealers gathered informally later became the site of:** *(Easy) (Skill 8.4)*

    A. Broadway and 44th

    B. The Statue of Liberty

    C. Avenue of the Americas

    D. New York Stock Exchange

Answer: D. New York Stock Exchange

The construction of the wooden wall that was intended to keep out aggressors became both an actual and a symbolic center of economy and commerce. The tree at the end of the street where traders and dealers gathered informally later became the site of the (D) New York Stock Exchange. This marked the beginning of New York's importance in the state's economy and the national economy. In time, it made the city a central point in international economy.

78. **Which island was used as an immigrant processing center?** *(Easy) (Skill 8.5)*

    A. Ellis

    B. Staten

    C. Manhattan

    D. Liberty

Answer: A. Ellis

While immigrants may live on either Staten (B) and Manhattan (C) islands, those who arrived from overseas in the late 19th and early 20th Century would have first gone through the processing center on Ellis (A). Liberty (D) Island houses what would arguably be America's largest immigrant (from France): the Statue of Liberty.

79. **What was the name of the cultural revival after the Civil War that took place in New York?** *(Average Rigor) (Skill 8.6)*

    A. The Revolutionary War

    B. The Second Great Awakening

    C. The Harlem Renaissance

    D. The Gilded Age

Answer: C. The Harlem Renaissance

As African Americans left the rural South and migrated to the North in search of opportunity, many settled in Harlem in New York City. By the 1920s Harlem had become a center of life and activity for persons of color. The music, art, and literature of this community gave birth to a cultural movement known as the Harlem Renaissance. (A) The Revolution War (1776) occurred prior to the Civil War. (B) The Second Great Awakening occurred in the 1920s but like the (D) Gilded Age (1878 – 1889) affected the entire United States.

80. **The idea that everyone has the right to education was expressed in which document?** *(Average Rigor) (Skill 9.1)*

    A. Declaration of the Rights of Man and Citizens

    B. Declaration of Independence

    C. UN Convention on the Rights of Children

    D. UN Declaration of Universal Human Rights

Answer: D. UN Declaration of Universal Human Rights

Neither the French Declaration of the Rights of Man and Citizens (A) nor the US Declaration of Independence (B) mentions anything about the right to an education for everyone. The UN Convention on the Rights of Children (C) primarily concerns itself with the safety and welfare of children, and it is in the UN Declaration of Universal Human Rights (D) that the universal right to education is expressed.

81. **Which group was interned in "War Relocation Camps" during WWII?** *(Easy) (Skill 9.2)*

   A. Japanese

   B. Germans

   C. Chinese

   D. Italians

Answer: A. Japanese

Although the US fought against both Germany and Italy, it was only those Americans who shared ancestry with the third Axis nation, Japan, who were placed into internment camps during World War II. Approximately 120,000 Japanese and Japanese-Americans, 62% of whom were US citizens, were detained.

82. **"Genocide" was first used to describe the deaths of:** *(Average Rigor)* *(Skill 9.3)*
   A. Native Americans at Wounded Knee

   B. The Holocaust

   C. Armenians at the hands of the Turks in WWI

   D. Warring tribes in Rwanda

Answer: C. Armenians at the hands of the Turks in WWI

Although all four events were tragic in terms not only of the circumstances but also the lives lost, the term "genocide" was coined by jurist Ralph Lemkin when he attempted to describe the extermination and displacement of Armenians by Turkey from 1915-1921. Lemkin would also later apply the term to the Holocaust, and it has unfortunately never fallen out of usage.

83. **Slavery arose in the southern colonies partly as a perceived economical way to:** *(Rigorous) (Skill 9.4)*

   A. Increase the owner's wealth through human beings used as a source of exchange

   B. Cultivate large plantations of cotton, tobacco, rice, indigo, and other crops

   C. Provide Africans with humanitarian aid, such as health care, Christianity, and literacy

   D. Keep ships' holds full of cargo on two out of three legs of the "triangular trade" voyage

Answer: B. Cultivate large plantations of cotton, tobacco, rice, indigo and other crops

The southern states, with their smaller populations, were heavily dependent on slave labor as a means of being able to fulfill their role and remain competitive in the greater U.S. economy. (A) When slaves arrived in the South, the vast majority would become permanent fixtures on plantations, intended for work, not as a source of exchange. (C) While some slave owners instructed their slaves in Christianity, provided health care, and some level of education, such attention was not their primary reason for owning slaves; they wanted a cheap and ready labor force. (D) Whether or not ships' holds were full on two or three legs of the triangular journey was not the concern of southerner plantation owners as the final purchasers of slaves. Such details would have concerned the slave traders.

84. **Europeans generally bought slaves who had been captured by:**
   (Average Rigor) (Skill 9.4)

   A. Americans

   B. Europeans

   C. Asians

   D. Africans

Answer: D. Africans

A sad fact of the slave trade was that the majority of slaves were initially captured by other Africans (D). Americans (A) and Europeans (B) fueled the trade and fanned the flames of tribal wars to further the practice so they would not have to venture deep into Africa to obtain slaves. Asians (D) were not involved in the slave trade.

85. **The Irish Famine resulted in part from a failure of what crop?** *(Easy) (Skill 9.5)*

   A. Potatoes

   B. Corn

   C. Rice

   D. Cabbage

Answer: A. Potatoes

Although there were other factors that contributed to the Famine, a blight on the potato crop (A) was at the very least the spark that set it off. Neither corn (B) nor rice (C) grows very well – if at all – in Ireland's climate, and while cabbage (D) is a favored vegetable, it is not the mainstay of the traditional Irish diet that potatoes are.

86. **The founder of the birth control movement was:** *(Easy) (Skill 9.6)*

    A. Margaret Sanger

    B. Eleanor Roosevelt

    C. Jane Addams

    D. Elie Wiesel

Answer: A. Margaret Sanger

Margaret Sanger (A) not only founded the movement, she coined the term. She struggled against the hostility of the medical profession and fought for the repeal of laws which existed in most states that prohibited contraception. Eleanor Roosevelt (B) was respected for her humanitarian and diplomatic efforts, Jane Addams (C) was a social reformer who founded Chicago's Hull House, and Elie Wiesel (D) is a 20th century Jewish novelist, philosopher and humanitarian.

87. **Which of the following most closely characterizes the Supreme Court's decision in *Brown v. Board of Education*?** *(Rigorous) (Skill 9.7)*

    A. Chief Justice Warren had to cast the deciding vote in a sharply divided the Supreme Court

    B. The decision was rendered along sectional lines with northerners voting for integration and southerners voting for continued segregation

    C. The decision was 7-2 with dissenting justices not even preparing a written dissent

    D. Chief Justice Warren was able to persuade the Supreme Court to render a unanimous decision

Answer: D. Chief Justice Warren was able to persuade the Court to render a unanimous decision.

The Supreme Court decided 9-0 against segregated educational facilities.

88. **A geographer wishes to study the effects of a flood on subsequent settlement patterns. Which might he or she find most useful? (Rigorous) (Skill 10.1)**

   A. A film clip of the floodwaters

   B. An aerial photograph of the river's source

   C. Census data taken after the flood

   D. A soil map of the A and B horizons beneath the flood area

Answer: C. Census data taken after the flood

(A) A film clip of the flood waters may be of most interest to a historian, (B) an aerial photograph of the river's source and (D) soil maps tell little about the behavior of the individuals affected by the flood. (C) Census surveys record the population for certain areas on a regular basis, allowing a geographer to tell if more or less people are living in an area over time. These would be of most use to a geographer undertaking this study.

89. **Which location may be found in Canada? (Rigorous) (Skill 10.2)**

   A. 27 N 93 W

   B. 41 N 93 E

   C. 50 N 111 W

   D. 18 N 120 W

Answer: C. 50 N 111 W

(A) 27 North latitude, 93 West longitude is located in the Gulf of Mexico. (B) 41 N 93 E is located in northwest China. (D) 18 N 120 W is in the Pacific Ocean, off the coast of Mexico. (C) 50 N 120 W is located near the town of Medicine Hat in the Canadian province of Alberta.

.

90. **Geography was first studied in an organized manner by the:** *(Average Rigor) (Skill 10.1)*

    A. Egyptians

    B. Greeks

    C. Romans

    D. Arabs

Answer: B. Greeks

The Greeks were the first to study geography, possibly because of the difficulties they faced as a result of geographic conditions. Greece had difficulty uniting early on as their steep, treacherous, mountainous terrain made it difficult for the city-states to be united. As the Greeks studied their geography, it became possible to defeat more powerful armies on their home turf, such as the great victory over the Persians at Marathon.

91. **Meridians, or lines of longitude, not only help in pinpointing locations, but are also used for:** *(Average Rigor) (Skill 10.2)*

    A. Measuring distance from the Poles

    B. Determining direction of ocean currents

    C. Determining the time around the world

    D. Measuring distance on the Equator

Answer: C. Determining the time around the world

Meridians, or lines of longitude, are the determining factor in separating time zones and determining time around the world.

92. **Which of the following is an example of relative location?** *(Average Rigor) (Skill 10.2)*

    A. The Post Office is at the NW corner of 1st and Main

    B. The Post Office is down the street from the courthouse

    C. The Post Office is at 422 Elm

    D. The Post Office is at 48 N°2°E

Answer: B. The Post Office is down the street from the courthouse

A, C, and D are all examples of absolute location because they give an exact description. B is less exact, and just as importantly, includes the location with reference (in relation) to a second object – hence it is a relative location.

93. **A description of how things are grouped in a given area (for example how people live) is known as:** *(Average Rigor) (Skill 10.3*

    A. Geography

    B. Spatial Organization

    C. Geometry

    D. Topography

Answer: B. Spatial Organization

Geometry (C) is the mathematical study of shapes. While geography (A) in general is the study of places, it is Spatial Organization (B) that is most concerned with how items are grouped in a place. Topography (D) is used for describing surface features, especially for maps.

94. **One of the foremost areas to which geography applies is:** *(Average Rigor) (Skill 10.4)*

   A. Sociology

   B. Mathematics

   C. Economics

   D. Politics

Answer: C. Economics

Geography plays a large role in economics (C), not least in the basic decisions involved in where to put a business. When it comes to product distribution, even distribution of resources, geography matters (think of the oil fields of the Middle East, for example). Geography is less important to politics (D), where it may influence the way a politician approaches a particular area or situation, for example when giving a speech or providing aid. In sociology (A) geography is little used, as the emphasis is placed on the interaction of people. And while mathematics (B) applies heavily to certain fields of geography, the reverse is not true.

95. **Which one of the following does not affect climate?** *(Average Rigor) (Skill 11.1)*

   A. Elevation and altitude

   B. Ocean currents

   C. Latitude

   D. Longitude

Answer: D. Longitude

Latitude is the primary influence of earth climate as it determines the climatic region in which an area lies. Elevation or altitude and ocean currents are considered to be secondary influences on climate. Longitude is considered to have no important influence over climate.

96. **Soil erosion is most likely to occur in large amounts in:** *(Average Rigor) (Skill 11.2)*

A. Mountain ranges

B. Deserts

C. Tropical rainforests

D. River valleys

Answer: C. Tropical rainforests

Soil erosion is most likely to occur in tropical rainforests as the large amount of constant rainfall moves the soil at a greater rate across a greater area. Mountain ranges and river valleys experience some soil erosion but don't have the levels of precipitation found in a tropical rainforest. Deserts have virtually no soil erosion due to their climate.

97. **Almost half of the world's population lives in which areas?** *(Average Rigor) (Skill 11.3)*

A. Rural Areas

B. Cities

C. Suburbs

D. Megalopolises

Answer: B. Cities

Cities (B) are the fastest growing areas of the world, as more people flock to urban centers from the rural countryside (A) in search of jobs or better living. Not every city has suburbs (C), as not every city follows the American model. Megalopolises (D) are those places where two or more areas run together, so there is no clear boundary between them.

98. **Which one of the following is not a use for a region's wetlands?** *(Rigorous) (Skill 11.4)*

    A. Produces fresh clean water

    B. Provides habitat for wildlife

    C. Provides water for hydroelectric power

    D. Controls floods

Answer: C. Provides water for hydroelectric power

A region's wetlands provide a number of uses and services not limited to but including production of fresh water, habitat and natural preserve of wildlife, and flood control. Wetlands are not used in the production of hydroelectric power the way dams or other power structures do.

99. **The end to hunting, gathering, and fishing of prehistoric people was due to:** *(Rigorous) (Skill 11.5)*

    A. Domestication of animals

    B. Building crude huts and houses

    C. Development of agriculture

    D. Organized government in villages

Answer: C. Development of agriculture

Although the domestication of animals, the building of huts and houses and the first organized governments were all very important steps made by early civilizations, it was the development of agriculture that ended the once dominant practices of hunting, gathering, and fishing among prehistoric people. The development of agriculture provided a more efficient use of time and for the first time a surplus of food. This greatly improved the quality of life and contributed to early population growth.

100. **Which branch of geography is concerned with the location of features and how they affect human activity?** *(Average Rigor) (Skill 12.1)*

    A. Physical

    B. Cultural

    C. Sociological

    D. Historical

Answer: A. Physical

Physical geography (A) is concerned with the locations of such earth features as climate, water, and land; how these relate to and affect each other and human activities; and what forces shaped and changed them. Cultural geography (B) studies the location, characteristics, and influence of the physical environment on different cultures around the earth. Neither sociology (C) nor history (D) play an important role in the study of geography.

101. **Which continent contains just one country?** *(Easy) (Skill 12.2)*

    A. Asia

    B. Austria

    C. Antarctica

    D. Australia

Answer: D. Australia

Australia (D) is the only country in the world that has an entire continent to itself. Asia (A) has many countries, Antarctica (C) has none, and Austria (B) is a small country on the European Continent.

102. **The conversion of Constantine to Christianity is an example of the spreading of a belief system through:** *(Rigorous) (Skill 12.3)*

    A. Conquest

    B. Commercial Exchange

    C. Education

    D. Cultural Exchange

Answer: A. Conquest

After Constantine converted, he then forced acceptance Christianity upon the Roman Empire in the year 313, relying on military might to enforce his wishes. (Ironically, the reverse would later happen in Constantine's own city, Constantinople, when Islamic Turkish forces captured it in 1453. However, Constantinople wasn't officially renamed Istanbul until 1930.)

103. **Which of the following is not a natural resource industry?** *(Rigorous) (Skill 12.4)*

    A. Fishing

    B. Farming

    C. Forestry

    D. Mining

Answer: B. Farming

Of the four, although farming (B) relies upon certain natural resources, such as water, it is not such a resource itself. Man has to plant and maintain the crops, as opposed to natural resources which are created by natural forces and then harvested by man after the fact. In order to harvest corn, for example, a farmer must plow, seed, water, and maintain his (or her) fields until the time comes to reap his crop. In order to harvest fish or timber, those who work in the industry head out into the ocean or the forest and collect what is already there.

104. The ___ model envisions cities in concentric circles. *(Average Rigor)* *(Skill 13.2)*

    A. Sector

    B. Von Thunen

    C. Burgess

    D. Hoyt

Answer: C. Burgess

The Burgess (C) model (also called the concentric model), is one in which cities are seen to develop in a series of concentric circles with the central business district at the center, ringed by the factories and industrial usage area, ringed by the low class residential area, then the middle class residential area, and finally the high class residential area (often suburbs). The Hoyt (D) model (also called the Sector (A) Model), is one in which the central business district occupies a central area of a circle, and other areas then abut the central district in a variety of patterns. The Von Thunen (D) Model applies to rural development and observes a city as the center of a state or region, from which a series of concentric circles – outside the city -emanates, each devoted to particular rural land usage patterns

105. The Hudson River is named for Henry Hudson, an Englishman who was exploring for the _____. *(Easy)* *(Skill 13.3)*

    A. Dutch

    B. English

    C. French

    D. Spanish

Answer: A. Dutch

Henry Hudson was employed by the Dutch East India Company to find an eastern passage to China. He entered what is now New York Harbor and sailed up the Hudson River as far as the site of Albany. Hudson later explored Hudson's Bay for the English.

106. **The growth of the suburbs often creates which type of segregation in cities?** *(Average Rigor) (Skill 13.4)*

A. Political

B. Economic

C. Ethnic

D. Racial

Answer: B. Economic

Though all four divisions existed within cities before the development of the suburbs, it was only after the Middle Class began fleeing the cities for outlying neighborhoods that significant economic (B) differences began to appear, and cities began to be seriously segregated by income levels.

107. **Which branch of statistics is most concerned with people's social well-being?** *(Average Rigor) (Skill 13.5)*

A. Demography

B. Paleography

C. Causation

D. Graphology

Answer: A. Demography

Demography is the branch of science of statistics most concerned with the social well being of people. Demographic tables may include: analysis of the population on the basis of various factors, changes in the population as a result of birth, marriage, and death, statistics on population movements, statistics of crime, illegitimacy and suicide, and levels of education and economic and social statistics.

108.	The designation of individuals or groups as they are influenced by their belonging to a particular group is known as: *(Average Rigor) (Skill 13.6)*

	A. Cosmopolitanism

	B. Cultural Identity

	C. Melting Pot

	D. Ethnography

Answer: B. Cultural Identity

A person's cultural identity (B) comes from their belonging to a particular group. Ethnography (D) is the study of cultures. The Melting Pot (C) is the blending of cultures brought together in a common place, like the United States. And cosmopolitanism (A) is the state of having a worldly view, as opposed to one limited by a single culture.

109.	Which canal was built to link Lake Erie with the Hudson River? *(Easy) (Skill 13.7)*

	A. Erie Canal

	B. Suez Canal

	C. Hudson Canal

	D. St Lawrence Seaway

Answer: A. Erie Canal

The Suez Canal (B) is in Egypt, there is no Hudson Canal (C) or at least not one which links the Hudson River to Lake Erie, and the St Lawrence Seaway is on the St Lawrence River, which does not connect to either Lake Erie or the Hudson River. It was the Erie Canal (A) which was built to connect the two waterways.

110. **Potential customers for any product or service are not only called consumers but can also be called a:** *(Average Rigor) (Skill 14.1)*

    A. Resource

    B. Base

    C. Commodity

    D. Market

Answer: D. Market

Potential customers for any product or service are not only customers but can also be called a market. A resource is a source of wealth; natural resources are the basis for manufacturing goods and services. A commodity is anything that is bought or sold, any product.

111. **Shopping centers represent which economic model?** *(Rigorous) (Skill 14.2)*

    A. Perfect Competition

    B. Oligopoly

    C. Monopoly

    D. Monopolistic Competition

Answer: D. Monopolistic Competition

Monopolistic competition (D) is the situation you see in shopping centers. There are numerous firms, each selling products that are similar, but not identical, like brand name shoes or clothing. Oligopoly (B) is a market structure in which there are a few sellers of products that may be either homogeneous, like steel, or heterogeneous, like automobiles. A monopoly (C) is where a single seller produces a product that no other seller provides and has control over the price. Perfect competition (A) is mostly theoretical but most closely approximated by agriculture

112. **The economic system promoting individual ownership of land, capital, and businesses with minimal governmental regulations is called:** *(Rigorous) (Skill 14.3)*

    A. Macro-economy

    B. Micro-economy

    C. Laissez-faire

    D. Free enterprise

Answer: D. Free Enterprise

(D) Free enterprise or capitalism is the economic system that promotes private ownership of land, capital, and business with minimal government interference. (C) Laissez-faire is the idea that an "invisible hand" will guide the free enterprise system to the maximum potential efficiency.

113. **The "father" of modern economics is considered by most economists today to be:** *(Average Rigor) (Skill 14.3)*

    A. Thomas Robert Malthus

    B. John Stuart Mill

    C. Adam Smith

    D. John Maynard Keynes

Answer: C. Adam Smith

Adam Smith (1723-1790) is considered by many to be the "father" of modern economics. In the *Wealth of Nations,* he advocated for little or no government interference in the economy, claiming that individuals' self-interest would bring about the public's welfare. John Maynard Keynes 1883-1946) advocated an economic system in which government regulations and spending on public works would stimulate the economy and lead to full employment. John Stuart Mill (1806-1873) constantly advocated for political and social reforms, including emancipation for women, labor organizations, and farming cooperatives. Thomas Malthus (1766-1834) was a British economist who introduced the study of population and early on considered famine, war, and disease to be the primary checks on world population.

114. **The idea that continued population growth would, in future years, seriously affect a nation's productive capabilities was stated by:** *(Average Rigor) (Skill 14.3)*

    A. Keynes

    B. Mill

    C. Malthus

    D. Friedman

Answer: C. Malthus

(C) Thomas Malthus was the English economist who had the idea that population growth would seriously affect a nation's productive capabilities. (A) Keynes advocated an economic system of government regulations and spending on public works to stimulate the economy and lead to full employment. (B) Mill was almost a Socialist and wrote the early work in Political Economy while Friedman (D) was a financial advisor in the arch conservative government of President Ronald Reagan.

115. **The idea or proposal for more equal division of profits among employers and workers was put forth by:** *(Average Rigor) (Skill 14.4*

    A. Karl Marx

    B. Thomas Malthus

    C. Adam Smith

    D. John Stuart Mill

Answer: D. John Stuart Mill

(D) John Stuart Mill constantly advocated for political and social reforms, including a more equal division of profits among employers and workers. (A) Karl Marx advocated the inability of capitalism to provide for the workers, the idea of class struggle, and the central role of economy. (B) Thomas Malthus was a British economist who introduced the study of population and early on considered famine, war, and disease to be the primary checks on world population. (C) Adam Smith advocated for little or no government interference in the economy.

116. **One method of trade restriction used by some nations is:** *(Rigorous)* *(Skill 14.5)*

    A. Limited treaties

    B. Floating exchange rate

    C. Bill of exchange

    D. Import quotas

Answer: D. Import quotas

One method of trade restriction used by some nations is import quotas. The amounts of goods imported are regulated in an effort to protect domestic enterprise and limit foreign competition. Both the United States and Japan, two of the world's most industrialized nations have import quotas to protect domestic industries.

117. **If the price of Good G increases, what is likely to happen with regard to comparable Good H?** *(Rigorous)* *(Skill 15.1)*

    A. The demand for Good G will stay the same

    B. The demand for Good G will increase

    C. The demand for Good H will increase

    D. The demand for Good H will decrease

Answer: C. The demand for Good H will increase

If Good G and Good H are viewed by consumers as equal in value but the cost of Good G increases, it follows that consumers will now choose Good H at a higher rate, increasing the demand.

118. **The study of ways in which different societies around the world deal with the problems of limited resources and unlimited needs and wants is in the area of:** *(Rigorous) (Skill 15.2)*

    A. Economics

    B. Sociology

    C. Anthropology

    D. Political Science

Answer: A. Economics

The study of the ways in which different societies around the world deal with the problems of limited resources and unlimited needs and wants is a study of Economics. Economists consider the law of supply and demand as fundamental to the study of the economy. However, Sociology and Political Science also consider the study of economics and its importance in understanding social and political systems.

119. **The macro-economy consists of all but which of the following sectors?** *(Rigorous) (Skill 15.3)*

    A. Consumer

    B. Business

    C. Foreign

    D. Private

Answer: D. Private

The private sector (D) refers to that area of politics and society not controlled by the public (i.e. the government). While it may include businesses and individual consumers, it is not considered part of the macro-economy.

120. **Which of the following is an example of why the United States does not operate as a closed economy?** *(Rigorous) (Skill 15.6)*

   A. Coffee

   B. Rice

   C. Cotton

   D. Oil

Answer: A. Coffee

Rice (B), cotton (C), and oil (D) are all products that the US either grows or, in the case of oil, has access to as part of its own territory and does not need to rely on foreign sources to provide them. Therefore, the US does not need to operate as an open economy for those items (though in practice it does for various other reasons). Coffee (A), on the other hand, is not grown within the United States and is an example of a product the US must trade with other nations to obtain.

121. **In the United States government, the power of taxation and borrowing is:** *(Rigorous) (Skill 16.1)*

   A. Implied or suggested

   B. Concurrent or shared

   C. Delegated or expressed

   D. Reserved

Answer: B. Concurrent or shared

In the United States government, the power of taxation is concurrent or shared with the states. An example of this is the separation of state and federal income tax and the separate filings of tax returns for each.

122. **The US economic system combines all but which of the following? (Rigorous) (Skill 16.2)**

    A. Capital

    B. Cost

    C. Profit

    D. Competition

Answer: C. Cost

Profit (C), capital (A) and competition (D) all go together in the U.S. economic system. Competition is determined by market structure. Since the cost (B) curves are the same for all the firms, the only difference comes from the revenue side.

123. **In the United States government, the power of coining money is: (Rigorous) (Skill 16.3)**

    A. Implied or suggested

    B. Concurrent or shared

    C. Delegated or expressed

    D. Reserved

Answer: C. Delegated or expressed

In the United States government, the power of coining money is delegated or expressed. Therefore, only the United States government may coin money, the states may not coin money for themselves.

124. **In the United States, federal investigations into business activities are handled by the:** *(Average Rigor) (Skill 16.3)*

   A. Department of Treasury

   B. Security and Exchange Commission

   C. Government Accounting Office

   D. Federal Trade Commission

Answer: D. Federal Trade Commission

The Department of Treasury (A), established in 1789, is an executive government agency that is responsible for advising the president on fiscal policy. There is no such thing as a Government Accounting Office. In the United States, Federal Trade Commission or FTC handles federal investigations into business activities. The establishment of the FTC in 1915 as an independent government agency was done so as to assure fair and free competition among businesses.

125   **The American labor union movement started gaining new momentum:** *(Average Rigor) (Skill 16.4)*

   A. During the building of the railroads

   B. After 1865 with the growth of cities

   C. With the rise of industrial giants such as Carnegie and Vanderbilt

   D. During the war years of 1861-1865

Answer: B. After 1865 with the growth of cities

The American Labor Union movement had been around since the late 18th and early 19th centuries, though it remained relatively ineffective until after the Civil War. In 1866, the National Labor Union was formed, pushing such issues as the eight-hour workday and new policies of immigration. This gave rise to the Knights of Labor and eventually the American Federation of Labor (AFL) in the 1890s and the Industrial Workers of the World (1905). Therefore, it was the period following the Civil War that empowered the labor movement in terms of numbers, militancy, and effectiveness.

126. The Fed will ___ interest rates to avoid inflation and ___ interest rates to stimulate the economy. *(Average Rigor) (Skill 16.5)*

    A. lower ... raise

    B. raise ... lower

    C. raise ... also raise

    D. lower ... also lower

Answer: B. raise ... lower

Contractionary monetary and/or fiscal policies (raising interest rates) are used to slow an economy that is expanding too quickly. Expansionary monetary and/or fiscal policies (lowering interest rates) are used to stimulate a sluggish economy to eliminate unemployment.

127. Economic mobility refers particularly to what factor's ability to move? *(Rigorous) (Skill 16.6)*

    A. Resources

    B. Money

    C. Labor

    D. Management

Answer: C. Labor

Economic mobility refers to the ability of factors, particularly labor (C) to move around the country in response to employment opportunities. The U.S. economy is so big that there can be unemployment in one part of the country while there are labor shortages in other parts of the country. In many cases there are institutional rigidities, like lack of information, that prevent workers from migrating in response to employment opportunities.

128. The study of the exercise of power and political behavior in human society today would be conducted by experts in: *(Average Rigor) (Skill 17.2)*

    A. History

    B. Sociology

    C. Political Science

    D. Anthropology

Answer: C. Political Science

Experts in the field of political science today would likely conduct the study of exercise of power and political behavior in human society. However, it is also reasonable to suggest that such studies would be important to historians (study of the past, often in an effort to understand the present), sociologists (often concerned with power structure in the social and political worlds), and even some anthropologists (study of culture and their behaviors).

129. Which of the following is an example of a direct democracy? *(Average Rigor) (Skill 17.3)*

    A. Elected representatives

    B. Greek city-states

    C. The United States Senate

    D. The United States House of Representatives

Answer: B. Greek city-states

The Greek city-states (B) are an example of a direct democracy as their leaders were elected directly by the citizens and the citizens themselves were given voice in government. (A) Elected representatives in the United States as in the case of the presidential elections are actually elected by an electoral college that is supposed to be representative of the citizens. The United States Congress, the Senate, (C) and the House of Representatives (D) are also examples of indirect democracy as they represent the citizens in the legislature as opposed to having citizens represent themselves.

130. **The programs such as unemployment insurance and health insurance for the elderly are the responsibility of:** *(Average Rigor) (Skill 17.4)*

    A. Federal Government

    B. Local Government

    C. State Government

    D. Communal Government

Answer: C. State Government

Assistance programs, such as unemployment insurance and free health insurance for the elderly is the responsibility of state governments.

131. **A political philosophy favoring or supporting rapid social changes in order to correct social and economic inequalities is called:** *(Rigorous) (Skill 17.4)*

    A. Nationalism

    B. Liberalism

    C. Conservatism

    D. Federalism

Answer: B. Liberalism

A political philosophy favoring rapid social changes in order to correct social and economic inequalities are called Liberalism. Liberalism was a theory that could be said to have started with the great French philosophers Montesquieu (1689-1755) and Rousseau (1712-1778). It is important to understand the difference between political, economic, and social liberalism, as they are different and how they sometimes contrast one another in the modern world.

132. The principle of "life, liberty, and the pursuit of happiness" was borrowed from the ideas of which figure? *(Average Rigor) (Skill 18.1)*

    A. Locke

    B. Rousseau

    C. Aristotle

    D. Montesquieu

Answer: A. Locke

When Thomas Jefferson penned those words, he was paraphrasing the philosopher John Locke, whose original quote was "life, liberty, and property." Of all the thinkers who influenced the Founders, it was Locke whose ideas were most emulated in the drafting of the Constitution.

133. The foundation of modern constitutionalism is embodied in the idea that government is limited by law. This law was stated by: *(Average Rigor) (Skill 18.2)*

    A. John Locke

    B. Rousseau

    C. St. Thomas Aquinas

    D. Montesquieu

Answer: C. St. Thomas Aquinas

(A) John Locke (1632-1704), whose book *Two Treatises of Government* has long been considered a founding document on the rights of people to rebel against an unjust government, was an important figure in the founding of the US Constitution and on general politics of the American Colonies. (D) Montesquieu (1689-1755) and (B) Rousseau (1712-1778) were political philosophers who explored the idea of what has come to be known as liberalism. They pushed the idea that through understanding the interconnectedness of economics, geography, climate and psychology that changes could be made to improve life. Therefore, it was St. Thomas Aquinas (1225-1274) who merged Aristotelian ideas with Christianity, who helped lay the ideas of modern constitutionalism and the limiting of government by law.

134. **To be eligible to be elected President one must:** *(Easy) (Skill 18.2)*

    A. Be a citizen for at least five years

    B. Be a citizen for seven years

    C. Have been born a citizen

    D. Be a naturalized citizen

Answer: C. Have been born a citizen

Article II, Section 1 of the Constitution clearly states, "No person except a natural-born citizen, or citizen of the United States at the time of the adoption of this Constitution, shall be eligible to the office of President."

135. **After Ratification, the most urgent of the many problems facing the new federal government was that of:** *(Rigorous) (Skill 18.2)*

    A. Maintaining a strong army and navy

    B. Establishing a strong foreign policy

    C. Raising money to pay salaries and war debts

    D. Setting up courts, passing federal laws, and providing for law enforcement officers

Answer: C. Raising money to pay salaries and war debts

Maintaining strong military forces, establishment of a strong foreign policy, and setting up a justice system were important problems facing the United States under the newly ratified Constitution. However, the most important and pressing issue was how to raise money to pay salaries and war debts from the Revolutionary War. Alexander Hamilton (1755-1804) then Secretary of the Treasury proposed increased tariffs and taxes on products such as liquor. This money would be used to pay off war debts and to pay for internal programs. Hamilton also proposed the idea of a National Bank.

136. **Which of the following is considered the basis of English constitutional liberties?** *(Average Rigor) (Skill 18.3)*

    A. Bill of Rights

    B. Petition of Rights

    C. Declaration of Rights

    D. Magna Carta

Answer: D. Magna Carta

The Margna Carta (A) has been considered the basis of English constitution liberties. It was granted to a representative group of English barons and nobles on June 15, 1215 by the British King John, after they had forced it on him. The Bill of Rights (A) is an American document. The Petition of Rights (B) was the title of a petition that was addressed to the King of England Charles I, by the British parliament in 1628 concerning taxes. And the Declaration of Rights (C) spelled out the rights that were considered to belong to Englishmen and was granted by King William III in 1869.

137. **The term that best describes how the Supreme Court can block laws that may be unconstitutional from being enacted is:** *(Average Rigor) (Skill 18.3)*

    A. Jurisprudence

    B. Judicial Review

    C. Exclusionary Rule

    D. Right of Petition

Answer: B. Judicial Review

(A) Jurisprudence is the study of the development and origin of law. (B) Judicial review is the term that best describes how the Supreme Court can block laws that they deem as unconstitutional as set forth in Marbury vs Madison. The (C) "exclusionary rule" is a reference to the Fourth Amendment of the Constitution and says that evidence gathered in an illegal manner or search must be thrown out and excluded from evidence. There is no (D) "Right of Petition"

138.   **The most basic level of participation in the political process is:** *(Average Rigor) (Skill 18.4)*

   A. Obeying laws

   B. Donating time or money

   C. Voting

   D. Running for office

Answer: C. Voting

Citizens of a democratic society are also expected to participate in the political process, either directly or indirectly. In theory, anyone who is a citizen of a democratic society can run for office and be elected (D). Other ways to participate in the political process include donating time and/or money (B) to the political campaigns of others and speaking out on behalf of or against certain issues. The most basic level of participation in the political process is to vote. (C) Obeying the laws (A) is not part of the political process.

139.   **The source of authority for national, state, and local governments in the United States is:** *(Average Rigor) (Skill 18.5)*

   A. The will of the people

   B. The United States Constitution

   C. Written laws

   D. The Bill of Rights

Answer: A. The will of the people

The source of authority for national, state, and local governments in the United States is the will of the people. Although the United States Constitution, the Bill of Rights, and the other written laws of the land are important guidelines for authority, they may ultimately be altered or changed by the will of the people.

140. **Which of the following is a recent attempt to encourage voter registration?** *(Average Rigor)* *(Skill 18.6)*

   A. Motor-Voter acts

   B. Poll Taxes

   C. Exit Polls

   D. Literacy Tests

Answer: A. Motor-Voter acts

Both poll taxes (B) and literacy tests (D) were restrictions put in place to limit voter registration, specifically black voters in the South prior to the Civil Rights Movement. Exit polls (C) are samplings of voters after they have voted and have nothing to do with registration. Motor-Voter acts (A) are designed to encourage voter participation by allowing people to register to vote when they get their driver's license.

141. **On the spectrum of American politics the label that most accurately describes voters to the "right of center" is:** *(Average Rigor)* *(Skill 19.1)*

   A. Moderates

   B. Liberals

   C. Conservatives

   D. Socialists

Answer: C. Conservatives

(A) Moderates are considered voters who teeter on the line of political centrality or drift slightly to the left or right. (B) Liberals are voters who stand on the left of center. (C) Conservative voters are those who are "right of center". (D) Socialist would land far to the left on the political spectrum of America.

142. **Which of the following lobbying tactics is illegal?** *(Rigorous) (Skill 19.2)*

   A. Paying for Congress members to travel

   B. Direct communications with Congress members

   C. Paying for meals or other entertainment for Congress members

   D. Paying cash to Congress members

Answer: D. Paying cash to Congress members

Surprisingly, you can pay for just about anything for your local (or even not your local) Congress member. Travel (A), dining, entertainment, (C) it is all legal up to actually paying members of Congress cash (D). That last category is officially known as a bribe, and illegal. And anyone is allowed to communicate directly with any member of Congress. (B)

143. **Which one of the following is not a function or responsibility of the US political parties?** *(Rigorous) (Skill 19.3)*

   A. Conducting elections or the voting process

   B. Obtaining funds needed for election campaigns

   C. Choosing candidates to run for public office

   D. Making voters aware of issues and other public affairs information

Answer: A. Conducting elections or the voting process

The US political parties have numerous functions and responsibilities. Among them are obtaining funds needed for election campaigns, choosing the candidates to run for office, and making voters aware of the issues. The political parties, however, do not conduct elections or the voting process, as that would be an obvious conflict of interest.

144. **What is the one thing that drives American politics more than any other?** *(Average Rigor) (Skill 19.4)*

    A. Money

    B. Race

    C. Issues

    D. Party Lines

Answer: A. Money

Race, issues and party lines are all factors in political campaigns and play an important role in political debate. However the success of a political candidate relies mainly on the amount of money the campaign can raise to gain exposure for the candidate and his or her views. Therefore (A) is the correct answer.

145. **Which group in the Executive Branch advises the President on foreign policy?** *(Average Rigor) (Skill 20.1)*

    A. NSC

    B. NSA

    C. CIA

    D. FBI

Answer: A. NSC

The National Security Council or NSC (A) advises the President on all manner of foreign affairs, and the NSC Advisor occupies a cabinet-level post. The NSA (B) handles electronic surveillance, while the CIA (C) conducts operations for intelligence gathering. The FBI (D) operates strictly in domestic situations and has no involvement in foreign policy or affairs.

146. **Which program was established to aid Europe's economic recovery after World War II?** *(Easy) (Skill 20.2)*

   A. The Kennan Plan

   B. The Marshall Plan

   C. The Truman Doctrine

   D. The Cold War

Answer: B. The Marshall Plan

After 1945, social and economic chaos continued in Western Europe, especially in Germany. Secretary of State George C. Marshall came to realize that the U.S. had serious problems and to assist in the recovery, he proposed a program known as the European Recovery Program or the Marshall Plan(B). George Kennan (A) proposed the policy known as Containment. The Truman Doctrine (C) offered military aid to those countries that were in danger of communist upheaval. The Cold War (D) was the ideological struggle between the US and the USSR.

147. **The United Nations Security Council has __ members, of which ___ are permanent members.** *(Average Rigor) (Skill 20.4)*

   A. 10 ... 3

   B. 10 ... 5

   C. 15 ... 5

   D. 20 ... 7

Answer: C. 15 ... 5

The United Nations Security Council consists of fifteen member nations. Ten of those countries rotate regularly, while five nations: Russia, the US, China, England, and France occupy five permanent seats. Though there has been talk in recent years of changing the permanent members, so far it has not happened, perhaps do in no small part to the ability of any one of the five to veto measures proposed by the Security Council.

148. The best place to find historical data is most often: *(Average Rigor)* *(Skill 21.1)*

   A. The library

   B. The locale where the event happened

   C. The internet

   D. Public Records

Answer: B. The locale where the event happened.

While the library (A), internet (C), and public records (D) are all great sources of information, historians are always well served, whenever possible, to visit the locale (B) they are researching. Whether it's to chat with the local residents or just get a feel for the land, the best place to get data is where it all started.

149. For the historian studying ancient Egypt, which of the following would be least useful? *(Rigorous)* *(Skill 21.2)*

   A. The record of an ancient Greek historian on Greek-Egyptian interaction

   B. Letters from an Egyptian ruler to his/her regional governors

   C. Inscriptions on stele of the Fourteenth Egyptian Dynasty

   D. Letters from a nineteenth century Egyptologist to his wife

Answer: D. Letters from a nineteenth century Egyptologist to his wife

Historians use primary sources from the actual time they are studying whenever possible. (A) Ancient Greek records of interaction with Egypt, (B) letters from an Egyptian ruler to regional governors, and (C) inscriptions from the Fourteenth Egyptian Dynasty are all primary sources created at or near the actual time being studied. (D) Letters from a nineteenth century Egyptologist would not be considered a primary source, as they were created thousands of years after the fact and may not actually be about the subject being studied.

150. **A team approach to a research project should include which position?** *(Average Rigor)* *(Skill 21.3)*

    A. Statistician

    B. Dietician

    C. Mortician

    D. Mathematician

Answer: A. Statistician

No research team can be considered complete nowadays without a statistician (A) on board to process the numbers. A general mathematician (D) might be helpful, but statistics is a specialized field and a general mathematician (or one specializing in a particular field) will probably not be needed. A dietician (B) might be useful for historians who are overweight, and hopefully no research team would ever require the services of a mortician (C).

151. **Which is not part of the scientific method?** *(Average Rigor)* *(Skill 21.4)*

    A. Formulation

    B. Testing

    C. Observation

    D. Interpretation

Answer: D. Interpretation

The heart of the scientific method is the absence of interpretation (D), or bias. The purpose of the method is to conduct experiments that yield a true/false result for a proposed hypothesis, based on observations, not interpretations.

152. **A project looking at the progress of school children must also take into account changes for which of the following?** *(Rigorous) (Skill 21.5)*

    A. The school

    B. The teachers

    C. The home

    D. The society

Answer: A. The school

Although an argument could be made for looking at all four factors, both home (C) and society (D) would result in far too many variables for a study to be useful. The same is true for teachers (B), though to a lesser extent. Looking at changes in the school (A), however, say in the curriculum that all teachers are expected to teach, or improvements made to the learning environment, would be helpful in measuring the progress made by students.

153. **What are used to show how either theoretical or real world data interrelate using two or more variables?** *(Average Rigor) (Skill 22.1)*

    A. Graphs

    B. Charts

    C. Maps

    D. Diagram

Answer: A. Graphs

Graphs (A) are used to show data with two or more variables (a common variable is time, with a graph showing how something has changed over time), Charts (B) may show more than one variable, but frequently only represent a single variable, such as a pie chart that shows percentages. Maps (C) generally do not show the interrelation of data, and diagrams (D) can mean almost anything shown in picture form.

154. **A good political cartoon will have all but which of the following? (Average Rigor) (Skill 22.2)**

   A. Wit and humor

   B. Foundation in truth

   C. Moral Purpose

   D. Party Affiliation

Answer: D. Party Affiliation

While many political cartoonists do have, if not a party affiliation (D) at least a party leaning, many others take equal opportunity shots at all facets of American politics. And even those with leaning, like Doonesbury, for example, will often take issue with both liberals and conservatives, or deal with issues which have no particular party slant. The other three criteria are, however, indispensable for a good cartoon (particularly a foundation in truth (B) if the cartoonist wishes to avoid charges of libel).

155. **A map of oil fields in the Middle East might be useful for discussing which of the following? (Rigorous) (Skill 22.3)**

   A. OPEC

   B. NATO

   C. ASEAN

   D. NAFTA

Answer: A. OPEC

The Organization of Petroleum Exporting Countries, OPEC, is the only one of the above whose primary concern is Middle Eastern oil fields. A military map of Europe might be useful for discussing the North Atlantic Treaty Organization, NATO; a map of Southeast Asia for discussing the Asia and Southeast Asian Nations organization, ASEAN (C); and a map of the US, Canada, and Mexico for discussing the North American Free Trade Agreement, NAFTA (D).

156. **Maps based on gnomonic projections are also know as what kind of maps?** *(Easy)* *(Skill 22.4)*

   A. Great Square

   B. Great Circle

   C. Great Sailing

   D. Great Route

Answer: B. Great Circle

Flat-plane projections are often used to show the areas of the north and south poles. One such flat projection is called a Gnomonic Projection. On this kind of map all meridians appear as straight lines, Gnomonic projections are useful because any straight line drawn between points on it forms a Great-Circle Route (B).

157. **For which age group would pictures be most vital in a presentation?** *(Average Rigor)* *(Skill 22.5)*

   A. Elementary School

   B. Middle School

   C. High School

   D. University

Answer: A. Elementary school

While pictures are a good idea in any presentation to any group, in order to hold the interest of (and for ease of explaining to) elementary school children, pictures are indispensable.

158. **The adjustment of various electoral districts in order to achieve a predetermined goal is referred to as:** *(Average Rigor) (Skill 23.1)*

    A. Racial Quotas

    B. Salamandering

    C. Gerrymandering

    D. Mercator Projections

Answer: C. Gerrymandering

The strange shapes that dot political maps are named after a former governor of Massachusetts, Elbridge Gerry, who helped create the odd, salamander-shaped districts. Gerry + salamander became gerrymandering (C). Mercator projections (D) are an actual way of making maps, though it has nothing to do with redistricting. Neither does racial quotas (A).

159. **Which of the following is a fact?** *(Average Rigor) (Skill 23.2)*

    A. That cloud looks dark.

    B. It looks like rain.

    C. It looks like snow.

    D. It looks like a rabbit.

Answer: A. That cloud looks dark.

Of the four statements, only the first one describes something that could be objectively agreed upon. (A better statement would be "The cloud IS dark.") The other three are all much more subjective and a matter of personal perspective.

160. **Which of the following would best apply to both primary and secondary sources with regard to careful usage?** *(Rigorous) (Skill 23.3)*

    A. Understanding the use of period language

    B. Consulting the original text

    C. Check bias

    D. Do not rely on one source

Answer: D. Do not rely on one source

Whether talking to eyewitness, consulting a historical source written at the time of the event, or even going back to an original text after looking at a second-hand account, the one rule for all sources is that historians cannot rely on a single source. Multiple sources, multiple accounts, and multiple approaches are always the best method.

161. **The purpose of ___ is to understand the works of others and to use that work in shaping a conclusion.** *(Rigorous) (Skill 23.4)*

    A. Synergy

    B. Synthesis

    C. Synchronicity

    D. Syllogism

Answer: B. Synthesis

The purpose of a synthesis (B) is to understand the works of others and to use that work in shaping a conclusion. The writer or speaker must clearly differentiate between the ideas that come from a source and his/her own. Synergy (A) is when two or more things work together for mutual advantage. Synchronicity (B) is the coincidental occurrence of two widely separated but related events. And a syllogism (D) is a form of deductive reasoning.

162. **Which of the following is an example of an inadequate (as opposed to a misleading) reason?** *(Rigorous) (Skill 23.5)*

    A. Ad hominem

    B. Ad populum

    C. Red Herring

    D. False Dilemma

Answer: A. Ad hominem

Ad populum (bandwagon) (B), red herring (C), or false dilemma (D) are all examples of misleading reasons. Only ad hominem (A), which is an attack on the arguer rather than the argument, is considered an inadequate reason.

XAMonline, INC. 21 Orient Ave. Melrose, MA 02176

Toll Free number 800-509-4128

TO ORDER Fax 781-662-9268 OR www.XAMonline.com

NEW YORK STATE TEACHER CERTIFICATION
EXAMINATION   - NYSTCE - 2008

PO#   Store/School:

Address 1:

Address 2 (Ship to other):

City, State Zip

Credit card number_____-_____-_____-_____   expiration_____

EMAIL _____

PHONE   **FAX**

ISBN	TITLE	Qty	Retail	Total
978-1-58197-866-7	NYSTCE ATS-W ASSESSMENT OF TEACHING SKILLS- WRITTEN 91			
978-1-58197-260-3	NYSTCE ATAS ASSESSMENT OF TEACHING ASSISTANT SKILLS 095			
978-1-58197-289-4	CST BIOLOGY 006			
978-1-58197-855-1	CST CHEMISTRY 007			
978-1-58197-865-0	CQST COMMUNICATION AND QUANTITATIVE SKILLS TEST 080			
978-1-58197-632-8	CST EARTH SCIENCE 008			
978-1-58197-267-2	CST ENGLISH 003			
978-1-58197-858-2	CST FRENCH SAMPLE TEST 012			
978-1-58197-344-0	LAST LIBERAL ARTS AND SCIENCE TEST 001			
978-1-58197-863-6	CST LIBRARY MEDIA SPECIALIST 074			
978-1-58197-623-6	CST LITERACY 065			
978-1-58197-296-2	CST MATH 004			
978-1-58197-290-0	CST MUTIPLE SUBJECTS 002			
978-1-58197-864-3	CST PHYSICAL EDUCATION 076			
978-1-58197-873-5	CST PHYSICS 009			
978-1-58197-265-8	CST SOCIAL STUDIES 005			
978-1-58197-619-9	CST SPANISH 020			
978-1-58197-258-0	CST STUDENTS WITH DISABILITIES 060			
			SUBTOTAL	
	FOR PRODUCT PRICES VISIT WWW.XAMONLINE.COM		Ship	$8.25
			TOTAL	

LaVergne, TN USA
26 January 2010
171161LV00001B/104/P